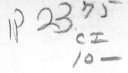
CHEMISTS
BY PROFESSION

Figure 1.   The Institute building, c. 1914
Architect: Sir John J. Burnet, LL.D.

CHEMISTS
BY PROFESSION

The origins and rise of
The Royal Institute of Chemistry

Colin A. Russell
with
Noel G. Coley
Gerrylynn K. Roberts

THE OPEN UNIVERSITY PRESS
in association with
THE ROYAL INSTITUTE OF CHEMISTRY

The Open University Press
Walton Hall, Milton Keynes
MK7 6AA

First published 1977

Printed in Great Britain by
Staples Printers Limited at The Priory Press, St Albans, Hertfordshire

ISBN 0 335 00041 X

CONTENTS

LIST OF ILLUSTRATIONS

FIGURES

PLATES

Plates 15 and 18–28, and Figures 1 and 2 are from the RIC collection.
Plates 11 and 17 are from the Chemical Society collection.
Plate 9 is from the collection of Mr M. T. Hall, British Rail, Derby.

In notes and references after each chapter names of publishers are given only for books published after 1900. The following abbreviations are used for standard biographical sources:

Boase: Frederic Boase, *Modern English Biography*, Cass, London, 1965.

DNB: *Dictionary of National Biography*, Oxford, 1917 onwards.

DSB: *Dictionary of Scientific Biography*, ed. C. C. Gillispie, Scribners, New York, 1970 onwards.

WWW: *Who Was Who*, A. and C. Black, London, year varies.

WW: *Who's Who*, A. and C. Black, London, year varies.

Titles for periodical publications are given in abbreviated form. The Journal of the (Royal) Institute of Chemistry appeared with various titles as indicated below:

  up to 1943: *Proc. Inst. Chem.*
  1944 to 1949: *Proc. R.I.C.*
  1950 to 1964: *J.R.I.C.*

From 1965 the *Journal* was absorbed in *Chemistry in Britain*.

FOREWORD

It is possible that lack of historical sense is responsible for most of the mistakes we make; in other words, an historical sense is a first-class destroyer of idols.

F. A. Freeth, in a lecture to the Manchester District Section of the Institute of Chemistry, 11 January 1934 (*Proc. Inst. Chem.*, 1934, 58, 53).

In 1977 the Royal Institute of Chemistry celebrates its centenary. To mark the event it has commissioned the present book, which traces the development of the chemical profession in Britain up to 1976. The story which unfolds is largely the history of the Institute, although suitable attention is paid to the events and trends leading up to its foundation in 1877.

I wish to record my sincere gratitude to the Institute for inviting me to be responsible for this volume, and my pleasure at the help given by two of my colleagues at the Open University, Dr G. K. Roberts and Dr N. G. Coley. Both have shared in planning and production as well as writing some of the chapters. The authorship of these is indicated by the initials of one of us at the end of the main text of each.

It is no mere formality to express our indebtedness to the administrative officers and Council of the Institute for their unfailing courtesy and goodwill throughout our investigations. Not only have they insisted upon our complete freedom to write what we wanted and to say anything we wished, they have gone out of their way to make available all the Council's minutes and documents relating to the formation of the Institute, the membership records, correspondence, and the now rare back numbers of the Institute's *Journal*. We are especially grateful to Mr D. A. Arnold, Deputy Secretary to the Institute until October 1975, for his kind encouragement and help in a multitude of ways.

For permission to examine and cite early minute books and other unpublished material, we extend our warm thanks to the Councils of the Chemical Society, the Society of Chemical Industry, the Pharmaceutical Society of Great Britain, the Managers of the Royal Institution, the General Secretary of the Association of Professional Scientists and Technologists, the Librarian of University College, London, and the County Archivists of Durham and Northumberland. We are also grateful to Mr M. T. Hall, Scientific Services Manager, British Rail, Derby, for access to his collection of early material relating to chemistry in the railway industry and to Mr George Rolleston for permission to quote from the Davy letters in his possession. Similarly, we thank Mr G. A. Bloxam for access to his private collection of papers relating to his grandfather, the chemist C. L. Bloxam. In addition we have consulted manuscript material in the British Library, the Public Record Office, King's College, London, the University of

London (Senate House), and Imperial College, London. We are very grateful to the librarians and staff of all these institutions and also to those of the Institute of Historical Research, the Wellcome Institute of the History of Medicine, the City Library of Newcastle-upon-Tyne, and public libraries in Sunderland and Bedford.

We are especially grateful to the staff of the Open University library for their cheerful acceptance of many outrageous demands upon their time and for their willingness to locate source material of all kinds, often with only the minimum of notice.

We are grateful for much additional material supplied to us by interview and would wish to express our special thanks to the following gentlemen who kindly went to much trouble to answer our questions: Sir Harry Melville, Sir James Taylor, Sir Ewart Jones, Dr G. H. Beeby, Col F. J. Griffin, Dr D. H. Sharp, Sir George Porter, Dr L. H. Williams, Dr R. E. Parker, and Mr D. A. Arnold.

The production of this book with its various drafts has been the major preoccupation for over a year of each of us and of several secretaries in the Faculty of Arts, amongst whom we would especially mention those who have served in the History of Science: Mrs S. Batten, Mrs E. A. Dickey and Miss P. E. White. It is more than formal thanks that we would offer to these ladies, who have had to cope with complex and sometimes scarcely legible manuscripts. We must also thank Mr A. W. R. Seward of the Open University Press for both encouraging and restraining where necessary, Mrs Caroline Land for preparing the manuscript for publication, and Mr A. J. Coulson for picture research. I am grateful to my wife Shirley for preparing the Indexes.

Any historical study which attempts to deal with comparatively recent times is attended with rather special difficulties. It is never easy to know how much or how little to say of those who are still alive when the book is published. For this reason we have adopted the definite policy of making very little reference by name to living persons, the only exceptions being where it would be impossible to produce a coherent and fair account without doing so. This avoided the necessity of making value judgements on the work of living individuals and at the same time of coming to premature conclusions about certain events in the recent past. In writing our book we have been very conscious of the critical times through which the Institute is passing, even as the book goes to press. In following the fortunes of the Institute since 1877 we have tried to paint a fair picture, 'warts and all', rather than to give the uncritical hagiography that was once the custom. But, having said that, we recognize the great service which it has given to British chemistry and cordially wish it well in its next hundred years, under whatever title it may continue to exist.

Colin A. Russell

The Open University, January 1977.

CHAPTER 1

THE IDEA OF A PROFESSION

The notion that chemistry was not only a science but could also be a profession is more recent than even the chemical atomic theory. So far as Britain is concerned it is undoubtedly a Victorian invention, though few people would share the opinion of Alexander Findlay that 'it is doubtful whether one could speak of the existence of a *profession* of chemistry before the founding of the Institute of Chemistry in 1877'.[1] Clearly, much depends upon one's precise conception of what a profession might be, and, as this book will show, it is a complex notion whose several constituents did not develop at the same time, in the same place, or at the same rate.

The starting-point for most discussions on the rise of the chemical profession has usually been two books by R. B. Pilcher, who served the Institute for half a century as Assistant Secretary (1894), Secretary (1895) and Registrar and Secretary (1900–45). His *Profession of Chemistry* first appeared in 1919 and came out as a 4th edition in 1938; it was in its time a valuable guide to prospective candidates for a career in chemistry, the changes in content over the various editions signifying several important developments in the profession.[2] However it must be stated that the book was primarily recruiting propaganda for the Institute, and in no sense did it lay claims to being a scholarly study of the evolution of the profession of chemistry. Much the same can also be said of Pilcher's *History of the Institute: 1877–1914* which was published at a time when, as will be seen, the Institute was being hard-pressed on several sides and a morale-raising history was deemed appropriate. The book tends to be rather a 'blow-by-blow' account of what happened than an analytical enquiry as to the causes behind events or a critical history.[3] Today both of these books should still be treated with respect and seriousness, but as historical raw material in their own right instead of 'official history' to be accepted without cavil or criticism. Although in the process Pilcher's value to us as an historian may be slightly diminished, there will emerge with greater clarity and force the administrative skill, dogged persistence, unflagging energies, clarity of vision and consummate devotion of this man who, more than anyone else, helped to create the history of the Institute of Chemistry.[4]

In the pages that follow an attempt is made to explore the development of the chemical profession in that spirit of enquiry. Especially in the early years of the Institute there is no need to chronicle detailed activities under each successive President, for Pilcher has already done this for us. Where such details are germane to the argument they will, of course, be supplied, together with some that Pilcher omits. At the same time this account will deny itself an indulgence of the opposite kind and frequently encountered today, namely the setting up of a sociological model and the incorporation of only such data as are seen to fit and 'confirm' such a model. Inevitably in an account about 'institutions' sociological categories of description will be needed, for the Institute of Chemistry, the Chemical Society and all the others in this narrative are (in a loose sense) sociological units. Primarily, however, the skills and sympathies of the historian have seemed more relevant to the present task, always taking for granted the sympathies (if not all the skills) of the chemist.

The rise of the profession of chemistry must be seen as part of a larger movement in which *science* in general acquired a professional status.[5] It occurred when, as the Victorians liked to put it, people no longer lived *for* science so much as *by* it. This professionalization of all the major sciences was in its turn related to both a growing awareness of the value of science to technology,[6] and the rise of the professions in general.[7] Consequently it makes no sense at all to begin the present account with 1877 for, by that time, the foundations of the Institute had been well and truly laid; this can be seen in the increasing applications of chemistry to both productive industry and analytical work that had marked the first forty years of Victoria's reign, and, on the other hand, the development of chemical institutions. The multifarious happenings in the latter area may seem merely amusing to a modern chemist, with tales of feuds, squabbles, animosities, alliances and regroupings, but they have much to tell us of the *modus vivendi* of a Victorian chemist and the social pressures he experienced. Certainly the Institute's foundation cannot be understood properly if they are to be ignored, nor can its later development.

The concentration of this book upon the British experience needs little comment. A treatment of (say) European developments would have dictated a much larger volume but the chief reason against it was the simple fact of the British priority in most of the developments of the chemical profession. As Chapter XV indicates it is no mere jingoism to assert this with confidence. Furthermore when other countries are concerned the very definition of professionalism raises acutely difficult questions, since it means manifestly different things in different places.[8] Certainly there have been attempts to discuss the development of professional careers in science elsewhere than in Britain but their categories have been different from those employed here.[9] In Britain, for example, the distinction between academic and professional qualifications has led to a rather specific use of the term 'profession' for those employed in the application of chemistry. Most university teachers would (rightly) regard themselves as fully professional though perhaps more as members of the university teaching profession than of the profession of chemistry.

It remains therefore to indicate the complex of ideas that are generally conveyed today by the term 'professional' and which underlie the discussion in the present book in the case of the chemists in Britain. The term 'profession' referring to a particular group of people carries certain definite connotations, though not always with equal force. As will be seen they emerged gradually and at different rates for the chemical community. They are as follows:

Intellectual qualifications   The adherence by members to a certain body of 'received knowledge', imparted by a teaching process that is subject to careful monitoring, and guaranteed by recognition from the professional organization (often by examination).

Social responsibility   The acceptance of obligations to the general public in respect of the maintenance of standards of technical service, as well as by personal integrity; the guarantees may vary from a Hippocratic oath, through carefully written codes of conduct, to a general consensus of corporate opinion – often with sanctions for non-compliance.

Remuneration   The expectation, in return, of certain monetary rewards which would not be allowed to fall below certain minima, and which would be related to those enjoyed by other similar groupings or 'professions'; this expectation carried with it the perpetual danger that such minima, once agreed, would then be regarded by authority as maxima, and reactions to this hazard varied widely between the professions.

Community relationships   The existence of a feeling of corporate identity, which largely manifests itself in a complex of social and cultural relationships appropriate to the time.

Authority   The recognition by other professional groups, and, more important, by Government, of the authoritative nature of the pronouncements by accredited representatives of the group on matters relating to their special area of expertise.

CAR

NOTES AND REFERENCES

1 A. Findlay, 'The Royal Institute and the Profession of Chemistry', *Proc. Inst. Chem.*, 1944, **68**, 211–16 (211). On Findlay see ch. XIII, note 56.

2 R. B. Pilcher, *The Profession of Chemistry*, Constable, London, 1919, (2nd. edn. 1927, 3rd. edn. 1935, 4th edn. 1938 pub. by the Institute of Chemistry 'having been prepared by the Registrar under the supervision of the Publications Committee').

3 *Idem, History of the Institute: 1877–1914*, Institute of Chemistry, London, 1914.

4 On Pilcher himself see ch. XII (note 19).

5 Among recent writings see E. Shils 'The Profession of Science', *Adv. Science*, 1968, **24**, 469–80; J. Ben-David, 'The Profession of Science and its Powers', *Minerva*, 1972, **10**, 362–83; E. Mendelsohn, 'The Emergence of Science as a Profession in Nineteenth Century Europe', in K. Hill (ed.), *The Management of Scientists*, Beacon Press, Boston U.S.A., 1964, pp. 3–48; D. M. Knight, 'Science and Professionalism in England, 1770–1830', *Proc. XIVth Int. Congress Hist. Sci.*, Tokyo, 1974, **1**, 53–67.

6 The interface between science and technology in the period from 1800 is the subject of an Open University half-credit course, AST 281 *Science and the Rise of Technology since 1800*. Extensive bibliographies are available in connection with that course.

7 The classic work is A. M. Carr-Saunders and P. A. Wilson, *The Professions*, Clarendon Press, Oxford, 1933. It was issued as a Cass Reprint in 1964, pp. 165–75 dealing with 'Chemists'. See also W. J. Reader, *Professional Men: The Rise of the Professional Classes in Nineteenth-Century England*, OUP, New York, 1966.

8 Thus D. M. Knight commenting on a 'Professionalization of Science' symposium in 1974 concluded 'it is still difficult to know what we mean by the terms "professionalization" and "science". . . . So "professionalization" is a vague term, which must be applied differently in different countries; but perhaps we can use it to mean the emergence of a scientific community'. As will be seen from this chapter the modern concept of professionalization is considerably broader and more complex than that. It is, of course, possible to object to the application of modern concepts in an anachronistic way to past situations, and such objections are perfectly proper. But if one seeks to understand how a *modern* multi-strand idea has arisen it is surely necessary to trace the development of *all* of its components, not just one or two. And it is not then desirable to apply a modern omnibus term to some components in isolation from the rest (unless the term has since changed its meaning and contemporaries used it differently). In that case the onus is on the historian to prove it to be so. Knight (note 5), 4, 159.

9 A recent example is M. P. Crosland, 'The Development of a Professional Career in Science in France', in *The Emergence of Science in Western Europe*, ed. Crosland, Macmillan, London, 1975, pp. 139–59; also in *Minerva*, 1975, 13, 39–57.

CHAPTER II
ALCHEMISTS, ASSAYERS AND APOTHECARIES

1   The Alchemical Tradition

One of the oddest but most persistent features of chemical thinking over the last 150 years is the air of embarrassment with which chemists generally contemplate their intellectual origins in alchemy. This was not the only—or even the most important—movement in the prehistory of modern chemistry. But the popular opinion of the alchemist at work is in the strongest contrast to the image a modern professional chemist seeks for himself. The conception that chemistry can be a profession as well as a subject goes no farther back than the Victorian era, and it is arguably the case that this awareness has still not developed to its maximum extent. The Institute of Chemistry, founded in 1877, was the incarnation of this new professional spirit, and its first seal depicted not an alchemist but Priestley, a proposed new design incorporating suggestions of alchemical symbolism being rejected in 1944.[1]

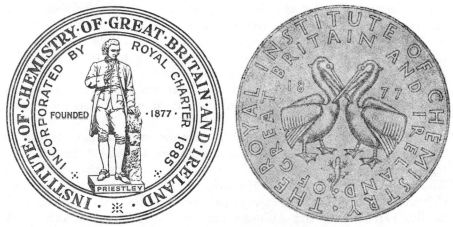

Figure 2(a)   The first seal of the Institute of Chemistry.
*   (b)   The rejected design, 1944.*

It is not hard to see how inappropriate the adjective of 'professional' must be for the alchemist[2] of popular convention, proceeding on the basis of inspired hunches or half-baked empirical knowledge, having regard to the welfare of no one but himself, with no assured prospects of having success, operating completely on his own and regarded by society, save his own, as a quack and charlatan. How far this popular understanding of the archetypal alchemist is correct and how far he lacked *any* kind of professional status we shall now proceed to examine.

So much scholarly study has now been made of alchemical ideas that their appalling complexity and diversity are a permanent warning to avoid generalization and over-simplification. Its diverse origins, the deliberate obscurity of much of its language, its strange blend of empiricism and mysticism all go to make alchemy one of the most formidable subjects for any historian to tackle.[3] Thus a belief in the efficacy of gold in prolonging life is very characteristic of Chinese alchemy but almost totally absent in the Greek variety. This in its turn varied from century to century and generally became less obscure as time went on.

At the basis of most alchemy lay the belief that matter, or at least its outward forms, can be changed. This, after all, is what nature is doing all the time, particularly in the processes of biological generation and decay. The mutation of nature became an obvious goal, whether by 'seeding' solutions with small amounts of the desired product or by applying external heat to hasten the processes of ripening or growth, or even by observing the heavens for propitious signs as in sowing and reaping. Indeed, there was frequently an association between the seven 'planets' and the seven metals then known (gold, silver, mercury, copper, lead, iron, tin).[4]

It is all too easy for modern science to write this off as mystical nonsense, yet the fact remains that chemistry did have such origins and that, in the context of the time, such ideas were nothing like as silly as they may seem to us. It would be going too far to claim that alchemy had an empirical basis (implying a similarity to, say, nuclear magnetic resonance spectroscopy) but it is true that a considerable mass of experimental data gave at least the appearance of credibility to some of the alchemists' most cherished beliefs. And some of the experiments performed by the Arab alchemists led to many important technical advances.

The practice of alchemy in the West cannot be dated much before the twelfth century. By the year 1200 there were available about six alchemical texts in Latin, derived from Arab sources through translations made at Toledo or some other centre of Moorish culture in Spain. From now on the alchemist enters on his long career in Europe and becomes an increasingly familiar part of the scene. Although certain central aspects of alchemy do not change noticeably during about six centuries the term alchemist has to cover at least three different classes of person. Firstly it was applicable somewhat loosely to those whose work was largely with metals and who can be regarded as the predecessors of the metallurgical developments of the sixteenth century (pp. 11-14). These men were the practitioners of alchemy, more concerned with its empirical basis than its metaphysical projection, and for this reason, almost always involved with operations at hearth or furnace. Here was the legendary 'puffer', earnest, credulous, motivated by a mixture of piety and avarice, yet a stranger to the holy mysteries of his more informed masters or rivals. He is a common feature of much alchemical art and is depicted thus by Chaucer in his Canon's Yeoman's Tale:[5]

> I am so used in the fyre to blowe,
> That it hath chaunged my colour I trowe . . .
> Though I was wont to be right fresh and gay
> Of clothing, and of other good array,
> Now may I were an hose upon myn heed;
> And where my colour was both fressh and red,
> Now it is wan, and of a leden hewe.

In contrast to these 'puffers', were the alchemical adepts, dabblers in esoteric mysteries, secret practitioners in the occult and custodians of the vast mass of Western alchemical literature. Being dependent on the written tradition they had to be literate and were usually clerics, often in a monastery. Over the centuries this group embraced a bewildering range of opinions and the outlines of these are just beginning to emerge from the clouds of verbiage which they gave forth. Their motives will have varied, but it seems that a genuine desire for knowledge and experience for their own sake as well as a strong interest in magic, usually exceeded the lust for gold. With greater understanding than the 'puffers' they had, as we shall see, greater reason to conceal what they knew. Their other-wordly naïveté contrasts strongly with the characteristics of a third group—the charlatans and con-men of pre-chemical science. If the adept was deceiving himself these were concerned to deceive others; if the adept whispered his secrets to a few initiates these would shout their own methods and their own merits from the house-tops. Many are the records of deliberate fraud and misrepresentation, and, so far as alchemical techniques are concerned, there were a few well-worn tricks, with appropriate variations.

The thirteenth century saw the pace of literary production show a noticeable quickening. Apart from a greater appetite for learning in general, there may have been a particular stimulus to alchemy in the money shortage that was manifest at the end of the century. Certainly the 'manufacture' of gold, real or imagined, was beginning to pose a sufficient threat to the stability of society though ecclesiastical opposition was expressing itself in many forms. In 1317 a Papal Bull was issued by John XXII from Avignon, prohibiting alchemical practice; it is an interesting comment on popular attitudes to record the widespread belief that the immense fortune left by the same Pope when he died was largely alchemical in origin. In similar vein modern chemists may ruefully reflect that their thirteenth-century predecessors were consigned by Dante together with other forgers and falsifiers of things to the tenth gulf of the Inferno.[6] This was the century of several outstanding figures in the history of chemistry: Albert Magnus and his English contemporary, Roger Bacon (1214–92), both outspoken critics of ancient authorities.

The fourteenth century witnessed several important technical advances and the appearance of hundreds more alchemical works, many of them saying little that was new but most managing to say it rather more clearly than before. The recognition of at least two of the three mineral acids (nitric and sulphuric) occurred during this period and their very reactivity and versatility seems to have promoted an odd reluctance to discuss them. As Multhauf observes,[7] the alchemists 'seemed to have believed that so profound a revelation should be theorized upon as a closely guarded secret'.

A characteristic of alchemy at this time was a strong desire for recognition and no better way could be imagined for achieving this than to append to one's work the name of a distinguished authority. The occurrence of such pseudepigrapha is characteristic of times of intense intellectual activity when enthusiasm gets the better of reason and honesty.

Despite mounting hostility on all sides the art proliferated in the fifteenth century and in England reached its zenith *c.* 1450. Thomas Norton, writing a few years later, in his *Ordinall of Alchemy* spoke of his subject in these terms:[8]

> Of every estate that is within Mankind
> If yee make search much people ye may finde,
> Which to *Alkimy* their Corage doe address
> Only for appetite of Lucre and Riches.
> As *Popes* with *Cardinalls* of *Dignity*,
> *Archbyshopes* with *Byshopes* of *high* degree;
> With *Abbots* and *Priors* of Religion,
> With *Friars, Heremites,* and *Preests* manie one,
> And *Kings* with *Princes* and *Lords* great of blood,
> For every estate *desireth* after good;
> And *Merchaunts* also which dwell in the fiere
> Of brenning Covertise, have thereto desire;
> And *Common workemen* will not be out-lafte,
> For as well as *Lords* they love this noble Crafte!

It was no doubt in this spirit that King Henry VI appointed a commission to inquire into the feasibility of replenishing his treasury by alchemical means.

It would be surprising if alchemy had been able to remain unaffected by the powerful forces released at the Renaissance and the Reformation and there is much evidence that it had not. Recent scholarship has emphasized the importance for science generally of the so-called *Hermetica*. This was a large body of Greek literature, probably from about A.D. 100, believed in the Renaissance to be the effusions of an Egyptian priest, Hermes Trismegistus, who was also supposed to have been the inspiration of Plato and the Greeks. In these highly mystical writings, freshly apprehended in the Renaissance, nature is viewed with a pantheistic devotion and therefore worthy of reverent study. An understanding of the importance attached to these writings has led to a re-interpretation in recent years of the events of the 'Copernican Revolution' and will certainly offer new insights into the literature of some of the alchemists, especially those who called themselves Hermetic philosophers. From now on, part of the literature of alchemy becomes increasingly suffused with a rather wild kind of mystical fervour. Nor was reformed Christianity without its impact and other recent work has demonstrated the impetus given to alchemy by Protestant theology.[9] The reasons are not yet fully clear, but may be connected with the Calvinistic general approval of experimental science and special approbation of that great transitional figure of the sixteenth century Theophrastus Bombastus von Hohenheim, otherwise known as Paracelsus. His career was as bizarre as his name (most of which he himself invented for purposes of publicity). More will be heard of him later but we will simply note here that he advocated a form of alchemy that was directly significant in many other ways for the development of chemical science, having been hailed as the 'father of chemotherapy and foreshadower of modern psychiatry'.[10] At very least he could be credited with liberating alchemy from a monomaniac obsession with gold production and an exclusive reliance on the four element theory of antiquity, as well as a failure to realize the importance of purity in chemical reagents.

In the seventeenth century alchemy was to enter its final period of prosperity. By now it had become sufficient of a public nuisance to earn the satirical wrath of Ben Jonson in his play *The Alchemist* (1610). At the other end of the century (and of the social scale) its claims are still sufficiently strong to endear itself to no less a personage than Charles II of England who attempted the 'fixation' of mercury in his private laboratory. But a much more impressive token of the fascination exerted over great minds is the known preoccupation with alchemical experiments of no less a personage than Sir Isaac Newton himself at the very end of the seventeenth century.

In general economic terms their expectations were as varied as their skills. The 'puffers', anxious to effect genuine transmutations for their own betterment were, in the nature of the case, almost always disappointed in the long run, and without the 'job satisfaction' that might have been the lot of those who, though unsuccessful in their ultimate objective, could produce many interesting changes and perhaps even identify with them. But for the 'puffer' all that could be expected was grinding poverty and this seems to have been as true in the sixteenth century as in the fourteenth century. This was the case of Chaucer's alchemist whose coat 'is not worthe a myte . . . it is al filthy and to-tore'.

For the genuine adepts society offered a strangely mixed response. On the one hand there is plenty of evidence that despite widespread scepticism many were prepared to give them the benefit of the doubt and to regard them as useful investments. Consequently we find them in Court appointments all over Europe from the fourteenth century to the seventeenth century, some even being lent or traded from one monarch to another. In England Edward III received two alchemists, prevented one from being imprisoned in 1336, and, in 1350, became arguably the first British monarch to give an endowment to chemical research. So intense was the interest aroused in Rudolph II of Prague that he is said to have neglected affairs of state in the interests of alchemy. Elsewhere the fortunate few who could gain a monarch's favour would enjoy great prosperity, even ennoblement. But in the nature of things they were a tiny minority although others in less exalted employment maintained a comfortable, if precarious, existence.

Against this we must set the fact that for much of the time alchemists of all kinds were execrated by society in both West and East. In fifteenth-century Europe the best that many could look forward to was a short itinerant career, terminated by crippling poverty. The worst was permanent exile, murder, the gallows or even crucifixion. If the Chinese provided some of alchemy's doctrines they also procured its destruction. An imperial edict of 144 B.C. decreed public execution for those who counterfeited gold, while a commentator three centuries later ascribes this to a disenchantment with alchemy itself.

In the West they suffered a further setback in the sustained opposition to alchemy from the Roman Catholic Church. Alchemy was first prohibited in the religious Orders: Franciscans (1272), Dominicans (1273), and Cistercians (1317). Then in 1317 came the Decretal of Pope John XXII attacking the art because of its defective theory (gold cannot be produced by art) and fraudulent practice. Thereafter the persecution of alchemists increased, although the Decretal appears to have been ignored in many of the subsequent debates among the faithful, e.g. on 'Whether an alchemist is a sinner and whether his art is prohibited'. Often a qualified approval was given. Had this not been the case the continued employment of alchemists would hardly have been as widespread as it became.[11]

More serious than this, however, was the cloud of suspicion hanging over the followers of Hermes by virtue of their secrecy and furtiveness. Some were known to make special claims for divine revelation and generally failed to conform to the standards of theological orthodoxy. So the fourteenth-century alchemists were in a heads-I-win-tails-you-lose kind of situation. If they failed to make real gold they were imposters and frauds; if against all expectation they succeeded they were heretics and deviants and, as such, even more dangerous to the Church. It has been suggested that after the initial rumblings of the Reformation the Hermetic philosophers might be able to constitute some kind of ecumenical bridge between Catholic and Protestant alchemists. This, of course, was a highly sensitive issue.

The clerical opposition undoubtedly caused a closing of the ranks and an even greater turning in upon themselves, at least as far as the adepts were concerned.[12]

A hundred years later Thomas Norton writes of 'a most sacred dreadfull oathe' required of those who had learned the 'secreats of Alkimy' although his work reveals a more rational and practical approach demonstrated by the organization of his laboratory, even to the extent of shift work for his 'ministers': 'One halfe of them must werke While the other Sleepeth or goeth to Kerke'.[13]

It was inevitably hard to reconcile the necessity for secrecy with the need for good communication between groups of adepts and one feels that anything approaching what we might call today 'professional unity' was entirely absent. Yet there is evidence that groups of alchemists met together right through the period, from a secret society at Basa in A.D. 950 to an alchemical Rosicrucian society at Nurnberg founded in 1654 with Leibniz as secretary and member for part of the time. The intention of such societies can hardly have been to advance the status of their members but it certainly included the exchange of information and ideas and this continued until the activities of the Hartlib circle in seventeenth-century England. As for the literary exchange of information the proliferation of literature bears ample testimony to this. The re-printing, or printing for the first time, of alchemical works in the sixteenth and seventeenth centuries has been of as much benefit to modern historians as to the adepts in those centuries. But how far all of this amounted to any kind of true professionalization is highly doubtful. What remains certain is the diversity of activities covered under the term 'alchemy' and it is in this sense alone that the words 'amateur' and 'professional' can be certainly applied. Two recent authors[14] speak of the distinction 'between those professional craftsmen who accepted the alchemical theories, and those who did not theorize about their art at all. The wildly impractical *amateur* alchemist, wasting his substance on fruitless researches, was emphatically a creature of medieval Europe: one more by-product of the intellectual indigestion which afflicted Europe from the twelfth century on'. This is effectively the distinction we have already made between the adept on the one hand and the 'puffer' on the other. Perhaps the distinction can be made sharper still. Thus a man like John Kunckel (who discovered the preparation of white phosphorus), holding a series of appointments of responsibility in alchemical laboratories, may be entitled to the epithet professional in the sense that his employment was that of a full-time alchemist. But in any other sense the day of professionalization for alchemy was never to arise.

2   The Metallurgical Tradition

The belief that alchemy was the only important precursor of modern chemistry has been held sufficiently long for it to have an air of respectable authenticity. That the facts are otherwise has been known for many years, although it is only in this century that an alternative view has begun to emerge strongly.

Shortly after the year 1500 an apparently new kind of technical literature began to appear.[15] This was a series of practical manuals for metallurgical and chemical operations. Unlike all except the most recent alchemical works these were printed books, often with a wealth of wood-cut illustrations. Two of the earliest of these were a *Bergbüchlein* (Augsburg, 1505) and a *Probier-büchlein* which saw many editions from about 1510. The authors of these and similar works are unknown and few copies survive—hardly surprising in view of their function as laboratory or workshop manuals. More famous is the *De La Pirotechnia* of 1540. Written by V. Biringuccio it dealt with a vast range of metallurgy, applied chemistry and pyrotechnics. The array of technical detail, in both text and illustration, was much vaster than anything before, and theories were kept well in the background. The author clearly has little brief for chemical speculations. Regarding alchemy he wrote 'The more I look into this art of theirs, so highly praised and so greatly desired by men, the more it seems a vain wish and fanciful dream'.

In much the same tradition, and clearly dependent upon it, was the *De Re Metallica* of Agricola, otherwise Georg Bauer, physician to several mining communities of Bohemia and Saxony. Here again was little theory and a massive account of metallurgical procedures (cupellation, liquation, cementation, amalgamation and the like), together with details of methods for assaying ores and metals, techniques for the preparation of 'strong waters' (mineral acids) and much else. A great deal of the book, though not all, comes straight from laboratory experience. As J. R. Partington observes 'The works chemist will sympathise with the direction that the laboratory should have no door, "lest anyone coming in at an inopportune moment might disturb his thoughts" '.[16]

These two great works—by Biringuccio and Agricola—enshrine a very different part of the prehistory of modern chemistry: technical laboratory experience, often in the area of metal production and assaying. It would be quite inaccurate to regard this tradition as one of rational science in contradistinction to metaphysical alchemy. Those who dealt in metals in the Middle Ages were as susceptible as anyone else to the beliefs and superstitions of their times. Indeed there was a specially mysterious association with mines and metals and it was hard to resist the conclusion that metals and stones did grow in the bowels of the earth. Hence came 'the idea that mining and metallurgy involved a kind of obstetric interference in a natural gestatory process, thus accelerating the natural growth of metals towards perfection—namely, gold'.[17] This persistent belief makes the sudden appearance of these prosaic technical manuals in the sixteenth century all the more remarkable—though all the more necessary! Distinctly light on theory, this literature has tended to be ignored by historians of chemical *ideas*. But its influence on chemical *practice*—particularly quantitative analysis—has been considerable.

It might seem that the accounts of assaying and of other techniques represented a sudden development in knowledge around 1500. Yet it is unlikely that this was so. There are traces of a continuous tradition of practical recipes relating to the various chemical arts going as far back as the eighth century. Thus a (probably) twelfth-century work by 'Theophilus', *Schedula Diversarium Artium*, does contain details of some preparative and analytical metallurgical techniques.

More direct evidence for the existence of a continuous tradition of chemical metallurgy before 1500 lies in the simple fact of debasement of the coinage and official reactions to it. Looking no further afield than England we can state the argument quite simply like this.

As far back as the twelfth century records from the Royal Mint demonstrate the need for controlling the quality of the coinage. Before the time of Henry II a great number of authorities—civil and ecclesiastical—had minted their own coins. By the middle of the thirteenth century the King's currency had been so maltreated that a new coinage had to be introduced and, in 1248, a jury of citizens and goldsmiths was formed to assure the country that the standards of the coinage were being maintained. This is the first recorded 'trial of the Pyx' (a ceremony that continued at intervals until 1870 when the Coinage Act stipulated an annual examination). Such trials must have included from the very beginning a chemical analysis or assay. Standards cannot be prescribed unless they can also be ascertained. This is borne out by the knowledge of such standards indicated in writings by Richard Fitzneal, Treasurer to Henry II, and Nicole Oresme, who in his *De Monetarum* (1355–8) discusses the morality of debasement of the coinage.[18]

Returning from this digression to the state of the art in the sixteenth century we can see that a continuous tradition of assaying must have existed through most of the Middle Ages. As Greenaway has pointed out it differed from all other chemical techniques in that it provided a service rather than a ropduct,[19] so perhaps we should expect the evidence to be of a rather different kind. The flood of literature in the sixteenth century can then be seen not as reflecting substantial advances in metallurgy but rather as a consequence of the invention of printing. Multhauf appears to underestimate the strength of the assaying tradition when he says that the new literature 'represents not a craft tradition but a rising interest of the community of learning in the arts'.[20] But these and other 'arts' were to become a proper subject for those gentlemen and amateurs who eventually found their way into the Royal Society.

Much still remains to be learnt of the conditions under which the assayers and metallurgists worked in the centuries before modern chemistry emerged. Their positions may have seemed less romantic than those of the court alchemists but some did exceedingly well nevertheless. One highly successful assayer in the sixteenth century was Lazerus Erker who enjoyed a series of appointments in Saxony and Bohemia as Assay Master and Warden of The Mint. It is amusing to recall that his final post was with that alchemical addict Rudolph II; doubtless his analyses of alchemical 'gold' were reported with tact and delicacy for he enjoyed much royal favour and was knighted in 1586. In the following century the literature on assaying increased still further, especially in Germany, as for example the *Elementa Artis Docimasticae* (1739) of J. A. Cramer, said to have been the best assayer of his day. Like many others he had to flee from his post (at Brunswick) because of personal vendettas and jealousies and it seems that assayers were remarkably successful in attracting to themselves this kind of treatment, presumably on account of the nature of their employment. If their occupation lacked a certain job security at least it kept alive a vital ingredient of the chemical tradition—quantitative analysis—that was to be crucially important several centuries later, in the first real moves to professional status that resulted in the foundation of the Institute of Chemistry.

3   The Medical Tradition

The modern chemist often tends to trace his pedigree back to the misty-eyed seekers of alchemical gold. Rather less obvious, though no less important, is his heritage of analytical techniques and attitudes from the craftsmen of the mines and metal-working shops in medieval Europe. A third line of ancestry may be identified in the assorted traditions of the medical and para-medical professions,[21] as suggested by the modern layman's use in that context of the very word 'chemist' itself. Indeed linguistic confusion on the proper use of that term eventually played a significant part in the struggle for professional recognition of 'chemists' of many kinds in the last century and even in the present one.

A rather extreme presentation of this case was expressed in the early nineteenth century by W. T. Brande, Humphry Davy's successor at the Royal Institution.

> The foundations of chemical science are to be found in the medical and pharmaceutical writers of the sixteenth century, who rescued it from the hands of the alchemical pretenders, and gave it a place and character of its own.

Brande took a particularly low view of alchemy: 'It presents nothing that the mind rests upon with satisfaction; nothing that it reverts to with interest or profit'.[22] He had been steeped in the tradition of pharmaceutical chemistry, his father having been Apothecary to George III and he, himself, the Professor of Chemistry to the Society of Apothecaries and its Master (1851). While his view of alchemy was undoubtedly defective his enthusiasm for the medical tradition in chemistry marks one of the earliest attempts to emphasize its special historical importance.

The trade of apothecary or druggist goes back to remote antiquity. It was chiefly, though not exclusively, concerned with the preparation of perfumery and cosmetics, as may be seen from the handful of biblical references to the apothecary's art (especially the eloquent comment of Ecclesiastes 10:1). Gradually substances of therapeutic significance (real or imagined) would be added to the stock of perfumes, eye paints, and sacred incense, and the apothecary gained a lowly foothold in the practice of healing. But we must not over-emphasize his role in ancient medicine. For all its achievements 'the weakest part of all ancient medicine was its pharmacology'.[23] The 'drugs' available to Galen and his predecessors included many that are now known to be totally useless, some that are distinctly revolting and a very few that still retain some use (such as castor oil).

These concoctions were rarely used on their own; the great characteristic of Galenist medicine was the prescription of mixtures of drugs of bewildering complexity, whose overall effect was supposed to produce exactly the right balance of humours. Cure-all nostrums might contain as many as eighty separate ingredients. How these medicines were prepared, and by whom, is still much of a mystery. But it is almost certain that somewhere in the shadows surrounding the practice of early medicine must have stood that enigmatic figure, the apothecary of the ancient and mediaeval worlds. Certainly from the eleventh century, when the first Arab pharmacopoeia appeared in Europe, the fruits of his labour became widely known through the numerous works on *materia medica* composed by the physicians of Spain.

In England the apothecaries were to become the first of the 'chemists' to seek and gain professional recognition, a process that began in 1617. But for several centuries before that another movement had been gathering momentum outside their ranks and, as it turned out, was of rather greater importance for the future development of the chemical profession. This new development can best be described as 'medical chemistry' and was, as Brande suggested, a derivative of alchemy. Its origins are a characteristic blend of mystical speculation and empirical knowledge.

By the early sixteenth century the range of materials on the apothecaries' shelves was extending for at least three reasons. First, there was, as we have seen, a new emphasis on chemical preparations—products of what we should now call 'reactions' in the shop or laboratory. One may cite the oft-quoted use of mercury in the treatment of syphilis which was just reaching epidemic proportions in Europe. Secondly, the liquors obtained by distillation were acquiring a new prominence; these included alcohol and alcoholic extracts of plant materials, as well as products obtained by subjecting these materials to heat and subsequent condensation ('essences'). Thirdly, new materials were being continually added as explorers returned from voyages overseas, some without any real therapeutic action, others potent beyond belief. The list included such substances as guaiacaum, opium, quinine, ipecacuanha and coca.

The great figure in this tradition is of course Paracelsus.[24] Born in Zürich in 1493 he pursued an itinerant and erratic medical career through Europe collecting a vast assortment of ideas from the multitudes of vagrants and others whom he met: astrologers, barber-surgeons, executioners and (especially) 'medical chemists' for whom he expressed particular admiration. At the age of thirty-three he became City Physician at Basle. In keeping with his contempt for the medicine of the past he assumed the name Paracelsus to indicate his superiority over the Roman physician Celsus and made a spectacular start to his new career in Basle by urging the study of 'nature and her works' rather than the books of Hippocrates, Galen and Avicenna, condemning their doctrines as false and at the midsummer bonfire celebrations of 1527 consigning their works to the depths of the flames. 'Thus the realm of medicine has been purged.'

The violent barn-storming antics of this colourful mountebank brought him many enemies and his departure from Basle was as sudden as it was necessary. Caught up in the intellectual convolutions of the Renaissance he still remains much of a mystery. No chemist, and perhaps not much of an experimenter himself, he has been termed 'the prince of quacks and imposters' but he bequeathed to chemistry a twofold legacy. First were his modifications of Aristotle's four elements theory which need not detain us here. Secondly, he gave a powerful re-direction to the whole course of chemical inquiry. He offered it a new objective:

> Many have said of alchemy that it is for making gold and silver. For me such is not the aim but to consider only what virtue and power may lie in medicine.

He also gave it a new name: 'iatrochemistry', chemistry applied to medicine. And, in a strange way, something of his own contentious spirit entered the practice of iatrochemistry as physicians and universities aligned themselves for or against the Paracelsan teaching. Paracelsus himself had early incurred the wrath of the Roman Catholic Church and that body remained largely antagonistic to medical chemistry for many decades. Thus it was of little importance outside the largely Lutheran Germany until well into the seventeenth century. There, however, it flourished. At Jena Andreas Libavius (c. 1540–1616) from his University Chair of History and Poetry was preparing a vast literary output on chemical matters including writings not uncritical to iatrochemistry and a work *Alchemia* (1597) that has been described as 'the first systematic textbook on chemistry'. More important still was J. R. van Helmont (1597–1644) who, though largely critical of much Paracelsan doctrine, has yet been called his greatest follower. A Roman Catholic himself he suffered at the hands of the Inquisition then active in his native Brussels. He marks much more clearly than Paracelsus a broadening of the movement of iatrochemistry into a noticeable transition stage between alchemy and chemistry. Not least of his achievements was that of being probably the first chemist to deal with gases as such.

But the iatrochemists did not have it all their own way. Certainly there was religious opposition though the traditionalists in medicine took a strong anti-Paracelsan line also. Often it is hard to disentangle the two reasons as in the case of the Protestant theologian, Erastes, who was both strongly anti-Calvinist and anti-Paracelsan. By the seventeenth century relations between the iatrochemists and the traditional physicians had reached such a bad state that the controversy became known as the 'Antimony War'. The name arose from the inclusion in so many medicines of preparations containing antimony. There was nothing new in the medical use of minerals like antimony sulphide but it was an innovation to take such trouble preparing what was hopefully taken to be a 'pure' simple substance. Here in fact lay a crux of the medical conflict, because the Galenists had taken the opposite line of preparing enormously complex mixtures. This was in complete contrast to the approach of the iatrochemists though they obviously lacked our full understanding of 'chemical purity' and, even more so, 'chemical identity'.

The medical chemists replied vigorously to their attackers. No longer content to defend medical objectives as worthy for a chemist they declared much more positively 'without this chemical philosophy, all Physik is but lifeless' (O. Kroll, 1608). Perhaps the most remarkable piece of polemics from the medical chemistry side is to be found in the oddly titled *The Triumphal Chariot of Antimony*. Ascribed to a fifteenth-century monk, Basil Valentine, the work is in fact a literary fraud, certainly one hundred years later than it purports to be and possibly the work of one Johann Thölde. Whoever he may be the author struck an effective blow for the iatrochemists in general and the medical use of antimony compounds in particular.

The antimony war was fought and won by the middle of the seventeenth century. From then on chemistry was at the service of medicine. Yet, sadly, men had to wait a few centuries more before chemotherapy was able to make a real impact on the diseases which ravaged them.

But if medicine enjoyed few short-term gains from the efforts of the chemist, chemistry itself must have profited enormously. There were many spin-off advantages in a deepening understanding of chemical processes and composition. Also chemistry became gradually recognized as a subject for study that was worthy in itself. Above all, the new changes demanded and secured new efforts for chemical instruction and training.

The apothecary was the first to benefit. Jean Beguin was a medical chemist in France in the early seventeenth century; he may well have been the discoverer of calomel (Hg_2Cl_2), and he certainly was one of the first to teach the production of chemical medicine, publishing his book *Tyrocinium*

Chymicum in 1610. He worked in Paris, noted for its traditional opposition to Paracelsan ideas. Yet a few years later the Jardin du Roi, originally a herb garden, received its first demonstrator in chemistry.

At the same time as Beguin was lecturing his pharmaceutical apprentices in Paris other developments were taking place in Germany. In 1609 Johann Hartmann was appointed Professor of Iatrochemistry at Marburg—the first university chair in a chemical science. Although the appointment lasted only until 1620 Hartmann quickly won a European reputation and elsewhere in Germany other similar appointments were made. Further afield chemistry had to wait rather longer for recognition in the form of university chairs. But in 1673 one was founded at Montpellier, the traditional rival to Paris and a stronghold of anti-Roman Catholicism. In the Low Countries at Utrecht (1694) and Leiden (1702), and at Oxford (1683) and Cambridge (1703) the foundation of chemical chairs again illustrates the tendency for the subject to flourish in Protestant rather than Roman Catholic universities. Thus it seems clear that the growth of the medical tradition in chemistry in one way or another led to a further step forward in its progress towards professionalization: the establishment of the subject as a university science and the provision of means whereby its practitioners could be properly trained.

That this was the major contribution of the growth of medical chemistry to the changing status of chemistry itself can hardly be doubted. Yet its impact might be expected to have been so much greater, for the apothecary was the first kind of 'chemist' to display a professional consciousness and to engage in significant corporate activity to improve the lot of his profession in society. In the event, however, other forces than those emanating from the practice of pharmacy were to prove more powerful in raising chemistry to professional rank. Nowhere does this emerge more clearly than in the case of the Society of Apothecaries in London.[25]

It must be admitted that any connection between the practice of the earliest English apothecaries and what would be recognizable as chemistry was slender indeed. They appear in the Middle Ages as rather superior retainers in wealthy households, successors to the Spicers and Pepperers whose duties they took over, together with the care of drugs and those spices and perfumes which made life tolerable in insanitary and ill-ventilated houses. The *Apothecarius* in the great house or at Court had comrades in the world of commerce whose activities in importing and selling commodities led naturally to liaison with those who practised 'the craft and mistery of the Company of Grocers', and they were admitted to that ancient institution of the City of London at least as early as the sixteenth century. Thanks to the increase in foreign trade, and doubtless to their own business acumen as well, many of these apothecaries advanced high in the social scale. Others, particularly outside London, might have been more instantly recognizable in this description by Shakespeare's Romeo[26] (ostensibly in Mantua but also typically in England):

I do remember an apothecary,
And hereabouts 'a dwells, which late I noted
In tattered weeds, with overwhelming brows,
Culling of simples; meagre were his looks,
Sharp misery had worn him to the bones;
And in his needy shop a tortoise hung,
An alligator stuff'd, and other skins
Of ill-shaped fishes; and about his shelves
A beggarly account of empty boxes,
Great earthen pots, bladders, and musty seeds,
Remnants of packthread, and old cakes of roses,
Were thinly scatter'd to make up a show.

In addition to their selling, most, if not all, the apothecaries would spend much of their time compounding medicines as well as 'culling of simples'. Not surprisingly this led to a differentiation within the Company of Grocers and the beginning of a secession movement that was to become a familiar feature of later stages in the rise of the chemical profession. Centrifugal forces began to be generated from within the Company but their effect was greatly magnified by pressures exerted by another body, the College of Physicians. To appreciate the factors which were involved in this stage of professional evolution of 'chemistry' it is necessary to look first, but briefly, at the struggles taking place in the related field of medicine.

Until the sixteenth century the practice of the medical arts was pursued by great varieties of people, clerical and lay, but because of his indispensability to society the 'doctor' enjoyed an increasingly high social status and (not unnaturally) resented tendencies which would deprive him of these benefits. Since the establishment and maintenance of a privileged status can only be accomplished with reference to those who are *not* to be admitted to the élite circle, people who were in a traditionally more powerful position began to make monopolistic claims so as to exclude their less effective rivals. In the case of medicine this became expressed in the attempted subjugation of the surgeons by the physicians. Given the absence of anaesthesia it is not hard to understand that the services of a physician were more frequently to be called for than those of a surgeon, and of course the whole tradition of Galen and Avicenna was predominantly medical rather than surgical. Furthermore the surgeons were usually associated with barbers and generally regarded in the same way, i.e. as skilled craftsmen rather than custodians of ancient knowledge. And it was rare, both in this country and abroad, to find a surgeon who knew Latin, that universal *lingua franca* of medical communication. For all these reasons, and doubtless others as well, the surgeon was the poor relation of the physician, but in England decisive steps were not taken to assert the asymmetry of their relationship until the reign of Henry VIII. It seems more than likely that a hidden driving-force behind the moves that then took place was the increasing secularization of society and the general weakening of the church's domination. So it was that, in 1518, the College of Physicians was incorporated, given a superintending role over the practice of medicine as a whole (including the privilege of licensing practitioners), and granted freedom from ecclesiastical interference. This last benefit is given added significance in the light of an Act, passed only seven years before, limiting the practice of medicine or surgery, within seven miles of London, to those examined and approved by the Bishop of London or the Dean of St Paul's.

The surgeons lost no time in pressing their own case and, in 1540, were, together with the barbers, incorporated as Masters or Governors of the Mistery and Commonalty of Barbers and Surgeons of London. But they still remained in an inferior position. Members could be called in to a case by a physician, but could not prescribe medicine; on the other hand a member of the College of Physicians was allowed to perform surgical operations.[27]

> Forasmuch as the science of Physick doth comprehend, include and contain the knowledge of Surgery, as a special member and part of the same, Therefore be it enacted, That any of the said Company or Fellowship of Physicians, may from time to time, as well within the City of London, as elsewhere within this Realm, practise and exercise the said science of Physick in all and every his members and parts.

The consequences were totally predictable. Jealousies on the part of the surgeons led to widespread flouting of the restrictions imposed upon them, while the physicians spent much of their energies seeking to maintain their monopoly in the London area, examining candidates and indulging in an almost ceaseless stream of prosecutions against those who were deemed to have practised illicitly. Amongst those involved in these proceedings in the early seventeenth century was a Censor of the Royal College of Physicians, the discoverer of the circulation of the blood, William Harvey.[28] Long after his time wrangles continued, though gradually the position of the lowly surgeons improved. In 1745 they were constituted a separate company, the barbers forming their own, and in 1800 the surgeons' company became the Royal College of Surgeons in London. But for nearly three centuries the medical profession was ruled by the members of the College of Physicians.

Against this background of professional in-fighting and rivalries the apothecaries' moves towards recognition were taking place, under the watchful eye of the physicians. Their separation from the grocers in some ways presents a parallel to the eventual differentiation between barbers and surgeons, though it happened far more quickly. An Act of 1540 seems to have been the first *de jure* recognition of the *de facto* difference between them and the other members of the Grocers' Company; their Wardens, together with Censors from the College of Physicians, were empowered to search apothecaries' shops in London and destroy any materials found to be defective. This must be one of the earliest legal enactments relating to professional standards of a chemical nature. The next step forward was not until 1607 when an amendment to the charter of the Grocers' Company gave formal recognition to the existence of the Apothecaries as a separate section within it. From there it was but a step to the logical conclusion of complete secession from the grocers with the prize of Court representation almost within their grasp. The Apothecaries moved swiftly and enlisted as their spokesman Gideon de Laune, apothecary to Anne of Denmark, wife of King James I of England. De Laune (1565–1659) was the son of an emigré French Protestant pastor who had studied medicine at Montpellier and Paris.[29] His aid was sought—and given—for a direct petition to the King for a Charter as a Livery Company. Just as the physicians had tried to exclude the surgeons, so the apothecaries now attempted to suppress the quack producer of medicines. Their reasons were properly altruistic:[30]

> Very many Empiricks and unskilful and ignorant men do abide in the City of London . . . which are not well instructed in the Art or Mystery of the Apothecaries, but do make and compound many unwholesome, hurtful, dangerous and corrupt medicines and the same do sell . . . to the great peril and daily hazard of the lives of the King's subjects.

A plea so reasonable, supported by precedents from many other European states, might have seemed quite unexceptionable. But that would have been to reckon without the powerful forces in the City. The grocers were not overjoyed with the distinction proposed by the King—'Grocers are but merchants [but] the business of an Apothecary is a Mistery'—and did all they could to retain the unwilling apothecaries.[31] In any case the secession movement was not unanimous. There were attractions in continued association with the great Livery Company of the Grocers and those who preferred to remain are said to have described their errant colleagues as mere 'tobacco-sellers' in the hope that the non-smoking James might be impressed with their evil intentions.

In the event a Charter was awarded and, from 6 December 1617, the City of London boasted a new Livery Company, the Society of Apothecaries. By 1632 they had amassed sufficient capital to acquire Cobham House, Blackfriars, as their Hall. This was destroyed in the Great Fire of 1666, but the new Apothecaries' Hall built on the site a year or two later, proclaimed its owners' determination to survive, whether assailed by fire or physicians. It still stands, the repository of many relics from those tempestuous days.

By a strange paradox a decisive factor that tipped the scales in favour of the apothecaries was the ever-growing hostility of that other city institution, the College of Physicians. For some time a mutual antipathy had been growing between physicians and apothecaries, the former having scored a notable point in the following resolution by the Common Council of the City of London in 1523: 'th' apothecaryes maybe swore and uppon a payne commaunded that they shall not serve any byll of any physicians not examyned and approved' by the College.[32] In similar vein the apothecaries had responded to the news that their rivals had opened a Physic Garden (with which to produce their own drugs) by protesting to the Queen. This was unsuccessful and the already strained relations were made no better by numerous excursions of individual apothecaries into the area of medical prescription. Undoubtedly their unofficial efforts were often successful, though at other times they did much harm. In either event they occasioned deep hostility from the physicians, but this very fact was to prove a valuable asset at the time of their petition for their own Charter. It won them two formidable allies in the King and his Lord Chancellor, Sir Francis Bacon, each of whom regarded the physicians with dislike, thus favouring their natural enemies the apothecaries. The reason for James I's dislike of physicians is not very clear but the fact is certain.[33] With such powerful support it is not surprising that the apothecaries' cause was able to triumph in 1617. Much more remarkable is the fact that the College of Physicians lent their weight to that cause.[34]

In 1614 the College indicated its approval of a separation of apothecaries from the grocers. Perhaps it was by now obvious the way things were going, and the College did not wish to oppose the inevitable. But they certainly saw advantages for themselves in the new situation. Thus the College petitioned the King to consider the malpractices of the apothecaries and urged that they be bound to dispense drugs solely under prescription by physicians. In the actual Charter an oath to this effect was dropped (at the instigation of Bacon himself, it seems), but the seven-year period of apprenticeship[35] was continued, to be terminated in examination by nominees of the College. In this way the 'chemists' were to exchange the tutelage of the grocers for that of the physicians, although in real terms their independence was considerably advanced.

In the years that followed the granting of the Charter, the apothecaries constantly tried to make their independence complete. At first they confined their challenge to the treating of patients without a fee, payment being asked only for the medicines they prescribed. Increasingly their services were in demand, especially for London's poor. When, during the Civil War and later in the Plague, most of the physicians left London, the apothecaries remained and flourished. The physicians, however, in financial difficulties after losing their Hall in the Great Fire (and blaming their rivals for much of their loss of income), stepped up their harassment. In 1675 they tried, unsuccessfully, for exclusive rights to search out apothecaries' shops for poor materials. Twenty years later, taking a leaf from their rivals' book, they established a Dispensary at Warwick Lane for the poor of London, selling their own medicines at rates which undercut those of the apothecaries. This institution lasted for thirty years and further embittered relations. Nor was this all, for a fierce literary assault was also launched upon the apothecaries' cause. Most notable at the time, though now almost totally forgotten, was the mock-heroic poem *The Dispensary* (1699) by the high-born poet and physician Sir Samuel Garth (1661–1719):[36]

> Long has he been of that amphibious Fry,
> Bold to prescribe, and busie to apply;
> His Shop the gazing Vulgar's Eyes employs,
> With foreign Trinkets and domestick toys.
> Here, *Mummies* lay most reverendly stale,
> And there, the Tortois hung her Coat of Mail;
> Not far from some huge *Shark's* devouring Head
> The flying Fish their finny Pinions spread.
> Aloft in rows large Poppy Heads were strung,
> And near, a scaly Alligator hung.
> In this place, Drugs in Musty heaps decay'd
> In that, dry'd Bladders, and drawn Teeth were laid,

and so on, Apothecaries' Hall itself being described as

> a structure on a rising Hill
> Where *Tyros* take their freedom out to kill.

Dryden was scarcely less abusive:[37]

> Th' Apothecary-Train is wholly blind.
> From Files, a Random-*Recipe* they take,
> And many deaths of One Prescription make,

while Alexander Pope asserted:[38]

> So modern 'pothecaries taught the Art
> Through doctors' bills to play the doctors' part,
> Bold in the practice of mistaken rules,
> Prescribe, apply, and call their masters fools.

A decisive turn of events in the apothecaries' favour occurred in the celebrated case of William Rose. A member of the Society, he was successfully prosecuted by the College of Physicians for prescribing as well as compounding medicines. On taking an appeal to the House of Lords, however, he secured a reversal of the judgement on the basis that such treatment was common practice and in the best public interest (1703). From then on the right to prescribe (though not to charge for it) was unassailable. Further improvements in the apothecary's status occurred in 1748 (when the Society was empowered to appoint ten examiners responsible for issuing dispensing licences in the London area) and in 1815 when its powers were extended over all England and Wales and it received for the first time the independent right to issue licences for the practice of general medicine. But for those who chose to continue the practice of pharmaceutical chemistry (as opposed to medicine) that victory must have seemed a hollow one indeed, for in 1815 the Society had scarcely one of them in its ranks! Elated by its successes during the eighteenth century the Society had become more and more exclusively medical and, in 1774, had [39] limited its Livery to those members engaged in medical practice. This merely consummated a tendency of some decades in which the compounders and manufacturers of drugs had left in large numbers to ply their trade independently, sometimes in the new firms that were to provide the foundations for Britain's pharmaceutical chemicals industry. No longer linked to a powerful parent body most of them were to remain unfederated until the foundation of the Pharmaceutical Society in 1841, the same year that saw the birth of the Chemical Society. So when, in 1816, Jane Austen writes in *Emma* that 'Mr Perry the Apothecary was an intelligent gentleman-like man whose frequent visits were one of the greatest comforts of Mr Woodhouse's life', the one thing we may be sure of is that Mr Perry was in no sense a predecessor of the modern chemist.

It simply remains to add that the apothecaries of London, like their counterparts overseas, played an important role in the education of their apprentices and that this, at least until mid-eighteenth century, embraced a considerable training in that branch of chemistry we term pharmacy. A laboratory for Galenic medicines was founded in 1623 and another one for 'chemical' medicines was established in 1671. The Physic Garden at Chelsea was first rented in 1673; it was accessible by the State Barge of the Company and, more to the point, was of value in training apprentices in their studies on *materia medica*. Later rented from Sir Hans Sloane it still remains a tranquil reminder of the days when the advancement of the profession of pharmaceutical chemistry and the training of English apprentices in its skills lay largely in the hands of a picturesque Livery Company of the City of London.

4 The Amateur Tradition in research: the End of an Era

It remains to note briefly the existence of a class of chemists who owed much to the threefold tradition of the past, yet were, in the early nineteenth century, having to give place to the new type of chemist. These were the amateur research workers, soon to become an almost extinct species. [40] The transition—and the constrast—can be clearly seen in two great figures of English chemistry at this period, Davy and Dalton.

The young Cornish chemist Humphry Davy [41] had many virtues, but it must be confessed that modesty was not one of them. In the year 1800 he wrote to his mother 'My future prospects are of a very brilliant nature'. [42] Time was to prove that this was no idle boast. Before him lay discoveries in electrochemistry that include the isolation of sodium and potassium and were to open up the way to an electrical view of chemical change, research in tanning and agricultural chemistry, invention of the safety lamp and much else besides. And the public acclamation that meant so much to him was to be accorded by the fashionable audiences who graced his lectures at the Royal Institution and even by his country's mortal foe, Napoleon I who, in 1807, awarded him the prize for the best research in galvanic electricity. The career that lay ahead of him was to include a Professorship at the Royal Institution, consultancies and medals from far and near, and finally, the coveted Presidency of the Royal Society. Clearly few of his contemporaries could look forward to quite such good fortune, but few would have espoused a life-style so much in contrast with that of Davy as did his Manchester rival, John Dalton.[43]

Dalton, like Davy, has received the homage of posterity. His own massive contribution to the science of the chemical atomic theory began to be recognized in his own lifetime and at his civic funeral commercial life in Manchester came virtually to a standstill. Yet apart from their deserved fame there was little in common between Dalton and Davy. The Manchester Quaker lived comfortably, but no more, and earned his living by taking in pupils until, eventually, a modest pension was granted to him from the Civil List. He rarely travelled to London and was mostly content with intellectual stimulus offered by the Literary and Philosophical Society of his own city.

In many ways these two men, representing as they do the apogee of English chemistry in the early nineteenth century, could hardly have been more different. Dalton was the embodiment of a long-standing tradition of amateur science, not being paid to do scientific work, of sufficient means to pursue independent research, equally at home in other branches of science as in chemistry (he did noteworthy research in colour-blindness and in meteorology), and genuinely seeking scientific truth for its own sake rather than for any material advantage it might bring to himself or mankind as a whole. By contrast Davy claimed 'philosophy, chemistry, and medicine are my profession'.[44]

But another two years later he had obviously felt that this was not an adequate description, for he wrote to Davies Gilbert of his new post with 'as much power as I could reasonably expect, or even wish for at my time of life, secured to me without the obligation of labouring at a profession'.[45] Until about 1805 he toyed with the idea of a medical career but after that time the call of chemistry was too strong to be denied. His predecessor, Thomas Garnett, had found to his cost that the managers would not permit a duality of roles, medical and chemical; it had to be one *or* the other.

Despite their differences Davy and Dalton nevertheless had several things in common. Neither man had received a formal scientific training, Dalton having learnt what science he knew from his schoolmaster Elihu Robinson and the blind philosopher John Gough, Davy having been a surgeon's apprentice before becoming assistant to Beddoes at the Bristol Pneumatic Institute. Secondly, neither received any unambiguous testimonial to his excellence as a chemist other than the plaudits of his audience and (in due course) the various tokens of royal or civic favour; for in fact no corporate body then existed that could have furnished such evidence. Finally, notwithstanding the Royal Society and the Manchester 'Lit and Phil', no welcome to its ranks was extended to Davy or Dalton by any independent British society or institution devoted specially to the science of chemistry. Such an institution did exist in their lifetimes but, as we shall see, it was not graced by their presence. It is no disrespect to Dalton to assert that in almost no way can he be described as a professional chemist (any more than Lavoisier, Priestley, Cavendish or Boyle), while Davy represents a transition towards something that the later nineteenth century was to make distinctively its own—the professional chemist.

CAR

NOTES AND REFERENCES

1 *Proc. Inst. Chem.*, 1944, **68**, 135–6. The emblem of the pelicans—an alchemical term for early distillation apparatus—was regarded by some as reminiscent of Tenniel's illustrations to *Alice in Wonderland*.

2 The literature on alchemy is vast, the following being a very short selection: (a) Mircea Eliade, *The Forge and the Crucible*, Harper, New York, 1971; (b) E. J. Holmyard, *Alchemy*, Penguin, London, 1957; (c) R. P. Multhauf, *The Origins of Chemistry*, Oldbourne, London, 1966; (d) John Read, *Through Alchemy to Chemistry: a Procession of Ideas and Personalities*, Bell, London, 1961; (e) *Idem*, 'Alchemy and Literature', *Proc. Chem. Soc.*, 1957, 138–43; (f) *Idem, ibid.*, 1958, pp. 162–6; (g) H. J. Sheppard, 'Alchemy: origin or origins?', *Ambix*, 1970, **17**, 69–84; (h) F. Sherwood Taylor, *The Alchemists*, Schuman, New York, 1949; (i) L. Thorndike, *A History of Magic and Experimental Science*, 8 vols, Columbia UP, New York, 1923–58.

3 For a summary of this problem see Read, note 2 (d), p. 14.

4 Such mystical notions were often intertwined with those from astrology and there were others more recondite still. The deeper symbolism of all chemical changes was in death and resurrection, for which Christian theology had no doubt some responsibility. Amongst many others the psychologist Jung has seen alchemy as a response to a universal, if subconscious, projection of a basic human instinct for renewal and clarification. The builder becomes identified with his materials and his quest becomes the redemption of matter itself. See, e.g., L. H. Martin, Jr., 'A history of the psychological interpretation of alchemy', *Ambix*, 1975, **22**, 10–20.

5 Geoffrey Chaucer, Canon's Yeoman's Tale, lines 666–7 and 724–8.

6 Dante, *The Divine Comedy*, Part I, 'The Inferno', Canto XXX.

7 Note 2 (c), p. 179.

8 From F. Sherwood Taylor, *A Short History of Science*, Heinemann, London, n.d., p. 112.

9 This could be Lutheran, as suggested by J. W. Montgomery, 'Cross, Constellation and Crucible: Lutheran astrology and alchemy in the Age of the Reformation', *Ambix*, 1963, **11**, 65–86; or Calvinistic, as proposed by W. Hubicki, 'The religious background of the development of alchemy at the turn of the XVIth century', *Actes de XII Congrès International d' Histoire des Sciences*, Paris, 1968, **3a**, 81–6.

10 See, e.g., H.M. Pachter, *Paracelsus, Magic into Science*, Schuman, New York, 1951.

11 For a discussion of religious attitudes to alchemy in the early fourteenth century see Chiara Crisciani, *Ambix*, 1973, **20**, 165–81.

12 In the *New Pearl of Great Price* by Petrus Bonus (about 1330) the author praises the obscurity and ambiguity of alchemical writing on two grounds. First, it enables the God-given secrets to be adequately protected from the uninitiated. Secondly, it makes possible in practice a distinction between the true and false brethren; the latter will fail to comprehend it and will stand revealed for what they are. The others will show by their understanding that they too share in the divine illumination.

13 Read (note 2 (d)), p. 87.

14 Stephen Toulmin and June Goodfield, *The Architecture of Matter*, Hutchinson, London, 1962, p. 119.

15 On the metallurgical tradition see especially Multhauf (note 2 (c)) and J. R. Partington, *A History of Chemistry*, Macmillan, London, vol. ii, 1961, ch. II.

16 J. R. Partington (note 15), p. 48.

17 For a full treatment of this theme see Eliade (note 2 (a)).

18 Until the fifteenth century the duties of the King's Assay Master were performed by the Warden of the Mint, though later this post was filled by an accredited assayer, in other words, a professional. This officer was later joined by the Master's Assayer whose concern was the composition of raw materials. Further changes took place in 1851, 1870 and again in 1888 when the title of Chemist and Assayer was conferred on the successor to the Queen's Assay Master. W. A. C. Newman, *British Coinage*, RIC Lectures, Monographs & Reports, London, 1953.

19 F. Greenaway, 'The Historical Continuity of the Tradition of Assaying', *Actes of Xth International Congress of the History of Science*, Ithaca, 1962, pp. 819–23.

20 Multhauf (note 2 (c)), p. 258.

21 On the medical tradition in chemistry see especially Holmyard (note 2 (b)), Multhauf (note 2 (c)) ch. X, Partington (note 15) chs. III–IV, and A. G. Debus, *English Paracelsians*, Oldbourne, London, 1961.

22 These two citations from Brande's *Historical Sketch of the Origins and Progress of Chemical Philosophy*, 1840, are included in H. W. Picton, *The Story of Chemistry*, London, 1889 (pp. 85 and 55), a 'Whiggish' piece of history which persistently underplayed themes which later science was to deem 'wrong'.

23 Sherwood Taylor (note 8), p. 46.

24 On Paracelsus see especially Partington (note 15), ch. III, Holmyard (note 2 (b)) ch. VIII, H.M. Pachter (note 10) and W. Pagel, *Paracelsus*, Karger, Basel and New York, 1958.

25 See W. S. C. Copeman, *The Worshipful Society of Apothecaries of London: a History 1617–1967*, Pergamon Press, London, 1967; C. R. B. Barrett, *The History of the Society of Apothecaries of London*, Elliot Stock, London, 1905; and note 32.

26 *Romeo and Juliet*, Act V, Scene 1.

27 Act of Henry VIII, 1541, in Charles Goodall, *The College of Physicians Vindicated*, London, 1676, p. 20.

28 Harvey's discovery dealt the death-blow to the medicine of Galen.

29 On both de Launes, father and son, see *DNB*.

30 Cited in Copeman (note 25), p. 18.

31 Grocers . . . are but Merchants . . . they . . . bring home rotten wares from the Indies, Persia and Greece . . . and think no man must control them because they are not Apothecaries.

J. A. Rees, *The Worshipful Company of Grocers, an Historical Retrospect, 1345–1923*, Chapman and Dodd, London, 1923.

32 C. Wall, H. C. Cameron and E. A. Underwood, *A History of the Worshipful Society of Apothecaries of London*, vol. i, *1617–1815*, OUP, London, 1963, p. 8.

33 The clinical notes of his personal physician, Sir Theodore de Mayerne, conclude with the following note of resignation: 'The King laughs at medicine and holds it so cheap that he declares physicians to be of very little use and hardly necessary. He asserts the art of medicine to be supported by mere conjectures and useless because uncertain.' The substance of Bacon's objection to the physicians seems to have been their sheer lack of progress as a profession: 'Medicine is a science which hath been more professed than laboured, and yet more laboured than advanced, the labour having been, in my judgement, rather in a circle than in progression.' (Translation in Norman Moore, *The History of the Study of Medicine in the British Isles*, Clarendon Press, Oxford, 1908, p. 106.)

34 On the conflict between physicians and apothecaries from a different standpoint, rather more sympathetic to the former (including the attitude of Bacon, pp. 158–9) see Sir Geoffrey Keynes, *The Life of William Harvey*, Clarendon Press, Oxford, 1966 (especially ch. VIII).

35 This system had been introduced in Elizabethan times for all trades.

36 Samuel Garth, *The Dispensary*, 1699, Canto II, lines 107–18; Canto III, lines 113–14.

37 John Dryden, *Epistle: To my Honour'd Kinsman John Driden*, 1700, lines 104–6.

38 Alexander Pope, *Essay on Criticism*, 1711, lines 108–11.

39 C. Wall, H. C. Cameron and E. A. Underwood (note 32), p. 188.

40 These were men who dominated the history of British chemistry from the seventeenth century to the early nineteenth century: Boyle, Hooke, Mayow, Cavendish, Priestley and many others. They have been so well reported that further commentary is unnecessary here.

41 On Davy see (a) Sir Harold Hartley, *Humphry Davy*, Nelson, London, 1966 (reprint SRP, 1971); (b) Anne Treneer, *The Mercurial Chemist*, Methuen, London, 1963.

42 Letter dated 27 September 1800, in Rolleston collection (copy in Royal Institution).

43 On Dalton see ch. IV, note 76.

44 Letter dated 1799, in Rolleston Collection.

45 Letter dated 8 March 1801, in Treneer (note 41 (b)), p. 74.

CHAPTER III
WHO IS A CHEMIST?

1   Introduction

To those responsible for official analyses of the occupations pursued in these islands, the existence of chemists has long been a source of perpetual and grave embarrassment. The term 'chemist' had a multiplicity of connotations that were the despair of the statistical recorders, as may be seen without much difficulty in those invaluable sources of social statistics, the decennial censuses of Great Britain and Ireland from 1841 onwards.[1] Earlier census returns had lacked the attempted precision of later ones and had therefore not posed the same problems.

A division of chemists into 'chemists and druggists' on one hand and something like 'manufacturing chemists' on the other appeared in 1841. By 1861 manufacturing chemists had been assigned to the 'Industrial Class',—the class of workers and artisans. Not so the chemists and druggists, however, for these were placed in the 'Professional Class', 'persons who are rendering direct service to mankind and satisfying their intellectual, moral and devotional wants'.[2]

At first glance the census returns for the years prior to the formation of the Institute of Chemistry give a clear enough indication of the progress of chemistry as an occupation. The graph on p. 30 indicates the increase in total numbers of the two classes.

For anyone interested in the practice of chemistry these census returns are more remarkable for what they conceal than what they reveal. In 1841, for instance, the 684 'manufacturing chemists' did not include bleachers (7196), copper manufacturers (52), dye manufacturers (265), metal manufacturers (1596), soda manufacturers (39), soap boilers and makers (738), etc. Again, in 1851, the term 'chemist (manufacturing)' explicitly includes employers and labourers. How many of these would be recognized as chemists today? More to the point, how many were so regarded by the pharmacists or laboratory workers of their own day? We may sympathize with the Registrar General in his taxonomic difficulties, and at the same time glimpse something of the confusion that cried out for resolution for over forty years.

Buried within these statistics is one small item that is in fact most revealing. In 1851 appeared a category of 'Scientific Persons', with a modest membership of 491. Obviously not all of these were in any sense chemists. In 1861 there was a new group of forty-seven 'others working and dealing in chemicals', while the 'Scientific Persons' included in their number nine analytical chemists. Ten years later the latter number had risen to fifty-six.

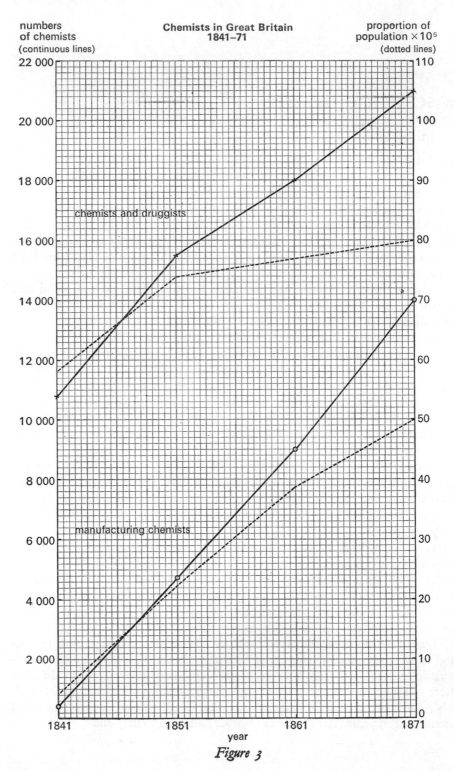

numbers
of chemists
(continuous lines)

**Chemists in Great Britain
1841–71**

proportion of
population ×10⁵
(dotted lines)

chemists and druggists

manufacturing chemists

year

Figure 3

The significance of this last entry will be apparent later. What is clear now is that census data are of little help in any respect except that of highlighting the confusion.[3] The rest of this chapter will therefore be concerned with an alternative approach. We shall endeavour to identify the main areas of national life until about 1870 in which anyone actively practising chemistry was employed, and to discover the kind of work he might be expected to be doing.

The great advances in chemical theory in the late eighteenth century and early nineteenth century might have been expected to lead to an increased application of chemistry to all kinds of industry. Such was the belief of Thomas Thomson, the Scottish professor whose ambition it was 'to erect a laboratory upon a proper scale, to establish a real chemical school in Glasgow and to breed up a set of young practical chemists'.[4] He wrote of his subject (1820):

> As an art, it is intimately connected with all our manufactures. The glass blower, the potter, the smith, and every other worker in metals, the tanner, the soap maker, the dyer, the bleacher, are really practical chemists; and the most essential improvements have been introduced into all these arts by the progress which chemistry has made as a science.[5]

2 Calico-printing and Dyestuffs

The rapid expansion of the textile industry in the early stages of the industrial revolution brought with it a host of problems that were essentially chemical in character. This was particularly true of the trades of bleaching and dyeing, notably in the printing of calico. Yet it took a considerable time for the relevance of chemistry to be seen generally—or at least accepted—and longer still for the actual employment of chemists in the print works. In the late eighteenth century very few owners or operators had more than the most rudimentary knowledge of chemistry, the function of various chemicals employed in the traditional recipes being sometimes discovered only when they were accidentally omitted.[6]

The earliest progress in the textile industry appears to have come from a few owners or managers who, for one reason or another, saw the relevance of 'scientific chemistry' and sought to acquire a smattering of the subject for themselves. Only in rare cases could they do this by some kind of formal tuition; the only exceptions were those who could attend Thomson's courses at Glasgow. Nearly always the only progress lay along the hard road of self-improvement. One of the earliest and most successful cases was that of John Mercer (1791–1866) who in 1809 became apprentice at the Oakenshaw Print Works at Clitheroe, nine years later being appointed as their first chemist and in 1825 attaining partnership in the firm.[7] This pioneer of textile chemistry was almost entirely self-taught, beginning with Parkinson's *Chemical Pocket Book* (1803) picked up at a secondhand stall in Blackburn Market. He acquired sufficient skill to develop a whole range of new technical processes and sufficient insight to enable him to adumbrate such diverse concepts as cosmological evolution and chemical catalysis. His near neighbour at Clitheroe's other print works (the Primrose Works) was 'the Duke of Wellington of calico printing', James Thomson (1779–1850), who developed important methods of destroying dyestuff colours by oxidation.[8] Together with Crum in Scotland, Mercer and Thomson are justly regarded as having transformed calico-printing in the first half of the nineteenth century by the use of metallic compounds in the application and discharge of colours.[9]

The chemical knowledge possessed by these self-taught Lancashire pioneers was inevitably fragmentary and idiosyncratic. Of Mercer it was said in 1835: 'This ingenious individual possesses a store of knowledge and facts unknown to scientific chemists, and sought for in vain in their latest works'.[10] But the industry could not boast many individuals of the calibre of Mercer who, according to Playfair, could have become 'a Dalton or a Faraday had he been differently placed'.[11] In any case the responsibilities of administration meant that even the most scientifically minded owners and partners could hardly have found time for all the experimentation that seems desirable. So about 1817 the first textile chemists appeared in Lancashire print works. It was a small beginning. Mercer himself wrote:

> When I became connected with calico-printing in 1818, the only printing firms in this country who employed a man possessing a knowledge of chemistry were the Thompsons [Thomsons] of Clitheroe and the Hargreaves of Accrington.[12]

Thomas Hargreaves, at Broad Oak, Accrington, had engaged a French chemist, Frederick Steiner, whose discoveries in turkey red printing gave his firm a notable lead over its larger rivals. The chemical tradition at Broad Oak was continued by Hargreaves' son John (a pupil of Dalton) and Steiner's assistant J. E. Lightfoot, later to achieve fame for his development of aniline black.

It is tempting, but unwise, to ascribe the new employment of the chemist to a buoyant market and the pressure of competition. Yet the early nineteenth century was a period of great difficulty for the industry owing to the upheavals on the Continent which made the European trade extremely precarious, the great Lancashire strike of 1815 against the use of cylinder printing,[13] frequent under-capitalization of projects and managerial incompetence. Many firms collapsed—up to a third of those in Lancashire by the 1840s[14]—and others had to lay off workers extensively. Instead it seems that the first employment of chemists owed far more to personal initiative and far-sightedness than to this kind of economic pressure which could well have had the opposite effect and made a chemist seem an unnecessary and expensive luxury.

A great boost was given to the English textile industry by the repeal, in

1831, of the duty of 3½d per square yard on printed calico. Moreover the successes of the new processes were vindicating the role of the chemists who had discovered them: the use of antimony(III) sulphide to procure the first good orange colour (Mercer 1817), the discharge of turkey red by bleaching powder (Thomson 1813 and 1815), the production of bronze colours with manganese (IV) oxide (Mercer 1823 onwards and Lightfoot 1826), the dichromate discharge of indigo (Thomson 1826), and so on. Thus the prospects for a chemist were considerably enhanced. Thomson affirmed in 1833 that 'chemical discoveries affecting the manufactures have been made in England much more important than those which have been made in France', and agreed that there were 'several great manufactories in England carried on by gentlemen perfectly understanding chemistry'.[15]

Two years later it was recorded that several Lancashire proprietors of calico-printing works were 'scientific men',[16] as were many of the managers of the bleach works in the county.[17] Yet it is still hard to find evidence for the *widespread* employment of chemists as such. Certainly they would not have been more than a tiny minority of the total work-force and do not appear in official statistics for persons employed in factories. The chemist was still more often than not a capitalist, part-owner of the establishment. Nearly always he was the only chemist at the works, and his isolation from colleagues elsewhere was often a matter of commercial prudence; it also stemmed from the absence of effective channels of communication. Thus it was recorded of Mercer that he enjoyed 'very little intercourse with scientific chemists' until 1841.[18] That was the year in which he made the acquaintance of Lyon Playfair,[19] newly appointed chemist to his neighbour and rival James Thomson. Playfair must have been the first textile chemist in England to have a PhD—recently awarded for his work with Liebig,[20] at the University of Giessen. With this experience behind him he could hardly fail to recognize the genius of Mercer or to start a scientific dialogue with him. As a result there came into being a series of informal discussions in the area (the 'Whalley meetings'), not the least benefit of which was the hint dropped by Mercer that led eventually to Playfair's discovery of the nitroprussides. 1841 also saw the birth of the Chemical Society, of which Mercer was a founder member. From now on a change of mood in the industry is unmistakeable.

Around the mid-century many of the smaller works were still without any kind of trained chemist on their staff, while in the larger ones tensions developed between old and new attitudes. Nowhere is this diversity more pointedly illustrated than in a young chemist's experience in North East Lancashire during the Christmas holidays, 1847, when Edward Frankland[21] endeavoured to enlighten himself on 'manufacturing operations to which chemical science was applied'.[22] Beginning with Thomson's works at Clitheroe he noted that one chemist (Playfair) had now been replaced by two—a refreshing sign of the times. At Haworth's establishment at Church, near Accrington, he confessed:

> I did not like to make too many inquiries as the parties seemed very much afraid lest I should obtain too much information; at least this was the case with one of the men who accompanied me, and who, as I after-wards learned was the patentee of several processes there in operation.[23]

In contrast was his reception by Mercer, 'one of the most interesting and clever men I have ever met with'. The once isolated pioneer freely conversed for 'Mr. Mercer's house was always open to chemists, although he never gave invitations'.[24]

By the 1850s 'the importance of having an educated chemist at print works, chemical works and bleach works was then generally recognized'.[25] But their presence brought its own problems as the tensions between 'academic' and 'practical' men were expressed in strained relationships between chemists and management. In 1853 Mercer wrote:

> . . . A case of this kind which occurs to me was that of a young man named Fletcher, who came to visit me from one of the chemical schools of London, with the object of obtaining a situation in print works. I endeavoured to obtain a situation for him, and he himself tried at various places, but all failed through the opposition of the managers or colour-men. Yet this young man, in my estimation, was one as likely to succeed in a chemical or print works as any I ever met with.[26]

From 1850 to 1855 the employment of chemists produced many new im-provements in calico-printing, as may be witnessed in the increasing numbers of patent applications.[27] But the most spectacular contribution of chemistry was not to come until 1857 when Perkin discovered the first synthetic coal-tar dyestuff, aniline purple or mauve.[28] From then on the aspiring young chemist would be far more attracted to the opening fields of organic research than to the still esoteric mysteries of printers' recipes. Thus it is interesting to note that of the 366 entries relating to former students of the Royal College of Chemistry, given as part of Frankland's evidence to the Devonshire Com-mission in 1871,[29] only seven can be clearly identified as being in any kind of dyeworks, while at least seventeen were to be found in the production of colours and dyes. The figures are probably not very accurate, but the trend is clear. While it was still possible for a bright young man to make his way in a calico-printers' establishment without a chemical training, it was totally impossible for this to happen in coal-tar dye research and so it is to the chemical industry proper that we must look for the main job opportunities for 'colour chemists'.

3 Chemistry as Applied to other Industries

(a) Gas production

The first decade of the nineteenth century saw the establishment, in London, of the first plant for making coal-gas for public distribution. An entrepreneur from Moravia, F. A. Winzler, launched the Gas Light and Coke Company in 1810 and thereafter gas lighting spread rapidly to many parts of London and the provinces.[30]

Numerous problems awaited the pioneers of gas lighting. Many of these we can now see to have been essentially chemical in nature, but the most obviously pressing ones were more clearly of an engineering character. So the early years of the century saw the rise of a new technical specialist, the gas engineer. His was the responsibility of producing, transporting and storing vast quantities of inflammable gas, a whole new problem demanding a totally novel approach. Where matters of chemistry arose there were several things that might happen. A gas engineer might improvise himself, as in the removal of hydrogen sulphide (H_2S) from coal-gas by means of lime. Outside help might be called in, as when Faraday was invited to advise on the lamentable effects of gas lighting in the Athenaeum—soporific for the members and corrosive for the leather bindings of their books (sulphur dioxide was at least partly to blame). The chemical utilization of tar was left to others—most gas engineers were only too glad to get rid of both the problem and the tar.

From this it will appear that the early gas industry was quite able to function without employing chemists. The great Winzler himself set the tone by expressing a strong preference for practical men as opposed to men of science, no doubt at least partly because of the opposition to his schemes from chemists like Davy. But one must not underestimate the scientific competence of some of his successors, men like the engineers Samuel Clegg and George Lowe. It was the versatility of such men that helped postpone the need to employ chemists. Occasionally efforts were made to tackle the chemical problems seriously. In 1814 the Gas Light and Coke Company established an 'elaboratory' for by-product research, but dismantled it the following year. The person employed, Winzler's son, shared paternal ignorance in matters of chemistry and the result was inevitable.[31] Where someone with a genuine knowledge of chemistry was to be found in the gas industry, he was usually in a position of some authority. Such was the case of Fredrick Accum, whose evidence as a chemist had been given to a Parliamentary Committee investigating the Gas Light and Coke Company,[32] who later became a director of that company; or John Leigh, Chemical Director of the Manchester Gas Works. But there is very little evidence to suggest chemists were frequently to be found on the staff of early Victorian gas-making establishments.

As will be seen subsequently, chemists began to enter the gas industry in some numbers in the 1860s. But these chemists were employed for analysis. The idea of using chemists in the gas industry for research had to await the present century. Again the Gas Light and Coke Company serves as an example, for they were entirely typical. The foundation of by-product research was not really laid until 1903 when a chemist on their staff, J. G. Clark, began research on his own initiative. But it was not until twenty years later that he became officially entitled 'Chemist to the Company' with responsibilities for research, and in that year the Central Laboratories were opened at Fulham.[33]

(b) Soap making

In the soap-making industry one finds several small chemical laboratories appearing in the 1840s although there is no suggestion that trained staff were appointed to work in them. Thus one soap works in 1842 was reported to have a small laboratory for analysis and experiments, needed because of the 'chemical nicety' involved in much soap-making theory and practice.[34] The famous firm of Joseph Crosfield and Sons in Warrington could boast a copy of Graham's *Elements of Chemistry*, owned by the proprietor's eldest son and co-partner, George, in 1843.[35] A few years later the firm was reported to have a tiny laboratory about 8 ft by 5 ft, not much bigger than a double bed.[36] The first reference to a chemist in the firm appears in 1880[37], while the West Country establishment of Thomas's have been described as the first soap makers to produce glycerol from spent lyes, having employed a 'general and analytical chemist as early as 1872'.[38] Generally speaking it appears to be true that the soap-making industry did not begin to use chemists on a large scale until about that time or even later, but by 1890, the Crosfield works had been put on a 'thoroughly scientific basis'.[37]

It seems to have been the case that the calls for analytical chemists in the soap-making industry were rather less vociferous than in other manufactures, while the pressing needs for research did not make themselves fully felt until the soap makers began to see the relevance of the new Solvay process for their industry, and that was not until towards the end of the nineteenth century.

(c) The brewing industry

One hardly needs to state that of all the industries remotely connected with chemistry this is surely one of the oldest. Yet of the chemical nature of the process called fermentation nothing was known with certainty until the late nineteenth century; brewing was not an industry renowned for its ready acceptance of scientific principles.[39] The eighteenth century had witnessed the introduction of numerous instruments such as thermometers and hydrometers to monitor the progress of the complex of reactions, but in the end the quality or otherwise of the product was ultimately determined by the palate. Brewing remained for many centuries a culinary art and by the early nineteenth century was still chiefly to be found in private houses and domestic establishments generally. The day of the large brewery had yet to come. It is perhaps surprising that the first appointment of a chemist to a brewery appears to have been that of Robert Warington[40] in 1831 to the firm of Truman, Hanbury, Buckton and Company. He was appointed on the recommendation of Turner whom he had assisted at University College, London, but little is known of his activities as a brewing chemist. Warington became far more important as a founder of the Chemical Society. So far as is known brewing chemistry in Britain began with the appointment in 1845 of Henry Böttinger to Allsopp's Brewery at Burton-on-Trent. He became their scientific adviser but his job appears to have been primarily the analysis of water. This study of the quality of water upon which a beer is based is of prime importance and one reason for the concentration of the industry in Burton-on-Trent is the peculiar characteristic of water obtained from wells in that region. But no pupil of Liebig's, as Böttinger was, would wish to spend his life on water analysis alone and it was not long before Böttinger was prying into the mysteries of fermentation, no doubt with his former tutor's theories in the back of his mind. But his name was made by the famous events known as the 'strychnine scare' of 1851. Payen in France had proposed that the bitterness of English beer arose from the addition of the alkaloid, strychnine. Such a story, if substantiated, would have had a catastrophic impact upon the British brewing industry. Böttinger was able to refute this monstrous allegation, and, on the advice of Hofmann,[41] he obtained the backing of Thomas Graham[42] for his denials. The result was widely publicized and led to record sales of Allsopp's products and a greatly enhanced reputation for the chemistry conducted in Burton-on-Trent. As with many industries, however, a scientific approach had to compete with age-old empiricism, a fact well illustrated by the following remarks of Muspratt in the late 1850s:

> Many operative brewers, in some of the largest town establishments, even now ridicule and despise the idea of chemistry being in any way connected with the art of brewing. Such ignorant prejudices only perpetuate bigotry, and cause an enormous waste of property; the progress of useful art is impeded; and its promoters are ungenerously maligned by a spirit, which knows not the limited range of its own capacity.[43]

Muspratt had his own axe to grind, of course, and one can see why the concept of a chemical brewer was so hard for the public to accept. T. S. Bremner, a recent chief chemist to Allsopp's, offers an explanation:

> Böttinger's laboratory was tucked away in a comparatively dark corner of the brewery in the Allsopp block. Whether this was done by accident or design, it is difficult to say, but it does seem as if the appointment of a chemist to a brewery was something to be regarded as a necessary evil

which should be advertised as little as possible. The public attitude to a brewery chemist was one of deep suspicion.[44]

So well did Böttinger get on, however, that in due course he was promoted to the post of head brewer, his place in the laboratory being taken by Peter Griess (1829–88),[39] This German chemist, a pupil of Kolbe and Hofmann, was to achieve his highest reputation for researches on diazonium compounds in 1858. But he was also an extremely effective brewery chemist and from his appointment dates the revolution in brewing science that so marked the latter part of the nineteenth century. More than that, his success soon led to a remarkable flow of personnel from London to Burton-on-Trent: 'The Burton breweries became permeated with brewers and chemists who were trained under Hofmann or his successors'.[45] Undoubtedly part of the reason was that brewery chemists had ample time for the pursuit of their private research interests, at least until the end of the century, and this would constitute a post in a brewery an attractive proposition to many aspiring young chemists. So true was that, in the 1870s and 1880s H. E. Armstrong[46] regarded Burton-on-Trent as 'the most stimulating scientific centre in the country'.[47]

Away from Burton progress was less marked, though in London the establishment of Whitbread's research and control laboratories has been dated to the visit of Pasteur in 1871.[48]

4   The Manufacture of Chemicals

The manufacture of chemicals in the nineteenth century took many forms and included the production of both metals and fine chemicals, and in later years dyestuffs. But the core of the industry, as well as its most substantial part, was unquestionably the manufacture of alkalis and sulphuric acid. This 'alkali industry', as it came to be called, varied from small concerns to firms with hundreds of employees; the merger in 1890 of forty-five companies into the United Alkali Company, a predecessor of the Alkali Division of Imperial Chemical Industries (ICI), created a mammoth concern of unprecedented size in the chemical industry anywhere.[49]

In attempting to discuss the role of the chemist in such a variegated scene we shall concern ourselves largely with the alkali industry on account of its size, though the reference will not be exclusive. It was chiefly concerned with the manufacture of soda (especially for soap and glass) and of sulphuric acid which was used for many purposes including the Leblanc process itself.

By the nineteenth century the industry was concentrated in three main centres: Glasgow, Merseyside and Tyneside, all of which had indigenous coal and excellent communications by sea and/or rail.

As will have been seen from the graph on p. 30 the British chemical industry had a slow start in the nineteenth century, and this was particularly true of that part of it concerned with alkalis. One factor was the punitive taxation that many chemical products had to suffer. Not least may we quote the taxes on soap (until 1853) and on glass (until 1845). But above all it was the punitive duty on salt that prevented the development of the Leblanc process in Britain. At the end of the eighteenth century this duty amounted to £30 per ton. It was removed in 1825 and by 1844 the total cost of salt was 10s to 12s per ton. These fiscal measures offer sufficient explanation for the late development of the British, as opposed to the French, chemical industry.[50]

While the broad shape of the alkali industry is clear, and its changing fortunes have been carefully charted by several reputable historians,[51] the actual role of the chemist is a subject on which information is exceedingly hard to obtain. There appear to be three main reasons for this. Chemists on almost any definition were a minute proportion of the total workforce and are often not even mentioned in descriptions of factories even though there may be evidence that they existed there; their roles were so varied that no perceptible pattern of activity occurs until very late in the century; but above all there was the central question with which this chapter is concerned, 'who is a chemist?' By way of illustration we may note in passing two passages from that indispensable volume by L. F. Haber, *The Chemical Industry during the Nineteenth Century*. At one point the author asserts:

> It was only later, say from about 1840 onwards, that British chemical engineers began to make their weight felt and it was largely the work of Gossage, MacTear, Dunlop, Deacon, Glover, and Weldon which formed the basis for the later growth of the heavy-chemical industry.[52]

Setting aside the possible anachronism in the term 'chemical engineer' we may ask what it was that these men had in common *other than* their undeniable impact on chemical industry. In fact it was very little, several of them having little or no training in chemistry and one of them (Weldon) vociferously denying that he was anything but an amateur. Elsewhere Haber speaks of 'the work of British chemists, above all of Weldon, Deacon, MacTear, and Chance',[53] the first two named being somewhat doubtful contenders for that title, except for the fact that the journalist (Weldon)[54] and engineer (Deacon)[55] each happened to make a chemical discovery that proved of great economic value. Does that constitute being a chemist?

Because of the extraordinary vagueness of this term, and the complexity of the industry, we shall attempt an alternative approach, looking at different groups in terms of their chemical expertise and commitment without necessarily designating some 'chemists' and some not.

Most familiar to chemists, and certainly to historians, are the proprietors. These were the men of imagination, enterprise and capital who staked a great deal on the profitability of alkali production. In an age when the profit motive is sometimes called in question it is pertinent to observe that, for all their preoccupation with money, the progress of chemistry[56] and the prosperity of

Victorian Britain are alike in their debt. They were a diverse group but nevertheless had much in common. Because of their financial success and because of the need for constant expansion many of them became landowners of some significance, and with that often went civic responsibility and office. Deacon was Chairman of the Local Board in Widnes and, in 1874, enjoyed a gross rental of £2687 from his nine acres.[57] Understandably there was also a marked tendency to support the issue of Free Trade and the cause of the Liberals.[58]

In the early part of the century the proprietors sometimes ventured their capital on the basis of what would seem to us an incredibly small chemical competence. Such was probably the case with James Muspratt[59] who, after an incompleted apprenticeship to a Dublin druggist and a turbulent career with first the army and then the navy in the Peninsular War, desertion, and return to Ireland, set himself up as a small chemical manufacturer in Dublin. Crossing to Liverpool in 1822 he established himself as a soda manufacturer at Vauxhall Road and prospered mightily. More striking, perhaps, was the experience of Christian Allhusen[60] who, from 1834, manufactured chemicals on Tyneside. Eventually his enormous works were to make him a personal fortune of over £1 million yet his own chemical education was non-existent and throughout his life he was content to adopt good ideas from others, regarding his own role as financial and managerial rather than technically chemical.

Such a situation was fairly common in the early days of the nineteenth century and again after about 1860. As Haber pointed out, the only people on the Boards of most chemical firms in Britain who had themselves an interest in chemistry tended, after about 1860, to be immigrants, especially from Germany.[61] In 1873 the President of the Newcastle Chemical Society, Dr Lunge[62] deplored 'the indifference of chemical manufacturers to the claims of science'.[63]

This however was not by any means true of all the proprietors in the nineteenth century, and a second class may be recognized as those who had acquired some degree of chemical expertise before they launched their products and who maintained a close interest in technical chemistry throughout their working lives. William Losh is an example of this class. He had studied chemistry at Cambridge and metallurgy in Sweden. Aware of the French research in alkali production, he spent some time in Paris and returned to his native Scotland only when events in France made it unsafe for him to remain there. After some experiments in conjunction with Lord Dundonald he settled in Newcastle-upon-Tyne and became the first man to introduce the Leblanc process in England (1797).[64] Many others followed suit and displayed a somewhat similar career pattern. Thus Peter Spence,[65] having worked in several gas works and learned a great deal about the chemistry of carbonization products, set up his own business in Carlisle in 1840 and his Manchester works (founded 1847) became the largest manufacturers of alum in Great Britain. Throughout this time Spence was constantly on the look-out for technological improvements. Yet again William Gossage[66] had gained some chemical training as a druggist in Leamington. After this he opened his own chemical works in Worcestershire in 1830 and six years later designed the famous Gossage tower to absorb water-soluble effluent gases from the Leblanc process. His story is well known. He packed a nearby disused wind-mill with brushwood, forced hydrogen chloride gas up against a counter current of water flowing down the tower and thus removed most of the noxious vapours as hydrochloric acid. Perhaps one of the most successful cases of the chemical entrepreneurs was that of Hugh Lee Pattinson[67] of Tyneside. His prior experience had been chiefly in metallurgical analysis (he had designed the desilverization process for lead). On the strength of that and other experience he created the famous alkali works at Felling-on-Tyne and later a further one at Washington a few miles away. Pattinson had also served an apprenticeship with Anthony Clapham, a soap and alkali manu-facturer, and he continued his experiments long after the factories were opened. In this category of proprietors probably came the very much smaller makers of fine chemicals, such as the pharmacist J. F. Cooper of London (who in 1820 was marketing such novelties as iodine, sodium and potassium) and his later colleague in Newcastle, J. C. Eno, whose Fruit Salt has been a highly successful mild purgative until the present day (sodium bicarbonate and citric acid).

Not all the great names in the chemical industry were however proprietors and a third group of people who may be discerned is those managers who were appointed to run the firms of men like Allhusen and Pattinson and whose chemical flair had to be developed from small beginnings. Such a case was John Glover [68] who, having been apprenticed to a plumber and enjoyed no formal education whatever, was appointed by Pattinson to Felling-on-Tyne to concern himself with the maintenance of the lead chambers. It was here that he encountered that rarity in the 1840s, a works chemical laboratory. His experience here, together with a more than usual capacity for self-help, enabled him to acquire a detailed chemical knowledge and, after many ex-periments, to devise the famous tower which bears his name. This invention, first put into effect in 1859, enabled the lead chamber process to operate with much greater efficiency by concentrating the acid and enabling some of the oxidation of the sulphur dioxide to take place before the chambers. This device has been estimated to have saved British manufacturers £300,000 per year although Glover declined to patent it. Reminiscent in some ways, though with less spectacular results, is the case of Henry Deacon at Widnes. He was a qualified engineer but his only experience of chemistry seems to have been attending some of Faraday's lectures in London. Nevertheless he was able to serve Pilkington's at St Helens as manager and then in a similar capacity in Widnes to devise a means of oxidizing the waste hydrochloric acid by means of air and a copper catalyst. It also seems probable that many of the chemists on Tyneside who joined the Tyne Social Chemical Society[69] in the 1870s were people who, without formal training themselves, felt acutely the necessity for learning by mutual help. Most of these were working either in the alkali industry or as servants of the famous Tharsis Company, which was concerned with metal extraction.[70]

A fourth group of persons became more famous in England as the century wore on and they were the trained managers. Several of the great entre-preneurs, realizing the deficiencies of their own education, ensured that the next generation would not be so limited. Thus Muspratt sent three of his sons to study with Liebig at Giessen. They were then expected to return to Merseyside to take over the works. Unfortunately the eldest, James, despite his education felt little aptitude for this and eventually found his destiny as an educator at the Liverpool College of Chemistry. But his youngest brother Edmund is an excellent representative of the new type of professional chemical managers towards the end of the nineteenth century.[71] In a rather similar way Kurtz,[72] the Liverpool manufacturer of lead chromate, sent his son to study in Paris. There were some notable men amongst this group of managers who would surely on any definition merit the title chemist— indeed in some cases this was part of their job descriptions. As the century progressed such men became a more conspicuous feature of the industry, tending to be both older and better trained than the previous generation. The most remarkable of them all was probably Georg Lunge [62] who came over to this country from Germany with a Breslau PhD and post-doctoral experience at Heidelberg. In the mid-1860s, after searching for a suitable post for some time, he secured an appointment at the Tyne Alkali Company at South Shields, becoming chemist and works manager. His comments on the deplor-able indifference of chemical manufacturers to his subject may therefore be well understood. He will be met again frequently in this book, but may be noticed now as one of the leading chemists in the alkali industry. He became Professor of Chemical Technology at Zurich in 1876.

We may identify a fifth group of persons as those who, though lacking managerial status, were nevertheless employed as chemists and whose func-tions appear to have been accurately so described. They do not appear in any numbers until the second half of the nineteenth century. This can be seen from the rarity of such facilities as chemical laboratories and chemical libraries, both of which were to be found at the Felling works in 1844,[73] but were chiefly notable in being so exceptional. A report of the Alkali Inspector in 1876 observes that 'when the Alkali Act was introduced [1863], few of the alkali makers had good laboratories, still fewer had chemists sufficiently free to test the gases for themselves, and I may almost say that few had chemists fit to do so'.[74] Part of the reason was that few facilities existed for training such men; in Tyneside in 1861 only fifty of the whole industrial population were being trained in chemistry,[75] while the lists from the Royal College of Chemistry in London suggest only a minute proportion of students going to the heavy chemicals industries.[29] Undoubtedly one reason was the poor financial prospects, £100 being the kind of salary such a chemist could look forward to.[76] This lack of opportunity was again echoed by Lunge in 1873 where this country was unfavourably compared with his native Germany:

> A great many chemical manufacturers in this country still look on their chemists as a somewhat expensive and not very useful encumbrance; at any rate, as soon as their business goes beyond the merely mechanical business of testing the raw materials which come in, and the products which go out. But the *rôle* of the chemist, apart from chemistry, in a chemical works ought to be a very different one indeed, and is a very different thing abroad. There, the chemist is considered as equally important with the practical manager; and he proves his importance too.[63]

However things did not remain quite as bad as that for much longer and it was only two years later that the Alkali Inspector was able to say exultantly 'now things are entirely changed'[74] though it must be confessed he is far more interested in chemical analysis than on-going research.

In a sixth group of persons to be found in the alkali industry were those who may be loosely described as 'consultants'. Often these were academics who hired their services to industry, although at first this was regarded as rather beneath their proper dignity. Frankland was often to be found acting in this capacity, as in the classic case when he designed a chimney for Peter Spence and when this was discovered to be unsatisfactory, was found (to Spence's fury and indignation) to have been retained as a consultant by the prosecution.[77] Occasionally, very non-academic consultants were able to contribute to the progress of the industry, the most notable being undoubtedly Walter Weldon[54] whose true vocation was that of journalist, being the proprietor of Weldon's *Ladies Journal* and sundry other literary periodicals. However he it was who became the originator of an alternative method for oxidizing hydrochloric acid, namely with manganese (IV) oxide. But it is not without interest to note that Weldon's invention could hardly have been of practical value without the assistance of Ferdinand Hurter[78] who, having studied with Bunsen, came to Widnes as his chief chemist.

Having spoken of all these classes of worker within the nineteenth-century heavy chemical industry it must be confessed that we have mentioned only a miniscule proportion of those who laboured and sweated in the production of metals, acids and above all alkalis. The vast mass of the working populace of the chemical industry were of course those whose manual efforts contributed to its success but whose chemical prowess was non-existent. Much has been written of the appalling conditions in which some of these 'white slaves of England' had to work, many of them exposed to quite lethal vapours and unable in some cases even to eat their food because hydrochloric acid had corroded away all their teeth. However there was a wide variety of work which, it must be emphasized, offered an opportunity for the really determined, ambitious and able man. One does not have to look further to see the truth of this than to remember the case of John Glover.

5 The Pharmaceutical Chemists

The remarkable flexibility of meaning that may be found in the word 'chemist' has already been noted (p. 29). This peculiarity of English usage has meant that for most of the nineteenth century the majority of those 'chemists' practising in England and Wales were engaged in what we might equally well term pharmacy. However it is not simply on account of a linguistic anomaly that we need to glance briefly at these people now; it will be apparent that their fortunes presented some striking parallels with those of their other chemical colleagues, and (more important) affected the course of chemical professionalization in general.[79]

(a) The organization of pharmacy

At the end of the eighteenth century the trade in medicines was in a state of some confusion. By rights, the practice of pharmacy was the exclusive prerogative of the apothecaries, for their Charter of 1748 had the intention not merely of preventing physicians from selling and making medicines but also of retaining for themselves the monopoly of *prescribing* drugs. This was aimed at a new class of rival, the Chemists and Druggists, 'a body of men unknown to the world till about the end of the last [seventeenth] century, unauthorized by any public charter, and almost undefined by any public Act'.[80] However this Charter was honoured more in the breach than in the observance, especially towards the end of the eighteenth century. From 1774 the pressure was on for all apothecaries to be medically qualified, and the preparation and prescription of medicines were becoming increasingly divorced, and the druggists were becoming more necessary. In some areas their numbers had quadrupled in ten or twelve years. But the apothecaries, understandably enough, tended to want it both ways and displayed signs of alarm over both the encroachment on to their territory by chemists and druggists and the lack of regulation over pharmaceutical practice. An indignation meeting held in 1794 affirmed that the infringement of their monopoly was costing the London apothecaries as much as £200 per annum each, presumably since most of their income was determined by the quantities of medicine supplied.

Accordingly there was formed a General Pharmaceutical Association of Great Britain. Its members would

> engage to deal with such Druggists only as would immediately consent to relinquish the composition of all medical prescriptions—to retain to themselves their wholesale occupations alone—and to receive no Apprentice, and employ no Assistant, who had not had a classical education.[81]

The necessity for such chemists to know Latin was a great feature of the apothecaries' argument; how else could prescriptions be translated?

With an ambitious programme of reform the Association lacked the means to carry it through and within a few months it had disappeared, one of the many transient groups whose rise and fall characterize the history of chemical institutions.

As we shall see on more than one occasion there is nothing like a strong external pressure from a third party to bring erstwhile rivals together in somewhat metastable union. Such was the case with the Medicine Act of 1802. Seeking to impose new duties on a wide range of medicines that had hitherto been exempt from such impositions, the measure called forth a 'Petition of Apothecaries, Chemists, and Druggists'. Their opposition was partially successful, but a more important consequence was the establishment of a 'Society' by the chemists and druggists, with a Standing Committee to look after their interests in the future. Its existence was splendidly justified when the next crisis broke—the proposed Bill in 1813 'regulating the practice of Apothecaries, Surgeon-apothecaries, Practitioners in Midwifery, and Compounders and Dispensers of Medicines throughout England and Wales'. The effect of such a measure would have been to constitute a fourth monopolistic medical body which would examine and license apothecaries and other medical ancillaries, yet would at the same time exclude from its Committee those chemists and druggists who would be subject to its enactment. Needless to say the chemists and druggists, alerted by their Standing Committee, took up arms and appointed an action committee of five. They advertised in seven leading newspapers, retained the services of Brougham as counsel and alerted public and parliamentary opinion as effectively as they could. Their case rested upon the 'long experience' of their trade, the injustice of an unrepresentative executive and the injury that would be done to the poor, for whom 'in large towns it is usual for Physicians to prescribe *gratis* . . . and to send them to a Chemist and Druggist for the medicines'.[82]

It was certainly true that many who could not afford orthodox medical treatment would resort to self-medication with the much cheaper proprietary medicines that were then available. The Stamp Act of 1804 gives a list of no less than 450 such items.[83] Many of these were antacid remedies from the eighteenth century which, 'whatever else it may have been, was the great century of overeating, and indigestion powders were the best-selling lines in the apothecary's shop',[84] and, we may add, at the chemist and druggist's establishment around the corner.

The outcome of the carefully orchestrated indignation was that the apothecaries' lobby, frightened at the opposition roused at the first reading of the Bill, made a number of modifications before the second reading, the most important ones being the exclusion of 'everything affecting the compounding chemist and druggist'. In the event the Bill was withdrawn for further reconsideration.

Its reappearance next year was with the support of the Society of Apothe-caries, though still with the opposition of the physicians. This hostility, together with amendments introduced by the Lords, caused delays and it had to be rushed through almost at the end of the Session. It was not an unqualified success for the apothecaries. A clause denying that the Act should be taken 'in any way to affect the trade or business of a Chemist or Druggist' robbed the Bill of most of its force. Indeed it has been described as 'almost a charter for the unqualified chemist'.[85] The *ad hoc* Committee of Associated Apothecaries which had fathered the measure played little further part in subsequent events.

Another transient intermediate in the institutional scene was the General Association of Chemists and Druggists of Great Britain, created on the last day of 1829 to oppose vexatious practices—including the use of common informers—in connection with the Medicine Act. A tightening up of the regulations concerning stamp duties on items such as lozenges had led to a genuine sense of injustice and, within a few months, the law was altered in response to the activities of the Association; whereupon it quietly expired.

A far more serious threat to the practice of pharmaceutical chemistry came in 1841, with a Bill introduced by the Liberal MP Benjamin Hawes.[86] Reflecting a general dissatisfaction with many aspects of the medical pro-fession the Bill proposed that no one should practise medicine without proper certification after 1 February 1842. To this unexceptionable item was added the further proposal that no chemist or druggist should practise after 1 December 1842 without a licence, renewable annually. Failure to obtain a licence for any reason could render a chemist liable to a fine of £20 if he was caught performing the most innocuous service to a customer, such as advising on how to take a medicine.

The chief objection lay in the nature of the proposed administering body in which general practitioners would inevitably outnumber the chemists.

It is interesting that the immediate reaction to the Bill came, not from the thousands of one-man businesses throughout the country, but chiefly from the wholesalers of London: Allen, Hanburys and Barry, Savory, Moore and Co, Charles Dinneford, John Bell & Co, and many others. Presumably these were better informed. Yet again a committee was set up, this time headed by William Allen, FRS, a distinguished Quaker chemist of Plough Court Pharmacy, London. The usual protest mechanisms were set in motion —nationwide publicity, parliamentary lobbying and so on—and the ob-noxious Bill was talked out. The immediate object had been achieved but a longer-term danger remained, the ever-present possibility of renewed take-over bids by the medical profession. This of course, was no new thing in itself, but the novel element lay in the increasing separation between pre-scription and dispensing of drugs, fewer doctors every year being involved in making up preparations for their patients (except in the most remote country districts). Partly for this reason the exertion of medical control was even less acceptable than before.

Clearly it was essential for the status of the chemist and druggist to be permanently raised in society. Without that safeguard there was no security from this kind of attack—and next time it might be successful. But now a mechanism had been set up for rapid, nationwide consultation between chemists and druggists, 3000 copies of the Committee's resolution having been circulated. It is hardly likely to have been a coincidence that the birth of both the Pharmaceutical *and* Chemical Societies took place in 1841, the year of origin of the Penny Post.

On 15 April 1841, a public meeting at the Crown and Anchor Tavern in the Strand committed itself to the following resolution:

> That for the purpose of protecting the permanent interests, and increasing the respectability of Chemists and Druggists, an Association be now formed under the title of the 'PHARMACEUTICAL SOCIETY OF GREAT BRITAIN'.

It was proposed by Allen and seconded by Jacob Bell, the thirty-year-old son of John Bell, chemist of Oxford Street, London. It was at the Bells' house three weeks previously that some members of the Committee had met informally at a 'Pharmaceutical tea-party' (as posterity dubbed it) and from which the idea of this public meeting had emerged. Thereafter the Pharmaceutical Society was to become virtually a full-time commitment for Jacob Bell who wrote, lectured, organized meetings and stumped the country on its behalf until death claimed him at an early age in 1859.[87] He is rightly regarded as the founder of the Society.

In an address to the chemists and druggists of Great Britain in July the new Council of the Pharmaceutical Society alerted them 'to the immediate necessity of uniting their strength and influence to meet the emergencies of the present crisis'. They did not mince words as to their intention:

> Those among us who take a real interest in our scientific art, rejoice at the opportunity which is now afforded of placing the 'trade' of a Chemist and Druggist on a professional footing, and effecting a union of our scattered forces for mutual benefit and advancement . . . The Council recapitulate the advantages contemplated in the Society; namely, the union of all the members of the body, for the purpose of self-government and self-protection; the establishment of a uniform system of education, which will promote the advancement of science and the elevation of the profession of Pharmacy; the restraint which will be placed upon the incompetent for the benefit of the public; and, lastly, the alleviation of the sufferings of the unfortunate.[88]

The first tangible result of their activities, alluded to in the last few words, was the immediate establishment of a Benevolent Fund, a very characteristic gesture of nineteenth-century professional institutions. Other objectives took longer to fulfil. The question of licensing drug-sellers was supported even before this date; thus in April 1841, W. Proctor, a founder member of the Society and Chairman of the Newcastle group of chemists and druggists was advocating this most strongly.[89] But little could be done without parliamentary sanction. A Royal Charter in 1843 was welcome, but it was not enough.

Accordingly, in 1850, Jacob Bell stood for Parliament, as Liberal candidate for St Albans. He was elected and in the following year presented a Bill 'for regulating the qualifications of pharmaceutical chemists'. Unfortunately for the Pharmaceutical Society the proposer's intention to restrict pharmaceutical practice to those on a register maintained by the Society was thwarted. In the compromise Bill which eventually became law on the last day of the Parliamentary session in 1852 the register was set up, and the monopoly was rejected as incompatible with free-trade principles in a year when these were to be among the chief issues in the forthcoming General Election.[90]

In the following years the Pharmaceutical Society did not make the universal appeal that had once been hoped. At an optimistic estimate its 2,000 members in the early 1860s were only about one third of those pharmacists in business on their own account. A discussion in the pages of the *Pharmaceutical Journal*[91] was based on the census returns for 1861 when it was argued that, of the 12,638 persons over twenty employed in pharmacies only about half were likely to be in business on their own account, i.e. about 6000. Such comforting manipulation of the statistics was necessary in view of the claims of a new upstart body, the United Society of Chemists and Druggists, formed in 1861 and 'based upon the principle of cooperation, as essential to the strength and progress of chemists and druggists as a trading community'.[92] With an annual fee of 5s and no other entrance conditions it would claim to be open to the poorest worker in a pharmacist's establishment. At first its aims appeared to be almost complementary to those of the Pharmaceutical Society, being more concerned with working conditions and appealing to a different section of the trade. Its moment of opportunity came with the Juries Act which granted exemption from jury service to those on the Pharmaceutical Society's Register. A meeting of its Manchester branch in October 1862, identified the source of the problem as 'the difficulty of defining, to the satisfaction of Her Majesty's Government, the qualifications of a chemist and druggist'.[93]

In the following summer a resolution of the central committee sought some general act of incorporation for the trade in order to avoid dispossession of 'upwards of 30,000 chemists and druggists' by the recently constituted General Medical Council that was now flexing its muscles with a view to exercising control over the hitherto uncontrollable pharmacists. The number of 30,000 had more than a touch of rhetoric about it and was subsequently reduced to about 18,000 (in conformity with the census data).

For the next few years both sides, the medical and the pharmaceutical, were massing their forces for the conflict of interests that came to a head in the Pharmacy Act of 1868.[94] But by now the pharmacists were in two camps, the Pharmaceutical Society and the United Society of Chemists and Druggists. They were, however, united in their detestation of the eventual proposal by the General Medical Council that it should examine and register *all* concerned with medicine or pharmacy. Eventually a compromise was reached between all interested parties in the formulation of an Act that regulated the practice of pharmacy for the next forty years. Amongst its provisions were the creation of a register of pharmaceutical chemists and druggists, together with their assistants and apprentices, enrolment on which would in future depend upon the passing of an examination set by the Pharmaceutical Society. Only those on that Society's Register were to be entitled to the designations 'Pharmaceutical Chemist', 'Pharmaceutist' or 'Chemist and Druggist'—an enactment that had important consequences for the rest of the chemical profession.

Shortly after this epoch-making Act the United Society, having lost its *raison d'être*, disappeared. A similar Act for Ireland was passed in 1875. The impact of these events on the Institute of Chemistry will be examined later (p. 151).

(b) The practice of pharmacy

During the period under review the practice of pharmacy was marked by several developments that were related to the changing status of the profession. Most obvious, perhaps, was the changing nature of the medicines available. While long-established nostrums continued, new remedies appeared. The alkaloids (as morphine, quinine, atropine etc.) are first encountered in the London Pharmacopoeia in 1836, though digitalis has been known since the eighteenth century through the researches of Withering.

The moves towards a more 'scientific' approach were not usually in the area of chemical constitution. Thus quinine, though isolated in 1808 had over a century to wait for the unravelling of its structure (and till the 1940s for its synthesis). In the area of nomenclature the pharmacopoeias reflected chemical trends. Thus the 1809 London Pharmacopoeia used Lavoisier's systematic nomenclature, and two years later Berzelius used the imminent appearance of a Swedish equivalent to argue the case for a universally understood Latin nomenclature of similar kind.[95] A new element of standardization of drugs may be detected in the last two editions of the London Pharmacopoeia, in 1836 and (especially) 1851.

In 1858 the Medical Act established the General Medical Council one of whose responsibilities was eventually to publish a British Pharmacopoeia to replace the local varieties hitherto available. This duly appeared in 1864, a landmark in the emergence of a national profession of pharmaceutical chemistry.

It was well into the nineteenth century before British pharmacists had their own specialist journals. Germany, by contrast, had given birth to Hanle's *Magazin* in 1823, and Liebig took over Geiger's *Magazin de Pharmacie* in 1831, the ancestor of his *Annalen der Pharmacie* (1832) which since 1873 has been *Annalen der Chemie*. However in 1840 a monthly publication appeared, *The Chemist* (not to be confused with the ill-fated weekly of that title fifteen years earlier). This was edited by Charles Watts and, though not exclusively devoted to pharmacy, did carry several pages in each issue on that subject. It continued until 1858, but from 1841 it had a rival in the *Pharmaceutical Journal*, a monthly edited by Jacob Bell that began almost as an accident, with the original intention of simply giving information on the Pharmaceutical Society's meetings, but which soon became that Society's official organ. Possibly for this reason *The Chemist* adopted an unfriendly stance towards the new Society, asserting that 'it never will possess an atom of power to compel chemists to become members'.[96] Other pharmaceutical papers came and went, but *The Chemist and Druggist*, beginning in 1859, has continued until this day.

During all this period the recognized route for training in pharmacy was by indenture to an apprenticeship for (usually) six years. This was of a very variable quality. Frankland once anathematized his service with a druggist in Lancashire from 1840–5 as 'six years continuous hard labour from which I derived no advantage whatever, except the facility of tying up parcels neatly',[97] but there is reason to suppose that this assessment fifty years after the time may lack something in objectivity. In any case it was by no means a typical reaction. But such a training was obviously dependent upon the ability of the masters and this was enormously varied at that time.

In 1840 the apothecaries were advocating two years' study in place of an apprenticeship, but the old method was to last well into the present century. However a start on full-time training was made with the establishment of the Pharmaceutical Society's laboratories and lecture courses in 1842 at their School of Pharmacy. The first professors were A. T. Thomson (pharmacy), George Fownes (chemistry) and J. Pereira (*materia medica*). Soon all the available places were taken up and several independent training establishments grew up in London and the provinces. In addition some pharmaceutical education was available at the Royal College of Chemistry, founded in 1845. The proliferation of all kinds of private tuition, including correspondence courses, followed the 1868 Pharmacy Act which imposed an examination on all future aspirants to a career in pharmacy.

Thus it will be seen that by the mid-nineteenth century pharmacy was obtaining the status of an independent profession in Britain, a state of affairs only made possible by the desirable intention to concentrate on that subject and not to treat it as a handmaid to medicine. CAR

NOTES AND REFERENCES

1 *Census Returns for Great Britain*: for 1841 (P.P. 1844, XXVII, 1), 1851 (P.P. 1852–3, LXXXVIII, 1), 1861 (P.P. 1863, LIII, 1), 1871 (P.P. 1872, LXVIII, 1).

2 *Ibid.*, P.P. 1863, LIII, 231.

3 However once an institution has been established it may well affect classification in a subsequent census, as in the case of engineers and surveyors (F. M. L. Thompson, *The Chartered Surveyors: Growth of a Profession*, Routledge, London, 1968, pp. 159–61).

4 Letter from Thomson to Robert Jameson, 9 September 1817, quoted in J. B. Morrell, 'The Chemist Breeders: the Research Schools of Liebig and Thomas Thomson', *Ambix*, 1972, 19, 1–46. On Thomson see *DSB*, *DNB*.

5 Thomas Thomson, *A System of Chemistry*, 6th edn, London, 1820, 1, 3.

6 C. M. Mellor and D. S. L. Cardwell, 'Dyes and Dyeing 1775–1860', *Brit. J. Hist. Sci.*, 1963, 1, 265–79.

7 On Mercer see E. A. Parnell, *The Life and Labours of John Mercer, the self-taught Chemical Philosopher: including numerous recipes used at the Oakenshaw Calico-Print Works*, London, 1886.

8 On James Thomson see *J. Chem. Soc.*, 1852, 4, 347–9.

9 P. Floud, 'The English Contribution to the Chemistry of Calico Printing before Perkin', *Ciba Review*, 1961, pt. i, 8–14.

10 Edward Baines, *History of the Cotton Manufacture in Great Britain*, 2nd edn., London, 1835, p. 278 (Cass Reprint, 1966).

11 Playfair, quoted in J. G. Crowther, *Statesmen of Science*, Cresset, London, 1965, p. 119.

12 Note by Mercer on chemical education (1853) quoted in Parnell (note 7), p. 241.

13 G. Turnbull, *A History of Calico Printing*, Sherratt, Altrincham, 1951, pp. 81–5.

14 K. L. Wallwork, 'The Calico Printing Industry of Lancastria in the 1840s', *Trans. Inst. Brit. Geographers*, 1968, no. 45, 143–56.

15 *Report of the Select Committee appointed to inquire into Manufactures, Commerce and Shipping*, P.P., 1833, III, 224.

16 Baines (note 10), p. 285.

17 *Ibid.*, p. 253.

18 Parnell (note 7), p. 102.

19 On Playfair see Crowther (note 11) pp. 105–71, and A. Scott, *J. Chem. Soc.*, 1905, 87, 600–5.

20 On Liebig see ch. V, note 4.

21 On Frankland see ch. VI, note 3.

22 Autobiographical, *Sketches from the life of Sir Edward Frankland*, 2nd edn. 1902, p. 87 (see ch. VI note 3).

23 *Ibid.*, p. 90.

24 *Ibid.*, p. 93.

25 Parnell (note 7), p. 241.

26 Mercer in Parnell (note 7), p. 245.

27 Mellor and Cardwell (note 6), p. 274.

28 On Perkin see *J. Chem. Soc.*, 1908, 93, 2214; also R. Brightman, 'Perkin and the Dye-stuff Industry of Britain', *Nature*, 1965, 177, 815–21. The significance of his work for later chemistry is discussed in *Perkin Centenary*, Pergamon, London, 1958.

29 *Royal Commission on Scientific Instruction and the Advancement of Science*, (c. 536), P.P. 1872, XXV, pp. 357–60 (evidence given 2 February 1871, q. 5683).

30 On the early history of coal-gas production see (a) D. Chandler, *Outline of History of Lighting by Gas*, Chancery Lane Printing Works, London, 1936; (b) S. Everard, *The History of the Gas Light and Coke Company 1812-1949*, Benn, London, 1949; (c) E. G. Stewart, *Town Gas, its Manufacture and Distribution*, HMSO, London, 1958.

31 Everard (note 30 (b)), p. 126.

32 *Ibid.*, p. 23. On Accum see ch. IV, note 12.

33 Everard (note 30 (b)), p. 323.

34 'A Day at a Soap and Candle Factory', *Penny Magazine*, 1842, **11**, 42.

35 A. E. Musson, *Enterprise in Soap and Chemicals, Joseph Crosfield & Sons Limited, 1815-1965*, Manchester UP, Manchester, 1965, p. 68.

36 *Ibid.*, p. 38.

37 *Ibid.*, p. 80.

38 Charles Wilson, *The History of Unilever: A Study in Economic Growth and Social Change*, Cassell, London, 1970, vol. i, p. 14.

39 See (a) H. S. Corran 'Brewing Technology in Britain, 1820–1900', in *A History of Brewing*, David and Charles, Newton Abbot, 1975, pp. 183–211; (b) T. S. Bremner, 'The Laboratory in Brewing', *The Red Hand*, 1952, **6**, pt. iv, 4–11; (c) H. T. Brown, 'Reminiscences of Fifty Years' Experience of the Application of Scientific Method to Brewing Practice', *J. Inst. Brewing*, 1916, **22**, 267–353; (d) E. R. Ward, 'Peter Griess (1829–1888) and the Burton Breweries', *J.R.I.C.*, 1958, **82**, 383–9, 458–63.

40 On Warington see J. H. S. Green, *Proc. Chem. Soc.*, 1957, 241–6.

41 On Hofmann see ch. V, note 18.

42 On Graham see *DNB*, *DSB* and *J. Chem. Soc.*, 1870, **23**, 293.

43 S. Muspratt, *Chemistry, Theoretical, Practical and Analytical*, Glasgow, 1857–1860, vol. i, p. 236. This was James Sheridan Muspratt (1821–71), eldest son of the pioneer of the alkali industry, James Muspratt (note 59).

44 Bremner (note 39 (b)), p. 6.

45 Ward (note 39 (d)), p. 387.

46 See J. V. Eyre, *Henry Edward Armstrong*, Butterworth, London, 1958; and E. H. Rodd, *J. Chem. Soc.*, 1940, 418–39.

47 H. E. Armstrong, *J. Inst. Brewing*, 1916, **22**, 349 (in proposing vote of thanks to Brown, note 39 (c)).

48 *The Story of Whitbreads*, 3rd. edn., Whitbread & Co, London, 1964, p. 37.

49 See, e.g., W. J. Reader, *Imperial Chemical Industries, A History*, vol. i, *The Forerunners 1870-1926*, OUP, London, 1970.

50 See A. Clow, 'Fiscal Policy and the Development of Technology', *Ann. Sci.*, 1954, **10**, 342–58.

51 (a) W. A. Campbell, *The Chemical Industry*, Longman, London, 1971; (b) L. F. Haber, *The Chemical Industry during the Nineteenth Century*, Clarendon Press, Oxford, 1958; (c) D. W. F. Hardie and J. Davidson Pratt, *A History of the Modern British Chemical Industry*, Pergamon, Oxford, 1966; (d) T. I. Williams, *The Chemical Industry, Past and Present*, Penguin, London, 1953 (reprint, E. P. Publishing, Wakefield, 1972).

52 Haber (note 51 (b)), p. 10.

53 *Ibid.*, p. 189.

54 On Weldon see D. W. F. Hardie, *Chem. Age*, 1957, **78**, 691.

55 On Deacon see *idem, ibid.*, p. 598; also *Chem. Trade J.*, 1889, **5**, 191–6.

56 This came about from (a) the greater availability of chemicals in purer condition, and (b) industrial problem solving with valuable 'spin-off' results of all kinds.

57 Haber (note 51 (b)), p. 196n.

58 D. W. F. Hardie, *A History of the Chemical Industry in Widnes*, ICI, London, 1950, pp. 124–5.

59 On James Muspratt see (a) *idem, Chem. Age*, 1957, **77**, 715; (b) J. Fenwick Allen, *Some Founders of the Chemical Industry*, London, 1906, pp. 69–100, (reprint of *Chem. Trade J.*, 1889, **5**, 240–3); (c) *J. Soc. Chem. Ind.*, 1886, **5**, 314.

60 On Allhusen see Allen (note 59 (b)), pp. 233–48 (reprint of *Chem. Trade, J.*, 1890, **6**, 222–3).

61 Haber (note 51 (b)), p. 189.

62 On Lunge see *J. Chem. Soc.*, 1923, **123**, 949–51.

63 *Trans. Newcastle Chem. Soc.*, 1871–4, **2**, 175.

64 On Dundonald and the Losh brothers see D. W. F. Hardie, *Chem. Age*, 1957, **77**, 342.

65 On Spence see (a) *idem, ibid.*, **78**, 219; (b) Allen (note 59 (b)), pp. 251–89 (reprint of *Chem. Trade J.*, 1890, **6**, 9–12).

66 On Gossage see Allen (note 59 (h)), pp. 1–36 (reprint of *Chem. Trade J.*, 1889, **5**, 111–14).

67 On H. L. Pattinson see E. E. Aynsley and W. A. Campbell, *Chem. & Ind.*, 1958, 1498–9.

68 On Glover see D. W. F. Hardie, *Chem. Age*, 1957, **78**, 816.

69 This is further discussed in ch. IV (p. 61).

70 S. G. Checkland, *The Mines of Tharsis*, Allen and Unwin, London, 1967.

71 On the Muspratt brothers see note 43 (for J. S.) and ch. V note 44 (for E. K.).

72 On Kurtz see Allen (note 59 (b)) pp. 103–50 (reprint of *Chem. Trade J.*, 1889, **5**, 287–92).

73 'A Day at the Felling Chemical Works, Newcastle', *Penny Magazine*, 1844, **13**, 208.

74 Alkali Inspector, *Intermediate Report*, P.P. 1876, XVI, 2.

75 *Report from the Select Committee on the Provisions for giving Instruction in Theoretical and Applied Science to the Industrial Classes*, P.P. 1867–8, XV, 352.

76 Haber (note 51 (b)), p. 190.

77 Allen (note 59 (b)), pp. 278–9.

78 On Hurter see ch. X, note 25.

79 On the development of pharmacy in Britain see (a) L. G. Matthews, *History of Pharmacy in Britain*, Livingstone, London, 1962; and (b) Jacob Bell and Theophilus Redwood, *Historical Sketch of the Progress of Pharmacy in Great Britain*, London, 1880.

80 Bell and Redwood (note 79 (b)), p. 34.

81 *Ibid.*, p. 36.

82 *Ibid.*, p. 53.

83 44 Geo. III c. 68.

84 W. V. Farrar, K. R. Farrar and E. L. Scott, 'The Henrys of Manchester', R. *I. C. Reviews*, 1971, **4**, 40.

85 Matthews (note 79 (a)), p. 115.

86 On Hawes see *DNB* and note 30 (b) (he was Governor of the Gas Light and Coke Company, 1851–60); also *Gent. Mag.*, 1862, pt. ii, 101–3.

87 On Bell see *J. Chem. Soc.*, 1860–1, **13**, 167–8.

88 Bell and Redwood (note 79 (b)), pp. 108–10.

89 Matthews (note 79 (a)), p. 128.

90 The same underlying attitude which finds monopolistic practices abhorrent may be seen in Babbage's polemic on *The Great Exposition of 1851* where England is lamented for departing from its first promotion of free trade and being 'the first nation to prohibit its very basis, "competition", at the world's great bazaar' (*op. cit.*, London, 1851, p. vi).

91 Bell and Redwood (note 79 (b)), pp. 334–5.

92 *Ibid.*, p. 300.

93 Bell (note 79 (b)), p. 323.

94 31 & 32, Vict. c. 121.

95 J. J. Berzelius, *J. de Phys.*, 1811, **73**, 253–86.

96 *The Chemist*, 1843, **4**, 175. The Pharmaceutical Society is described as 'this self-constituted and ill-managed body, which consists of only about one eighth of the trade' (p. 172), its pretentions as 'this monstrous piece of humbug' (p. 175), and its *Journal* as 'a trashy and boyish affair' (p. 176).

97 Frankland (note 22), p. 21.

1   *Alchemical laboratory of sixteenth century.*

2   *Assaying in the sixteenth century.*

3   *Apothecaries' Hall in early nineteenth century.*

4   *English pharmacy laboratory (1747).*

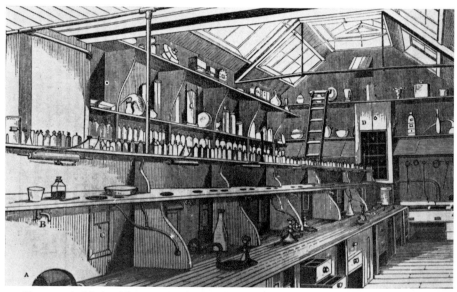

5   *Pharmaceutical Society laboratory, London (1844).*

6 *Access to factory chimney for analyses of effluent gases.*

7 *United Alkali Company's Central Laboratory, Widnes (est. 1891).*

8   *Roscoe's chemistry teaching laboratory, Manchester (1873).*

9   *Great Western Railway laboratory, Swindon (1907).*   **4**

CHAPTER IV

THE GROWTH OF CHEMICAL INSTITUTIONS

The practice of chemistry has often been characterized by a tension between two opposing tendencies. On one hand there has been a cautious isolationism in which the solitary practitioner has guarded the secrets of his art by keeping his own counsel and declining the company of possible rivals and competitors, be they alchemical mystics or Victorian industralists. Often, however, the natural gregariousness of chemists has overcome their scruples and the most wary entrepreneur has emerged from his shell to enjoy the company of his fellow chemists. This was specially obvious in the early nineteenth century, and there came into being all kinds of groupings which we can call 'chemical institutions'. Whatever their purpose—convivial, scientific or technical—they set a fashion that helped to make possible the rise of the professional chemist. In this chapter we consider several important kinds of chemical institution existing before 1877.

1 Chemistry at the Grass-roots

One of the remarkable features of English chemistry in the nine-teenth century is the importance of what may be described as the popular initiative. From the 1860s this was to manifest itself in publications like the *English Mechanic*, produced at 1d a week for an enormous readership of working-class men, boys and even girls. Its ample pages were replete with well-informed and perceptive comment on the current state of chemistry (together with mechanics and the 'useful arts' generally), and many contri-butors to its correspondence columns displayed an awareness of critical chemical issues that the 'professionals' in university departments were reluc-tant to consider. Thus the concepts of valency and structure were discussed volubly and without inhibition at precisely the time that many academic chemists were agonizing over the propriety of the even more basic idea of the atom. The *English Mechanic* was several years ahead of the *Journal of the Chemical Society* in that respect.[1]

Such cases of proletarian precocity were a manifestation of the great urge for self-improvement that characterized the Victorian working masses, or at least a substantial proportion of them. The supreme monument to this zeal can be seen in the mechanics' institutes and their modern descendants the colleges of technology and polytechnics. Their checkered history dates back to the early years of peace when Europe was recovering from the Napoleonic wars.[2] One of the earliest was in Glasgow (1823). The London Mechanics' Institute was founded in 1824 and within two years over a hundred similar institutions had sprung into existence. The forces that generated such momentum were enormous, and their effects were very diverse. Long antedating the *English Mechanic* was the *Mechanics' Magazine*, and this was accompanied by a considerable number of worthy volumes on the sciences, including Lord Brougham's 'Library of Useful Knowledge', at 6d a book. Another result was the establishment of the London Chemical Society.[3]

This Society must not be confused with its more august successor of 1841. Its origins and fate have, until recently, been buried in almost total obscurity, for it lasted hardly a year and was from start to finish without any perceptible impact on the course of chemistry itself. Yet it does seem to have been the first example of an independent institution dedicated exclusively to chemistry. Although at first sight few phenomena could have been less relevant to the profession that was to come in the future, on closer examination it can be seen that it does mark in several ways an important development. But before we look briefly at this strange and ephemeral body it is necessary to glance at the source of our information, a periodical if anything even more strange and more ephemeral than the society whose fate it chronicles.

The Chemist made its first appearance on 13 March 1824. Despite its modest price (3d a week) its aims were ambitious: 'to give an outline of the principles of chemistry, with their numerous applications, as well as a history and description of all the arts which are connected with this science', and to become 'a repository of every valuable discovery, either in chemistry or the sciences connected with it, which might be made, either at home or abroad'.[4] It is hardly necessary to add that such high objectives were not to be fulfilled; but the unpretentiousness, and even crudity, of its few closely packed pages conceal its significance for British chemistry. It was, in fact, one of the first English periodicals devoted specifically to chemical science, though later than Nicholson's *Journal of Natural Philosophy, Chemistry and the Arts* founded in 1798. However, *The Chemist* kept more to its declared subject-matter and, unlike anything before it, was aimed at the uninitiated and obscure rather than the cognoscenti and the famous. It was published by Knight and Lacey, more renowned for the *Mechanics' Magazine*.

To read *The Chemist* today with a view to understanding the science of the 1820s can be an unrewarding experience. It is highly selective, bitty, badly illustrated, inaccurate and as prone to lapse into sententious argument as it is to report new chemical discoveries. One learns far more in that respect from Nicholson's *Journal* or the *Philosophical Magazine*. But to see it in the light of the new Mechanics' Institute movement, and to hear much of its verbosity as a *cri de coeur* from those deprived by social accident of the chemical knowledge for which they long, to regard it more as a social than a chemical document—this is to gain a totally different impression. The journal does not talk about professionalism as such, nor does it complain about working conditions or standards or wages or salaries. But it does demonstrate one of the pressures that eventually forced chemists to unite as a professional body, and that was the need for effective channels of communication between those who pursued the subject *at all levels*.

This point repeatedly emerges in the journal. It occurs on the very first page—the editor's 'Apology and Preface'—with a tilt at the scientific establishment of the day, so evidently and painfully divided into 'sects' that he cannot decide whose portrait should adorn his preface! Davy was a possible contender but was excluded by his remoteness.

> As we have not observed any very great zeal, among those who are at the tip-top of science, to assist the working classes in the numerous and glorious efforts they have lately made to procure instruction for themselves, we confess a suspicion is excited that they look with no kindly eye on these efforts, and would rather have mankind for pupils than fellow-students of the great volume of nature. If this be correct, it might perhaps be an insult to our readers to place in the front of our pages the portrait of a man who, however learned, is not learned for their utility, and who seems to take little or no interest in their improvement.[5]

Davy stood condemned, as President of the Royal Society (PRS), for his profession of 'a sort of royal science'. The editor repeatedly attacked the Royal Society long before Babbage made his celebrated onslaught in 1830.[6] Concerning the leaders of such societies he assures a correspondent that 'if he will furnish us with a single instance of their assisting to promote scientific knowledge among the people, we will readily publish it, and, as far as we can, make it known to the world'.[7] Elsewhere he complains:

> Neither Mr Brande, nor any more eloquent man, will now persuade the world that the Royal Societies are of any use but to bestow false honours on those persons who are the most skilful (*sic*) intriguers.[8]

Anxious 'to reduce aristocracies in science to their proper level'[9] he inserted a letter that concluded:

> The spirit of the age does not accord with the views of the dandy philosophers; they may black-ball at Somerset House, segregate from Albemarle Street, or shut themselves up in the Atheneum (*sic*) . . . but they will only . . . have the mortification of seeing that the world goes on better without them.[10]

The complaints were not merely that the artistocracy of science existed, but also that it was divided amongst itself—hence the numerous fulminations against the 'sects', for 'almost every scientific journal of any reputation is in our country merely the organ of some sect or party'.[11] Such comments cannot be dismissed as wholly partisan and they are a devastating critique of one aspect of early nineteenth-century chemistry that smacked of an incipient professionalism, its exclusiveness.

Much sympathy is expressed for those struggling to acquire the rudiments of a chemical education despite 'the system'. Cheap and simple apparatus is described and popular lectures are reported. Attacks by correspondents on Accum's book on food adulteration[12] are sustained because of its inference 'because some men have been guilty of frauds, that all tradesmen are rogues',[13] etc.

The identity of the editor has been a matter of some speculation as he always assumed anonymity. However Brougham in his *Practical Observations upon the Education of the People*, praises *The Chemist* which was, he said, 'judiciously conducted by Mr. Hodgkin'.[14] This was presumably Thomas Hodgskin, for a short time co-editor of *The Mechanics' Magazine*, and radical economist who in some respects anticipated the conclusions of Karl Marx.

If the editor is correctly identified as Hodgskin the radical attitudes of *The Chemist* need occasion no surprise. Nor need its failure after less than a year of life, for an inexperienced editor with insufficient capital was in no position to sustain a periodical that cocked a snook at the chemical establishment and gained no support whatever from it. The hard fact was that the services and approval of the quasi-professionals were needed, if only to ensure the maintenance of an adequate quality. In its absence subscriptions gradually dropped and the whole project sank from sight in early 1825. But before it did so it gave news of another venture that emphasized very similar attitudes: the London Chemical Society. In fact *The Chemist* did more than just give news of the Society; it could be said that it gave it its birth.[15]

On 22 May 1824, *The Chemist* printed the following letter:[16]

> To the Editor of the Chemist
> Sir, You must be aware, that the majority of the readers and admirers of your little Work is composed of persons who can devote but a small portion of time to chemistry, and who at the same time are not in circumstances to lock up part of their capital in apparatus, &c. for prosecuting the study of that science; would it then not be advisable for you, who appear so much the encourager of beginners, to form, as it were, a nucleus for a society of young chemists, who might, at their common expense, purchase chemical tests, instruments, &c. as they want them, and that without bringing down ruin on any of them. I should like the society to be respectable and select, and to meet at a stipulated number of times every week.
> I have the honour to be,
>
> Sir,
> Your most obedient,
>
> May 7th   A. W.

The initials of the author were subsequently amended to 'A. M'.[17]

The proposal was favourably received both by the editor and his readership. The lively correspondence that followed included suggestions for a self-help course based on Henry's textbook, offers of apparatus, money and even a room. Declining an invitation to organize a meeting ('being always engaged of an evening')[18] the editor backed gracefully out, but his journal continued to supply information about the new venture; indeed this was the only means whereby potential members could be in touch with developments.

On 15 July a steering committee was formed. Its chairman was A. J. F. Marreco, possibly the 'A.M.' of the first correspondence; the secretary was W. Jones who was host for the exploratory discussions. A room in Aldermanbury was hired and became the venue for a series of lectures by J. B. Austin (one of the committee members) and C. F. Partington of the London Institution.[19] One lecture was reported by *The Chemist* as having been delivered 'in a very pleasing style, agreeably illustrated by experiments. Several ladies were present, taking a warm interest in all that was said, encouraging the lecturer by their smiles, and ensuring order and decorum by their presence'.[20] When the inaugural lecture was delivered by Birkbeck he made a special point of the suitability of chemistry for feminine study and indicated that the Society intended that ladies should be admitted as members. Had this progressive policy been implemented it would have anticipated by nearly a century our own Chemical Society's extension of Fellowship to women in 1920.[21]

This inaugural lecture was a great occasion with over 300 people ('amongst them a great many ladies')[22] assembled at the City of London Tavern to hear the founder of the Mechanics' Institute movement. It was a wide-ranging discourse, devoted to the highly topical theme of *change*, emphasizing its role in chemistry, denying that its study should 'be confined to learned men',[23] stressing the Society's desire to foster experimental practice and urging on his audience the appropriateness of studying the 'processes and operations of common life'.[24]

Birkbeck's reception must have been rapturous and his text was printed almost in full in *The Chemist*. Yet less than three weeks later came the following complaint, in a letter from one who signed himself 'Visitor'.[25]

> I have attended more than once at the meetings of the 'London Chemical Society', and, taking them *en masse*, with as much profit as could reasonably be expected; but now that the inauguration has taken place with so much *éclat*, and the officers are regularly appointed, I trust you will afford me sufficient space to express a hope that they will prevent any recurrence of lectures being delivered by persons who are not sufficiently pregnant with the matter to give information in an intelligible manner.

Perhaps this offers us a clue to the strange fact that no further reference to the Society appeared in the pages of *The Chemist*, and, of course, within a few more months that worthy journal had disappeared almost without trace.

Yet the Society, like *The Chemist*, was important for what it did *not* accomplish. The failure of both was undoubtedly due to lack of both experience and resources, and (Birkbeck notwithstanding) isolation from the scientific community at large. The foundation of the Society was a fresh demonstration of the centripetal forces drawing chemists together, just as its demise signifies the centrifugal forces which made coherence impossible with the existing community. The whole episode emphasizes the monopolistic character of aristocratic science, with its quasi-professional exclusiveness; and it offers a rare glimpse of the strength of reaction against it. Marreco and his friends represent the identity crisis of chemists who were, by any criterion, amateurs. This was a crisis that has as much to do with the internal differentiation of science into chemistry, physics, etc., as with the burgeoning radicalism of Hanoverian England.[26]

The composition of the Society is of some interest. Certainly we know that being a beginner in chemistry was no bar to admission, but how far it was populated by those whose vocation was in a general way chemical it is simply impossible to say. How far the Council was truly representative of either abilities or interests is also an open question, but those members who can be unequivocally identified would certainly not have been at home in chemical employment. Marreco is a case in point. From 1821 to 1829 he appears in Post Office Directories as a merchant in the City; he then appears on Tyneside as a shareholder in a Joint Stock Bank,[27] then Secretary and eventually Director of the Stanhope and Tyne Railway.[28] Finally, in the 1840s he returns to his native Portugal with a bride (his employer's daughter) and presumably a fortune.[29] Like some of his friends in the Chemical Society he was able, ambitious and eventually prosperous though he began in a small way. Finding opportunity lacking in chemistry he sought to provide it for himself; thwarted in this object by the sheer difficulty of beating the chemical establishment he sought and found his fortune elsewhere. We shall meet him again.[30]

2 Provincial Chemical Societies

(a) On Tyneside

If the formation of the London Chemical Society in 1824 shows that chemistry was no longer the prerogative of the 'charismatic genius',[31] the events we shall now describe show that it was not the monopoly of the metropolis either. Throughout the nineteenth century many scientific associations of one kind or another had flourished in the provinces, such as the Yorkshire Philosophical Society which gave birth to the British Association, or the even more famous Literary and Philosophical Society of Manchester. Certainly in the latter case, and in some others, chemistry was much to the fore. But the sharp differentiation of science into specific 'subjects' did not occur in the genteel gatherings of most provincial societies of this kind. For this to happen a strong external pressure was needed, and this was to be applied, in the 1860s, by the insistent demands of chemical industry. What was really remarkable was that the area concerned, Tyneside,[32] was within a couple of years to have not one but two Chemical Societies.

In June 1868 a meeting was convened in Newcastle to establish 'a Chemical Society, with the object of the promotion of chemistry and its allied sciences in this district, more especially with regard to their practical application'. Within a year it numbered nearly a hundred members, the vast majority being from Tyneside or its immediate vicinity.[33]

The Newcastle Chemical Society offered from the first an impressive array of talent. Its first President was Isaac Lothian Bell, a pioneer of the Cleveland iron trade and eventually baronet, MP, President of the Iron and Steel Institute, the Institution of Mechanical Engineers and the Society of Chemical Industry.[34] The Treasurer was a well-known local analyst, J. Pattinson.[35] One of the two joint secretaries was the German-born Georg Lunge, then chemist and works manager of the Tyne Alkali Co, and rapidly acquiring an international reputation for his encyclopedic knowledge of the alkali industry. His colleague in the secretariat was Reader in Chemistry at the Newcastle College of Medicine, one Algernon Freire-Marreco.[36] A most remarkable character, and later a member of the first committee of the Institute of Chemistry, Marreco (whose hyphen was often omitted) was in fact the son of none other than A. J. F. Marreco of the London Chemical Society. This was the man, more than any other, who was to guide the affairs of the Newcastle Chemical Society for the next decade. His obituarist in *Chemical News* many years later singled out one aspect of his work that uncannily, and unconsciously, reflected the early enthusiasm of his father:

> He . . . laboured with characteristic zeal to knit together North Country chemists in the bonds of fraternity.[37(f)]

Within a few months the Society launched its *Transactions* and so became one of only three societies in the North of England then to publish original researches.[38] The tone of the *Transactions* was to become heavily industrial, with emphasis on developments in the alkali industry. The Society continued to flourish for the next few years, despite the appearance of a rival organization and journal in the same neighbourhood.

The Tyne Social Chemical Society was formed in 1870 with, it is said,[39] 'similar aims and an overlapping membership', although only eight members can be unambiguously assigned to both societies. Study of its *Transactions* suggests a 'self-help' group of persons responsible for the day-to-day running of much of Tyneside's chemical industry. As its functions became more technical the name 'Social' was dropped from its title.[40] The Newcastle Chemical Society was a very different affair, with a much more influential membership and strong links with the prosperous Literary and Philosophical Society of that city.

The 'means for training chemists' had already been an important issue before the Newcastle Chemical Society.[41] The foundation of the Durham

College of Science at Newcastle (eventually to become that city's University), in 1871 owed much to pressure from several members of the Society, notably including Marreco who became its first Professor of Chemistry. The academic commitment of the Newcastle Chemical Society was further strengthened by Marreco's election to the Presidency in 1876.

One of the direct results of the concern of this society for academic matters was an important discussion, in 1874, on the necessity for professional examinations for public analysts.[42] When the Institute was formed in 1877 four of its fifty-two founder members had connections with the Newcastle Chemical Society.[43]

During February 1876 overtures were made to the Tyne Chemical Society by the Newcastle Chemical Society 'relative to a proposed union, and it was unanimously resolved that the question should not be reopened'.[44] The disparity in aims, membership and size was so great that the outcome is hardly surprising. Doubtless the larger society, now becoming more aware of the issue of professionalism in chemistry, saw a takeover as some small step towards greater unity amongst chemists. They were not to be rebuffed. However, nearly four years later, amalgamation was proposed to a meeting of the two committees and carried unanimously.[45] By January 1880 the President of Newcastle Society, R. C. Clapham, could claim 'the two Chemical Societies are now practically united'.[46] Few of the original Tyne Social Chemical Society were now active and the independence which had been so jealously guarded a few years before was now readily surrendered.

Ironically within a few months of the amalgamation both Clapham and Marreco died and the combined Society was faced with a new and urgent challenge: to be absorbed within the new Society of Chemical Industry. Since this organization was itself an offspring of local activity in another area, Merseyside, we must first note briefly the pattern of events in that part of England.

(b) South Lancashire

On 28 June 1872, the *Chemical News* carried a letter urging the formation of an Association of Manufacturing Chemists. Unfortunately the pseudonym of its writer, 'Frank', conceals both his identity and location—as no doubt he intended they should.[47] He was an 'English chemical manufacturer', situated in a district with many other manufacturers 'within a few miles', clearly at loggerheads with 'illiterate Local Board inspectors', and much disturbed by 'the secretiveness and isolation' of his neighbours. It does not seem likely that the last item would be a feature of the Tyneside chemical scene, and the only probable alternative is therefore South Lancashire.[48] Be that as it may, the suggestion of an Association to bring together 'the great body of manufacturing chemists' was warmly welcomed by several correspondents from that area as well as by the inevitable anonymous writers and a sympathetic editorial.[49]

It is interesting that the correspondence picks up a number of issues already encountered on Tyneside. The 'manager of one of the largest chemical works in Lancashire' points to the advantage of efficient communication even between rivals without loss to either; Peter Hart writes from Manchester to eliminate from the discussion that city's Literary and Philosophical Society— 'its tone is more high science, with only comparatively a sprinkling of technology'; a London engineer hoped that a new society 'will not be limited to the profession strictly';[50] and a bold note is struck by 'Black Ash' in hoping that a new united society could address itself to all relevant matters 'even to wages questions'.[51]

All this was familiar to the members of the Tyne Chemical Society, as that institution's honorary secretary was not slow to observe.[52] There was 'the nucleus of such as Association' already in being, and 'the chemists of Newcastle will be most happy to greet their professional brethren here, if they will make this town the scene of the first meeting of the Association'. In similar vein 'Black Ash' commended papers by Thomas Gibb in the Newcastle Transactions as examples of the new openness amongst manufacturers in the north east.[53] In a footnote to this letter the editor announced that steps were to be taken in Newcastle to start such an Association. But two weeks later he had to report that the Tyne Social Chemical Society had declined the task; it was 'a society of managers and chemists only, and not of manufacturers; and the Council think that the organisation of the proposed association should proceed in the first instance from the manufacturers themselves'.[54] This is an eloquent demonstration of the social homogeneity of the Society and of social tensions within the chemical industry at that time.

So the idea came to nothing; not even the enthusiasm of Lancashire and the experience of Tyneside were sufficient to overcome the prevailing inertia. In America a Manufacturing Chemists' Association did in fact start up that same year, but Britain had to wait until 1916 for the Association of British Chemical Manufacturers to emerge. It is interesting that the more powerful Newcastle Chemical Society seems to have taken no part in the discussions, and one can speculate that its aloofness may have been a major factor in their eventual failure. Its President, Lunge, gave 'my best wishes' to the project but claimed 'Our own Society cannot in any case merge in such an Association, because, after all, its scope is somewhat different from that of purely technical chemistry; for even though, from our local circumstances, the latter will always form the chief, yet it will not and ought not to form the exclusive subject of our Transactions', adding that 'the presence amongst us of chemists, other than manufacturing ones, is of the greatest possible benefit'.[55] In other words, transformation into such an Association would be to the detriment of the academic interests in the Newcastle Chemical Society. A basically similar conflict of interests may be detected in Lancashire. Here manufacturers were reluctant to allow their employees to get together, mainly, it seems, for fear of trade secrets passing from one to the other.

Academic chemistry had been seen as a boon in Newcastle; on Merseyside it was deemed a threat. But in each case the conflict between academic and practising chemist is plain for all to see.

However all was not lost and the chemists of Merseyside and South Lancashire were able to take some steps towards an association. In 1875 George E. Davis,[56] a recent recruit to the South Lancashire chemical industry from the south, formed the Faraday Club, an informal association of chemists in Widnes and St Helens who, he said, scarcely knew each other. They met fortnightly, alternately at the two towns, and later at Liverpool,[57] though some difficulties were experienced at first owing to the employers' reluctance to allow their chemists to attend.[58] The Faraday Club seems to have been similar to the Tyne Social Chemical Society, but on an even smaller scale, without printed transactions and (presumably) with greater suspicion on the part of the employers. The suggestion[59] that its existence 'shows that the example of the Tyneside chemists had spread to the Lancashire district' appears to be without sufficient support. That there was a traffic in ideas between the two areas is certain, but its effects were chiefly shown in a different organization, the South Lancashire Chemical Society.

There is good reason to suppose that a key role in the establishment of good relations between Tyneside and Merseyside chemists was played by John Morrison. One of the founders of the Tyne Social Chemical Society, he was at the Arklow Chemical Works in 1871[60] but two years later was at Runcorn, returning once in 1873–4 to read a paper on 'Gossip from Widnes' understandably marked 'For private circulation only':

> Of all towns for an unprotected stranger with any predisposition to mental depression to enter on a cold, wet winter's evening, Widnes is about the very last I could recommend.[61]

Apparently this uninhibited son of the Tyne was free from such depressive tendencies for within a year he was to be found at the Atlas Chemical Works in Widnes, working the Hargreaves process for making saltcake from sulphur dioxide (SO_2) directly. However by 1875–6 he was back on his native Tyneside running his own highly mechanized Forth Bank Chemical Manure Works and in due course becoming President of the Tyne Chemical Society. It is not improbable that he was instrumental in persuading James Hargreaves to address the Tyne Chemical Society in 1875 on his sulphate process[62], and in 1879 John Hargreaves[63] visited the Society again while on a visit to Newcastle. This had important consequences which are best conveyed in his own words:

> Realising the great advantages accruing from the intimate association and frequent conferences of those engaged in chemical manufacture, on my return to Widnes I convened a meeting of chemists and managers of this district, which was held in the Y.M.C.A. rooms of this town, on

November, 21 1879, to consider the advisability of forming a local chemical society similar to the one referred to.[64]

A local press report adds that 'the meeting was well attended by managers and chemists of the district' and that the secretary of the Tyne Chemical Society, A. Campbell, was also present to exlpain the working of the now amalgamated society in Newcastle.[65] The Tyne model was consciously adopted, with monthly social gatherings, the reading of papers and formation of a library.

An allegation that the new South Lancashire Chemical Society arose from jealousy of the Faraday Club[57] is wide of the mark, for Hargreaves asserted that he never heard of the Club until after the preliminary meeting.[66] However a meeting at the Drill Hall, Widnes, in December 1879, chaired by James Muspratt, was attended by Davis and a few henchmen apparently with the intention of breaking it up.[67] The upshot was, however, their conversion to the new cause and the election of three of them on to the new Committee (Davis, Hurter and Herman)! Numerous other meetings were held in Liverpool and Manchester and it soon became clear that, this time, the tide was running strongly in the organizers' favour. Amongst others G. E. Davis (then honorary secretary) and H. E. Roscoe of Owens College were known to be strongly in favour of a national organization, with a local branch in Lancashire. A further issue widely debated was whether it should be known as the Society of Chemical Engineers but, at the inaugural meeting in the Chemical Society's rooms in London on 4 April 1881, it was finally decided to call it the Society of Chemical Industry. Of the discussion that took place and the issues raised more will be heard later (p. 189). In view of the confusion once reigning over the origins of this Society it may be useful to quote from its own *Journal* on the occasion of its Jubilee:

> It seems clear after reading many conflicting statements in our Journal and in old correspondence that the idea of forming the society that subsequently became the Society of Chemical Industry originated with Mr Hargreaves . . . It is equally obvious that Mr George E. Davis, so soon as he realized the nature of the proposed society, did a great deal of very valuable work in the actual formation of the society and that he had a larger share of this work than anyone else.[68]

3 National Associations of Chemists

(a) The British Association

Attempts to unite chemists in some kind of organization were not confined to undergraduate clubs, splinter groups of the Royal Society or popular movements like the London Chemical Society. The need was also recognized by some whose scientific reputations were international, only it was seen in terms of something more than just chemistry. The 1830s and 1840s witnessed notable progress in the institutionalization of chemistry, but such changes can only be correctly understood in the light of a larger movement dedicated to the development of British science as a whole.

The formation, in 1831, of the British Association for the Advancement of Science [69] was a conscious response to the agitations of those who became known as 'Declinists'—men who lamented the poverty of contemporary British science and saw it in a state of sad decline from its former greatness. Their most vociferous spokesman was Charles Babbage whose *Reflections on the Decline of Science in England and Some of its Causes* (1830) was a scorching indictment of the Royal Society which for years had been managed by a 'party' far more determined to maintain its own position and to resist change than to give genuine support and encouragement to science. In this respect Babbage repeated very similar sentiments to those of *The Chemist*, six years later (p. 57). For Babbage the lamentable result was that 'The pursuit of science does not, in England, constitute a distinct profession, as it does in many other countries'.[70]

Charles Babbage was a Cambridge graduate of independent means, much of which was consumed in developing his 'Calculating engine'—the first mechanical computer. His plea was taken up by the Scottish philosopher David Brewster, himself a Fellow and Medallist of the Royal Society. Not surprisingly, Brewster's wrath found a slightly different target; he concerned himself particularly with the British universities, and went so far as to assert, though with rather less than justice that:

> Within the last fifteen years not a single discovery or invention of prominent interest has been made in our colleges, and that there is not one man in all the eight universities in Great Britain who is at present known to be engaged in any train of original research.[71]

The real sting in the Declinists' argument lay in the assertion that science was in a worse state in England than elsewhere. In 1829 Brewster's *Edinburgh Journal of Science* contained a report by Babbage of his visit the previous year to a 'great congress of philosophers at Berlin', i.e. the annual meeting of the Deutsche Naturförscherversammlung. In early 1831 the same journal printed an account by J. F. W. Johnston of the Hamburg meeting of German philosophers the previous year. The implication was obvious. Britain must form a similar body, people who are united by being 'cultivators of science' rather than an assortment of 'nobility, clergy, gentry and philosophers'. Such a body, Brewster wrote to Babbage, could well be formed from a gathering of British men of science due to meet at York in the summer of 1831.

That meeting duly took place though, despite the attendance of over three hundred wellwishers, 'the body scientific' was ill-represented. Many of the great names of English science were conspicuously absent. The host body was the Yorkshire Philosophical Society[72] and the eventual formation of the new organization owed much to that Society's President, William Vernon Harcourt, amateur scientist and Canon Residentiary of the Cathedral Church of York. Like Babbage, he condemned the Royal Society: 'as a body which scarcely labours itself, and does not attempt to guide the labours of others'.[73] And so the new association must arise 'having for its objects to give a stronger impulse and more systematic direction to scientific inquiry, to obtain a greater degree of national attention to the objects of science, and a removal of those disadvantages which impede its progress, and to promote the intercourse of the cultivators of science with one another, and with foreign philosophers'.[74]

How far the origins of the British Association may really be traced to Babbage and Brewster or Harcourt is still a matter for debate. Certainly Harcourt was influential in playing down the Declinists' line to win the somewhat grudging support of the universities; and the notion of a permanent association, rather different from the German model, owes more to him than to Brewster. It is sufficient to say that, whatever its parentage, the new British Association did not enjoy an untroubled growth, drawing upon itself the wrath of established organs like *The Times* ('When shall this monstrous bubble burst?'), lampooned by Charles Dickens as 'the Mud-fog Association for the Advancement of Everything', ostracized by many at Oxford and Cambridge and considerably impeded by internal disagreement as to how best to achieve its objectives.

The subsequent fortunes of the British Association as a whole do not need to detain us here, except in so far as they affect the changing social relationships of chemists. One of the most striking features about the Association has always been its commitment to science *as a whole*. Harcourt spoke strongly in favour of this attitude:

> It is easy to conceive, on the one hand, how much advantage might be derived to geological debates from the presence of a sober and rigorous mathematician; and how, on the other hand, the abstract analyst and geometer might have his calculations restricted or promoted by listening to the detail of facts, which those could give him who cultivate the sciences more directly dependent on observation and experiment.[75]

Despite this laudable desire to promote the unity of science the exigences of the situation demanded that, from the beginning, sub-committees should be appointed to look after subject interests. Chemistry was one of those thus designated in 1831 with members including the Professors of Chemistry at Oxford, Cambridge, London and (later) Durham, and, of more enduring fame than them all, John Dalton.[76] Next year the six sub-committees were replaced by four full committees, Dalton now becoming chairman of a group devoted to chemistry, mineralogy, electricity and magnetism. Not until 1835 was chemistry to find its permanent home in the famous Section B, devoted to that subject and mineralogy alone. This, like other sections, though to a greater extent than most, played an important role in future years with its commissioned reports into the state of chemistry. This activity had a long-term significance considerably greater than the organization of the more set-piece events that constituted the Association's Annual Meetings in different provincial centres.

A curious extension of the activities of Section B was the B-Club, an informal association of chemists that lasted from about 1860 until at least the late 1870s. The B-Club was a successor to an earlier offshoot of the British Association, the Red Lions, founded by the Edinburgh botanist Edward Forbes.

The Red Lions continued, on and off, until quite recent times. The B-Club, though continuing their convivial tradition, was distinctively chemical in membership and more bohemian in style. Its formation was a protest against the 'scientific don' and represents the growing disenchantment with the high seriousness and self-importance of the academic chemists. Few of the B-Club members were academics, and those few could be fairly categorized as 'middle rankers'. Those printed records of their activities that have survived throw an interesting light on attitudes held by ordinary chemists.[77]

At a different level Section B left its mark on the organization of chemists. Speaking on the early activities of that section the President of the Chemical Society in 1916, Alexander Scott, observed:

> The chemists in Section B assembled to discuss their various investigations and the difficulties met with in their prosecution before proceeding to the formal publication of their work. These meetings, from their helpful nature, no doubt suggested the formation of a formal and central Society ten years later, the chief object of which would be the communication and discussion of chemical papers.[78]

The formation of that Society will be the concern of the following pages.

(b) The Chemical Society of London

In 1841 the birth of the Chemical Society of London was probably the most important single event in the history of chemical institutions to this day.[79] It set a trend that was later followed in many other countries for national societies devoted to chemical science, notably France (1855), Germany (1866), Russia (1869) and the U.S.A. (1876). Moreover it became the immediate ancestor of the Institute of Chemistry in 1877, and thereafter the relations between the two bodies were of great importance for both the progress and the professionalization of chemistry.

After considerable informal canvassing, much correspondence and preliminary meeting to set up a provisional committee, the Society was formally constituted with seventy-seven members under the Presidency of Thomas Graham. Designated 'The Chemical Society of London' its objective was declared to be 'the advancement of chemistry and those branches of science immediately connected with it'. To that end discoveries announced at members' meetings were to be published by the Society in Proceedings or Transactions. There was also to be a library, research laboratory and museum.

The new society settled down to its routine of meetings, published its first *Proceedings* and *Memoirs* within a few months, elected its first few distinguished Foreign Members (Liebig was the very first) and in 1848, with a membership of over two hundred, obtained its first charter. From now on it was to be known by the shorter title still in use and its Members became Fellows. Its new *Quarterly Journal* was now graced with increasing coverage of foreign developments in chemistry. This had been one of the original intentions of the Society. Others were less easy to fulfil. Until 1857 the Society had no permanent home, occupying a succession of rooms in London, none of them wholly satisfactory. It then moved to Burlington House, of which it has occupied different parts to this day, along with the Royal and Linnean Societies. Despite its early peripatetic existence the Society was able to build up the nucleus of what is, today, one of the world's great chemical libraries. The museum lasted until only 1867, while the laboratory project was subsumed in the movement leading to the Royal College of Chemistry (1845). The subsequent history of the Society will be touched on in some of the following chapters.

The formation of the Chemical Society in 1841 was, as we have said, highly significant for the growth of chemical institutions generally. It would therefore be foolish not to inquire a little more fully into the reasons for this event in the light of wider developments in the nineteenth century.

Perhaps the first and most obvious factor is the *specialization within science*. We have already seen how in both London and the provinces the differentiation of science into chemistry and other subjects was creating needs for new channels of communication. Nor was chemistry the only science to be so placed. The formation of the Linnean Society (1788), the Geological Society (1807) and the Astronomical Society (1820) had marked the same tendencies and, in a sense, established a precedent. The successful resistance by the last two bodies to absorption by the Royal Society had suggested that chemists now had nothing to fear from that quarter.

However, it was not obvious to all in 1841 that chemistry *had* reached that stage of specialization. One of the recipients of an exploratory circular was W. H. Fox Talbot, inventor of the negative/positive method in photography. In declining the invitation to a preliminary meeting he wrote that chemistry alone is not a sufficient basis for a Society: perhaps it should be combined with electricity?[80] Certainly one does not have the impression that English chemistry was growing so fast in the 1830s that it was now too big to be allied with anything else. Yet despite the sceptics a large majority of those approached did believe that chemistry had 'come of age' as a separate subject.

Specialization within science may explain why, eventually, a Chemical Society appeared. But it cannot suggest why chemists had to wait until 1841 (or, for that matter, physicists until 1874). Clearly the *internal organization* of the newly differentiated subject is another factor of some relevance.

Now it might be pleasant to record that chemistry was now being so unified that chemists naturally came together in symbolic expression of that unity. But it would be quite untrue. Certainly it may be argued that the 1830s in general witnessed a convergence of organic and inorganic theory under the influence of atomism and the electrochemical theory of Berzelius.[81] But this was much more a Continental than a British phenomenon. In the United Kingdom what really seems to have happened is a recognition not that chemistry *was* unified but that it *ought to be*. In other words the formation of the Chemical Society reflected not the union but the fragmentation of chemistry.

This becomes immediately obvious if one peruses the list of twenty-five gentlemen 'interested in the prosecution of chemistry',[82] at that preliminary meeting in February 1841. They represent a wide variety of interests. Academics of one sort or another preponderated but there was a considerable sprinkling of industrial chemists, several pharmacists and three medical men. What had brought them together was the growing recognition of what they had in common: chemistry. More precisely, perhaps, we could say that this recognition was of the relevance of chemistry as taught and studied in colleges to that which is practised in the wider world of industry and medicine. None of these pressure groups could have accomplished much for chemistry and its organization on its own; together they had a chance.

Closely related to the need for promotion of a subject amongst its practitioners is its need for educational advance. So it can hardly be a coincidence that precisely the same pressure groups can be identified in the formation of the Chemical Society as the almost contemporaneous Royal College of Chemistry.

This educational priority may offer a partial explanation for the rather obvious change in emphasis on the governing body. Nine people were not elected to the provisional committee from the first *ad hoc* meeting and none of these held academic posts. The first Council excluded the only businessman left (H. J. Brooke) and added academics from Aberdeen, Cambridge and Oxford. Later on some of the non-academics retrieved their reward with positions on Council, and the membership from the start included men like Mercer, Macintosh[83] and H. L. Pattinson.[84] But it is hard to avoid the impression that, even if there was no overt academic/non-academic conflict, the early Chemical Society went out of its way to acquire an academic 'image'— and of course this it still retains in large measure.

Behind these tendencies may be seen a third factor of some importance: *an external force making urgent the need to combine*. Human nature would appear to need rather more than academic persuasion that large masses have a lot in common; it seems an occasion to require something of a jolt to urge it to take action.

Such a jolt may well have been acquired from the almost simultaneous banding together in 1841 of the pharmacists to protect their professional interests in the Pharmaceutical Society. In that connection it is significant that none of the 'twenty-five gentlemen' was solely a pharmacist by profession. However an alternative explanation has long been current to the effect that Liebig's visits to England in 1837 and later were chiefly responsible.[85]

However it has been argued elsewhere[86] that Liebig's visits had the effect more of confirming the faithful in views they already held than of converting the sceptics. One can hardly disagree with this view of R. Warington Junior, son of the Society's founder:

The readiness with which the idea of a Chemical Society was taken up by the majority of the chemists in Great Britain, shows that the conditions necessary for forming such a Society were already present.[87]

The same commentator has these remarks to offer concerning the *special circumstances* which further facilitated the events of 1841:

There are two circumstances which helped to determine the formation of the Chemical Society in 1841. The preceding year had seen the commencement of the penny postage, and this fact undoubtedly gave an impetus to all attempts at organization requiring much correspondence. The year 1841 was also part of a short period of leisure in the life of my father. Between 1839 and 1842 he held no official position, and was at liberty to turn his energies in any direction which he might desire. It is probably that neither before nor after this period would he have attempted the serious task of uniting the chemists of Great Britain and Ireland in one Society.[88]

Undoubtedly these circumstances played a part in the Chemical Society's birth. But with the benefit of greater hindsight we can perceive something of the long-range forces at work in Victorian science and Victorian society that helped to form this most notable of all chemical institutions.

CAR

NOTES AND REFERENCES

1 On the chemical role of the *English Mechanic* see C. A. Russell, *The History of Valency*, Leicester UP, Leicester, 1971, chs. IV and V.

2 On the mechanics' institute movement see e.g. Thomas Kelly, *George Birkbeck, Pioneer of Adult Education*, Liverpool UP, Liverpool, 1957.

3 W. H. Brock, 'The London Chemical Society 1824', *Ambix*, 1967, 14, 133–9.

4 *The Chemist*, 1824, p. viii (Preface).

5 *Ibid.*, p. vii.

6 C. Babbage, *Reflections on the Decline of Science in England*, London, 1830.

7 *The Chemist*, 1824, **2**, 80.

8 *Ibid.*, p. 37.

9 *Ibid.*, p. 46.

10 *Ibid.*, p. 47

11 *Ibid.*, p. 44.

12 F. Accum, *A Treatise on the Adulteration of Food and Culinary Poisons*, London, 1820. On Accum see D. W. F. Hardie, *Chem. Age*, 1957, **77**, 1009.

13 *The Chemist*, 1824, **2**, 254.

14 H. Brougham, *op. cit.*, London, 6th edn., 1824, p. 3. Hodgskin's interest in chemistry had political overtones. He spoke of 'the mechanic in the gas works' as 'a chemist of considerable skill', who converted coals 'into products ten times their value' (*Mech. Mag.*, 1824, 11 December, p. 191). See E. Halévy, *Thomas Hodgskin, 1787–1869*, Société nouvelle de librairie et d'edition, Paris, 1903.

15 This is evidenced by the Report of the General Meeting (*Chemist*, 1824, **2**, 162):

> 'Thanks of the Society were also voted to Mr Mongredieu, the Editor of The Chemist, Mr W. Jones the Secretary of the Committee, and the Chairman, for his able conduct in the Chair.'

The misspelt name of A. Mongrédien, later prominent in the London Political Union, occurs in Pigot's Directories for 1826–7 and 1828–9 and Robson's Directory for 1830—all at '44 George St'. In the papers of Francis Place reprinted in *London Radicalism 1830–1843*, ed. D. J. Rowe (London Record Soc. 1970), he is correctly spelt (except for the accent) but given the same address. The name is so evidently rare that there appears to be a certain link between the London Radicals, *The Chemist*, and the London Chemical Society.

16 *The Chemist*, 1824, **1**, 167.

17 *Ibid.*, p. 221.

18 *Ibid.*, pp. 237–8.

19 *Ibid.*, **2**, p. 162.

20 *Ibid.*, p. 56.

21 The Institute opened its doors to women in 1892.

22 *Ibid.*, p. 162.

23 *Ibid.*, p. 164.

24 *Ibid.*, p. 166.

25 *Ibid.*, p. 168.

26 It has been suggested that the affair 'is a sad comment on the divorce between the chemical natural philosophers and the professional chemists who staffed the country's breweries, dye-works, and emerging gasworks' (W. H. Brock, note 3, p. 138). How far these full-time employees of the chemical industry can be truly called 'professional' is clearly a matter for some debate.

27 C. B. Hodgson, *The Borough of South Shields*, Andrew Reid, South Shields, 1903, p. 402.

28 *Ibid.*, p. 180.

29 Buddle Correspondence at Durham County Record Office, MSS 950, 951, etc.

30 Marreco is the subject of a biographical study by the author, now in preparation.

31 cf. J. Ben-David, 'The Profession of Science and its Powers', *Minerva*, 1972, **10**, 362.

32 (a) N. McCord and D. J. Rowe, *Northumberland and Durham: Industry in the Nineteenth Century*, Graham, Newcastle, 1971, p. 5; (b) W. A. Campbell, *A Century of Chemistry on Tyneside, 1868–1968*, SCI, London, 1968.

33 W. A. Campbell, 'The Newcastle Chemical Society and its Illustrious Child', *Chem. & Ind.*, 1968, 1463–6.

34 *DNB*; also J. S. Jeans, *Pioneers of the Cleveland Iron Trade*, Middlesbrough, 1875.

35 On J. Pattinson see *Analyst*, 1912, **37**, 166; and *Proc. Inst. Chem.*, 1912, pt iii, 9.

36 (a) *History of the Berwickshire Naturalists' Club, 1882–4*, Alnwick, pp. 68–72; (b) *Lancet*, 1882, **1**, 409 and 670; (c) C. E. Whiting, *The University of Durham, 1832–1932*, Sheldon Press, London, 1932; (d) D. Embleton, *History of the Medical School*, Newcastle, 1890, pp. 96–7; (e) *J. Chem. Soc.*, 1882, **41**, 238; (f) *Chem. News*, 1882, **45**, 108; (g) *Durham University Journal*, 1882, p. 22. Contrary to every published notice about him he was born at South Shields on 5 November 1835 (Parish register of St Hilda's Church, South Shields, entry for 16 December 1835).

37 Note 36 (f).

38 *Trans. Newcastle Chem. Soc.*, 1868–9, **1**, 95–6.

39 Campbell (note 33), p. 1465.

40 The first reference is 31 October 1873.

41 Eg. *Trans. Newcastle Chem. Soc.*, 1871–4, **2**, 172–6.

42 *Ibid.*, pp. 220–6.

43 I.e., Bell, Marreco, Pattinson and Wright (who had been Secretary in 1871).

44 *Trans. Tyne Chem. Soc.*, 1876, Secretary's Report.

45 *Trans. Newcastle Chem. Soc.*, 1878–80, **4**, 327.

46 *Ibid.*, p. 335.

47 *Chem. News*, 1872, **25**, 239.

48 See D. W. F. Hardie, 'The Chemical Industry of Merseyside', *Proc. Chem. Soc.*, 1961, 52; *idem, A History of the Chemical Industry in Widnes*, ICI, London, 1950.

49 *Chem. News*, 1872, **26**, 1.

50 *Ibid.*, p. 21.

51 *Ibid.*, p. 46.

52 W. Crowder, *ibid.*, pp. 10–11; he became FIC in 1878.

53 *Ibid.*, p. 46.

54 *Ibid.*, p. 57.

55 *Trans. Newcastle Chem. Soc.*, 1871–4, **2**, 87–8.

56 Obituary in *J. Soc. Chem. Ind.*, 1907, **26**, 588.

57 D. de L. Herman, *ibid.*, 1921, **40**, 29R.

58 E. B. Hughes, *J.R.I.C.*, 1956, **80**, 534.

59 R. P. Bedson, *J. Soc. Chem. Ind.*, 1921, **40**, 47R.

60 *Trans. Tyne Chem. Soc.*, 1871–2, paper read 5 January 1872.

61 *Ibid.*, 1873–4, paper read 21 November 1873.

62 *Ibid.*, 1874–5, paper read 20 July 1875.

63 John was the younger brother of James Hargreaves.

64 J. Hargreaves, *J. Soc. Chem. Ind.*, 1921, **40**, 86R–87R.

65 *Widnes Weekly News*, 29 November 1879, quoted in *J. Soc. Chem. Ind.*, 1931, **50**, 9.

66 Nevertheless there was a certain exclusiveness about the Faraday Club; according to Davis it 'consists solely of chemists'. By contrast he wondered how a new Institute could exclude 'Quacks in general' (*Chem. News.*, 1876, **34,** 39).

67 Hargreaves (note 64), p. 87R.

68 *J. Soc. Chem. Ind.*, 1931, **50,** 10.

69 (a) O. J. R. Howarth, *The British Association for the Advancement of Science: a Retrospect 1831–1931*, British Association, London, 1931; (b) H. T. Tizard, 'The British Association for the Advancement of Science', *J.R.I.C.*, 1954, **78,** 503; (c) A. D. Orange, 'The Origins of the British Association for the Advancement of Science', *Brit. J. Hist. Sci.*, 1972, **6, 152.**

70 Note 6, pp. 10–11. Babbage used the term 'profession' in a very restricted sense, with primary reference to mathematical and physical sciences in an academic context.

71 *Qu. Rev.*, 1830, **43,** 327.

72 This was one of several important institutions of similar character concerned with the dissemination of culture generally, including science, and patronized chiefly by the wealthier members of society. Other examples were the Literary and Philosophical Societies of Manchester and Newcastle.

73 *Rep. Brit. Assoc.*, 1831, **1,** 28.

74 *Ibid.*, p. 22.

75 *Ibid.*, p. 29.

76 On Dalton see, e.g., *DNB*, *DSB*, F. Greenaway, *John Dalton and the Atom*, Heinemann, London, 1966.

77 Papers relating to the B-Club are at the Chemical Society, London. Most of the members earned their living by chemistry in some way (industry, journalism, publishing).

78 *J. Chem. Soc.*, 1916, **109,** 342.

79 (a) T. S. Moore and J. C. Philip, *The Chemical Society 1841–1941*, Chem. Soc., London, 1947; (b) *The Jubilee of the Chemical Society of London*, Chem. Soc., London, 1896.

80 Note 79 (b), p. 118; note 79 (a), p. 14.

81 The Open University (1975) S304 *The Nature of Chemistry*, Units 1–3 *The Structure of Chemistry*, The Open University Press, Milton Keynes.

82 Note 79 (b), p. 118.

83 See D. W. F. Hardie, *Chem. Age*, 1957, **77,** 643.

84 Distant relative of J. Pattinson, father-in-law of both I. L. Bell and R. W. Newall, H. L. Pattinson discovered a desilvering process for lead.

85 E.g. W. J. Russell in note 79 (b), p. 10.

86 G. K. Roberts, *Hist. Stud. Phys. Sci.*, 1976, **7,** 437–85.

87 Note 79 (b), p. 116.

88 *Ibid.*, p. 117.

CHAPTER V
CHEMICAL TRAINING BEFORE 1877

Chemical training that contemporaries designated 'professional' became available in England during the 1840s.[1] It had of course long been possible to study chemistry in Britain at such varied institutions as the Mechanics' Institutes, the Scottish Universities, many medical colleges, University College, London (1826), King's College, London (1828), the University of Durham (1833), and even to some extent at Oxford and Cambridge. However, before the 1840s, chemistry was usually taught as either one of many optional subjects under the heading of general knowledge, or an ancillary subject in medical curricula. It was generally taught by means of lectures alone, and interested students had to make private arrangements for practical instruction. What distinguished the 1840s was that chemistry then began to be taught as the basis of a professional pursuit in its own right. At the same time, practical laboratory instruction became an important feature of this new training. A significant event in this transition was the establishment of the Royal College of Chemistry in London in 1845.

1 The Royal College of Chemistry

An independent, privately-funded venture, the College was established '... for promoting the science [of chemistry] and its application to agriculture, arts, manufactures and medicine'.[2] It soon became one of England's most productive scientific centres in terms of both the number of students who trained there and the amount of published scientific work which they generated. The establishment of the College was initially the project of two fairly insignificant early-Victorian figures, John Gardner and John Lloyd Bullock, an apothecary and a pharmaceutical chemist by training, who saw a possibility of considerable financial gain in arranging for the systematic utilization of the fruits of chemical research. In order to promote their own interests, they designed a project that would appeal to the chemical interests of other groups. Although they directed their propaganda to manufacturers as well, mainly medical men, pharmaceutical chemists, and agriculturists responded by contributing to the support of the College.[3]

The academic part of the proposed College (for it was initially meant to be more than just a teaching and research institution) was modelled on the highly successful department run by the already famous German organic chemist Justus Liebig at the University of Giessen. Liebig publicized his views on the application of organic chemistry to agriculture and to physiology during the early 1840s in England, and his work was widely known there.[4] The key to his success was his method of teaching. Lectures on chemical theory provided the basis of Liebig's course, but more important was the practical experience of analysis and synthesis which the student gained in the teaching laboratory. At Giessen, analytical training was organized in such a way that the student did more than rote repetition of techniques. Each analysis of an unknown was approached as though it were a research project. In this way, Liebig's students learned how to do research while acquiring fundamental practical techniques in both inorganic and organic chemistry. All students, regardless of their career intentions, did the same course. Liebig argued that training in the principles of chemistry and the methods of scientific inquiry equipped a student for any subsequent chemical pursuit. This was a prudent policy for a man who wanted time to do research. At the same time, his pedagogical programme provided him with a constant supply of research assistants.[5]

The promoters of the College suggested that the adoption of Liebig's methods would bring a number of advantages to those with chemical interests in England. For example in 1839, the University of London devised a new medical curriculum. This was essentially the culmination of a movement in the 1830s for the reform of the medical profession. There were to be two levels of medical degrees. Among the requirements for the first degree in medicine (MB) was one term's study of practical chemistry in the laboratory. The MD was a research degree.[6] Those promoting the College of Chemistry during the early 1840s pointed to the inadequate provision of facilities for analytical teaching in London, and the importance of training in research methods for the prospective MD, particularly in the field of organic chemistry and its applications to physiology.[7] They took similar advantage of the professional ferment among chemists and druggists during this period (p. 46). Practical chemistry was cast as the cornerstone of the new-style pharmaceutical chemists' professional training and the rather slow start of the Pharmaceutical Society's school was not overlooked.[8] In addition, English agriculturists had become increasingly interested in soil analysis during the 1830s.[9] This interest was reinforced by Liebig's parallel emphasis on the importance of plant-ash analysis. Thus the promoters emphasized that their College would train analysts as well as pursue organic chemistry. The propaganda pointed out that analytically-trained pharmaceutical chemists scattered throughout the country would provide a useful corps of consultant analysts for both agriculturists and medical men.[10]

The College's propagandists were not wrong so much as inaccurate in their claim that cilities such as they proposed were needed. Existing institutions were evolving slowly to deal with the conditions which those promoting the College noted. For example, well before the movement for establishing the College, both University College, London and King's College, London began to offer courses in practical chemistry for medical students, admittedly with little enthusiasm from their respective Professors of Chemistry because of the significantly increased labour and poor financial reward involved.[11] Similarly, the new Pharmaceutical Society had teething troubles; but by 1842 it launched its school, and by 1844 it began to offer practical instruction. From 1842, agriculturists could send samples to the government-financed Museum of Economic Geology for analysis by its chemist, who was also supposed to provide instruction in analytical chemistry.[12] In addition, the Royal Agricultural Society retained an analyst, as did the Royal Horticultural Society, although both societies were justifiably sceptical about the immediate applicability of organic chemistry.[13] Moreoever, in parallel with the movement for the establishment of the College of Chemistry, another group was promoting what in 1845 became the Royal Agricultural College at Cirencester. This included a laboratory for practical chemistry.[14] In another sphere, the Putney College for Civil Engineers opened in 1838, and practical chemistry was included in its curriculum, as it was in the engineering course at King's College, London.[15] The Royal Polytechnic Institution (established in London in 1838 to teach applied science to medical students, engineers, miners, manufacturers and agriculturists) also offered a course on practical chemistry.[16]

In addition to stressing the rather gradual and cautious nature of some of these developments, those promoting the College of Chemistry offered supporters a number of perquisites. The college was to run a journal, establish a chemical library, hold regular meetings at which recent research results would be announced to members who might want to develop them commercially, act as the centre of an analytical network which would systematically undertake the analysis of all soils in Britain, do consulting analytical work for supporters, provide research facilities for supporters who cared to use them, and establish affiliated local chemical societies.[17] The net result of the propagandists' efforts was that the Royal College of Chemistry opened in October 1845, with A. W. Hofmann,[18] a former pupil of Liebig's as its director. It remained a private institution until 1853 when it was taken over by the government.

The academic programme which Hofmann instituted at the Royal College of Chemistry was based directly on that of the Giessen school. The full course consisted of lectures on chemical theory, training in qualitative and quantitative analysis in both inorganic and organic chemistry, and ended with the student undertaking a small, probably analytical, research project. The laboratory was open six days per week, but students were not required to attend full-time; the system was very flexible. Lectures were not compulsory and each student was permitted to progress at his own rate in the analytical laboratory. The student could elect to spend anything between one and six days per week in the laboratory for which he was charged pro rata, £25 being the annual fee for full-time study. There were no examinations, and each student could decide for himself when he had gained sufficient analytical expertise for his purposes. It was Hofmann, however, who decided which students were ready to do research. Successful completion of the analytical course and production of a piece of publishable research earned a Testimonial of Proficiency; but perhaps more important, Hofmann recommended some students to Liebig for the award of a Giessen PhD. Otherwise, the College could only provide personal recommendations and Certificates of Attendance. The latter were useful to those studying chemistry as part of a medical or pharmaceutical curriculum, while the former were not without value to students applying for academic posts.[19]

The Royal College of Chemistry became deservedly famous for the galaxy of prominent Victorian chemists who studied there during its first eight years.[20] The list includes four presidents of the Chemical Society (Warren De la Rue,[21] F. A. Abel,[22] William Odling[23] and William Crookes[24]), eleven more who served as vice-presidents, and a further six who served as ordinary members of Council. In all some sixty-eight of the College's students from this period became members of the Chemical Society. Twenty-three became founder Fellows of the Institute of Chemistry and twenty-two joined the Society of Chemical Industry when it started in 1882. Sixty-five of the students from these early years published scientific papers; although thirty published nothing more after their work at the College, the rest were quite consistently productive throughout their careers. Until 1865, Hofmann and the pre-1853 students of the College taken together accounted for nearly twenty per cent of the papers published by the Chemical Society. Another thirty-one students took out various chemical patents. This was certainly an enviable record.

It is necessary to consider how far this eminent group was typical of the College of Chemistry's students and to what extent their success was due to their experience at the College. During the eight years when the Royal College of Chemistry was a private institution, some 356 students enrolled for varying periods. Thus, for a start, it is obvious that only about twenty per cent of the College's students joined the Chemical Society, about ten per cent maintained a consistent research output, and roughly a further nine per cent held patents. The activities of the well-known twenty per cent were not, therefore, typical of the student body. Furthermore, an investigation of the attendance at the College of Chemistry from 1845 to 1853 indicates that only twenty-one per cent of the students attended for more than three sessions; fifty per cent left after one half year, which was one session, or semester, by the College's reckoning. On average, each student attended for 3.6 days per week, or sixty per cent of the available time. Hofmann estimated that an average student should complete the qualitative and quantitative analytical programmes in one year of (presumably full-time) study.[25] However, he did not prescribe the length of time needed to become a competent research worker, but the only Testimonial of Proficiency awarded during this period was earned by William Crookes who had attended six days per week for three years.[26] Furthermore, of those who did become eminent only fourteen of the sixty-five authors and ten of the patentees studied at the College for three or more sessions. Two of the most productive, George Downing Liveing,[27] later Professor of Chemistry at Cambridge, and William Odling, later Professor of Chemistry at Oxford, only spent one session each there.

These attendance figures do not necessarily give the whole picture since several of those who subsequently became eminent stayed on at the College as Hofmann's teaching or research assistants after relatively short periods of formal enrolment. However, the general outline is clear; the vast majority of the students attending the Royal College of Chemistry during its first eight years really only spent sufficient time there to receive basic analytical training. These 356 students were a very mixed group in terms of background and motivation. In his first semi-annual report to the Council, Hofmann divided the student body of twenty-six into three categories.[28] The first group, consisting of two students, were already sufficiently acquainted with chemistry to begin research projects immediately. The second group included several students who were '. . . already established in Professions or some department of business, manufactures, for example of chemicals, and Pharmaciens, who appear to have availed themselves of the College Laboratory in order to systematize their knowledge by passing through the course of study we have adopted'.[29] Several of these had progressed sufficiently far in the analytical course, Hofmann reported, to anticipate undertaking some simple analytical research projects during the next session. The third group consisted of students with 'varied futures' and limited chemical backgrounds; they were progressing more slowly through the analytical course as they needed a good deal of remedial textbook work.

The College's Register of Students recorded the backgrounds of most of the first session students; six were listed as pharmacien, five had medical backgrounds, three came straight from school where they had studied some chemistry, two were artists' colourmen, two were designated chemists, two were science teachers, two were printers, and one was a colonial agriculturist. There was not necessarily any similarity of background among those who belonged to the same broad groupings. Pharmacists and medical men in particular came at various stages in their careers; some were just beginning to seek modern professional qualifications, others wanted to do research. Their expectations of the College were consequently very different.

For example Warren De la Rue was included in Hofmann's first category of students. Some twenty-five years later, he reminisced that the original student body had consisted mainly of mature students like himself who attended to further their own research interests. For him, the College was a research institute rather than an analytical school; it was '. . . an assemblage of zealous men who were desirous of making investigations, and who carried them out with great ardour, aided by the advice and sometimes with the co-operation of Dr Hofmann'.[30] As Hofmann's description of the first session's students showed, De la Rue's reminiscences were somewhat optimistic. In addition to De la Rue, Hofmann had placed only one other first session student in the category of those ready to pursue research. Hardly a mature student at eighteen, E. C. Nicholson had originally set out to be a chemist and druggist via apprenticeship. Furthermore, De la Rue's reminiscences indicate that the advance of science was the students' primary goal. They undoubtedly did have this goal, but it is also impossible to overlook the fact that De la Rue was well established in the family printing business which was involved at mid-century in applying chemistry to printing problems and even financed a research laboratory at this time.[31]

There is some fragmentary evidence about the expectations of some of the less scientifically-prominent students. Henry Wardle, a brewer's son, for example, spent the greater part of three sessions studying six days per week in the laboratory. These were not three sequential sessions, but rather the spring session each year for three years. In a letter requesting information about the programme of another institution, Wardle's father explained his objectives.

> My son is very anxious to devote a little time to the study of chemistry at one of the London institutions with a view to its application to Brewing; he cannot possibly be spared from the brewery for more than 8 or 10 weeks; I shall be greatly obliged if you will inform me what will be the terms for such a period at the London University and at what time between this and September he would derive most benefit.[32]

The flexible system at the College was ideal for someone in young Wardle's position. Given Hofmann's views on the importance of sound basic training in the fundamentals of chemistry, it is unlikely that Wardle would have studied anything so specific as the chemistry of brewing while there, but there was no reason that some of his later analytical work could not have related to brewing. In 1848 for example, one student, who was a brewer's chemist, systematically analyzed a large range of British beers.[33]

Another student, Captain William Elliot spent three days per week at the College during one session in preparation for the Indian Service. Admitting that he had no ability for chemistry and little genuine interest in the subject, he merely wanted to learn a few analytical techniques needed for his posting. In fact, he could not manage day-time laboratory study with his other commitments and probably had no taste for the general analytical programme, so he left the College and continued to study privately with one of Hofmann's assistants. He learned very specialized techniques such as how to perform mineral analyses and assays, and how to investigate the wearing qualities of tent fabrics. Before leaving, he thanked his young teacher.

> ... I shall always retain a lively recollection of your anxiety to get a very stupid fellow on who disliked chemistry for its memoria technica etc. etc. .... I think there are corrections in Table II which you may let me

have perhaps to copy out and any other little [?] that may be useful—particularly the determination of FeO and Fe_2O_3 in the original mineral which d––n me if I have not forgotten for the thousandth time . . . and which will be so useful to me in my Magnetic survey.[34]

William Odling spent his one session at the College while preparing for the London MB degree and probably had only this limited purpose in view at the time. However, his introduction to organic chemistry at the College seems to have shaped his future career, eventually turning him away from medicine to academic chemistry.[35] It is also possible to speculate about the motives of G. D. Liveing. After finishing eleventh Wrangler in the Cambridge Mathematical Tripos in 1850 and first in the new Natural Sciences Tripos (with distinctions in chemistry and mineralogy) in 1851, Liveing enrolled at the College for six days per week during one session at the College. He probably wanted to observe a teaching laboratory in operation so that he could organize one himself. From the College, he went on to study in Berlin and on his return to England in 1852, he started teaching Cambridge's first course in practical chemistry.

The occupations of the students from this early period at the College were as varied as their backgrounds.[36]

Occupation	% of total enrolment	
	of the 79% who studied 2 sessions or less	of the 21% who studied 3 sessions or more
Academic	5.3	4.7
Agricultural chemist	1.1	0.5
Analyst	3.3	0.5
Brewer	3.9	0.5
Engineer	2.5	0.8
Government employee	3.6	0.8
Manufacturer (chemical)	7.3 (6.1)	6.1 (5.3)
Metallurgical chemist	2.8	0.2
Pharmaceutical chemist	9.5	0.8
Physician and surgeon	9.5	0.8
?	31.7	3.1

Perhaps instead of depending on the eminence of the minority, the college's real claim to fame should be that it was able to provide training relevant to so many different varieties of chemists.

2   Other Provisions for Practical Instruction

As soon as it was obvious that the Royal College of Chemistry would successfully be launched as a separate institution, both University College, London
and King's College, London took steps to provide laboratories for practical
instruction in chemical analysis.[37] At the same time, the school of the
Pharmaceutical Society expanded its laboratory. But perhaps the most significant development was that the government began to take a stronger interest
in applied science. In 1851, the publicly financed Government School of
Mines and of Science Applied to the Arts opened in London. This developed
out of the Museum of Economic Geology and was the particular project of
the head of the Geological Survey who had been singularly successful in
winning government funds for his projects. The new institution aimed to
combine theoretical studies with practical work in order to train applied
scientists, initially mainly for mining and related pursuits. Lyon Playfair a
former pupil of Liebig's was appointed Professor of Chemistry there.[38] In
1853, Playfair wanted to leave his post at the Government School. At the
same time, it was obvious that the Royal College of Chemistry was in severe
financial trouble. The result was that the College was taken over by the
government.[39] It became the chemical department of the School of Mines
with Hofmann as Professor, but it also retained its independent identity as
the Royal College of Chemistry with Hofmann as Director. After the take-
over it was still possible for a student to enrol at the College without en-
rolling at the Royal School of Mines. In 1865, Edward Frankland succeeded
Hofmann in this joint post, and the College continued to operate a flexible
programme of analytical teaching; the backgrounds and subsequent occupations of the students continued to be extremely varied.[40]

The other major development in chemical teaching during this period
was the establishment of Owens College in Manchester in 1851. Chemistry
was one of the foundation chairs and Edward Frankland, its first incum-
bent, was instructed:

> to give not only elementary instruction but also a more extended course
> in chemical science generally and as applied to the arts, with a view to
> afford greater facilities than at present exist in this neighbourhood, for
> obtaining instruction in a branch of science of so much local importance
> and general interest.[41]

The chair was well-financed and a teaching laboratory was provided.
Frankland was expected to teach technical chemistry including the techniques
of dyeing and calico-printing, as well as the general principles of chemistry.
As at the Royal College of Chemistry, students did not have to attend full-
time and there was an evening programme for those who could not be there
during the day. The emphasis at Owens was not all practical and a Dalton
Scholarship for research students was endowed in memory of the famous
Mancunian chemist to:

prove the earnest purpose of the founders to give to experimental science that place as a branch of scientific education to which it was entitled by its efficiency as a mental discipline, and not merely by its practical application; a plan not generally recognized hither by the conductors of higher education in this country.[42]

Chemistry at Owens was not an immediate success. It was the best attended and most popular subject at the College, but few students recognized its other than practical merits. An annual average of twenty students attended Frankland's lectures while some seventeen took advantage of the laboratory facilities each year between 1851 and 1857.[43] Typical of local industrialists' attitudes was that of E. K. Muspratt, son of the alkali manufacturer (p. 42). The younger Muspratt entered Owens in 1855 to learn some specific analytical techniques, but soon felt that Frankland could teach him nothing that he could not learn in the works. He remained at Owens for two months doing unsupervised laboratory work and left when he felt capable of setting up his own laboratory.[44] Frankland was dissatisfied with this situation, particularly since many students required very elementary instruction. He left Owens in 1857.

Henry Enfield Roscoe[45] who had studied at University College, London and in Germany succeeded Frankland. Roscoe reorganized the chemical curriculum into a three-year programme along the lines that he had observed in Germany, stressing the importance of a knowledge of the general principles of the science and the need for practical training in analysis as a means of transmitting both specific techniques and a way of seeking answers to chemical problems. In his courses on applied chemistry, particularly with regard to the local dyeing and printing industries, Roscoe emphasized the basic scientific principles underlying the applications, rather than attempting to teach vocational courses.[46] Gradually the chemical programme at Owens began to prosper, and it was recorded that by the time Roscoe retired from his professorship in 1886, some 2,000 students had been through his laboratory.[47] As was the case with the College of Chemistry, not all students were by any means full-time or embarked on complete programmes of training and their eventual occupations were extremely varied.[48]

3 The Growth of Examination Systems

Thus from the 1840s there were increasing opportunities for formal professional training in England, and there was an expanding pool of individuals who had at least some practical instruction in chemical analysis. In addition to these opportunities, from the 1850s, a number of examination systems which included scientific subjects arose for different purposes.

(a) *The University of London science degrees*

Until the turn of the twentieth century the University of London was only an examining board; it had no teaching functions. It was founded in 1837, primarily due to the agitations of medical reformers, to be a national degree granting body. This would eliminate the inequity whereby some colleges sought authority to grant higher status awards than others. Under the University of London system, students at numerous affiliated colleges were eligible to take the University's examinations for a recognized degree. From 1837, London degree examinations were envisaged in arts and in medicine.[49] Fairly basic chemistry was an optional subject in the former and a required subject in the latter. Students at Owens College were eligible for the London examinations. It was not until 1858, however, that the University of London science degree scheme, for the BSc and the DSc began. At the same time, London degrees were opened to all comers regardless of where they studied.

Both the BSc and the DSc were examined degrees. The science degree scheme was drawn up after consultation with most of the prominent science teachers in London.[50] The scheme attempted to reconcile the advantages of broad general training, the traditional English university hallmark, with a rising emphasis on specialist subjects. The BSc was divided into two parts, the first taken after two years' study tested the students' knowledge of the general principles of a range of subjects, mathematics, biology, chemistry, physics, and logic. The second BSc examination taken a year later, after which the student actually received the degree, concentrated on the student's choice of two or three sciences. At both levels, it was possible to sit honours examinations which concentrated on one science only. In the case of chemistry, until 1877, the only required practical examination was at the second BSc honours level. This seems to have been a fairly straightforward set of exercises in qualitative inorganic analysis. It was possible to obtain an ordinary degree without having done a practical examination. From 1877, such an examination was required at the second BSc ordinary level, and also added to the requirements of the first BSc examinations for honours.[51] All science degree candidates at the University of London had to pass the same matriculation examination as the arts students and the medical students. This included compulsory Latin, a choice of two languages from Greek, French and German, English language and history, mathematics, natural philosophy (physics) and chemistry. Thus, although it was making some tentative steps in the direction of specialization, the London science degree was none the less firmly based on the concept of a broad general education.[52]

(b) *Non-university examinations in science*

In 1856, the Society of Arts instituted examinations in science subjects, including chemistry. It hoped thereby to promote the application of science to manufactures by raising the standards of science education. The examinations were intended primarily for part-time students at Mechanics' Institutes.[53] Then in 1859, the Department of Science and Art (which had been established by the government some six years earlier as a result of the enthusiasm for science and technology generated by the Great Exhibition of 1851) also instituted a series of examinations in scientific subjects to encourage the application of the sciences to practical problems. At the same time, to foster science teaching throughout the country, the Department introduced a financing system known as 'payment-by-results'. Teachers were paid in proportion to the number of successful examinees that they had trained. This system encouraged elementary school teachers to augment their incomes by teaching science subjects in the evening. This in turn, highlighted the necessity of providing training for science teachers. Between 1859 and 1867, the Department also ran certificate examinations for teachers. Chemistry was a popular certificate subject; by 1866, there were 500 Science and Art Department certificated teachers.[54]

Thus throughout England, science classes were held in the evenings to cater for part-time students who were at work during the day. The Science and Art Department syllabuses focussed on the principles of the sciences rather than demanding a knowledge of practice in specific fields, lest manufacturers be alarmed that educated operatives would betray trade secrets.[55] Since they were backed by the state in tangible form, the Science and Art Department examinations became so successful that the Society of Arts dropped its own science examinations in the early 1870s. By the mid-1860s, upwards of 1,000 students per year entered the Science and Art Department examinations in chemistry alone. At the end of that decade, the entry in chemistry was more than 2,500; and in 1876, the figure was in the region of 5,800 students.[56] Thus, there was a large group of individuals with sufficient interest in chemistry to seek some basic training.

(c) *Technical examinations and qualifications*

In 1873, to replace its redundant examinations in scientific subjects, the Society of Arts launched a scheme of examinations in technological subjects. This scheme emerged from a conference on technical education which the Society held in 1868. The conference was a response to the furore created by Lyon Playfair's allegation that British manufacturers' performance at the Paris Exhibition of 1867 had fallen markedly from the standards reached in 1862. Playfair attributed this decline to a British failure to promote scientific training for those involved in manufactures. This in turn led to a failure to harness scientific and industrial advance together, in contrast to practice on the continent. The Society of Arts' conference established a committee on technical education and passed resolutions calling for improved scientific education from primary to university level, including the establishment of special technical institutions at government expense.[57]

Edward Frankland was a member of the Society of Arts Technical Education Committee which reported in July 1868.[58] It had devoted its attentions to higher technical education, arguing that Britain's industrial problem was a lack of scientific knowledge in its managerial classes. That is, the problem was with those who directed works rather than with those who operated them. The committee's definition of technical education was '. . . general instruction in those sciences, the principles of which are applicable to the various employments of life'. Although the definition explicitly excluded manual training in workshops and the like, the committee did suggest that formal academic training in the principles of science was not sufficient to provide complete training of a professional in any field. It merely provided the base on which his professional knowledge was to be built. Therefore, the committee recommended that, after formal scientific training, there should follow a period of apprenticeship or pupilage. During this period, the student would learn to put into practice the principles that he had acquired.

This system had the obvious strategic value of satisfying all educational factions. By preserving pupilage, it satisfied those who argued that manufacturing processes depended so much on unique circumstances that they could only be learned in the works, as well as those who feared that the teaching of specific applied science courses would lead to the betrayal of trade secrets. At the same time, the suggested scheme safeguarded the interests of the academics, who argued that general training in the principles of science prepared the student for any subsequent career, and who objected to the competition for students engendered by specialist state-run institutions. Since the committee saw the teaching of pure science as the corner-stone of technical education, it could argue that the most effective way of achieving its objects quickly, given limited resources, was to take advantage of the facilities of existing universities and colleges. The committee called for the institution of a system of examinations which would lead to the award of professional certificates. These certificates were to signify to potential employers that the student had acquired the theory on which his profession was based. The student's training would be completed by a further examination in his specific field, including practical work, after he had completed his period of pupilage. The completion of this second examination would entitle the student to a diploma in his chosen technical field. The committee suggested that these examinations should be administered jointly by the professional association for each occupation and the teaching institutions. Meanwhile, the professional associations would also function as an inspectorate, validating the educational institutions' courses and facilities.

Among the specific diploma schemes devised by the committee was a curriculum for the prospective chemical manufacturer, designed by Edward Frankland, A. W. Williamson[59] (Professor of Chemistry at University College, London), and D. S. Price (a Giessen-trained chemical manufacturer). The academic portion of the student's training for this diploma was to take three years. The first two years were devoted to basic physics, mathematics and chemistry, including practical laboratory training. The third year was to be a specialist year during which the student attended lectures and a laboratory programme based on the principles of the specific branch of applied chemistry which he hoped to pursue. A prospective brewer, for example, would study not how to make beer, but the principles of fermentation. In fact the academic requirements for the diploma were quite similar to those for the London BSc. The proposed diploma would essentially provide a way to augment this into a professional qualification by requiring a supervised period of works' experience.

Testifying before the Select Committee on the Provisions for Giving Instruction in Theoretical and Applied Science to the Industrial Classes (the Samuelson Committee) at the very same time that the Society of Arts Committee on Technical Education was preparing its report, Frankland indicated by implication some of the ways in which the existence of a national system of professional examinations in chemistry, such as that proposed by the Society of Arts' Committee, would be valuable.[60] Most of his students at the Royal College of Chemistry were manufacturers' relatives who hoped to enter some technical profession after their College training. The College awarded its own diploma on successful completion of the chemistry course, but this had no legal status as a qualification and was valuable to the student only as a personal testimonial. Frankland suggested that the existence of a recognized qualification would help to stimulate demand by manufacturers for trained chemists. This, Frankland felt, was sadly lacking. In fact, demand was so low, that existing facilities for training chemists, few though they were, were adequate for supplying the chemists needed. Another implication of his comments was that the Society of Arts' scheme of approved pupilage would help to bring about better contact between scientific men and those who had to apply their ideas. He saw the absence of such contacts as a serious weakness in the industrial utilization of science. Furthermore, the scheme would encourage students to obtain training in the basics of physics and mathematics, which he recognized as a weakness in the students who came to study under him.

In the event, the Society of Arts did not institute a scheme of technological examinations until 1873. This delay may have resulted from the recommendations of the Samuelson Committee which suggested that, to overcome Britain's lack of technical expertise, it was first necessary to provide adequate secondary education. This in turn depended both on the training of an adequate supply of teachers and provision of elementary education. The Samuelson Committee divided industrial personnel into three categories: managers, foremen, and workmen. All three categories would benefit from an improvement in the general level of education nationally, and this was where the Samuelson Committee felt the start should be made. After all, there was no point in providing an elaborate system of higher technical education for managers until their general education made it possible for them to take advantage of it. Similarly, it was necessary for foremen and workmen to achieve a certain minimum level of education in order to deal with instructions effectively.

The scheme of technological examinations which the Society of Arts instituted in 1873 was an attenuated version of the technical education committee's suggestions of 1868.[61] In 1872, Major Donnelly, Secretary to the Department of Science and Art, suggested that the Society should offer a series of technological examinations to supplement the Department's science examinations. The Society adopted the suggestion. Any student wishing to qualify in a particular branch of technology would have to go through three stages of examinations. The first stage was to be a general examination in the principles of the sciences relevant to the student's specialist applied field. This would be covered by the existing examinations of the Science and Art Department. The second stage was in the principles of manufacture and the third in the practical skills of manufacture. The Society's examinations, launched in 1873, were designed to test the second stage of training. The scheme grew slowly, was taken over by the City and Guilds of London Institute in 1879 (p. 164), and eventually became a very successful means of testing evening technical training.

In the meantime, the issue of what constituted a sound chemical qualification came under discussion from an immediately practical point of view, as contrasted with the rather idealized discussions of the relationship between technical education and industrial progress. The Pharmacy Act of 1868 required that all pharmacists, chemists and druggists have specific qualifications (p. 49). Similarly, the Sale of Food and Drugs Act of 1872 provided for the creation of Public Analyst posts and recommended that their incumbents have relevant medical, chemical, and microscopical knowledge (p. 107). Furthermore, the Public Health Act of 1875, stipulated that Medical Officers of Health should hold a Diploma of Public Health. Among the subjects required for this diploma was chemical analysis relevant to public health problems. These statutory requirements put the discussions about qualifications for chemists on a new plane, and were a central issue in the establishment of the Institute of Chemistry in 1877.

4   The Devonshire Commission

Parallel to these developments in the field of technical education, the early 1870s also witnessed a major investigation of science teaching and research, the Royal Commission on Scientific Instruction and the Advancement of Science. The brief of this famous Devonshire Commission was to investigate the funding of science in British colleges and universities and to determine whether government action was appropriate.[62] Witness after witness linked the future prosperity of industrial Britain to its capacity to produce scientific research and asked the government to play a major role in financing this expensive activity. Most academic witnesses agreed that the form of scientific education most appropriate to universities was general training in the principles of science with instruction in research methods given via practical laboratory experience. Thus at the same time that opportunities for technical education were expanding, the ideal of general training in the sciences was being reiterated.

Again, Edward Frankland was an important chemical witness, testifying both in his capacity as Chemistry Examiner for the Science and Art Department examinations, and as Professor at the Royal College of Chemistry. Frankland reported that the general standard reached by Science and Art Department examinees was satisfactory, but that there were obvious defects in their practical training. He also commented that what he designated the 'higher class of students' were not attracted to the Department's examinations. With reference to the facilities at the Royal College of Chemistry, Frankland argued, in contrast to his suggestion to the Samuelson Committee that they were adequate, that in fact they were in need of a major expansion. Furthermore, he suggested that the London BSc degree should require more practical and experimental knowledge as it was quite possible to earn the degree without ever having done an experiment. He favoured making the DSc a definite research degree, rather than just another examination.[63]

In the event, the Devonshire Commission brought about few specific changes. As a result of its recommendations, some of the government facilities for science teaching were rationalized and the government voted a £4,000 annual grant to be administered by the Royal Society for the support of individual research projects. However, the Commission did reaffirm the view that university level science education should not be specialized, rather supporting the style of the London BSc, and not really dealing with the arguments of those who supported more vocationally oriented training for prospective professional scientists, but putting this outside the sphere of universities.

5 Opportunities to Study Chemistry in 1877

With all the complaints about the state of scientific and technical education in the United Kingdom during the 1860s and 1870s, it is salutary to survey the opportunities open to the prospective student of chemistry in 1877. Every autumn, William Crookes, the editor of the *Chemical News* published a list of chemistry courses available. The following is Crookes's list for 1877:[64]

Universities and Colleges

    University of Oxford
    University of Cambridge
    University of Dublin, Trinity College
    Science & Art Department and Royal School of Mines (this included the
        Royal College of Chemistry)
    King's College, London

University College, London
University College, Bristol (established 1876)
Royal Agricultural College
The Yorkshire College, Leeds (established 1874)
College of Physical Science, Newcastle (established 1871)
Owens College, Manchester
Royal College of Science for Ireland, Dublin
Anderson's College, Glasgow

Chemical Lectures, Classes and Laboratory Instruction

Berners College of Chemistry and the Experimental Sciences, London
Birkbeck Literary and Scientific Institution, London
New Central School of Chemistry and Pharmacy, London
Royal Polytechnic College, London
Royal Veterinary College, London
Working Men's College, London
School of Pharmacy of the Pharmaceutical Society
South London School of Chemistry
Midland Institute, Birmingham
Queen's College, Birmingham
Bristol Medical School
Liverpool Royal Infirmary School of Medicine
School of Technical Chemistry, Liverpool
Leeds Mechanics' Institution
Manchester Grammar School
Manchester Mechanics' Institution
Queenwood College, Hampshire
Sheffield Borough Analysts' Laboratory
Sheffield School of Medicine

London Hospitals

St Bartholomew's Hospital and College
Charing Cross Hospital and College
St George's Hospital
Guy's Hospital
King's College Hospital
London Hospital
St Mary's Hospital
Middlesex Hospital
St Thomas's Hospital and School
University College Hospital
Westminster Hospital

Scotland

University of Aberdeen
Aberdeen School of Science and Art Mechanics' Institution
Dundee Literary Institution Chemical Laboratory
University of Edinburgh
School of Medicine, Edinburgh
Glasgow University
Glasgow Mechanics' Institution
Glasgow Veterinary College
School of Chemistry, Glasgow
Chemical Laboratory, Glasgow
Analytical Laboratory, Glasgow

Ireland

Queen's College, Belfast
Queen's College, Cork
Queen's College, Galway
Royal College of Surgeons in Ireland
Dublin, Carmichael School
Dublin, Catholic University
Dublin, Dr Steevens's Hospital and Medical College

Crookes did not make clear his reasons for listing seemingly equivalent institutions under different headings, and obviously all of these schools did not offer the same quality teaching. However, the fact was that the chemical student in 1877 was already faced with a bewildering choice of institutions.

GKR

NOTES AND REFERENCES

1 *Proposal for Establishing a College of Chemistry for Promoting the Science and its Application to Agriculture, Arts, Manufactures, and Medicine*, London, n.d., p. 4 (Brit. Mus., Add. MSS, No. 40553, ff. 21–9). This can be dated July 1844 in Royal College of Chemistry, Minutes of the Council of the College, 1845–51, preface, Imperial College London, College Archives, C/3/3. (Hereafter, RCC, Council Minutes.) For a general discussion of English scientific education and institutions during the nineteenth century, see D.S.L. Cardwell, *The Organisation of Science in England*, rev. edn. Heinemann, London, 1972.

2 RCC, *Proposal*, note 1. The founding of the College is examined in G. K. Roberts, 'The Establishment of the Royal College of Chemistry: An Investigation of the Social Context of Early-Victorian Chemistry', *Hist. Stud. Phys. Sci.*, 1976, 7, 437–85.

3 *Ibid.*

4 On Liebig (1803–1873), see J. Volhard, *Justus Liebig*, 2 vols., Verlag von Johann Ambrosius Barth, Leipzig, 1909; and *DSB*.

5 J. B. Morrell, 'The Chemist Breeders: The Research Schools of Liebig and Thomas Thomson', *Ambix*, 1972, 19, 1–46.

6 H. H. Bellot, *University College London, 1826–1926*, University of London Press, London, 1929, ch. 7.

7 *Lancet,* 7 September 1844, p. 736; 16 November 1844, pp. 231–2; 11 October 1845, pp. 403–4.

8 *The Chemist,* 1844, **2,** 276–82.

9 Sir E. John Russell, *A History of Agricultural Science in Great Britain, 1620–1954,* Allen and Unwin, London, 1966, pp. 81–6.

10 RCC, *Proposal,* (note 1), p. 13.

11 Roberts (note 2).

12 *Ibid.*

13 See Sir T. Wemyss Reid, *Memoirs and Correspondence of Lyon Playfair,* Cassell, London, 1899, pp. 77–9; and Harold R. Fletcher, *The Story of the Royal Horticultural Society, 1804–1968,* OUP, London, 1969.

14 Charles Daubeny, *A Lecture on Institutions for the Better Education of the Farming Classes, especially with Reference to the Proposed Agricultural College near Cirencester, 14 May 1844,* Oxford, 1844; 'Agricultural College', *Eng. J. of Ed.,* 1843, **1,** 383–4.

15 Putney College for Civil Engineers, *College for Civil Engineers and of General Practical and Scientific Training,* Putney, 1845.

16 Royal Polytechnic Institution, *Catalogue for 1844,* new edn., London, 1844.

17 Roberts (note 2).

18 On Hofmann (1818–92), see *Berichte,* 1902, **35,** pt. iv, sonderheft; and *DSB.*

19 This discussion of the academic programme and student body of the RCC is based on G. K. Roberts, *The Royal College of Chemistry (1845–1853): A Social History of Chemistry in Early-Victorian England,* PhD diss., The Johns Hopkins University, Baltimore, Md, 1973, ch. VIII.

20 *Ibid.,* Tables 8–13.

21 On De la Rue (1815–89), see *J. Chem. Soc.,* 1889, **57,** 441.

22 On Abel (1827–1902), see *ibid.,* 1905, **87,** 565–70.

23 On Odling (1829–1921), see *ibid.,* 1921, **119,** 553–64.

24 On Crookes (*c.* 1830–1919), see *ibid.,* 1920, **117,** 444–54.

25 RCC, Council Minutes, 12 August 1846.

26 Roberts (note 19), p. 323.

27 On Liveing (1827–1924), see *DNB.*

28 RCC, Council Minutes, 11 March 1846.

29 *Ibid.* The college used the French term *pharmacien* to distinguish the modern, professional pharmaceutical chemist whom it hoped to help train from chemists and druggists.

30 *Reports of the Royal Commission on Scientific Instruction and the Advancement of Science . . .,* (c. 598), P.P. 1874, XXII, qq. 13082; qq. 13055, 13079. (Hereafter, Devonshire Commission, II).

31 Roberts (note 19) pp. 316–17.

32 F. Wardle, letter to C. C. Atkinson, [1849], College Correspondence, University College London, College Archives.

33 RCC, Council Minutes, 31 May 1848.

34 William Elliot, letter to C. L. Bloxam, 3 October [1851], C. L. Bloxam, Diaries, 6, 11, 14, 15, 28 October 1850, 5, 11, 14 February 1851, etc., Bloxam Collection.

35 *DSB*

36 Based on Roberts (note 19) Table 12.

37 *Ibid.*, p. 337.

38 Sir Henry T. De la Beche, *Inaugural Discourse at the Opening of the School: Museum of Practical Geology, Government School of Mines and of Science Applied to the Arts*, London, 1851.

39 Roberts (note 19), p. 371.

40 *Report from the Select Committee on the Provisions for Giving Instruction in Theoretical and Applied Science to the Industrial Classes*, P.P. 1867–8, XV–1, qq. 8047–9, 8057–76. (Hereafter, Samuelson Committee).

41 H. B. Charlton, *Portrait of a University: 1851–1951*, Manchester U.P., Manchester, 1951, p. 30.

42 Joseph Thompson, *The Owens College: Its Foundation and Growth, and its Connection with the Victoria University, Manchester*, Manchester, 1886, p. 147.

43 *Ibid.*, p. 148; *Reports of the Royal Commission on Scientific Instruction and the Advancement of science . . .*, (c. 536), P.P. 1872, XXV, q. 7366. (Hereafter, Devonshire Commission, I).

44 E. K. Muspratt, *My Life and Work*, John Lane, London, 1918, pp. 91–2.

45 On Roscoe (1833–1915), see H. E. Roscoe, *The Life and Experiences of Sir Henry Enfield Roscoe*, Macmillan, New York, 1906; and *DNB*.

46 Devonshire Commission, I (note 43) qq. 7364–7.

47 T. E. Thorpe, *The Right Honourable Sir Henry Enfield Roscoe: A Biographical Sketch*, Longman, New York, 1916, p. 108.

48 Devonshire Commission, I (note 43) q. 7365.

49 Bellot (note 6), *loc. cit.*

50 Cardwell (note 1), pp. 92–4.

51 University of London, *Calendar*, London, 1861, pp. cclxxxii–iii, ccxcvi–viii, ccci–ii, ccciv–v; 1878, pp. clxix, clxxxv; 1879, p. cliv.

52 Cardwell (note 1) pp. 94–5.

53 *Ibid.*, pp. 83–5.

54 P. S. Uzzell, 'The Development of Science Teaching with Special Reference to Chemistry', Unpubl. PhD diss., University of Exeter, 1975, pp. 46–7.

55 Samuelson Committee (note 40), p. xxix; see also Michael Argles, *South Kensington to Robbins: An Account of English Technical and Scientific Education since 1851*, Longman, London, 1964, pp. 21–4.

56 Uzzell (note 54) pp. 44 and 161. For 1876, the pass-rate was of the order of 75 per cent.

57 Cardwell (note 1) pp. 111–15; see also *J. Soc. Arts*, 1868, 16, 184–209.

58 *J. Soc. Arts*, 1868, 16, 627–42.

59 On Williamson (1824–1904), see *J. Chem. Soc.*, 1905, 87, 605.

60 Samuelson Committee (note 40), qq. 8034–5, 8045, 8065–7, 8076, 8106, 8133–5, 8142.

61 *J. Soc. Arts*, 1872, 20, 261–3, 725–35; 21, 21–34.

62 Devonshire Commission, I (note 43), p. v; Cardwell (note 1), pp. 119–26.

63 Devonshire Commission, I (note 43), qq. 763–6, 5690–3, 5871–2, 5896.

64 *Chem. News*, 1877, 36, 123–32. The list for 1868 is very similar in quantity and range of quality to that for 1877; *ibid.*, 1868, 18, 134–42.

CHAPTER VI

THE GROWING ROLE OF CHEMICAL ANALYSIS

> On 2 October 1877 the Institute of Chemistry of Great Britain and Ireland became incorporated by licence of the Board of Trade, under the provisions of section 23 of the Companies Act, 1867.[1]

In that laconic sentence R. B. Pilcher described, with typical precision, one of the most important milestones in the long journey of chemists towards a truly professional status. Yet, as he himself fully realized, the foundation of the Institute could only be understood in the light of several significant events in the years immediately preceding 1877. Perhaps we, with the insights available to us after sixty more years, can see that an even wider perspective is desirable, taking into account the events recorded in the previous three chapters. It is also possible for us to give a rather different evaluation of the years leading up to the Institute's birth, years when its conception and gestation may be comprehended in terms of complex interactions between developments within chemistry and changes in the larger world outside. The period concerned is roughly from 1860 to 1877.

Within chemistry there had been a steady improvement in the quality and accuracy of chemical analysis, though on its own this is quite inadequate as an explanation of the great boom in analytical chemistry that was crucially important for the emergence of the Institute. On the production side of chemical industry there had been three trends of high significance: new methods of metal extraction applied to the immense tonnage of pyrites mineral residues (after combustion to yield sulphur dioxide) and the Bessemer process for steel (1860); the manufacture of synthetic dyestuffs dating from Perkin's chance discovery of 'mauve' in the late 1850s; and the use of nitroglycerin explosives starting with Nobel's patents for dynamite in 1867 and blasting gelatin in 1875. In the supposedly more tranquil world of academic research a chemistry that was now more united than ever before by the widespread acceptance of 'modern' atomic weights, the theories of valency and structure and much else, was also being riven—at least in England—by acrimonious arguments as to whether or not atoms existed, and, if they did, what to do with them.[2]

All these developments were taking place before a backcloth of events and trends, great and small, on the national and international scene. In Britain the population of 1871 was 26 million, as compared with 23 million ten years previously. The continued upward population trend, combined with increased communications and greater factory outputs, meant that environmentalist issues (though mercifully not by that name) could no longer be shelved by central or local government and the chemist found his subject embodied in the new legislation. Other broad issues in which he found himself involved were the proliferation of educational facilities in Britain and the movement towards professional associations amongst many other groups of skilled workers. And, like it or not, he would often find himself caught up in the 'scientific lobby' which was a series of informal networks that acted as pressure groups upon the government for greater recognition of the claims of science. Government responses were naturally varied as the political climate changed; the all-important question of free trade had far more significance for chemistry than is often realized, particularly at the times of the great international exhibitions of which the Victorians were so inordinately fond. And on the international scene the German victory of the Franco-Prussian war of 1870 was to have profound effects on the whole shape of the European chemical industry for decades to come, though its immediate impact on the prehistory of the Institute is rather less important.

In this chapter and the next many of these great issues and happenings will be seen to have interacted with those with which the chemist is much more at home. But, when all is said and done, the emergence of the Institute was no predetermined outcome from such interactions. The story—like all history—has a strong human and individualistic element, reflecting the idiosyncrasies, insights and fallibilities of real people. Thus it could be argued that the turn of events owed much to the personalities of a few men, most notably the first President, Edward Frankland. Born in humble circumstances in 1825, near Garstang, Frankland experienced a bewildering variety of schooling in Lancashire until he entered the apprenticeship of a Lancaster druggist in 1840. Five years later he entered Playfair's laboratory at the Department of Woods and Forests (somewhat incongruously situated in central London), and then studied with Bunsen and Liebig in Germany. One of the founders of the theory of valency, and certainly the founder of organometallic chemistry (he even coined the name), he became interested in theoretical organic chemistry, applied chemistry—especially water analysis—and above all chemical education. Having occupied Chairs at Manchester (1851), St Bartholomew's Hospital (1857) and the Royal Institution (1863), he succeeded Hofmann in 1865 as Professor of Chemistry at the Royal College of Chemistry. Although no orator he made it his business to know the right people and was a man of considerable influence. He also had remarkable business acumen and his consultancy work was extremely prosperous. He is by no means the only person of significance in our story but he is certainly the most outstanding.[3]

With these preliminaries over we shall trace the course of events by considering in turn several of the issues whose resolution may be fairly said to have been major factors in the foundation of the Institute of Chemistry. One of the most fundamental of these was analysis.

1 The Emergence of the Analytical Consultant

It has sometimes been urged that the origins of chemical analysis lay in the three commercial activities of assaying, drug analysis and industrial quality control. While these commercial origins are undoubtedly of importance they are certainly not exclusively so. In the nineteenth century analytical advances also owed much to developments of a more academic kind: the elemental analyses of organic compounds were instituted by Berzelius to test the universal applicability of atomism, their improvement by Liebig to foster his study of natural and synthetic organic compounds; the perfection of gravimetric and other techniques by Stas was in connection with atomic weight determinations while the early development of the spectroscope by Bunsen and Kirchhoff owed nothing at all to the demands of industry. But whatever may have been the origins of analytical techniques their extension and application to industrial needs was a conspicuous feature of applied chemistry in the period from 1860, as was their embodiment in a succession of Parliamentary statutes. So satisfactory was the outcome that analysis has retained its dominant position in chemical education almost until our own day. Part at least of the explanation seems to lie in its striking social utility in the later nineteenth century.

The picture that emerges of the practice of chemical analysis from the 1850s is a complex one. Much of the so-called 'analytical work' of industrial concerns seems to have been rule-of-thumb exercises performed, if at all, by foremen or other operatives who cannot have had any chemical training of substance at all. Very few concerns employed full-time chemists, let alone full-time analysts. Instead the independent analytical consultant begins to appear, making his services available to a wide variety of concerns as required. Often such consultancy work was undertaken by those also holding academic posts. An undated analysis of Teesside ironstone in the Tomlinson collection of early railway documents at Newcastle upon Tyne is by 'Mr R. Betley, Analytical Chemist and Lecturer at the Mining School, Wigan'.[4] Several other analyses in the same collection are from the Newcastle firm of Thomas Richardson. He was the first British student to matriculate at Giessen under Liebig, gaining his PhD in 1837, returning to Britain to set up in 1844 the first superphosphate works on Tyneside. He later became Reader in Chemistry at the Newcastle College of Medicine, simultaneously building up a highly successful consultancy practice at 5 Portland Place, and later Neville Hall, Newcastle.[5] In this he was helped by assistants, E. I. J. Browell and later A. F. Marreco. From 1858 his 'Assay Office and Laboratory' had a rival establishment in that of J. Pattinson whose name appeared in the Directory as early as 1860 as 'Analytical Chemist'.[6]

The use of consultants for occasional analyses extended to a wide range of industries which were unable to afford their own analyst. We have already noted the gradual employment of chemists by the brewing industry, but as late as 1905 it was being asserted that small breweries could not afford the services of a chemist other than on a consultancy basis.[7]

2 New Jobs for Full-time Analysts: Railways, Metallurgy, Explosives and Agriculture

At the other end of the scale of magnitude we find the vast railway industry moving more quickly away from the consultancy system. Initially they faced two major problems requiring chemical advice. One of these was the imperative need for good water supplies, with the minimum of temporary hardness, for use in locomotive boilers. Thus in 1860 a report from Richardson to William Bouch, Locomotive Engineer of the Stockton and Darlington Railway, commending 'water from Lartington Pond'[8] was followed immediately by instructions to secure that source for the railway.[9] The other great demand upon chemical analysis was the examination of raw materials for steel-making and determination of minor components in the steel which, from about 1860, was beginning to replace the puddled iron for rails.

Shortly after this the first railway laboratory was established by the London and North Western Railway at Crewe in October 1864. Surviving laboratory notebooks from that date testify to the nature of its work. One deals entirely with water analysis, being concerned not merely with the demands of locomotives but also with the domestic needs of the rapidly expanding town.[10] Another is more varied and records many analyses of carbon in steel, no doubt reflecting the laying of the world's first Bessemer steel rails at Crewe in 1861 and the installation of a Bessemer plant there three years later. Some lack of confidence is perhaps suggested in the copying of independent iron assays by Richardson and Browell (1864) and Pattinson (1866). But thereafter the laboratory seems to have managed on its own. It was here, in October 1867, that Joseph Reddrop was appointed, becoming chief chemist three years later. His application to the Institute for admission to the Fellowship in 1878 reveals the work he did: 'analysis of materials required for the production of Bessemer Steel . . ., analyses of the more common metals . . ., analyses of water for locomotive, also domestic use, analysis or testing of various articles of commerce . . ., analysis of waste products from the works'.[11]

Other railway companies followed the lead of the LNWR, notably the North Eastern in about 1877 with a primary remit to examine steel rails which were a special concern of the Teesside steelmaker Sir I. L. Bell. A manuscript from Bell of 1875 deals with the manufacture of rails and discusses their durability in terms of their chemical composition.[12] Gradually, through the 1880s and beyond other railways established their own laboratories, but the pioneering venture of the LNWR illustrates vividly the role of the analytical chemist in this vast area of British industry.

The breweries and the railways were industries where, at least at this time, chemical analysis was a matter of prudent management only; there was no legal constraint that *directly* demanded it. And of course they were not alone in this respect.

In metallurgy many firms by the mid-1870s were advertising for men who could analyse ores and metals. Some of these cases were to achieve notoriety in the pages of *Chemical News* as examples of the impoverished conditions of analytical chemists, the classic case being the £2-a-week man 'competent to make the analysis of zinc ores' (28 April 1876).[13] Even the Royal Mint itself was taking analysis more seriously than before, its first chemist being appointed at about this time.[14]

The explosives industry offered another example of analysis receiving a new importance at this time. From 1863 Britain was a market for nitroglycerin, the first explosive to be a serious rival to gunpowder. The much safer dynamite was available a few years later, being made in Nobel's factory at Ardeer in Scotland, but a series of devastating explosions led to the establishment of a Select Committee on Explosive Substances in 1874.[15] The evidence presented to that Committee showed an awareness amongst chemists of the need for high degrees of purity in dynamite and similar explosives. Some manufacturers, but by no means all, were employing chemists to conduct analyses, notably George M'Roberts at Ardeer. Where a chemist was not employed, or where he was incompetent, it sometimes became the melancholy task of outside consultants to testify at inquests after death by explosion. Thus A. Dupré,[16] a 'scientific chemist' assisted the coroner at Stowmarket after an explosion there. He observed that out of twenty-nine samples of nitroglycerin examined the previous year, eight contained free acid. The chemist in charge at first denied it, though later had to admit it.[17] The manufacture of explosives based on nitroglycerin was a much more demanding operation than gunpowder production as their formulation needed to be so much more precise. The analyst was to become essential to survival in a literal sense.

The mid-nineteenth century was a time when agriculture was becoming far more chemically oriented, partly through the activities of Liebig but still more (in England) through the availability of superphosphates from 1843. As time went on analysis of these and other chemical fertilizers became more necessary. The techniques were complex and in 1874 were debated in *Chemical News*[18] and were the subject of a request from the Glasgow Philosophical Society that the British Association form a sub-committee to look into the matter. In the discussion on this proposal at the Newcastle Chemical Society it was suggested that a professional examination for public analysts should be instituted, anticipating by many months the debates on this subject in London (p. 162).[19] Matters came to a head in 1875 when the Agricultural Holdings Act set up arbitration machinery to compensate outgoing tenants for unexhausted manures on their land.[20] Valuation required analysis and this led to much urgent experiment, signalled by a paper by J. B. Lawes[21] on the establishment, 1876, of the Woburn Experimental Section under A. Voelcker, Chemist to the Royal Agricultural Society.[22]

3   Analysis in the Gas Industry

Nearly all major gas undertakings were sanctioned by individual Acts of Parliament. In return for the right to lay gas-mains under streets etc. the companies were required to maintain certain minimum standards of quality; this usually related at first just to the illuminating power of the gas and to the removal of most of the sulphur. As there was no adequate system of enforcement such testing as there was tended to be a hit-and-miss affair, certainly not sufficiently rigorous to demand the services of an analyst. Each morning the superintendent of the works might check for hydrogen sulphide with lead acetate paper while the tests for illuminating power were hardly chemical in nature at all.

As the mid-century approached, however, the gas lighting industry began to feel the pressures exerted on many manufacturers—demands for better quality control. The chemical analyst began to appear in the 1850s as a somewhat rare phenomenon in the gas industry. Thus, in 1851, the Great Central Gas Consumers Act empowered the Lord Mayor and Common Council to appoint a chemist in order to test gas supplies.[23] The appointee was a Dr Letheby,[24] who drew attention to the continuing problem of sulphur compounds in coal-gas. At this time the hydrogen sulphide had been removed but carbon bisulphide was still present; removal of this obnoxious compound by the use of red-hot barium oxide was proposed by L. Thompson, significantly described as 'a practical chemist'.[23] However, in the previous year the Gas Light and Coke Company, aspiring to supply the City of London and anxious to give at least as good a product as its competitors, was forced 'to obtain the services of a professor of chemistry to report upon the purity and illuminating power of the gas from the eastern station'.[25] Nor was it always thought necessary to ask a chemist about chemical matters. Perhaps the most remarkable case was the source of advice upon gas measurement and quality called for by HM Government in relation to the Sale of Gas Act of 1860.[26] This resided in no less a personage than George Airy, the Astronomer Royal.[27] The Civil Service appears on this occasion to have surpassed itself for the disingenuousness with which it directed its inquiries, for it proceeded to ask for advice from the engineer Willis and the physicist Wheatstone. The former somewhat tartly observed that the subject of gas meters 'belongs rather to chemists than mechanics', while the latter suggested inquiries be made of Frankland and Lowe.[26] In the end Frankland did produce the advice requested, his experience of gas analysis under Bunsen having made him eminently well-qualified to give it. The sheer difficulties of some of the techniques are reflected in the following rueful comments of Samuel

Clegg and help to account for the passing of such responsibilities from engineers to chemists:

> The accurate analysis of gaseous mixtures is one of the most delicate operations of modern chemistry. . . . This branch of chemical analysis owes much of its present accuracy and perfection to Professor Bunsen.[28]

There were also reasons of a quite different kind for the new involvement of analytical chemists. Whereas there had always been some standard of quality imposed by legislation, from 1860 this was much more stringently enforced. In that year the Metropolis Gas Act imposed on all London undertakings a system of independent testing, with penalties for non-compliance with statutory levels of purity, quality and pressure.[29] This was effectively in exchange for the rights to monopolies in the areas being served. Other measures followed. Thus a report of the Select Committee concerned with the City of London Corporation Gas etc. Bills (1866) proposed a Chemical Board of three persons, appointed at the expense of the gas companies, by the Secretary of State, to regulate the analysis of purity and illuminating power of gas from different companies, with power to fix the mode and places for testing the gas, such Board to report to the Home Secretary.[30] In 1871 similar provisions were made for the whole country.

A typical case of increasing attention being paid to analytical chemistry is that of the Newcastle upon Tyne and Gateshead Gas Co Ltd as can be seen from the minutes of the directors' meetings.[31] After occasional analyses from local consulting firms the directors resolved to ask for weekly analyses from Thomas Richardson, then assisted by Marreco (13 December 1865). The firm offered to conduct purity tests for £25 per annum and, for another £50 p.a. 'to give advice on other matters relating to the chemical purity of the gas, manufacture of sulphate of ammonia &c.' The offer for purity tests was accepted (10 January 1866) together with an additional weekly test for illuminating power for £5 per annum. More general advice would, however, be sought from the partners on an *ad hoc* basis. On those terms it was then resolved 'that Messrs Richardson and Marrico [sic], as chemists to the Coy., be desired to test the qualities of Howard's West Hartley and the Pirnie Coals'.[32]

However this arrangement did not keep the company out of trouble for Newcastle Corporation had since 1863 employed Pattinson as an official analyst for water and gas and his figures did not agree with those of Richardson and Marreco. In March 1866 the directors were informed that information laid by them before the Magistrate would be withdrawn if the company paid the costs of different assays. Eventually the prosecution went ahead (October) and it was subsequently resolved to set up a meeting between the two sets of analysts so that agreement could be reached as to the mode of testing for purity (29 January 1867). Numerous other passages of arms are recorded with the authorities and Marreco's reports appear fairly frequently from early 1867 (Richardson had died that year). There was also an advisory visit from the famous London authority on ammonium sulphate manufacture, Dr Letheby (20 December 1869); perhaps Marreco's advice on that subject had been insufficient. But the most remarkable feature of the minutes is the sudden appearance, from 24 January 1872, of regular weekly reports from Marreco on sulphur content and illuminating power.[33] No doubt the Gasworks Clauses Act of the previous year was acting as a stimulus to more efficient testing on site. But it must be confessed that so routine was the operation that the figures are often carelessly reported, blank spaces being sometimes left for them with no addition made at the following meeting. It was still a period when a directorate could regard the services of its analytical chemist as scarcely worth noticing (unless of course, legal action was in the air), the business of high finance being much more interesting. Such analysts had everything to gain from a professional institution.

4   Analysis in the Alkali Industry

By this time, however, the law was not confining its attention to the chemical monitoring of coal-gas. In 1863 the first Alkali Act[34] directed that any soda-works pouring hydrogen chloride into the atmosphere had to condense at least ninety-five per cent of that noxious vapour. It is not quite true that this was the first regulation to be expressed in quantitative chemical terms (other than for revenue or taxation purposes), because the individual Gasworks Acts had attempted to do that. It would be nearer the truth to designate it as 'the first attempt to express in very definite terms the meaning of a nuisance at any particular class of chemical works'[35]. The Act was of limited application, being confined to hydrochloric acid (HCl) emissions and then only from alkali works; infringement of its provisions had to be established by a costly procedure at County Courts; and a poorly-paid Inspectorate of five men had to cover the whole country until 1882. Yet such was the quality of leadership by the Chief Inspector, Dr Angus Smith, that most manufacturers were willing to comply and cooperate, and soon began to realize the benefits of so doing in better social relationships with previously outraged neighbours and in the economic value of the hydrochloric acid obtained by scrubbing the effluent gases in a Gossage tower or its equivalent. One commentator has even suggested 'Angus Smith ought to be a national hero'.[36] A further Alkali Act of 1874 which included other noxious gases was no longer limited to alkali-works,[37] just as Smith had advocated in his annual reports and elsewhere. These Acts were, with the possible exception of the Salmon Acts, the only legislation at that time sanctioning inspection simply (or mainly) to protect private property.[38]

The work of the Alkali Inspectorate was not without its hazards, involving withdrawal of gaseous samples from specific points in flues or chimneys and determination of flow-rates at those points. Often these were extremely inaccessible and involved climbing 'lofty and awkward ladders and passages'. Then of course the samples had to be carefully analysed. Some inspectors seem to have been more accident-prone than others; one gentleman, having been laid off from an accident for eleven months,[39] shortly afterwards lost another three months through a misadventure with his horse while travelling to a works.[40] That was in 1898–9. Many years earlier, in 1874, another inspector 'broke a blood vessel by the exertion required in shaking his aspirator' while yet another fell over in the dark![41] But their efforts were well rewarded by remarkable improvements, as shown by the small numbers of prosecutions, and by the growing importance of the analytical chemist at the works themselves. As Smith observed in 1876 the days when such a person was a rare oddity were now over:

> The frequent entrance of the inspector has caused him to be watched, imitated or criticized, and nothing is commoner than a comparison of results with him. In some cases, and these increasing ones, the works are tested daily; and Mr Todd informs me that this plan is introduced almost universally on the Tyne, or at least it was so for a while, and I hope they are not becoming weary of it. In some cases, and these increasing, the escape book is kept as regularly as the ledger, and the chemist opens it to the inspector and shows the work done by him on this subject since the last visit. If the result on the day of the visit agrees with the result obtained by the inspector, it speaks well for the previous days.
> This is a great change, and one which never could have been brought about without inspection.[42]

That the Alkali Acts raised the stock of chemical analysis in the public mind cannot be doubted. Yet it would be quite wrong to suppose that, under the threat of legal action against them, the manufacturers had simply to appoint a well-trained analytical chemist and all would be well. Even in the 1880s appointing men of distinction who could become 'resident examiners of works' was 'not always easy',[43] still less so in the decades before. But the real problem lay in the degree of specialism involved. When Lunge read a paper on analytical methods in alkali works in 1875 he confessed that, ten years previously, he had been the only chemist at his works and had had to devise all his own methods.[44] In the somewhat narrow specialism of those methods lay a great danger to the would-be professional chemist. Given a sufficient level of education it would be quite possible for some workers to develop the manipulative skills that the chemist displayed, though without the understanding that lay behind them. Many years after the birth of the Institute, in 1890, the inspector suggested that 'so great has been the advance of education generally' that an ordinary workman could control complicated apparatus and thus be 'raised . . . to a skilled artisan', with the stoker handling burette and beaker and making 'rapid analysis of the gases of combustion'.[45]

Thus not only did analysis in the alkali industry offer a great opportunity to the aspiring professional; it also posed him a considerable threat.

5 The Rise of the Public Analyst

Neither the alkali industry nor any of the other industrial concerns which touched chemistry at its periphery were able to effect any profound change in the status of analytical chemistry in the eyes of the government or the public generally. The real advance that took place in the 1860s and 1870s was in those areas of analytical chemistry that affected every man, woman and child of the population directly, i.e. food, water supply and medicines.[46]

The great question for analysts in these areas was that of adulteration, either deliberate or accidental. This played a part in establishing a group of people who termed themselves analytical chemists and who first appeared in the London Directory, for example, in 1854. The points in Figure 4 overleaf show how their members rapidly increased until 1891.

The first major awakening of public awareness on this subject was due to the German apothecary and chemist, Fredrick Accum, whose famous treatise on adulterations of food, with its Biblical reference to 'Death in the Pot', was published in 1820.

The author sought to alert the public to a wide variety of dangers, such as the use of red lead to act as a cheese colourant, the use of lead equipment in which to prepare food and many other hazards. As he said 'for the abolition of such nefarious practices it is the interest of all classes of the community to cooperate'.[47] Unfortunately Accum's reputation was severely dimmed a few years later after a prosecution was threatened by the Royal Institution for defacing some of their books; rather than face the magistrate Accum fled the country, never to return. It has been suggested that the great hostility he aroused was because of his assault on the vested interests of the food manufacturers, but whether this lay behind the legal proceedings is not clear. What is certain is that with the departure of Accum little was done to remedy the state of affairs to which he had pointed.

The next stage in the alerting of the public to the dangers of adulteration came in the early 1850s with the warnings clearly articulated by A. H. Hassall, then physician at Royal Free Hospital, London, a man well described as the 'first food analyst'.[48] Hassall used the medical periodical *The Lancet* as the medium for his attack, and in a series of articles pointed to the dangers of impure food in London and elsewhere. Much of his writings come as reports of an Analytical Sanitary Commission in which he was the major figure. In 1855 the collected insights of this Commission appeared as a book by Hassall, *Food and Its Adulterations*. As a result of this agitation a Select Committee was appointed by Parliament to 'enquire into the adulteration of food, drinks and drugs'.

Early in 1856, before the report of this committee was available, the

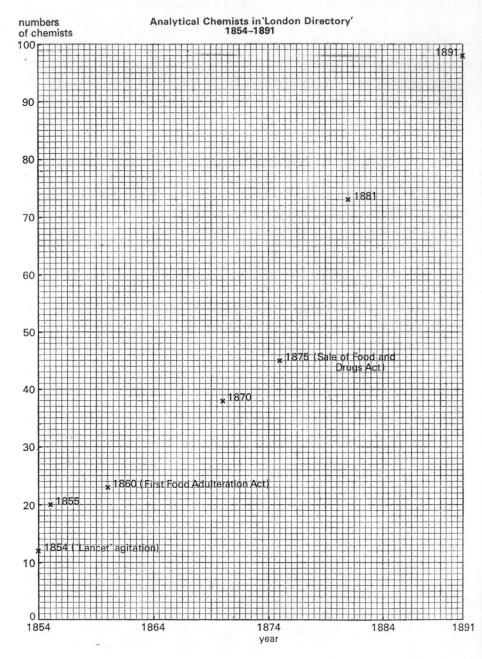

Figure 4

Pharmaceutical Society voiced its understandable misgivings: 'the sweeping and indiscriminate charges which have been brought against the entire body of chemists, and extensively circulated by the members, have caused no less surprise than annoyance to those who have been for many years successfully using all their endeavours to bring about an improvement'.[49] From a non-pharmaceutical committee not much could be expected, they thought, but they were somewhat reconciled by the committee's unexpected compliment to the Society 'the members of which, being specially educated in the knowledge of drugs, are better able than heretofore to make proper selections and to detect adulterations'.[50]

The outcome of the committee's deliberations was the 'Act for Preventing Adulteration in Food and Drink' of 1860.[51] This Act permitted the appointment of public analysts by Courts of Quarter Sessions and certain metropolitan authorities. But the Act was permissive rather than compulsive, and it applied to food and drink but not medicine. The many deficiencies of the Act were soon apparent and it became little more than a dead letter. The basic problems were first, lack of clear definition as to what was, or was not, adulteration, and the enormous difficulties of obtaining competent analysts. It was alleged that no more than twelve such people existed throughout the country although this statement was widely challenged.[52] Meanwhile further social roles for analytical chemists were beginning to appear. One of the most important new subjects for his research was the supply of drinking water to the population, particularly in London. On 7 July 1855 Faraday wrote to *The Times* complaining of the state of the River Thames, which had been allowed to become 'a fermenting sewer' and from which London's water supply was drawn. On dropping white visiting cards into the river edgeways he found the lower part was invisible before the upper was below the surface, so turgid was the water.[53] Various measures were taken to combat this problem both in terms of sewage disposal and in drawing water from higher up the river but not much was done by way of chemical analysis until Hofmann was charged with monitoring the metropolitan water supply on a monthly basis for the Registrar General. From 1865 this task was taken up by Frankland who continued the exercise until the end of his days and in 1868 was appointed to the Royal Commission into River Pollution. During the six years this Commission met he analysed over 5,000 samples during which time, as he rather immodestly put it 'the processes of water analysis were brought to their present condition of accuracy'.[54]

In 1862 a second Adulteration Act[55] was passed and proved to be an improvement on the earlier legislation. It provided for the procuring of samples by 'Inspectors of Nuisances' and extended the right to appoint analysts to boroughs having separate police establishments. Although the situation was improved there were many complaints, particularly of unjustified prosecution and again particularly because of a failure to give a clear definition of adulteration. A second Select Committee in 1874 suggested several useful amendments.[56] In addition, it was proposed that public analysts should meet together and this they did on 7 August 1874, ostensibly to consider the report but in fact to constitute themselves into yet another chemical organization.[57] They met under the chairmanship of Theophilus Redwood[58] and with secretarial assistance from two public analysts from London, C. Heisch[59] and G. W. Wigner.[60] Twenty-five persons were present on this occasion. Several propositions were made, the most enduring of which was to the effect that the analysts present should constitute themselves into a body whose name was eventually agreed as the Society of Public Analysts.[61] From now on this became a small but important pressure group for the organization of chemists. Its later history is well known. Eventually it turned into the Society for Analytical Chemistry and was absorbed into the Chemical Society in 1975.

Most of the members of this new society held their posts as analysts in plurality with other appointments, only a very few being at that time independent consultants on a virtually full-time basis. Their backgrounds were varied. Some had enjoyed a chemical training and turned to medicine in order to afford an opportunity for practising chemical analysis; others were Medical Officers of Health without much or any formal chemical training. Yet others held positions of trust in the pharmaceutical world.

This society was clearly born out of a conflict of interests or rather a series of conflicts. Three were particularly significant and very seriously taken. The first of these was a strong hostility between the Public Analysts as a body and a group who became known as the 'chemists of Somerset House'. These were men employed by the Inland Revenue who, though without broad chemical training, had nevertheless shown themselves to be deft workers when it came to determining the strength of alcoholic liquors or measuring other parameters important for the collection of excise duty. Often they were inspectors or officers whose appointment as 'chemist' was almost a routine matter if they had acquitted themselves well in these other duties. Indeed it was a proposal by the Select Committee that where analyses of results were challenged the chemist of Somerset House should act as the sole arbiter.

Such a proposal to anyone with any pretensions to professional expertise would be totally unacceptable and it is no wonder that the Society of Public Analysts was formed (1874) to deal with this menace. It must be admitted that efforts were made by the Somerset House authorities to make up for lack of expertise by in-service training and that the head of the laboratory, Dr James Bell,[62] enjoyed good personal relations with many Public Analysts. But this did not extend to collaboration in practice:

> The Somerset House Laboratory was not, like the Government Laboratory of today, an independent department. It was merely a branch of the Department of Inland Revenue, and its officers were more or less swathed in an entanglement of red tape, which was, unfortunately,

knotted by the legal advisers of the department in such a way as to limit their freedom of intercourse with those whom they might otherwise have regarded as their outside colleagues. There was imposed upon them the official view that if they became members of our Society or took part in our discussions, the independence of their position as referees might be jeopardized.[63]

Thus spoke Bernard Dyer, one of the early members of the Society of Public Analysts (SPA). He also identified part of the technical difficulty that arose when habitual discrepancies were noted between the two sets of analysts.[64]

A second unifying factor lay in the tensions existing between the analysts and the medical profession. Under the second Adulteration Act of 1872 it was decreed that Public Analysts should be competent practitioners in the medical, chemical and microscopical areas of analysis. Their difficulty lay in the lack of any recognized test of *chemical* competence, whereas their medically-qualified colleagues had no such disadvantage. On this count alone they could justifiably fear incursions from a rival profession. But that was not all, for their uncertificated applications for posts required individual scrutiny, and who should be appointed to perform this task but Angus Smith (unexceptionable enough) and John Simon, Medical Officer to the Local Government Board? Neither the excellence of the medical opinion (Sir John Simon became a leader in sanitation reform) nor the strength of the medical tradition in these matters (as embodied in Hassall) could console the analysts for the indignity of such subordination to another profession.[65] Perhaps in this may be seen part of the explanation for their continuing hostility to the Pharmaceutical Society, who, after all, had a strong medical orientation (pp. 44–50).

There was moreover a third conflict that helped to unite the members of the Society of Public Analysts; this turned out to be a far more intractable problem than the others and got worse rather than better as the century wore on. It was a conflict of classic structure, one between the academic chemists and the 'practising chemists' (as the members of the SPA liked to style themselves). It arose from a fundamental difference in the traditions of the two groups and the suggestions by the Select Committee that Public Analysts might well be examined by Frankland and his colleagues at South Kensington. The analysts themselves regarded the academics as being remote from reality and unfamiliar with all the detailed problems with which they were confronted; and the academics could—and did—sneer at the staggering incompetence of many of the unqualified analysts who testified to their ignorance in open court. Furthermore much of the analytical work involved in food testing was not chemical but rather microscopical. The great pioneer in using the microscope to this end was Hassall and when the government decreed that tests had to be carried out of quantitative character they would inevitably require chemical methods to arrive at the necessary figures. Thus although it may be true that in the alkali industry analytical skills preceded the legislation it is highly doubtful whether the same generalization holds for the workings of the Food and Drugs Act that became law in 1875. Techniques were quite primitive for many of the tasks that had to be performed; heavy metals would be identified by charcoal block tests; nitrogen determinations were tedious affairs until the days of Kjeldahl, and many of the pieces of equipment such as burners were not really suitable.[66] Perhaps the problem really stemmed from the medical origin of much of this work and of many of its practitioners. Some indication of the depth of feeling that did exist much later on may be obtained from Otto Hehner's article on the analytical chemist in the *Chemical Trade Journal* for 1891 (p. 166).[67]

Now it is an interesting fact that the resolution of all these difficulties might have been accomplished by the institution, under its own aegis, of special training for members and prospective members of the Society. Its achievements were many in the years ahead but they did not include the provision of a systematic training programme. This is all the more remarkable in view of some discussions that took place far away from London at this time, in Newcastle-upon-Tyne. Introducing these discussions A. F. Marreco proposed to elicit the views of the Newcastle Chemical Society 'as representing the chemical opinion of the North' on the following proposals:

1　That in the interest alike of the buyer, the seller, and the profession, it is desirable that only thoroughly competent persons should be appointed to the new office of public analyst.

2　That there is at present no recognized standard for the 'competent knowledge,' medical, chemical, and microscopical, required by the act.

3　That until some recognized examination exists, giving some guarantee of the knowledge of these various subjects required by professional analysts, this state of things cannot be remedied.

4　That it is desirable that such an examination under proper supervision should be instituted, and that only persons holding such diploma should be considered as duly qualified for the post of public analyst.[68]

In the ensuing discussion the Newcastle chemists got very near to the position reached three years later in London. As Marreco argued, 'let them have a board before whom a man can give clear evidence that he ought to call himself a chemist. . . . Let everybody be required to show proofs of this information before he was eligible—before he was, in the language of the Act "duly qualified" '.[69]

The question arises: why did the SPA hold back from this final, logical step? We should like to suggest that the reason may lie embedded in the complex relationships that were already being established with that great institution, the Pharmaceutical Society.

Shortly after these events something approaching a near panic broke out in the ranks of the pharmacists as one of the founder members of the SPA, A. H. Allen,[70] Public Analyst for Sheffield, undertook a series of spot tests over a very wide area and analysed the medicines that were dispensed for him according to the same prescription. The result was far from flattering to the pharmacists and a strong effort was made to suppress a paper which William Thomson of Manchester had written, extending the investigations begun by Allen 'On the degrees of accuracy displayed in the dispensing of physicians' prescriptions by druggists in different towns throughout England and Scotland'. However *The Chemist and Druggist* published it *in extenso*,[71] and the new organ of the SPA, *The Analyst*, hugged itself with delight at the prospect of such open discussion,[72] reflecting no little credit on its own members. But if relations with the Pharmaceutical Society were slightly strained it must not be forgotten that several of the most influential members of the SPA were also distinguished pharmacists, not least of whom was its President, Dr Redwood. But the real core of the problem was probably that in the Pharmaceutical Society qualifying examinations already existed—they were in fact the best thing available in lieu of anything specifically designed for the analyst. Thus at the Newcastle meeting Faraday's nephew, B. S. Proctor, observed:

> In the absence of other evidence, the best evidence of the fitness of a man for that post was the higher graduation of the Pharmaceutical Society . . ., far better than any medical evidence they professed and [he fancied] it embraced ground more valuable than that which they had got in a college of pure technical chemistry.[73]

It seems that the strange reluctance of the SPA to proceed to a system of examinations can well be explained in those terms. Had this not existed it is quite probable that the Institute would never have been formed but the relations between the embryo Institute and the SPA will be further considered in a later chapter.   CAR

NOTES AND REFERENCES

1 R. B. Pilcher, *History of the Institute, 1877–1914*, Institute of Chemistry, London, 1914, p. 50.

2 See W. H. Brock (ed.), *The Atomic Debates*, Leicester UP, Leicester, 1967.

3 Frankland is a central figure in the events of several subsequent chapters, though no major study of him has ever appeared. His autobiographical *Sketches from the Life of Sir Edward Frankland, edited and concluded by his two daughters, M. N. W. and S. J. C.*, was printed for private circulation, London, 1901 (almost all copies being quickly withdrawn and only one or two are now known to have survived) and 1902 (a similar but 'expurgated' edition). It is, naturally, highly selective and uncritical. See also *DNB* and *DSB*, several articles by H. E. Armstrong (e.g., *Chem. & Ind.*, 1934, 12, 459–66), but chiefly H. McLeod, *J. Chem. Soc.*, 1905, 87, 574–90; C. A. Russell, *Chem. Brit.*, 1977, 13, 4–7.

4 Tomlinson Collection (Newcastle-upon-Tyne City Library), vol. i, f. 66.

5 *Ibid.*, f. 65.

6 *Trans. Tyneside Naturalists Field Club, 1860–2*, 1863, 5, 322.

7 J. L. Baker, *The Brewing Industry*, Methuen, London, 1905, p. 141.

8 Tomlinson Collection (note 4) f. 65.

9 LNWR Notebook in the collection of Mr M. T. Hall, Derby, 'Water Analyses', 21 October 1864–21 June 1877.

10 LNWR Notebook in Hall Collection, 'Chemical Analyses', 21 October 1864–13 October 1869.

11 Application letter (29 January 1878) for Fellowship, in RIC records.

12 Tomlinson Collection (note 4) ff. 75–81. Bell was President of the Iron and Steel Institute (1873–5) as well as of the Newcastle Chemical Society in 1868 and the SCI in 1889.

13 *Chem. News*, 1876, **33**, 178, (letter from C. H. Alldred).

14 *1st Report of Deputy Master of the Mint, 1870*, (c. 303), P.P. 1871, XVI. Before this date analyses of finished coin were often delegated to outside chemists (W. A. C. Newman, *British Coinage*, RIC Lectures, Monographs & Reports, 1953, no. 3, 36).

15 *Report from the Select Committee appointed to inquire into the law relating to . . . all substances of an explosive nature*, P.P. 1874, IX.

16 On Dupré see *Analyst*, 1907, **32**, 314–6.

17 Note 15, p. 53.

18 *Chem. News.*, 1874, **29**, 190–3, 211.

19 *Trans. Newcastle Chem. Soc.*, 1871–4, **2**, 231.

20 Agricultural Holdings Act, 38 & 39 Vict. c. 92.

21 J. B. Lawes, *J. Roy. Agric. Soc.*, 1875, **2**, 1–38.

22 E. J. Russell and J. A. Voelcker, *Fifty years of Field Experiments at the Woburn Experimental Station*, Longman, London, 1936. On agricultural chemistry generally in the nineteenth century see K. Hudson, *Patriotism with Profit: British Agricultural Societies in the 18th and 19th Centuries*, Hugh Evelyn, London, 1972, ch. III. On A. Voelcker see ch. VIII, note 11; for the later role of agricultural analysts see ch. X.

23 C. Carpenter, *The Purification of Gas by Heat*, South Metropolitan Gas Co Ltd, London, 1914, p. 9.

24 On Letheby see *J. Chem. Soc.*, 1876, **29**, 618–19.

25 S. Everard, *The History of the Gas Light and Coke Company, 1812–1949*, Benn, London, 1949, p. 188.

26 *Papers relating to the Sale of Gas Act*, P.P. 1860, LIX, p. 9.

27 On Airy see J. G. Crowther, *Scientific Types*, Cresset, London, 1968, pp. 359–92.

28 S. Clegg, *A Practical Treatise on the Manufacture and Distribution of Coal-Gas*, London, 2nd edn., 1853, p. 45.

29 Everard (note 25) p. 200.

30 *Report of the Select Committee on London (City) Corporation Gas &c Bills*, P.P. 1866, XII, p. v.

31 Newcastle-upon-Tyne and Gateshead Gas Co. Ltd., minutes of Directors' Meetings (Northumberland County Record Office, NRO 303, NGB 1).

32 *Ibid.*, **10**, pp. 243, 249, 251, 253 etc.

33 *Ibid.*, p. 266; **11**, pp. 19–20, 38, 241, etc.; **12**, p. 14.

34 'Act for the more effectual Condensation of Muriatic Acid Gas in Alkali Works' (26 & 27 Vict. c. 124). It was made perpetual in 1868 (31 & 32 Vict. c. 36).

35 Alkali Inspector, *4th Report*, (3988), P.P. 1868, XVIII, p. 114.

36 F. Greenaway, 'Analytical Chemistry and Social Legislation in the 19th Century: a Case History', *Actes de XIIe Congrès International d' Histoire des Sciences*, Paris, 1968, **XB**, 35–9 (38). On R. Angus Smith (1817–84), a founder member of the Institute, see *J. Chem. Soc.*, 1885, **47**, 335.

37 38 Vict. c. 43.

38 *Report of Royal Commission on Noxious Vapours* (c. 2159), P.P. 1878, XLIV, 27, 31.

39 Alkali Inspector, *34th Report*, (141), P.P. 1898, XII, 6.

40 *Idem, 35th Report*, (160), P.P. 1899, X, 6, 80.

41 *Idem, 10th Report*, (in c. 1071), P.P. 1874, XXV, 405–6.

42 *Idem, 12th and 13th Reports*, (c. 2199), P.P. 1878–9, XVI, (Inter. Rep. for 1876, p. 2).

43 *Idem., 18th Report*, (c. 3583), P.P. 1883, XVIII, 6–7.

44 *Trans. Tyne Chem. Soc.*, 1875, p. 14 (10 December).

45 Alkali Inspector, *26th Report*, (c. 6026), P.P. 1890, XX, 16. This has, of course, been a perennial problem since that time, and a very characteristic one for the chemical industry.

46 See F. A. Filby, *A History of Food Adulteration and Analysis*, Allen and Unwin, London, 1934.

47 F. Accum, *A Treatise on Adulterations of Food and Culinary Poisons . . . and Methods of Detecting them*, London, 1820, p. iii; reprinted in C. A. Russell and D. C. Goodman, *Science and the Rise of Technology since 1800*, Wright and Sons, Bristol, 1972, p. 158.

48 R. C. Chirnside and J. H. Hamence, *The 'Practising Chemists': a History of the Society for Analytical Chemistry, 1874–1974*, SAC, London, 1974, p. 6. On Hassall (1817–94) see *Analyst*, 1894, **19**, 97–8.

49 Jacob Bell and T. Redwood, *Historical Sketch of the Progress of Pharmacy in Great Britain*, London, 1880, p. 246. See also T. D. Whittet, 'Some contributions of pharmacy to pure food and drugs', *Chemist & Druggist*, 1960, **174**, 378, 412, 441.

50 Bell and Redwood (note 49), p. 247.

51 Bill for Preventing the Adulteration of Articles of Food or Drink, 1860, 23 & 24 Vict. c. 84.

52 *Report of the Select Committee appointed into the Adulterations of Food, Drinks, and Drugs*, P.P. 1854–5, VIII.

53 *The Times*, 7 July 1855. There had been a mounting campaign for pure water since Chadwick's famous Report of 1842 on *The Sanitary Condition of the Labouring Population of Great Britain*, but, despite the Public Health Act of 1848 and other legislation, little had really been done to monitor public water supplies.

54 Frankland *Sketches* (note 3, 2nd edn.), p. 145.

55 Bill to Amend the Law for the Prevention of Adulteration . . ., 1872, 35 & 36 Vict. c. 74.

56 *Report of the Select Committee on the Adulteration of Food Act (1872)*, P.P. 1874, VI.

57 A full report of this meeting occurs in *Chem. News*, 1874, **30**, 73–8.

58 Redwood was from 1846 to 1885 Professor of Chemistry and Pharmacy at the Pharmaceutical Society's School of Pharmacy in London. His links with the Chemical Society (Council 1849–50, Vice President 1869–72) as well as with the Institute later make him into one of the few important figures with affiliations with all the important chemical bodies before the SCI. On Redwood (1806–92) see *Pharm. J.*, 1891–2 (3rd. Ser.), **22**, 763–6.

59 On Heisch (1820–92) see *J. Soc. Chem. Ind.*, 1892, **11**, 146; *Proc. Inst. Chem.*, 1892, pt. ii, 18; and *J. Chem. Soc.*, 1892, **61**, 489–90.

60 On Wigner (1842–84) see *J. Chem. Soc.*, 1885, **47**, 344.

61 On the SPA see B. Dyer and C. A. Mitchell, *Some Reminiscences of its first Fifty Years and a Review of its Activities*, Heffer, Cambridge, 1932, and, for a centenary history, Chirnside and Hamence (note 48).

62 Bell (1825–1908) was President of the Institute from 1888 to 1891; he was unaccountably 'knighted' by Dyer (note 61). See K. R. Webb, *J. R. I. C.*, 1958, **82**, 582–6.

63 Dyer and Mitchell (note 61), p. 16.

64 Many of the difficulties arose with analysis of milk. Wanklyn's method of analysis in fact gave an incomplete separation of fats and a correspondingly low estimate of them; while the Public Analysts used this method their results were bound to differ from those of their Somerset House rivals who did not. Added to this were problems of decomposition in samples after collection but before analysis. Neither the chemistry nor the microbiology was clearly understood, and confusion was inevitable. See Dyer (note 61), p. 15.

65 *Report of the Select Committee* (note 56) especially qq. 51–2, 110, 116, 127, 129 (the testimony of Hugh Owen).

66 On analytical techniques in use at this time see Chirnside and Hamence (note 48) ch. III. Much of the difficulty confronting analysts lay in defining what constituted acceptable limits of impurities.

67 *Chem. Trade J.*, 1891, **9**, 73–6.

68 *Trans. Newcastle Chem. Soc.*, 1871–4, **2**, 220–1 (26 March 1874).

69 *Ibid.*, p. 221.

70 Allen (1846–1904) was President of the SPA, 1887–9. See O. Hehner, *Analyst*, 1904, **29**, 233–42.

71 *Chemist & Druggist*, 1876, **18**, 114–7.

72 *Analyst*, 1877, **1**, 27.

73 *Trans. Newcastle Chem. Soc.*, 1871–4, **2**, 226.

CHAPTER VII

PRESSURES FOR REFORM

In the previous two chapters we have considered the two great themes of qualifications and analysis that together constituted the main issues under-lying the emergence of the professional chemist. In this chapter we look at several other issues which were, at the time, of great immediate importance and which in association with the problems of analysis and the growth of education were to lead up to the emergence of the Institute itself. These matters were hotly debated in and out of the chemical press. Particularly full coverage of debates can be found in the correspondence pages, the editorials and the reports of *Chemical News*. The three main national societies concerned with chemistry were keenly interested and, in their different ways, highly involved in the events leading up to 1877: the Chemical Society, the Pharmaceutical Society and the Society of Public Analysts. On the more local scale debates took place no doubt in many quarters; there are particularly clear reports of those that occurred in the Newcastle Chemical Society, for example. Undoubtedly the most important ones were never reported in print at all, although numerous manuscripts and other sources can enable us to see behind the scenes and learn something of the undercurrents that helped to determine the course of events. The total mass of information available is bewilderingly large; in this account we shall try to unravel the key issues as they appeared to the protagonists, to chart the multifarious happenings in the light of those issues, and also to enquire whether a modern re-evaluation of the importance of some of them might not be desirable. One thing is clear, and that is that the Institute arose out of a series of strong, even acrimonious, controversies. Unfortunately several of these arguments were so intertwined with each other, and many of them had protagonists in common, that it is not always easy to see why actions took place at any particular time. We begin with the most obvious and also the earliest question of the discussion.

1   The Meaning of Membership of the Chemical Society

The tranquil life of the Chemical Society was rudely disturbed by a series of events in 1867 that raised, apparently for the first time, matters of great im-portance for that Society's future. It had been a practice in the Chemical Society, as with many other learned societies at that time and since, for the outgoing Council to nominate its successor, but with the proviso that every Fellow could, if he so desired, substitute a name of his own suggestion in place of one proposed by the Council. What took place at the Annual

Meeting in March 1867 was strictly constitutional, but provoked a feeling of outrage that was well conveyed in the editorial of 5 April in *Chemical News* :

> Most Fellows of the Chemical Society will hear with considerable sur-prise that the proposed list of officers and Council which they received a few weeks ago has met with an organised opposition. A young gentle-man of little more than a year's standing in the Society, whose claims for distinction over any of the 500 other Fellows are absolutely *nil*, has had the presumption to set his own crude conception of what is best for the interests of the Society in opposition to the sagacity and matured ex-perience of the Council. In total ignorance of the principles which guide the selection of Council and officers, our revolutionary young friend ventured to nominate another President, another Secretary, another Treasurer, and sundry other Members of Council. This is sufficiently startling; but this is not all. He has not scrupled to go about soliciting votes to place upon the Council—himself! Need we stop to characterise conduct like this? However, the preposterous cabal signally failed. But for the proverbial impossibility of keeping a plot secret, he might, with the aid of a handful of supporters, in a scant general meeting, have snatched a short-lived triumph. As it happened, however, the friends of the Society mustered in force, and, by a majority of nearly four to one, decisively crushed the unwarrantable opposition.[1]

The name of this audacious usptart has not been revealed to us, but the im-portance of his action is that he demonstrated once and for all the ability of a small number of activists within the Society to cause a great deal of trouble, and the editorial of *Chemical News* wisely suggested a postal ballot to avoid a repetition of such disgraceful occurrences. It also raised in an acute form the problems of admission to the Fellowship. How could the Society prevent irresponsible youngsters from joining its ranks and exerting a subversive in-fluence upon its meetings? This question, rather than how to elect the Coun-cil, was to receive an embarrassing prominence within the next few weeks. The election of Fellows was by voting of those present at an ordinary meeting of the Society, a seventy-five per cent majority of those voting being neces-sary. At a poorly attended meeting a very small number of Fellows could vote against the candidate and thus ensure he was not elected—a process long known as 'black-balling'. Rarely had it happened in the past but now, in April and May 1867, there were several cases in which candidates were re-jected by this process. Again the editorial columns of the *Chemical News* throbbed with righteous indignation. The objections were the same as before: a tiny and irresponsible minority vetoing the wishes of the silent, or at least largely absent, majority.[2]

In the middle of the crisis the Council met but came to no decisive con-clusion:

Mr Crookes brought forward the question of the desirability of imposing some restrictions upon the admissions to the Society. He insisted
particularly upon the advantage of making it a qualification that a
Candidate should have contributed some paper which had been printed
in the Society's Journal, which would operate not only as a limitation
but as an inducement to those who desired to become Fellows of the
Society to engage in some scientific work or, at any rate, to communi-
cate work they had done to the Society.

The objection having been raised that such a qualification would
reduce the number of yearly elections too far, it was proposed that it
should be required of a Candidate to be recommended from personal
knowledge by not less than five Fellows of the Society. Finally, it was
reserved for consideration at the next meeting whether it might not be
well to admit both these qualifications. It was further proposed that
newly-elected Fellows should be required to pay their entrance fee and
first year's subscription within three months of the date of their election. [3]

A further repetition of black-balling next month was reported in *Chemical
News* in such a way that its rival paper *The Laboratory* carried a critical letter
by J. A. Wanklyn, denying certain impressions created by the report, particularly the implication that 'ten or a dozen young men should, by devious
strategy, attempt to overrule the wishes of the Council and the great body of
the members'. He asserted that less than half of the voting Fellows supported
the black-balled candidate, and added the interesting information that the
eleven black-ballers 'included one who has, within the last few weeks, pre-
sided at the Chemical Society, and also myself'. [4] Apparently the innuendo was
widely taken to apply to J. H. Gladstone who, however, vigorously denied it
in a subsequent edition of the paper. [5] But the admission by Wanklyn himself
is remarkably interesting for he was a member of the Chemical Society
Council.

A few days later, on 16 May, the Council met, Wanklyn being present,
and decided to delay the third reading of candidates' certificates for the time
being and to appoint a committee of five to consider the bye-laws relating to
admission.

The Committee eventually reported. It conceded the dual character of
fellowship of the Chemical Society, i.e. as being 'a distinction which should
be conferred only upon those who have given evidence of marked chemical
proficiency', but also since 'the object for which the Society exists is not to
confer honour upon any individual whatever, but to promote the general
advancement, distribution and application of chemical knowledge', fellowship should be open to all 'engaged in pursuits more or less dependent on or
connected with chemistry, and taking a sufficient interest in chemistry'. Their
sole immediate concession to the agitators who wished to limit the use of the
initials FCS as much as possible was to take up Crookes' proposals, sug-

gesting that five rather than three Fellows of the Society should sign a recommendation form for a candidate, at least three of them being required to do so from personal knowledge; it was suggested that the words 'qualification or occupation' should be substituted on that form for the words 'position, profession, or occupation'. They concluded this operation of delicate diplomacy by suggesting two alternatives:

> ... that the by-law should be altered so as to render valid the election by a mere majority, or else that the by-law should be temporarily abrogated, and that during its abrogation the election of Fellows should be delegated by the Society at large to a Committee appointed for the purpose.[6]

The Council on 7 November adopted the report and its recommendations and no doubt hoped that that was the end of the matter. And so it almost was, at least for another seven years, apart from a revealing letter in *Chemical News* dated 13 December 1867 from Wanklyn himself.[7] Although both a member of the Committee of five and of the Council of the Chemical Society he wished to dissociate himself from both the report and its adoption, having been absent from the later meetings of the Committee and from the meeting of the Council. He was particularly concerned about the final sentence of the report regarding as a far greater danger the perpetuation of the Council by 'a kind of apostolical succession' than even the possibility of some Fellows excluding a desirable candidate. His letter does not in fact deal at all with the issues raised by the Committee and is a swingeing attack upon the Council of which he was a member. What he was really looking for was 'a radical change in the manner of appointing the Council of the Chemical Society'.

Although the issues raised by this succession of incidents at the Chemical Society were genuine enough it appears that part at least of the explanation for their occurrence at this time may be found in the personality and attitudes of James Wanklyn. Born in 1834 and having studied both chemistry and medicine he worked with Frankland, Bunsen and Playfair, becoming in 1863 Professor of Chemistry at the London Institution and building up for himself a deserved reputation for chemical analysis. However as one of his former friends and admirers recorded: 'Unhappily, nature had endowed (or cursed) him with a spirit of pugnacity which seemed almost inevitably to involve him sooner or later in personal quarrels with those with whom, or for whom, he worked'.[8] In June 1867 he announced his ammonia process of water analysis, a technique which led to highly controversial results although it was basically sound.[9] In particular he had the misfortune to run into the hostility of his former chief, Edward Frankland, whose combustion method was also being developed about the same time.[10] Wanklyn was not a man to let things slide and at the Council meeting on 19 March 1868 proposed an official enquiry into water analysis to examine the discrepancies between his results and those of other people. The proposal was not seconded and so got nowhere.[11] Shortly afterwards he was angered by a savage, though anonymous, review of his book *Water Analysis* (1868). Wanklyn's subsequent retort was described by the editor as showing 'anything but a contrite spirit'.[12] He was removed 'in accordance with by-law' from the Chemical Society at a Council meeting on 19 May 1870,[13] possibly because he no longer regarded it worth his while to pay a subscription. He later became a founding father of the Society of Public Analysts and was a Vice-President in 1874, but shortly afterwards was involved in a row on the Publications Committee of *The Analyst*. He attempted to pass a vote of censure upon himself, failed to do so and left in high dudgeon. There followed the usual rancorous exchange of letters in the press and *The Analyst* announced with evident relief shortly afterwards that 'We notice that Mr J. Alfred Wanklyn has already announced his secession from the Society in the *Chemical News* and we are happy to be able to confirm the accuracy of his statement'.[14] A few days later the same journal printed a review of the fourth edition of his *Water Analysis*, concluding with an expression of 'deep regret that Mr Wanklyn has introduced controversial matter into the pages of his work'.[15]

The only purpose in now recording the passage of this stormy petrel through the Chemical Society's affairs is to suggest that at least in part one may understand them in terms of personalities as well as issues. But this is not to suggest that issues do not matter, for the same questions arose in a similar form several years later, after Wanklyn had forsaken the Chemical Society for the temporarily more congenial company of the Public Analysts.

From the end of 1874 until May 1876 black-balling occurred sporadically at Chemical Society meetings. At one of them five candidates were refused admission and on several occasions apparently worthy persons were rejected. This time, however, the black-ballers were exerting their legal rights after the main issue had been well debated. Following a speech by Frankland, to which we shall return, in 1872 pleading for the recognition of original research,[16] a correspondent ('A.T.') in *Chemical News* argued that the Chemical Society should confer some distinction on those Fellows who have contributed exceptionally to the science.[17] This letter came just at a time when the question of an association of manufacturing chemists was being mooted and, possibly for that reason, tended to be lost to view. But at the end of 1875 the *Chemical News* reported several outrageous incidents which appeared to call in question the whole value and meaning of the letters FCS. One bearer of these initials contrived to disgrace himself with hitherto unplumbed depths of chemical ignorance in a public examination in Swansea,[18] while another gentleman seeking the distinction of Fellowship, though doing a roaring trade in the sale of degrees by correspondence, was apparently chemically unqualified and therefore was black-balled; as one correspondent urged: 'No qualification should be accepted at the Chemical Society but chemical qualifications'.[19]

A further outbreak of 'black-balling' occurred at the end of 1874, continued sporadically over the next eighteen months and came to a head in May

1876, when six out of the nine proposed candidates were rejected. At the following meeting one of the Society's critics reported:

> the President condemned this act in language which, to say the least, was injudicious, and which most certainly would have been received in a different spirit had it not been for the great respect entertained for the speaker. In brief, it was intimated that the Fellows ought not to use their individual judgment, and that the blackballing was indiscriminate.[20]

One of the Society's supporters, C. E. Groves, a sub-editor of the *Journal*, attributed the fresh troubles to the activities of a small group of youthful reformists:

> These six or eight young men form themselves into a 'clique', and with more zeal than discretion proceed to blackball everyone they do not know. As their personal knowledge of the qualifications of the candidates is in most cases somewhat limited, the result is more curious and instructive than agreeable, although not unentertaining to a student of human nature if he be not interested in the welfare of the Society.[21]

He regarded it as 'scarcely justifiable to make use of the power given to the minority by the vote by ballot for the purpose of virtually altering the constitution of a society'.[21]

For those who exercised their right to veto admission of Fellows the issue was clear-cut:

> Recently awakened to the fact that their Society was in disgrace and was begun to be held in derision, and almost in contempt, even by themselves, a number of the Fellows have for some time past steadily refused to admit any but those who show unmistakable evidence of chemical attainments, and so at each successive meeting a larger and larger proportion have been blackballed, until, last meeting but one, two-thirds of the candidates were rejected.[22]

Writer after writer testified to the low standing of the Society. Its numbers looked healthy enough. At the Anniversary Meeting in March 'The President said he had to congratulate the Fellows on the flourishing state of their Society, the number of admissions during the past year having been 103, whilst the losses by death and other causes had been 23, so that the Society now numbered 881 members'.[23] But numbers were not everything, and one of the dissidents complained that the Chemical Society 'was not a body of chemists, but a motley mixture of all kinds of dabblers in science, and often, alas! very often, not even that'.[22] Such 'dabblers' would then abuse their privileges in the manner complained of by one member at the Anniversary Meeting. He enquired 'whether there was any bye-law which would give the Council some control over the use which Fellows might make of the privilege of membership, and then proceeded to detail three or four flagrant instances in which the letters FCS had been used for purposes of advertisement'.[24]

The only immediate outcome was a promise that the Council would consider the matter, and the raising of the admission fee from £2 to £4. Speaking of the 'chemists who are not gentlemen, and not the gentlemen who are not chemists', R. Warington urged:

> The only plan of dealing with this real, though happily limited evil, is by making some addition to the obligation clause signed by all Fellows, as already suggested by Dr Williamson.[25]

But the black-ballers were not to be so easily deflected: 'I differ from Mr Warington in believing that the Chemical Society was intended to be an association of chemists, and chemists alone, not a body of miscellaneous *dilettanti*—else why ballot for Fellows at all? Were it really a body of chemists it would surely forward the interests of our Society with much more ability and effect than at present, and so subserve better the purpose for which it was founded'.[26] A non-member wrote:

> My own case will probably be that of many chemists in this country. I have been in the actual practice of chemistry, both laboratory work and manufacturing, for the last twenty-five years; have published at least a dozen papers on analytical and kindred chemical subjects; possess no degree of any kind; would have offered myself for admission to the Chemical Society years ago, but was deterred by the fact that their title indicated nothing as to attainments, but had been distributed right and left with so lavish a hand as to become a bye-word; that the learned knew how valueless it was; and that, in many cases, it served only to gratify the vanity of would-be scientific men, with which they tickled the groundlings, or, if a deeper deep could exist, was bought for advertising purposes.[27]

And so the debate went on, gathering rather than losing momentum, and revealing further grievances, real or imagined. One correspondent identified a fundamental cause for misgiving: a lack of openness in government and an inadequate power structure:

> It is evidently felt that in the Chemical Society . . . the opinions of many Fellows obtain no adequate representation, and can therefore only find immediate expression through the medium of the Press. Where perfect understanding does not exist, secret opposition has arisen. The case in point is the protest which has made itself heard through the ballot, by so large a section of the Society, against the admission into its ranks of men who have no place there.[28]

An editorial reminder of the parallels with the 1867 troubles[29] aroused sympathy in the bosom of that rugged individualist J. A. Wanklyn, who entered the fray in July with a shrewdly judged letter:

> The structure of the Chemical Society, like that of other so-called learned societies, is very peculiar. Nominally the Chemical Society is a republic of the most democratic character, inasmuch as the Council and officers hold office solely by virtue of a majority of votes given by the Fellows, and each Fellow has only one vote.
>
> Really and in practice, however, the elective power of the Society remains permanently in abeyance; and the Council of one year re-elects itself and its nominees to form the Council of the next year. It is notorious how thinly the anniversary meetings are attended, and that not one-tenth (and probably not one-twentieth) of the 600 or 700 Fellows of the Society take any part in the election of the Council of the Society. Inevitably this state of things develops 'officialism', and leads to all those evils the existence of which is announced by the systematic black-balling which is so prevalent in the Chemical Society.[30]

It was obvious there was a widespread lack of confidence in the leadership, for which it must at least partly be held responsible. Warington rather petulantly condemned the black-ballers because they 'will not accept the testimony of a number of eminent men to whom the candidate is personally known', preferring to use their own judgement on the basis of documentation provided for them.[25]

Thus the Chemical Society was being assailed from without and within. Even the achievement for which it could claim to be legitimately proud was brought in to add to its discomfiture: 'Some time since the Chemical Society saddled itself with an expensive though valuable journal, the publication of which costs more money than can well be found. To meet this expense the portals of Burlington House were thrown open to all comers, and for a time there was witnessed a disgrace which, it is to be hoped, will never again be experienced'.[31] But the internal problems of the Chemical Society were only one factor in the emergence of the Institute. Another lay in the recognition of a fact that was 'on everybody's lips'.

> It is, in a word, that Chemistry is a profession as well as a science, and some members of the Chemical Society think that the Society should be the guardian of the professional as well as of the scientific functions of chemistry. The Society will certainly have fallen on evil days when these two functions shall have been permanently confounded; the honourable and important profession of the chemist will not have emerged from its anomalous and unrecognised position until, with or without the help of the Society, it has separated these functions completely, and organised the means of distinguishing the skilled practical chemist from the amateur or the purely philosophical student of the science.[32]

2 The Advance of Professionalism

The nineteenth century was a great period for professionalism in England. As F. M. L. Thompson has observed 'The very Victorians who condemned trade unions as vicious, restrictive, futile and as unwarrantable interferences with individual liberty, flocked to join professional combinations'.[33] The Engineers both Civil (1818) and Mechanical (1847) were flourishing, and when the Institution of Chartered Surveyors was formed in 1868 the President observed that everyone else 'having a common occupation' had formed associations so why not surveyors?[34] It is not surprising that chemists felt similarly. The rise of the Institute must be seen as part of a much wider tendency in Victorian society. But professional awareness usually requires some immediate pressures to bring it to a sufficient level for action to be likely. In the case of the chemists this triggering effect was supplied by the sudden surge in demand for analysts which threw into strong relief two closely related problems. They were both identified by C. R. A. Wright,[35] then Lecturer in Chemistry at St Mary's Hospital, Paddington, in a most important article in *Chemical News*, 21 January 1876, entitled 'On the necessity for organization amongst chemists, for the purpose of enhancing their professional status'. Writing of poorly-qualified men with analytical pretensions he said:

These semi-chemists inflict a double injury on the legitimate practitioners. In the first place, although they continue to go on tolerably smoothly when routine analyses or work of ordinary occurrence is in hand, yet as soon as anything out of the common run crops up, or if a quantitative determination requiring more than ordinary skill is required, they are at sea: in many cases they get out of the difficulty by sending the analysis on to some one more skilled than themselves, in others, they make the attempt, and produce a result which often is satisfactory enough to the unfortunate client, but which is, as likely as not, perfectly fallacious: occasionally their results are checked by more competent chemists, when woeful discrepancies come to light. Cases of this sort are familiar to nearly every chemist, but the unfortunate result is that the general public—being unable to decide between the qualified man and the semi-educated empiric—throws discredit on both, and on the chemical profession generally. In the second place, these quasi-chemists, not having to recoup themselves for the time and money spent in acquiring a thorough knowledge of their profession, are frequently willing to do work for fees absurdly low: the general public finding that Mr Smith or Jones FCS, will do analyses at a certain figure, expects the competent man to do the same; and if the latter does not come down to the fees for which his bastard professional brother will work, he loses his clients and his income altogether.[36]

In other words inadequate standards were associated with inadequate remuneration, and on the latter evil he went on to say:

> A good illustration of the lowness of the position chemists now occupy in the eyes of the public, as compared with members of other professions, is afforded by the amounts of the salaries offered to Public Analysts as compared with those of the Medical Officers of Health in the same districts. Frequently the Public Analyst is paid at a lower rate than a Nuisance Inspector, Surveyor of Roads, or even the Parish Beadle: the wonder is, accordingly, not that the best known names in the chemical world are—for the most part—conspicuous by their absence from the list of Public Analysts, but rather that there should be really a considerable percentage of skilled chemists amongst them. The bare fact that so many thoroughly trained chemists are willing to take posts as a rule much underpaid is a sufficient proof of the difficulty experienced in making a decent living out of professional chemistry.[36]

Many subsequent correspondents echoed Wright's denunciation of these twin evils. One example must suffice, that of C. H. Alldred who extended the argument to works' chemists as well.

> It is a very general thing, in many commercial laboratories, for youths to be employed entirely at one certain thing; for instance, at an 'Assay Office' with which I am acquainted one boy is kept to do all the weighing, another all the H_2S precipitations, so that in a single determination the manipulation will have passed through three or four different hands, and the results are then returned as gospel: if they should happen to turn out correct it is by a happy dispensation of Providence—if not it cannot be helped; and this is done by those holding high positions as commercial analysts.
>
> But then, Sir, the rate of fees quoted by these people will not admit of doing honest work. Will it pay a man (of any position above that of bottle-washer) *himself* to do an analysis of an iron ore, determining Fe, Mn, S, P, Ca, Si, Al, and Mg, for £3 10s. (which is the advertised price of many firms)—to do it in duplicate, and be able (as advised by Fresenius) to *swear* to his results? and yet how many brokers and manufacturers will quibble over £5 for an analysis, seemingly forgetting that every £1 saved by employing an inferior chemist may entail a loss of £100 on themselves. Take the case of copper ore. I imagine very few commercial assayers or analysts *bother* to determine the copper within ·025 per cent over or under the actual quantity present, and yet this would represent 4s. per ton; and as this ore is often bought in parcels of 1000 tons, would represent a loss or gain in the parcel of £200. . . .
>
> I perfectly agree with you, Sir, that those persons rejoicing in a sufficient private income had far better devote themselves to original

research than degrade themselves and the profession by doing work at wretchedly low fees. What would be thought of a barrister who pleaded causes at half-a-crown a head? I imagine he would be very soon ejected by his profession; and the cases are exactly similar.[37]

In Wright's proposal may be seen the first public expression of what became known as the 'Organization amongst chemists movement' from which the Institute is directly descended.

> The remedy which naturally suggests itself for these injuries to the public, and these and various other grievances of professional chemists, is that these latter should unite together, forming an *Association* or *Guild*, and that they should obtain a Charter enabling them to do as is done in what is virtually the Guild of Medical and Surgical Practitioners; *i.e.*, to *grant licenses to practise to duly qualified persons only.* The possession of the licentiateship of the Guild would then be a fair guarantee to the public of the efficiency of the owner; whilst non-licentiated practitioners should be debarred from the power of enforcing, by law, payment for the work which they are presumably incompetent to perform (just as in the medical profession).[38]

Such an association would have quite a different role from the Chemical Society:

> the first would have reference to chemistry solely as a *business*, as a means of livelihood; whilst the second looks on chemistry only as a *science*); only duly qualified persons would have the privilege of being registered on the rolls of the Guild; whilst, as is well known, any one who takes an interest in chemical science, whether connected with it as an experimental discoverer, as a druggist, science teacher or lecturer, or as a professional chemist, or whether unconnected altogether with chemistry in his occupation but taking an amateur interest therein, is ordinarily admitted to the Fellowship of the Chemical Society, provided (as in a recent case in point) there is no special reason to the contrary; and there is a great deal to be said in favour of this mode of proceeding.[38]

Regarding admission to the Guild 'all candidates unable to satisfy the original committee of their fitness for immediate registration and all subsequent applicants might be subjected to examinations of such a character as to test their fitness for the licentiateship, *practical quantitative work forming an essential part of such an examination*'.[38] A registration fee, perhaps five guineas, and possibly an annual subscription would enable the Guild to pay its way.

Wright's proposals got off to a slow start. Five weeks later they were commended by an editorial in *Chemical News* and a trickle of correspondence began, nearly all of which expressed agreement. A month or two later the trickle became a flood and, by the spring, letters about the Chemical Society and about 'Organisation' were side by side in the columns of succeeding issues. The interesting part is that few writers connected the two topics,[39] and one is left with a strong impression that they were, at first, regarded as separate. This is strengthened by the frequency of suggestions like the following:

> It appears to me that the necessary nucleus of the proposed guild already exists in the Society of Public Analysts; of course, I do not intend to assert that all members of that Society are fit to become members of the guild. The Public Analysts' Society was originally formed to discuss and influence the proposed legislation on Adulteration, and admirably it has answered its purpose. It is well known that the Public Analysts under the Sale of Food Act are many of them quite unused to general analytical work, and would never desire or expect to be recognised as members of a Guild of qualified Analytical Chemists. Still, the Public Analysts' Society, now numbers either among its honorary or its ordinary members, nearly all the consulting analytical chemists in the Kingdom, and if it were to take in hand the work of formation of a Guild of Professional Chemists, those analysts who are not yet enrolled as members would probably give it their influence and support.[40]

As we shall see the SPA was not to have the role envisaged. This suggestion came from A. H. Allen, Public Analyst for Sheffield, and it certainly seems that the 'Organisation' issue was felt most strongly by men in that kind of position, concerned with analytical standards and proper remuneration. It was also primarily (though not exclusively) the analysts who were aware of another issue, derivative to that of professionalism as such, the question of what might best be called 'professional encroachment'.

3   Professional Encroachment

In February 1876 *Chemical News* carried a review of the 1875 *Year Book of Pharmacy*, and the anonymous reviewer concluded his remarks with the following: 'We think it is impossible to glance through this volume without being struck with the amount of influence and prestige which have accrued to the pharmaceutists of Britain from union. Will the "analytical and consulting chemists" never follow this example to protect themselves against the encroachments which they suffer on various hands? We have often harped upon this string, but we wish to tune it'.[41] Since 1868 the pharmacists had been a shining example of professional unity—and professional monopoly. But the chemists were not so favoured, being subject to encroachments on at least two sides.

First, there were numerous cases where chemical analysis was being attempted by those whose training and experience were in the field of *medicine*.[42] On occasions, as Wright observed, such work was undertaken by 'medical men possessing only the small modicum of chemical knowledge gained during their studies in the medical school, and often wholly innocent of any notion whatever how general quantitative work should be conducted, although they may have picked up some acquaintance with the methods to be adopted in the examination of some few articles of food, of water, or air, &c.'.[36]

A. H. Allen expressed strong opinions on 'the pseudo-scientific medical men' as a

> class generally very ready to quack as chemists, though remarkably tenacious of its own privileges. . . . One of my acquaintance belonging to this class is very fond of talking of the 'quantitative analysis he saw when assistant to Professor Brande, forty years ago', while another recently expressed an opinion that 'iodide of potassium could not be accurately estimated in admixture, but he supposed it would be best accomplished by means of starch'! Unfortunately, the ignorance of these pretenders is not understood by the public, and their results and opinions are liable at any time to be quoted as gospel.[40]

He was also concerned with encroachments by unqualified druggists:

> Some years ago I heard a druggist say in the witness-box that he was an analytical chemist, though I have good reason to believe he never made an analysis in his life. The extent of his information may be imagined when I say that a youth, since then a pupil of mine, once went to his shop for some 'hydrosulphuric acid' for private use, and was instructed by the analytical chemist to 'put some water to sulphuric acid, which will make hydrosulphuric acid'![40]

A *Chemical News* editorial identified another kind of threat.

> In support of our view that the sphere of the chemical profession is being encroached upon by outsiders, we will bring forward two unmistakable modern instances. The Board of Trade have recently appointed a Water Examiner. Now a water examiner should be a chemist and a microscopist. Yet the gentleman appointed is an engineer! Turning to a closely connected matter, what can be more evident than that the treatment of sewage is a chemical question? The distinction between sewage and pure water is a chemical distinction. The methods of removing the impurities depend on chemical principles, and chemistry alone can decide whether any sewage or refuse water is sufficiently purified to be safely admissible into rivers. Yet at a meeting of the Society of Engineers, recently held in Westminster Chambers, the President, Mr Vaughan Prendred, in the course of his address observed:—'The sewage question was the great question of the day, and it would require their (the engineers') deepest thought and utmost skill'. There exists, in

fact, already a Society of Sanitary—not Chemists—but Engineers. Thus, without prompt and vigorous action, we shall see this important matter taken entirely out of our hands, the main credit and the main emoluments falling to those who merely execute the subsidiary portion of the work. . . .

The great principle of the division of labour, still more important in intellectual matters than in mere manual affairs, forbids any man from being at once chemist and engineer.[43]

The following issue carried a report on a further outrage.

A fresh instance of the encroachments referred to in our last issue has occurred in connection with the proposed removal of the Mint to the Savoy. The Government has employed Mr F. J. Bramwell, an engineer, to report on the possibility of the Mint proving a nuisance to the neighbourhood. Now, as the nuisance, if any should arise, must depend on the escape of fumes and gases, the question is strictly chemical, and can no more be solved by an engineer than by a lawyer or a clergyman. We are glad to find that this opinion was expressed by one of the speakers at a meeting held in the vestry-room of St Mary-le-Strand to protest against the New Mint. 'Mr Bramwell' it was remarked 'was a civil engineer and not a chemist, and his opinions, therefore, on the fumes which would arise from the melting of the metals could not be worth much'. An evening paper, discussing the question, makes the farcical suggestion that if Mr Bramwell's report is not considered satisfactory 'some other eminent engineer' ought to be consulted.[44]

A review of a treatise on gas manufacture concludes: 'Is it because Murdoch was by profession an engineer that the manufacture of gas, which, abstracting from the subsidiary process of its distillation, is essentially a chemical art, has fallen comlpetely into the hands of a body of engineers?'[45]

That this profession posed a greater threat than medicine may be judged from the following comment on a report about London water:

Parenthetically, and from an absolutely impersonal point of view, we must pronounce it strange that chemical and sanitary questions, such as the purity of a water supply and the efficiency of methods of sewage treatment, should be referred, not to chemists or medical practitioners, but to engineers, whether Royal or Civil.[46]

And for many years the engineers looked down upon chemists as a lesser breed of men. The advice given in the 1870s by W. Menelaus, President of the Iron and Steel Institute, was perhaps less extreme than it sounds: chemists 'should be kept in a cage until something went wrong!'.[47]

Finally, the worst encroachment of all was from those unqualified in any field. Kingzett was exaggerating when he wrote of 'quacks who rejoice in the possession of bogus degrees'[48] as a serious threat to the livelihood of chemists, but there undoubtedly were cases where charlatans were using a genuine FCS as a token of excellence.

These controversies may seem reminiscent of the more fatuous 'demarcation disputes' of modern times, and they sprang from very similar causes: a deep sense of insecurity and a rising feeling of injustice. But in fairness one must add that the chemists had solid grounds for believing that such encroachments would genuinely lead to a debasement of analytical standards and real disservice to the public.

4 Political Trends

In the early 1870s there was much that could have encouraged those eager to promote a new professional status for the chemist. In a general way several recent government enactments had provided useful precedents to many items in their own programme. The outstanding example of state recognition of a professional monopoly was fresh in the minds of those who had observed the triumphant passage of the Pharmacy Bill to its successful conclusion in July 1868. Shortly after that date, in December, Disraeli's Conservative Government was replaced by a Liberal administration under Gladstone, destined to rule for the next five years. This augured well for those in favour of free associations of workers, manual or otherwise. In fact 1869 saw the formation of a new Trades Union Congress, and two years later Gladstone's Trade Union Act gave protection to union funds as well as enhanced status for unions themselves. The Criminal Law Amendment Act of the same year, however, modified these benefits by effectively impairing the right to strike. But, as David Thomson has written,

> Together the two Acts meant Liberal recognition of the unions as friendly and benefit societies and as vehicles of peaceful collective bargaining, but severe restriction of their powers as fighting bodies.[49]

Such restrictions were of little relevance to those engaged in the organization of chemists, nor were they even concerned with collective bargaining as such; but they could scarcely have failed to take encouragement from measures aimed at strengthening liaisons of skilled workers with a common interest. The political agitation of the rest of the 1870s, partly at least in opposition to the Criminal Law Amendment Act, could only have strengthened their hands still further. So, in a different way, did the opening of the civil service to competitive entry, in 1870.[50] The establishment of competitive examinations for virtually all departments except the Foreign Office brought a new professionalism to the civil service just as it was to do, several years later, to the practice of chemistry.

Doubtless these events contributed in a general way to the creation of a climate of opinion favourable to the organization movement. But there were other changes that affected the fortunes of the chemists far more directly.

Most important of all was the growth of what is sometimes called the 'endowment for research movement',[51] whose beginnings may perhaps be dated to August 1868 with a paper read to the British Association (Physics and Mathematics Section) 'On the necessity for State Intervention to Secure the Progress of Physical Science'.[52] The author, Alexander Strange,[53] was a retired colonel from the Indian Army. As a juror at the Paris Exhibition he had been impressed by the way that Britain was rapidly falling behind other nations in scientific productivity and proposed an enquiry by the BA into whether this country had sufficient provision for the vigorous prosecution of physical science, and, if it did not, how the situation could be repaired. A committee was appointed, including the chemists Frankland, Stenhouse, Williamson, Playfair and some eleven other persons, most of them members of the unofficial pressure-group known as the X-Club.[54] The outcome was the appointment of a Royal Commission on Scientific Instruction and the Advancement of Science better known as the Devonshire Commission, from its Chairman the seventh Duke of Devonshire[55] (a distant relative of Henry Cavendish). From 1872 to 1875 the Commission produced eight massive reports, the last of which proposed support of science by the Government on a wholly new scale: state laboratories, research grants, with the creation as 'a matter of primary importance' of a Ministry of Science and Education.

Had these recommendations—and the many others in the earlier Reports—been accepted the professionalization of chemistry and of all branches of science and technology might have been enormously accelerated. Additional impetus might have been expected from the recent Franco-Prussian War (1870) in which the armies of the scientifically more advanced Germany were victorious. But it was not to be, apart from a research grant to the Royal Society of £4,000. Many were the reasons, and it is certainly not fair to lay all the blame at the door of the Liberal Government. Later administrations dallied with the same problem, and such progress as there was turned out to be very slow indeed. But in the 1870s Gladstone's dedication to free trade, self-help and those other virtues beloved by Victorian Liberals is probably a sufficient, if not the only, explanation. In a famous speech to the Institution of Civil Engineers in 1872 he argued:

> It was in the growth of individual and local energy and in freedom from all artificial and extraneous interference that the secret of the greatness of this country was to be found. That danger of centralization which had been a formidable and fatal difficulty in other lands had not yet obtained serious dimensions among ourselves, but it had lifted its head in this country also, and Englishmen would show at once their wisdom and their fidelity to the traditions of the forefathers by taking care not to hand over to the executive the discharge of functions which would be much better performed by themselves.[56]

Thus it was not without some reason that one correspondent in *Chemical News* wrote in 1876 'the proposal of a corporation of analytical chemists is perhaps more likely to receive the support of a Conservative than of a Liberal Ministry', though he was shrewd enough to add that 'while there is a Lyon Playfair in Parliament the interests of chemists are sure to be efficiently represented'.[40]

Although the members of the X-Club were strongly opposed to Gladstone's attitude to science (they did not like his Home Rule policy for Ireland either), not all chemists were inclined to blame the government for its parsimony. Some, like Marreco at Newcastle, (although his politics were Conservative[57]) felt the chief offenders were elsewhere:

> I do not say that this is a large step in the endowment of research. I do not say that a nation like ours might not well afford to do more, and might not, perhaps, find that the operation was a far more profitable investment than the purchase of one-hundred-ton guns. But such as this £4000 a year is, we shall judge, I think, that this is a step in the right direction. I cannot, however, help feeling that there are other sources more appropriate perhaps—certainly more adequate to the occasion—to which we might have looked, and to which indeed we have looked, and looked I regret to say to a great extent in vain, for some years. Prominent amongst these, the older universities at once suggest themselves. . . .
>
> Without going into details, I do not think any one will dispute the proposition that, were the older universities really animated with the desire to encourage original scientific research, the colleges would probably apply some fraction of that sum to the endowment of research, instead of the endowment of persons. I cannot, I confess, realise the condition of mind which can conceive it is desirable that a man, simply because at the age of twenty-two or three he has passed a better examination than his fellows; simply because he has happened to show he has some capability of being henceforth useful should be endowed with a sum of money, coupled in the majority of cases with no conditions as to future work.[58]

The universities should set their house in order for the simple reason that 'we have had an addition to the national taxation in order to endow research'.

It may seem strange that the scientific community did not regard government support with unrelieved joy. One reason was probably the fear that Whitehall's favours would be largely restricted to the scientists of London. The Newcastle chemists (to mention but one example) were at times quite strongly anti-metropolitan,[59] and later in the 1880s the fear that certain members of the South Kensington scientific community might be feathering their own nests at the expense of the taxpayer gave rise to expressive, if unedifying, vituperation.[60]

Reluctance to be dependent upon the government for finance had deeper undertones than mere provincial mutterings. While testifying before the Devonshire Commission Sir George Airy, Astronomer Royal and President of the Royal Society, had been distinctly lukewarm on the matter of government support. Writing for a popular paper, *The English Mechanic*, in 1881 he explained his misgivings:

> I think that successful researches have in nearly every instance originated with private persons, or with persons whose positions were so nearly private that the investigators acted under private influence, without incurring the danger attending connection with the State. Certainly I do not consider a Government is justified in endeavouring to force at public expense investigations of undefined character, and, at best, of doubtful validity: and I think it probable that any such attempt will lead to consequences disreputable to science. The very utmost, in my opinion, to which the State should be expected to contribute, is exhibited in the large grant entrusted to the Royal Society.[61]

So government support might lead to government interference. This idea was abhorrent to Victorian scientists of all persuasions; the chief difference between them lay in the fact that not all were prepared to accept Airy's inference. Their determination to be independent was not, as some have argued, a display of gross irresponsibility by and for science; it was rather a well-placed fear of the consequences of interference in scientific affairs by a bureaucracy that knew nothing of science. The least that could be hoped for was that 'if scientific men are to be legislated for and directed, justice requires that it should be by men possessed of scientific knowledge.'[62]

Thus state involvement gave new opportunities but it also posed a very real new threat. For chemists this offered another powerful reason for their association into a well-organized profession. But in the nature of things this was one reason which it would *not* be prudent to advertise, especially if government recognition of some kind of professional monopoly might be required. And in the 1870s there was before the chemists the salutary experience known as the 'Ayrton incident'.[63] This unsavoury affair concerned the dispute between Joseph Hooker, Director of the National Arboretum at Kew ('Kew Gardens') and the unpopular and autocratic First Commissioner of Works in Gladstone's administration, A. S. Ayrton. Although it became a *cause célèbre* in its day, the strife ended inconclusively in a stalemate with the crucial issue of 'who ran science' raised but not resolved. Because the issue was seen to transcend in importance particular details of the squabble (into which we need not enter) the whole scientific establishment was roused to passionate attacks on government interference in the early summer of 1872. One of these took place at an occasion memorable also for its connections with the Institute.

On 30 May 1872, the second Faraday Lecture to the Chemical Society was delivered by Cannizzaro: 'Considerations on some points of the theoretic teaching of chemistry'.[64] On the following evening the President, Frankland, entertained some 150 guests to a dinner in honour of the lecturer. Amongst those present were the Italian Ambassador and the Chancellor of the Exchequer, Robert Lowe.[65] Also amongst the guests was Frankland's close friend and X-Club confederate, John Tyndall.[66] Never a man to keep silence unnecessarily, Tyndall determined to turn the occasion to advantage. He wrote to the aggrieved Hooker:

> I blew off some steam *à propos* of Ayrton (without naming him) at the Chemical dinner of Friday. Lowe was there and when I spoke of the crass ignorance of men in authority (always excepting Lowe) and their doing things before High Heaven that would make the angels weep, Lowe said 'That's Ayrton—I quite agree . . .'[67]

It was in the context of that exchange that Frankland rose to speak from the Chair, an occasion that Pilcher rightly identifies as 'the real origin of the Institute. . . . In the course of his speech, the President drew attention to the increasing importance of chemistry in relation to the wants of communities, and pointed out how great would be the usefulness of an Institute which would be to chemists what the (Royal) Colleges of Physicians and Surgeons were to the medical profession, the Institution of Civil Engineers to civil engineers, and the Inns of Court to the legal profession'.[68]

Clearly it would be wrong to make too much of this one incident, however great its intrinsic importance. But it does offer at least presumptive evidence for a strong connection between the formation of the Institute and the growing awareness of the need of chemists for protection from undue government interference.   CAR

NOTES AND REFERENCES

1 *Chem. News*, 1867, **15**, 163.

2 E.g., *ibid.*, p. 243 (17 May).

3 Chem. Soc. Council minutes, 18 April 1867.

4 *Laboratory*, 1867, **1**, 117 (18 May). On Wanklyn, see *DNB*, *DSB*.

5 *Ibid.*, p. 206. On Gladstone see W. A. Tilden, *J. Chem. Soc.*, 1905, **87**, 591–7.

6 Printed paper inserted into Chem. Soc. Council minutes for 7 November 1867.

7 *Chem. News*, 1867, **16**, 303.

8 Bernard Dyer, *The Society of Public Analysts and other Analytical Chemists, some Reminiscences of its First Fifty Years*, Heffer, Cambridge, 1932, pp. 12–13.

9 E. T. Chapman, M. H. Smith, and J. A. Wanklyn, *J. Chem. Soc.*, 1867, **20**, 445.

10 E. Frankland, *ibid.*, 1868, **21**, 77.

11 Chem. Soc. Council minutes, 19 March 1868.

12 *Chem. News*, 1868, **18**, 151, and 165.

13 Chem. Soc. Council minutes, 19 May 1870.

14 *Analyst*, 1877, **1**, 157.

15 *Ibid.*, p. 165.

16 *J. Chem. Soc.*, 1872, **25**, 341 (30 March).

17 *Chem. News*, 1872, **25**, 189 (19 April).

18 *Ibid.*, 1875, **32**, 251.

19 *Ibid.*, p. 313.

20 *Ibid.*, 1876, **33**, 220 (26 May).

21 *Ibid.*, p. 229 (2 June). On Groves see *J. Soc. Chem. Ind.*, 1920, **39**, 83R, and *Proc. Inst. Chem.*, 1920, 14.

22 *Chem. News*, 1876, **33**, 220 (26 May).

23 *J. Chem. Soc.*, 1876, **29**, 617; *Chem. News*, 1876, **33**, 146.

24 *Chem. News*, 1876, **33**, 146. One of these was later identified by R. Meldola (*ibid.*, **34**, p. 7) as a pamphlet advertising:
'J. N. Hearder's Guide to Sea Fishing . . . and Descriptive Catalogue of his Prize River and Sea Fishing Tackle, Cricket, Archery, Croquet, Umbrellas, Parasols, etc'.
by 'J. N. Hearder, DSC., PHD, FCS'.
It was an unhappy example. A few days later a letter from 'FCS' described Hearder as 'a man of great ability' who was widely respected locally:
> Dr Hearder has been blind for many years, and anyone who has attended his lectures, carried out, as they must have been, under great difficulties, will agree that instead of bringing discredit on the Chemical Society he has been an honour to it. (*Ibid.*, p. 20).
Three days later the unfortunate man died from a sudden paralytic seizure (*ibid.*, p. 32)—perhaps a victim of the Chemical Society's internal strife?

25 *Ibid.*, 1876, **33**, 229–230 (2 June).

26 *Ibid.*, p. 238 (9 June).

27 *Ibid.*, p. 239.

28 *Ibid.*, p. 248 (16 June).

29 *Ibid.*, p. 263 (30 June).

30 *Ibid.*, **34**, 7 (7 July).

31 *Ibid.*, **33**, 248 (16 June).

32 N. S. Maskelyne, *ibid.*, pp. 246–7.

33 F. M. L. Thompson, *The Chartered Surveyors: the Growth of a Profession*, Routledge, London, 1968, p. 149.

34 *Ibid.*, p. 65.

35 On Wright see *Proc. Roy. Soc.*, 1894, **57**, v–vii.

36 *Chem. News.*, 1876, **33**, 27.

37 *Ibid.*, pp. 178–9 (28 April).

38 *Ibid.*, p. 28.

39 Perhaps the first to perceive a connection was Alfred Tribe who lamented the possibility of yet another chemical organization, saying 'what we really want now is unity' (*ibid.*, p. 250), though it was Wright himself who first explicitly drew attention to 'the relations between the Chemical Society and the Organization Movement' (*ibid.*, p. 269).

40 *Ibid.*, p. 94 (3 March).

41 *Ibid.*, p. 73.

42 This was not entirely a one-way encroachment. In 1873 the Chief Alkali Inspector recommended that the chemist must supplement medical methods for examination of air, 'taking probably out of the hands of medical men some of the work, according as experiment becomes more and more definite' (Alkali Inspector, *9th Rep.*, (*c.* 815), P.P. 1873, XIX, 2).

43 *Chem. News*, 1876, **33,** 89 (3 March).

44 *Ibid.*, p. 102.

45 *Ibid.*, 1877, **35,** 74 (16 February).

46 C. M. Tidy, *ibid.*, p. 194 (11 May).

47 J. C. Carr and W. Taplin, *History of the British Steel Industry*, Blackwell, Oxford, 1962, p. 218; the advice was given to the Directors of the West Cumberland Steelworks concerning the appointment of G. J. Snelus. Similar disdain was reported as late as 1908 at an Iron and Steel Institute meeting (*ibid.*, p. 218).

48 *Chem. News*, 1876, **33,** 107 (10 March). On Kingzett see G. T. Morgan, *J. Chem. Soc.*, 1935, 1899–1902.

49 David Thomson, *England in the Nineteenth Century*, Penguin, London, 1975 edn., p. 148.

50 *Ibid.*, p. 131.

51 On this see R. M. MacLeod, 'The support of Victorian Science: the Endowment of Research Movement in Great Britain, 1868–1900', *Minerva*, 1971, **9,** 197; D. S. L. Cardwell, *The Organisation of Science in England*, Heinemann, London, 2nd edn., 1972; and references cited in these two works.

52 *Rep. Brit. Assoc.*, 1868, **38,** Trans. Sections, pp. 6–8.

53 See J. G. Crowther, *Statesmen of Science*, Cresset, London, 1965, pp. 237–69.

54 See J. V. Jensen, 'The X-Club: Fraternity of Victorian Scientists', *Brit. J. Hist. Sci.*, 1970, **5,** 63; and R. M. MacLeod, 'The X-Club: a Social Network of Science in late Victorian England', *Notes & Records*, 1970, **24,** 181.

55 See Crowther (note 53) pp. 212–33.

56 *The Times*, 26 April 1872.

57 G. A. Lebour, *Hist. Berwickshire Nat. Club*, 1882–4, 71.

58 *Trans. Newcastle Chem. Soc.*, 1874–7, **3,** 226; *Chem. News*, 1876, **34,** 282.

59 Thus Marreco regretted the exhibition of Stephenson's original 'Geordie' lamp at South Kensington, and deplored 'that excessive centralisation with which we meet at every turn, and which would aim at concentrating the whole of art, science and literature in one corner of London, for that is what we are fast drifting into' (*Trans. Newcastle Chem. Soc.*, 1874–7, **3,** 233–4).

60 E.g. the correspondence in *The English Mechanic* documented by MacLeod (note 51), p. 224.

61 *English Mech.*, 1881, **22,** 586–7 (25 February).

62 G. Gore at Plymouth, 1872, cited (from *Trans. Soc. Sci. Assoc.*, 1872, p. 284) on p. 48 of note 63.

63 R. M. MacLeod, 'The Ayrton Incident: a Commentary on the Relations of Science and Government in England, 1870–1873', in *Science and Values: Patterns of Tradition and Change*, A. Thackray and E. Mendelsohn (eds), Humanities Press, New York, 1974, pp. 45–77.

64 S. Cannizzaro (trans. H. Watts), *J. Chem. Soc.*, 1872, **25,** 941–67.

65 *Chem. News*, 1872, **25**, 274 (7 June).

66 See *DNB*, *DSB* and J. G. Crowther, *Scientific Types*, Cresset, London 1968, pp. 157–88.

67 Letter from Tyndall to Hooker (3 June 1872) in Hooker papers at Kew (vol. i, f. 222), also cited in MacLeod (note 63) p. 61.

68 R. B. Pilcher, *History of the Institute, 1877–1914*, Institute of Chemistry, London, 1914, p. 24. It is curious that few, if any, other records of this speech are available today.

CHAPTER VIII
THE BIRTH OF THE INSTITUTE

One of the most remarkable features of the events leading up to the formation of the Institute was the atmosphere of secrecy with which discussions were conducted by the 'Organisation Committee', in marked contrast with the public debates in the chemical press. In March 1876, Charles Kingzett, a Fellow of the Chemical Society (and one of the black-ballers) remarked:

> That a provisional committee may be formed which shall invite chemists to attend a meeting, with the view of establishing such a guild, is much to be desired.[1]

and a week later C. H. Piesse, a London public analyst, enquired: 'Can we not hold a provisional meeting, say at the Scientific Club, to discuss our projects and our prospects?'.[2] In fact a meeting had been held the previous year[3] but seems to have been kept secret, and an Organisation Committee was already in existence. When, eventually, an Institute of Chemists was proposed, one Fellow of the Chemical Society complained:

> How is it, Sir, that we Fellows have never been consulted, called to any meeting, or officially communicated with in any way by the Council? Is a great movement to be dealt with without any reference to the constituency by our little Parliament? Is not this for our representatives to take upon themselves to be our masters rather than our servants? So far has this been carried out that I have been unable to obtain copies of counsel's opinion upon the powers of organisation under our charter, although I have applied for such, and have even been shown printed copies! And, though not at all behind the scenes of this absurd and needless mystery, I perceive that the very natural course of asking questions produces a state of irritation, as if one had some malevolent motive in presuming to learn what, as a Fellow, I may fairly term one's own business! Evidently, though a council, a board of directors, or any corporation would not be wise in making the details of their proceedings known to their constituents, yet on the eve of a great and irrevocable movement it is very far from wisdom, courtesy, or respect to allow no opportunity outside their own body of gaining information, of forming a judgement, or expressing an opinion on such vital matters as are now in question. I call upon the Fellows to express their opinions upon this policy of secrecy.[4]

The first, clandestine meeting was held, in 1875, at 15 Billiter Street, the house of Frederick Manning, an analytical chemist who had previously served as chemist to the Mint in Hong Kong.[5] In addition to Manning those present were:

> Michael Carteighe, Examiner to the Pharmaceutical Society
> W. N. Hartley,[6] Demonstrator at King's College, London
> Charles Tookey, another former Assayer at the Hong Kong Mint
> J. M. Thomson,[7] Demonstrator at King's College, London
> C. R. A. Wright, formerly of Newcastle and now Lecturer at St Mary's Hospital, Paddington.

All of these except Tookey (who disappears from the scene after this) played a prominent part in subsequent developments of the Institute. It seems from the scant description given by Pilcher[3] that an Organization Committee was appointed at this meeting, and, since all nominees subsequently appeared on both it and its successor, that there had been some preparatory talk beforehand. This Committee consisted of:

> Carteighe, Manning, Wright and (as Hon Sec *pro tem*) Hartley, as above
> Dugald Campbell,[8] Analytical chemist, London
> Edward Frankland, Professor at the Normal School of Science;
> Theophilus Redwood, Analytical consultant and Professor at the Pharmaceutical Society
> Thomas Stevenson,[9] Lecturer at Guy's Hospital
> R. V. Tuson,[10] Professor at the Royal Veterinary College
> Augustus Voelcker,[11] Consultant chemist, London
> J. A. Wanklyn, Public analyst, Bucks.

Carteighe, Voelcker and Wanklyn all testified to the Select Committee on the Adulteration Act in 1874, the first two being highly critical of analytical practice generally.[12]

Nothing appears to have been done by this Committee whose existence, as we have seen, was unknown to many who might have been expected to be aware of it. Eventually it seems to have been activated by the interest and support raised by Wright's remarks in *Chemical News* of 21 January 1876.[13] It printed a circular in the following terms.[14]

> A MEETING will be held on   , at
>   , to discuss the question of Organisation of the Chemical Profession. The Chair will be taken at   o'clock, by F. A. ABEL, Esq., F.R.S., President of the Chemical Society.
>   PROBABLE ORDER OF BUSINESS.
> Opening Remarks of the Chairman.
> Sketch of proposal for the formation of an 'Institute of Professional Chemists.'
> Sketch of proposal to obtain the desired ends by a development of the Chemical Society.

Remarks.
Motions may probably be to the following effect:—

(1) That it is necessary that an organisation of Professional Chemists should be effected, for the purpose of drawing a marked distinction between properly educated Practitioners and other unqualified persons professing to act as Analytical and Consulting Chemists.

(2) That in order to effect this organisation it is desirable that an electoral body should be formed for the purpose of admitting to the practice of Professional Chemistry such persons only as may be found to be thoroughly competent.

(3) That the qualifications for registration as a duly qualified practitioner should be either—

(a) Having passed through a course of three (?) years' study of theoretical and analytical Chemistry and allied branches of Science under competent recognised teachers, and having subsequently been engaged for three (?) years more either as assistant to some member of the electoral body, as "chemist" in a chemical factory, &c., or,

(b) having, after a due course of training, published an original research on some Chemical subject of sufficient merit in the eyes of the electoral body; or,

(c) having been trained and occupied in some other ways considered by the electoral body as equivalent to fulfilling one of the above conditions.

(4) That if the charter and constitution of the Chemical Society permit of this Society undertaking the responsibilities attached to the electoral body, it is desirable that the desired organisation be effected through the agency of that Society.

AMENDMENT.—That in view of the difficulty in distinguishing between ordinary Fellows of the Chemical Society and qualified Practitioners admitted and registered through the agency of that Society, it is expedient that the desired organisation should be effected by a body wholly distinct and separate from the Chemical Society.

Clearly the Committee had to brace itself for a number of meetings, as is suggested by the blank spaces left for times and places. It had obviously engaged in some preliminary discussion so as to formulate a probable agenda, some tentative motions and an important amendment. The contents of the paper, the rendezvous of the meeting and the identity of the chairman testified to a strong involvement by the Chemical Society even at this early stage. It will be recalled that the public debate so far had *not* connected the Society and the projected Guild or Association, so we may infer that the demand for this came from within the Chemical Society itself. This impression is reinforced by a consideration of the list of names selected by the Committee as recipients of the first circular. This hand-written document[15] contains 124 names, of whom all except four were Fellows of the Chemical Society. Of these no less than sixty—almost half—were or had been office-bearers in the Chemical Society, while over a dozen more were later to join them. The responses to the circular,[16] as indicated by attendance at the meeting called on 27 April, were as follows:

CS officers or Council (past or present)	18
Other CS Fellows at the time	22
Others invited	1

Thus both the original invitations and the responses to them indicate at the outset a heavy involvement by the Chemical Society in the proposed project. The advertised meeting took place on 27 April with forty-six present, forty-one from the original list and five others who do not appear to have been formally invited: W. E. Halse, W. Ramsay and the three analysts H. C. Bartlett, F. Maxwell Lyte and G. W. Wigner. The gate-crashing (if that is what it really was) by these members of the SPA had a significance that will be touched on later. For the first couple of items the meeting seems to have followed the suggested agenda. Doubtless with enthusiastic applause the resolution proposed by Odling and seconded by Frankland was carried unanimously:

> That it is desirable that an organisation of Professional Chemists be effected.

Then, in the spirit, if not quite the letter, of the agenda's suggestion, Gladstone, seconded by Howard, proposed:

> That in order to effect this organisation it is desirable that an electoral body be formed for the purpose of selecting as members of the organisation such persons as may be found to be competent chemists.

Before this could be put to the vote a note of dissension crept in, introduced in true character by J. A. Wanklyn, with the support of C. W. Heaton. With memories of his own black-balling activities nine years previously and his perennial protest against any suggestion of electoral malpractices by minority groups Wanklyn desired 'that the word electoral be omitted', and so the meeting unanimously agreed.

From the minutes in Hartley's bold handwriting[17] it is impossible to tell what impassioned speeches were made or how well the meeting was guided by Abel. What is certain is that from now on they entered turbulent waters as (presumably) they turned to consider the next item, the qualifications for membership of the new organization. No resolution on this subject was recorded for it was becoming apparent that little could be done without reference to the Chemical Society. Accordingly a step was taken that could then have been of momentous importance to relate the two current issues: the need for an organization of chemists and for a resolution of the difficulties of the Chemical Society. Significantly the resolution was proposed by Wright, whose letter on the first issue was beginning to make a stir, and seconded by Friswell who had been active the month before on the abuse of the letters FCS.[18] The meeting unanimously agreed:

That a committee be appointed for the purpose of conferring with the Council of the Chemical Society with a view to ascertaining how far that Society may be able and willing to carry out a scheme for the organisation of Professional Chemists and that this committee be requested to report to the adjourned meeting.[17]

The following names were agreed to, though with how much discussion we have no means of knowing:

Campbell, Carteighe, Frankland, Manning, Redwood, Stevenson, Tuson, Voelcker, Wanklyn, Wright, with Hartley as honorary secretary.[17]

This was identical with the first Organisation Committee. Every man of this 'second eleven' was a Fellow of the Chemical Society, Campbell, Tuson and Wright were on the Council, Wanklyn had been a member before disgracing himself in 1876, and Stevenson had finished in 1874; Voelcker was a Vice-President, while Redwood had only recently stepped down from that office, as had Frankland from the Presidency. Of the others only Manning would end his days without experience at government of the Society.

Judged from outside it must certainly have appeared almost as a 'put-up job' to ensure the Chemical Society's full involvement in the new movement. This is not quite fair because it would have been impossible to proceed very far without at least the goodwill of that Society, and a delegation of this kind would have a greater chance of successful negotiation than one in which non-members were predominant. In any case effectively the same committee existed *before* the meeting. But the circumstances in which the meeting was called make it look as though this may have been what the Council of the Society intended all along. However that may be, secrecy was preserved, and the *Chemical News* for the next few weeks contained the first flood of indignant letters about the Society's affairs with, occasionally, only the darkest of hints that the writers suspected something definite was afoot (Chapter VII).

Before this delegation could meet to consider its tactics the black-ballers turned on their pressure and called forth the wrath of the President by rejecting six out of nine candidates for the Fellowship.[18] Two of these activists were at the Organisation meeting on 27 April: Kingzett (who had already expressed himself forcibly to the Society in speech as well as in voting[19]) and Neison, later to be known as Nevill[20]. We may perhaps see their tactics as efforts to force the Chemical Society's hand into immediate action.

The day after the black-balling incident the committee met on 5 May in Frankland's private room at South Kensington. Rather predictably Frankland was voted to the Chair. A detailed scheme for forming an association was presented by Michael Carteighe and adopted by the Committee. Its main features have been summarized by Pilcher[21]. The main point was the establishment of an 'Institute of Professional Chemists (of Great Britain and Ireland)', with one class of members to be admitted by a Board of twenty-one examiners. This was reminiscent of the practice of the Pharmaceutical Society for which Carteighe was himself an examiner. The crucial question was the appointment and composition of such a Board. On this matter the committee was in favour of total commitment to the Chemical Society. The President and one Vice-President of the Chemical Society would have similar functions on both the new Institute and its Examining Board. Three members of the Institute's Council should be appointed by the Council of the Chemical Society, and sixteen others should be appointed by that Council 'conjointly with this or another enlarged committee' for the first year, all such persons to be Fellows of the Chemical Society; thereafter the Board was to be generated by its predecessor in much the same way as the Chemical Society's Council. Entry was conditional on perhaps three years' 'study of theoretical and analytical chemistry and physics' under recognized teachers, publication of 'an original research' and a further period (three more years?) experience of chemistry.

It was now necessary for these far-reaching proposals to be discussed with the Society itself. The date of the Council meeting was 18 May and it seems that the Organisation Committee were invited to attend in order to discuss the position.[22] The Council then resolved to appoint its own subcommittee to look into the question of whether it would be advantageous for the organization of chemists to be effected from within the Chemical Society, and if so, in what way. This was to consist of Crookes, Gladstone, Heaton, Russell, Tuson and Wright. Of these all except Crookes had been at the inaugural meeting, and his inclusion would ensure that kind of coverage in the *Chemical News* that was deemed appropriate. The nomination of Tuson and Wright is surprising for, according to the minutes of the Organisation Committee of which they were also members, the new subcommittee's role was 'to continue negotiations',[23] in which case they would have, as it were, to sit on both sides of the table at once. What kind of identity crisis they experienced we do not know, but the subcommittee went speedily to work, doubtless with full awareness of the moves being made by its colleagues in the Organisation Committee.

While the subcommittee was thus deliberating the Organisation Committee was far from idle and went so far as to instruct a solicitor to act for them, one J. Pettengill of Walbrook, London. On 9 June the *Chemical News* carried a letter from him, beginning in the following terms:

Sir – Many of your readers will be glad to know that the proposal to establish an Institute of Professional Chemists is assuming a definite form, a scheme for the establishment of the Institute having been already prepared in readiness to be submitted to the Organisation Committee already appointed if the Council of the Chemical Society come to a decision upon the questions now before them affecting that Institute adverse thereto.

Some gentlemen, well known chemists, for whom I am professionally concerned, and who take a great interest in the establishment of the Institute, desiring that the proposed scheme should be brought under the notice of all members of the profession before the Institute is actually formed, have instructed me to address to you this communication as the only means of reaching all persons interested in this important subject.

After outlining the main provisions of the committee's scheme he continued:

The above is a short statement of some of the provisions of the scheme for the organisation of an Institute which, if earnestly supported and judiciously managed, will advance alike the interests of its Members as well as the science to which they devote their talents and life. It is thought that when the name of the Institute and the high qualifications demanded from all persons seeking its membership are known the Institute will carry with it a reputation which will reflect honour upon its Members and will constitute membership a prize to be coveted and a necessity for professional success.

There are several plans of organising a society of this character and the plan to be recommended to their *confrères* has been carefully considered by my clients who are amongst the most active of the many promoters of this enterprise. The several methods of organising the Institute may thus be briefly stated.

1 By special Act of Parliament or Charter.

2 By Deed of Settlement.

3 By Incorporation under Section 23 of the Companies Act 1867.

4 By the publication of Rules and Regulations to be signed by every Member upon his admission as a Member.

Under one of the methods stated in the first and third cases alone can the Institute become a Corporation, but as the Government would not at the present time grant a Charter or support an application for a special Act of Parliament for the Incorporation of the Institute, the only course open to the promoters is to register the Institute as a Joint Stock Company in accordance with the Companies Act, 1867, or to form a Society with or without a Deed of Settlement, which would be in its nature a purely voluntary Society without legal existence and having none of the incidents of a corporate body. After mature reflection my clients think it better that the powers given to them by the Companies Act should be employed.

Such an arrangement, under the Companies Act of 1867 permitted charitable, scientific, religious and similar bodies to enjoy the advantages of being a limited company without having to use the word 'Ltd' in the name. Pettengill concluded by inviting consideration of this proposal before a public meeting which would be held to decide upon it.[24]

There was an immediate reaction to this letter in the periodical in which it appeared. One Council member wrote the next week that since 'this organisation is now being arranged by its natural leaders' black-balling should cease forthwith.[25] It was in the same issue that the *cri de coeur* for openness referred to previously (p. 119) by an anonymous Fellow of the Chemical Society appeared. Another letter touched on the same topic but introduced a new note of dissension:

> We do not know as yet who are Mr Pettengill's 'clients,' but it seems as if they were going to place themselves in a very ambiguous and some-what ridiculous position in one respect. Why on earth should Fellow-ship of the Chemical Society have anything to do with admission to membership of the proposed Institute? Surely this latter ought to be perfectly independent in every respect; and it is, at any rate, a very ill-chosen moment to propose any such rule as requiring candidates for the Institute to first be FCS, when the Fellows are disputing among themselves whether or not any *chemical* qualification is to be demanded before election to their Society, and when their President has distinctly stated that none such should be required.

He concluded:

> All well-wishers of the Chemical Society must be glad to see an agitation which will, perhaps, put an end to this bad state of things. All well-wishers of the proposed Institute will desire that it may in no way connect itself with the Chemical Society, unless the latter is very much reformed in some respects.

The signature at the foot of this missive was highly significant in view of the Chemical Society's apparent course of action: 'Analyst'.[26] Whether the author was a member of the SPA we cannot be sure, but that organization must have been increasingly disenchanted with the bid by its sister society for control of the professionalization issue.

Yet another letter on 16 June came from C. R. A. Wright revealing the nature and composition of the Organisation Committee. His purpose was obviously to allay the mounting suspicions but also to indicate in public (and thus to the Council) that they still had two options open to them:

> The letter of Mr Pettengill clearly shows that the desired results can readily be obtained even without the concurrence and co-operation of the Chemical Society as a body. If, however, at such a general meeting of the Chemical Society the Fellows should give their assent to such alterations in the bye-laws of the Society, and in the constitution and mode of election of its Council, as may be necessary to render fairly

practicable the scheme of uniting under one charter a purely scientific Society with a professional Association, there can be little doubt that this plan will commend itself to the acceptance of those present at the adjourned meeting of the promoters of the organisation movement.[27]

A few days later a communication appeared in *Nature* from W. N. Hartley, in which he forestalled opposition from within the Chemical Society by pointing out that *not* to appoint a Board of Examiners or grant some kind of recognition on those deserving it, would be hardly acting in the interest of the 'general advancement of chemical science for which it [the Society] had been created'.[28]

These letters reflected the discussions taking place in the Council and its subcommittee. The latter had also taken legal advice, including Counsel's opinion as to the feasibility of a separate grade of 'Practising Fellows' within the membership of the Chemical Society. The view of Mr W. Cracroft Fooks, QC, was that such a grade could be established and an examining body could be constituted and remunerated. This would require alteration to the bye-laws.[29]

In the light of this advice the subcommittee compiled a confidential Report to the Council, advocating 'a scheme for the organisation of Professional Chemists as a distinct section of the Fellows of the Society',[29] since this would help to achieve one of the Society's declared objectives, 'the general advancement of chemical science'. In this respect they differed radically from the Organisation Committee whose intentions, at least at first, had been to establish an independent Institute. The proposals incorporated in the Report included detailed draft regulations that owed a good deal to Carteighe's original ideas.

The Council received its subcommittee's report at its meeting on 15 June. It resolved that the Chemical Society should 'take such steps for the establishment of an organisation of professional chemists as are compatible with the terms of the Society's charter and the full control of the Council over the proposed organisation'.[30]

A week later (22 June) a special meeting of the Council approved a series of measures for recommendation to the Organisation Committee. This accepted most of the subcommittee's suggestions: the notion of 'practising fellows'; the Examining Board of fifty with at least ten members retiring annually; the Board to recommend replacements; the Treasurer to have charge of the fees, with payments made to examiners who were not members of Council, etc. The Council did not endorse its subcommittee's recommendation for a 25-year minimum age for candidates, nor did it spell out details of the course of training required.[31]

When this report reached the Organisation Committee its 'best thanks . . . to the Council . . . for the care and consideration shown in framing the scheme' were no doubt sincerely conveyed, but with also a firm indication that the unanimous wish of that committee was to change the title 'Practising Fellow of the Chemical Society'. This resolution on 1 July, proposed by Carteighe and seconded by Tuson, reflected the general feeling that the earlier title was not a sufficiently distinctive one and that 'Fellow of the Chemical Institute of the Chemical Society' was preferable.[32]

On receipt of this communication the Council sought further legal advice regarding the proposed change in name. The Counsel, Joshua Williams, regarded the new title as 'calculated to mislead and on that account objectionable'. Although Williams expressed himself in agreement with the opinion of Fooks he went on to make an additional point:

> We are of opinion, however, that the Society have no power to organise a separate Body of its Fellows under either of the titles indicated or any other title which shall have authority to confer upon its members any special privilege as incident to the title they may bear or which shall have authority to exercise powers of self-management regulation control and discipline (as appears to be contemplated by some of the foregoing suggested proposals) or any other powers which shall override or be otherwise than subordinate and subservient to the powers of the General Meetings of the Fellows and those of the Council as prescribed by the terms of the Charter.[33]

It is curious that Fooks did not make this point, but conflict of legal opinion is far from rare and the Council do not seem to have been unduly perturbed by those remarks which they probably took as advising caution only. However, at their next meeting on 29 July they did agree to convey the following information to the Secretary of the Organisation Committee:

> That the Council of the Chemical Society, having taken Counsel's opinion on the proposition to alter the proposed title 'Practising Fellow of the Chemical Society' to 'Fellow of the Chemical Institute of the Chemical Society' and having fully discussed its bearings with reference to the powers of the Chemical Society, are of opinion that such alteration is undesirable.[34]

The Organisation Committee, having received this communication at its meeting on 1 August, tendered its 'warmest thanks' to the Council and resolved to postpone any action until more members were available after the summer holiday.[35]

On 13 October the Organisation Committee set to work again. How long their deliberations took is not clear from the minutes but their conclusion was terse and decisive; that Frankland should inform the Chemical Society's President 'of the insuperable difficulties the Committee find in approving of that Scheme submitted to them by the Council of the Chemical Society and of the decision of this Committee that a separate organisation is desirable'.[36]

Accordingly Frankland wrote to Abel officially intimating that:

> The Committee regret that the obstacles of carrying out within the Chemical Society the wishes of the promoters of the Organisation Scheme appear after mature deliberation to be so formidable as to render it undesirable to prosecute the attempt further; but they trust that any independent scheme which may be inaugurated will be carried out in friendly alliance with the Society and will receive the sympathy and support of its Fellows.[37]

This momentous letter, dated 16 October 1876, closed the door to any immediate possibility of professional functions being undertaken by the Chemical Society.

The issues underlying these differences of view were deep and complex. Moreover, they were by no means exclusively of a purely temporary and local nature, and the following century has seen them arise time and time again, not least in connection with the movements of the 1970s. It may for that reason be of more than passing interest to note how they were seen in 1876 by one of the chief participants, C. R. A. Wright. His comments were expressed in a letter to *Chemical News* on 30 June, and are particularly valuable because he, of all people, was in a position to see things from the viewpoints of both parties.

He began with an extremely frank admission:

> I may as well premise that since the publication of my first communication on the subject (CHEMICAL NEWS, vol. xxxiii., p. 40) my own views have undergone more than one change. At first, I was disposed to think that the objects of the desired association or guild of chemical practitioners were entirely different from the ground hitherto covered by the Chemical Society; that the policy of that Society hitherto adopted rendered it unsuitable as an origin of the desired association; and that the Society and the Professional Association were entirely separate in their nature, and incapable of fusion together without injury to both. I subsequently was led to think that there were numerous difficulties in the way of establishing such a separate association: and that although a scheme for organisation through the Chemical Society would not by any means do all that seemed necessary and desirable to be done, it would nevertheless enable a distinction to be made between competent and incompetent men, and that it might be preferable to sacrifice a portion of the ends to be aimed at in order to facilitate the attainment of some of them. Finally, an attentive study of the nature of the steps which appear to be possible for the Society to take under the existing Charter has induced me entirely to revert to my former opinions. So few of the results aimed at by organisation appear to be likely to be effectively attained if this be attempted to be carried out through the Society that I am

reluctantly compelled to believe that in proposing to do anything of the kind the Society will only weaken itself by uselessly stirring up dissention amongst its members.

Before addressing himself to this particular problem he dealt with an objection to a professional association in general:

It has been objected that this is a 'Trades' Union'. So it is, in the same sense that the legal and medical organisations of this country, the Established Church, and many other institutions of repute are 'Trades' Unions'. An association of professional men (*i.e.*, brain-workers) for the mutual advantage of the community at large, and of themselves, does in truth bear considerable resemblance in many respects to an organisation for the same purposes amongst handicrafts men: in fact, the chief distinction lies in the nature of the work done, mental *versus* bodily. These correlations and differences are embodied in the very term 'Professional Association'.

Wright then proceeded to examine the principal arguments for and against the Association's origin in the Chemical Society.

Dealing with the arguments in favour of this approach he cited the desirability of achieving unity in the profession which would be more likely with than without the Chemical Society if that Society could permit itself to be the centre of such a movement. Were an entirely separate Institute to form, the Society might suffer financially and the Institute might find itself confronted with a rival association formed from its own rejected candidates and other opponents. In practical terms 'various influential men' were supposed to be prepared to support an Institute based on the Society but not one that was independent. However in all these arguments there is the necessity to make a judgement as to the balance of probabilities and, on the whole, Wright was not convinced by any of these considerations.

Turning to arguments that favoured a separate Institute, Wright remarked on the inadvisability of what inevitably must be a 'Movement of a most reforming character' with a Society that was in a condition of instability and liable to be rent asunder by future dissension. More particularly he saw grave drawbacks arising from the Charter of the Chemical Society. First, the system of personal voting at the annual election was not suitable for a professional association whose Board should be elected by *all* members; second, it was legal opinion that no other title than Fellow could apply to 'the body of professionally competent men', and the application of qualifying adjectives like 'Professional' or 'Practising', though possible, was likely to be unacceptable to the present membership; third a Board of Management could not exercise executive power because the Charter restricts that prerogative to the Council itself. As he saw it:

One natural result which would spring from the establishment of such a Board would be that the Professional Fellows of the Chemical Society would combine together so as to alter the mode of electing the Council, and so to influence the elections as always would ensure the decisions of the Board being of necessity ratified so far as the Council could ratify them; in other words, the Council would become not the managing committee of a purely scientific society, but that of a professional association pure and simple. Alterations in bye-laws other than those relating to the constitution of the Council would be gradually introduced; intestine squabbles in the Society would be rendered imminent; and, finally, neither the Society nor the Association would be an institution of stability. From the point of view of the interests of the Society, it seems extremely undesirable that such a course should be adopted as will inevitably lead to disputes and revolutionary measures. The tendency towards the latter is already strongly marked, but is as yet only taking the direction of useful reforms. The importation into the question of other considerations, however, might tend to pervert reform into total anarchy.

Given these difficulties in the Charter there remained the possibility of exchanging it for a new one. He did not see that the present membership would ever achieve the necessary unity for this to be practicable, 'whilst even if every existing Fellow desired it, it is very improbable that such a new charter would be granted'. Consequently, he said, 'it is now tolerably clear to me that if a Professional Association of an effective character is to be originated, it must be apart from the Chemical Society'.[38]

On this conclusion Pilcher has an illuminating comment. Sensitive to the aspirations of the Institute in 1914, when he was writing, he observed that Wright did 'not appear to have realized the influence which the Institute would have on the progress of scientific education and research'.[39] But to accuse Wright for lack of prophetic insight is as unfair as it would be to arraign Pilcher for a deficiency in historical understanding. As things stood in 1876 it was totally unclear what later developments might be; and in so far as Wright could identify future roles for Institute and Society it was the former, not the latter, that looked like being a custodian of radical new ideas. As we shall see things did not turn out quite as simply as that. In the political climate of the two groups *at that time* it looks as though Wright's judgement was essentially sound.

Much insight into the 'insuperable difficulties' may be gained from Wright's analysis. There is also another place in which a clue may be found, and that is in the opinion expressed by the second Counsel, Joshua Williams, retained to advise on the change of title. It is hard to conceive that the Organisation Committee was inflexibly committed to a title: 'Fellow of the Chemical Institute of the Chemical Society', yet we read they were unanimous in objecting to 'Practising Fellow of the Chemical Society'. It was, however, this new title that was decisively ruled out by Williams[33] and seems to have raised his suspicions as to the propriety of the whole enterprise. We can recall that the compliant Fooks was confronted with everything *except* this provocative title. What raised legal hackles seems therefore to have been the concept of an Institute within a Society and capable of exercising some degree of self-governance.

Now it would not appear impossible to have got round these difficulties (even in the opinion of the wary Williams) given sufficient goodwill and determination. What now seems apparent is that there was plenty of the latter but not too much of the former. In fact Williams had touched a very sensitive nerve: the question of power and control. The Council, as we have seen, were adamant on their right to 'full control' over the new institution. The Organisation Committee, however, seems to have thought otherwise. It will not have been forgotten that amongst their number was the idiosyncratic and independent Wanklyn, while in the wings lay the numerous black-ballers whose avowed aim was to cut the Council's powers down to size. But perhaps the person most to reckon with was Edward Frankland. Outwardly shy and having to be apparently bullied to take on the Presidency of the Chemical Society in 1871[40] he was nevertheless an extremely astute politician and a great man for exerting pressure behind the scenes. Was he not the most diligent attender at 'the Albemarle Street conspiracy'—that influential pressure group known as the X-Club?[41] Now in the mid-1870s he was in something of a personal crisis. His wife had died in 1874 and he remarried the following year. His research was apparently coming to an end for he was collecting together all his published papers for issue as a book.[42] His six-year term of service with the Royal Commission on River Pollution was completed in 1874 and now, almost for the first time since 1858 he no longer held office in the Chemical Society. Ludicrous though it would be to assert that the foundation of a separate Institute was simply an outcome of Frankland's need to exercise creative leadership, it cannot be far from the mark to suggest that it played some part in forging a temporary alliance with his old enemy Wanklyn, and breaking away from the Society he had served for so long. He did, of course, remain a Fellow of the Chemical Society, though after 1876 his few remaining papers graced the pages of the Royal Society's *Proceedings*.

By the autumn of 1876 it was fairly clear the way things were going. On 4 November the adjournment of the inaugural meeting was convened at the Chemical Society's room. A document was read out as the *Report of Committee appointed to confer with the Council of the Chemical Society* (too long to reproduce here). After briefly outlining the course of negotiations since May it now proposed 'formation of a new and independent body'. It is not clear how many were present on this occasion at the meeting, but after the usual expression of gratitude to the Chemical

Society Council the delegates gave unanimous approval to the following resolution:

> That having regard to the limited powers of the Chemical Society under its Charter, it is desirable that an Association be formed that shall be independent of the Chemical Society, and that the following gentlemen, or such of them as may be willing to act, form a new Committee (with power to add to their number) to settle the form and details of the scheme and to take all steps necessary to secure the formation and incorporation of the proposed new Association.[43]

There followed a list of fifty names, together with that of the President of the Chemical Society, Professor Abel. The membership is indicated in Table 1 on p. 150.

The new committee lost no time in settling down to work. On 25 November, twenty-eight of its members assembled at Burlington House for the first meeting. Frankland was appointed Chairman, Hartley, Secretary, Dittmar of Glasgow and Dr Graham of University College, London as additional members, Williamson, Abel and Voelcker as Vice-Chairmen and Wright as a second secretary. So far every decision was unanimous but tensions began to manifest themselves when Kingzett and Friswell proposed one of their black-balling colleagues, Neison, as another secretary. Whether or not their proposal was seen as an attempt to reintroduce radical extremism of an unwelcome kind is not sure, but Redwood and Paul moved in to propose an amendment to the effect that appointment of secretaries should be deferred. This was carried by a majority of six votes. The black-ballers had their revenge when a motion was put by Attfield and Voelcker to add another thirty names to the committee (most of them 'establishment' figures like Playfair and Brodie); Neison and Kingzett proposed the amendment that no further names should be added at present, and this was carried unanimously. But the most important decision of the meeting was to appoint a small subcommittee of seven to prepare a new draft scheme. It was a well-chosen array of talent and interest. Abel might be said to represent the Chemical Society establishment in an informal way; Wright brought un-doubted political expertise, and Hartley had already proved his worth as secretary to the previous committees; Carteighe was both a pioneer of the whole venture and a valuable link with the Pharmaceutical Society; Voelcker was *persona grata* with the analytical community. But in terms of academic versus practical chemistry the academics, i.e., those concerned with teaching or research, had a clear majority.[44]

Throughout the winter of 1876–7 the subcommittee was active, holding no less than seven meetings, and on 24 February 1877, they presented to the full committee their findings and recommendations.[45] These took the form of a printed pamphlet now in the possession of the Institute. It pro-

TABLE 1   Founders of the Institute of Chemistry

Highest offices held to 1877 (1882 for SCI):

M = Member	T = Treasurer
F = Fellow	FS = Foreign Secretary
H = Honorary Member	S = Secretary
P = President	C = Council Member
V = Vice-President	R = on Register of Pharm. Soc. but not MPS

		First Meeting (informal)	1st and 2nd Committees	Second Meeting	3rd Committee	First Council	Chem. Soc.	SPA	Pharm. Soc.	SCI	Royal Soc.
Abel, F. A.	Chemist, War Dept., Woolwich			M	M	V	P	H		M	F
Allen, A. H.	Public Analyst, Sheffield				M		F	C		M	
Armstrong, H. E.	Prof., London Institution			M	M		C			M	F
Attfield, J.	Prof., Pharmaceutical Soc.			M	M	M	C	M	R	M	
Bell, I. L.	Iron & steel mfr., Teesside				M		C			M	F
Bell, James	Principal, Inland Revenue Lab.				M	M	F	H			
Bloxham, C. L.	Prof., King's Coll., London				M		C				
Brown, A. Crum	Prof., Edinburgh University				M	V	C				
Campbell, Dugald	Chemist, Brompton Hospital		M		M		C				
Carteighe, M.	Examiner, Pharmaceutical Soc.	M	M	M	M	M	C		C	M	
Crookes, William	Editor, *Chemical News*			M	M	M	C	M		M	F
Davis, G. E.	Chemist, alkali works, Runcorn				M		F			M	
Dewar, James	Prof., Cambridge University				M		C			M	
Dittmar, W.	Prof., Anderson's Coll., Glasgow					M				M	
Dupré, A.	Lect., Westminster Hospital			M	M		C	P		M	F
Field, F.	Partner in candle manufacturers				M		C				F
Frankland, E.	Prof., Royal School of Mines			M	M	M	P	P	H	M	C
Friswell, R. J.	Chemist in pottery works			M	M	M	F			M	
Galloway, R.	Prof., Mus. Irish Ind., Dublin				M	V	F				
Gladstone, J. H.	Prof., Royal Institution			M	M	M	V	H		M	C
Gore, G.	Schoolteacher & researcher, B'ham			M	M						F
Groves, C. E.	Analytical chemist, London			M	M	M	C			M	
Hartley, W. N.	Dem., King's Coll., London	M	M	M	M	M	C			M	
Heaton, C. W.	Asst., Royal Veterinary Coll.			M	M		C	T		M	
Herman, D. de L.	Chemist, St Helens glassworks			M	M		F			M	
Howard, D.	Manufacturing chemist, London			M	M	M	C	H		M	
Kingzett, C. T.	Analytical chemist, London			M	M	M	F			M	
Manning, F. A.	Analytical chemist, London	M	M	M	M	M	F			M	
Marreco, A. F.	Prof., Newcastle Coll. Phys. Sci.			M	M		F				
Mills, E. J.	Prof., Anderson's Coll., Glasgow			M	M	M	C			M	F
Müller, Hugo	Partner in printing firm				M		FS			M	F
Neison, E.	Analytical chemist, London			M	M	M	F			M	
Odling, W.	Prof., Oxford University			M	M	V	P	H	M	M	F
Page, F. J. M.	Asst., St Thomas' Hospital				M		F			M	
Pattinson, J.	Analyst, Newcastle-upon-Tyne			M		M	F	M		M	
Paul, B. H.	Analyst, Westminster				M		F	M	R		
Perkin, W. H.	Dyestuff manufacturer, London				M		S			M	F
Piesse, C. H.	Chemist, St Thomas' Hospital			M	M		F	M			
Redwood, Theophilus	Prof., Pharmaceutical Soc.		M		M	M	S	P	M	M	
Reynold, E.	Prof., Trinity Coll., Dublin				M	M	S			M	
Russell, W. J.	Lect., Bart's Hospital			M	M		S	H		M	F
Smith, R. Angus	Alkali Inspector, Manchester				M	V	C	H			F
Sprengel, H.	Independent research worker				M		C			M	
Stevenson, T.	Lect., Guy's Hospital		M		M	M	C	T		M	
Tatlock, R. R.	Prof., Anderson's Coll., Glasgow			M	M		F	T		M	
Teschemacher, E. F.	Analytical chemist, London				M	M	F				
Thomson, J. M.	Dem., King's Coll., London	M					F			M,	
Tookey, C.	Museum worker, London	M					F				
Tuson, R. V.	Prof., Royal Veterinary Coll.		M	M	M	M	C				
Voelcker, A.	Consultant chemist, London		M		M	V	C			M	F
Wanklyn, J. A.	Public Analyst, Bucks.		M		M		C	V			
Way, J. T.	Consultant chemist, London			M		M	C				
Williamson, A. W.	Prof., University Coll., London			M	M	M	P	H		M	F
Wright, C. R. A.	Lect., St Mary's Hospital, London	M	M	M	M	T	C	H		M	

posed that 'The Institute of Professional Chemists of Great Britain and Ireland' should be formed:

1   To promote and encourage a thorough study of Chemistry and the allied branches of Science in their application to the Arts, Manufactures, to Agriculture, and Public Health.

2   To ensure that persons practising as Consulting Chemists, or as Analytical Chemists, are qualified by study and training for the competent discharge of the duties they undertake.

3   To carry out measures necessary for the maintenance of the profession on a satisfactory basis.

The now familiar grades of Fellowship and Associateship were introduced together with detailed regulations as to their admission.

With one minor amendment the document was accepted as it stood and the subcommittee was 'reappointed to take all necessary steps for the incorporation of the Institute'. The first list of Fellows was approved, the existing committee together with forty-eight other names of whom the vast majority held senior academic positions. Further suggestions were requested from the subcommittee. Frankland was elected President of the new Institute, with Vice-Presidents Abel, Crum Brown, Galloway, R. A. Smith, Odling and Voelcker, while Wright was appointed Treasurer. Twenty-seven persons were appointed to the first Council (Table 1).

On 19 June 1877, the Council of the Institute held its first meeting with fifteen present, together with the President and the acting Secretary, W. N. Hartley.[46] The main business was to consider the outcome of negotiations with the Board of Trade conducted by the solicitor Mr J. Pettengill, who was also in attendance. Considerable difficulties had arisen originating, it seems, in the position of the Pharmaceutical Society, and centring on the meaning of the word 'chemist'. According to the Pharmacy Act of 1868 that term was reserved for those who had passed the Pharmaceutical Society's minor or major examinations, respectively known as *chemists and druggists* or as *pharmaceutical chemists*. As R. B. Pilcher observed this meant that not even the President of the Chemical Society could, in law, be described as a 'chemist'![47] This was the view conveyed to the Board of Trade from the Privy Council to whom they had applied for advice and who were, under the provisions of the Pharmacy Act, the supervising authority over the Pharmaceutical Society. It was not, it seems, any expression of hostility on the part of the Pharmaceutical Society,[48] one of whose officers (Carteighe) had actually suggested the title. However, the Board of Trade were insistent and the Council had no alternative but to climb down gracefully and so it was resolved that the name be changed to THE INSTITUTE OF CHEMISTRY OF GREAT BRITAIN AND IRELAND. In conformity with the need to avoid all suggestion of trespass on the Pharmaceutical Society's preserves the Council also agreed 'that no Fellow or Associate be entitled to a Certificate of his Fellowship of Associateship'.[46] After a decision to recognize examinations of institutions recognized by the Council, the meeting terminated with a charge to the subcommittee to 'secure the registration of the Institute at the earliest possible opportunity'.[46]

Further correspondence with the Board of Trade ensued and at a meeting on 9 July the subcommittee was apprised by Mr Pettengill of a further objection.[49] It emerged that the object 'to ensure that Consulting Chemists and Analytical Chemists are qualified by study and training for the proper discharge of their duties they undertake' was unacceptable 'because it appeared to point to the granting of certificates and nothing else' and because it seemed 'to cast a doubt on the fitness of the Pharmaceutical Society to perform their duties' of seeing that consulting chemists are properly qualified.[50] Accordingly the Council had the option of further compliance or settling for establishment as a purely private society with all the disadvantages of that arrangement. They decided to comply on condition that the succeeding object was modified as follows:

> To adopt such measures as may be necessary for the advancement of the profession of chemistry and particularly for the maintenance of the profession of the consulting and analytical chemist on a sound and satisfactory basis.[49]

On 2 October 1877, the licence of incorporation was granted by the Board of Trade. An Extraordinary General Meeting on 1 November dropped the entrance fee from five to two guineas[51] and at a meeting sixteen days later the first officers of the Institute were declared Fellows, and, at a Council meeting on the same day, Hartley was (doubtless to his relief) replaced by a permanent secretary, C. E. Groves, a position he held until 1892.[52] At the first Anniversary meeting on 1 February 1878, the Secretary could report that over sixty inquiries had been received and ninety-three candidates had applied for admission.[53]

One final point needs to be made concerning the foundation of the Institute of Chemistry. Its relations with the Chemical Society and the Pharmaceutical Society have been touched upon, but little has been said of the role of the Society of Public Analysts. This is because the public manifestations of that Society's concern did not take place until after the main events recorded above, and also because, in some senses at least, these relations were to prove of the profoundest importance.

Although the correspondence columns of *Chemical News* and other periodicals contained occasional misgivings vented by 'Analyst' or similar authors, the chief onslaught on the new Institute came early in 1877 when *The Analyst* mounted a series of editorials and letters at the activities of the Organisation Committee. Most of the contributors were SPA members, though the paper was not yet the Society's official organ.[54] The paper itself exuded self-righteousness: 'In pleasant contrast to the hole and corner work of attempted private organisation, stands out the Society of Public Analysts'.[55] It called for a new public meeting, circulation to 'every professional chemist in the kingdom', and a 'really representative committee'.[56] This was the opposition decried by the *Pharmaceutical Journal*, but the *Analyst* was unrepentant.[57] Towards the end of November its rival observed that 'this excellent contemporary . . . although it has ceased to rail, still whines'.[58]

It is impossible not to have a good deal of sympathy with the grievances of the analysts. After all it was their cause that the Institute was supposed to be championing. But the Organisation Committee seemed to have an almost wilful disregard for their opinions and gave evidence time and time again that it was, in reality, far more in sympathy with the brand of chemistry more associated with the Chemical Society and traditionally named 'academic'. The tension between 'academic' and 'practising' chemists is never more apparent than here.

At the inaugural meeting many notable analytical consultants were not invited and three of the gatecrashers came into that category.[59] The composition of the Organisation Committees reflected a similar tendency, with academics in the majority. When it came to nominating Fellows even Pilcher admits that 'the Organisation Committee certainly overlooked some well-known chemists' though he went on to add that 'the matter was so widely discussed in scientific journals that there was little reason for complaint, and any chemist could have got in touch with the Founders had he so wished.'[60] But, as Chirnside and Hamence so aptly remark, 'this was to miss the real point at issue; there were not a few Public Analysts and Consulting Chemists who should have been included in the invitation issued by the preliminary Organizing Committee to become initial or founding members, but these had been left to make voluntary application for membership after the body had been actually formed'.[61] These authors charitably attribute the dissensions 'to failures in communication' and, in a technical sense, they are right. But there appears too much evidence to lead us to suppose that exclusion of perfectly competent analysts was not deliberate.

There is, however, another side to the picture which Pilcher does not mention. The academic chemists had in their favour a commitment to take definite steps to raise and maintain standards, using ultimately the examination system as an instrument. The SPA for its part seemed disinclined to do anything in this direction[62] and so could appear to have automatically ruled itself out of court as an effective agent. Again, there is considerable danger in inferring too much from short 'job titles' like those beloved by Victorian chemists and used in Table 1. The fact was that many of those founders— probably most of them—held posts in plurality. Many of the 'professors' also ran lucrative consultancies on the side, and none more effectively than Frankland himself. In other words the majority of the Organisation Committee could without prevarication assert that this consisted of analytical consultants. On the other hand such plurality was much less common amongst Public Analysts. Indeed they were sometimes regarded as only food analysts, which they tended to be at first. If this is so the issue is not even that between 'academics' and 'practising chemists'. It is between those who do many things and those who do one; it is between the generalist and the specialist. Such were the social and economic conditions of late Victorian England that it was the former who inevitably won.　　　　　　　　　　　　　　CAR

NOTES AND REFERENCES

1 *Chem. News*, 1876, **33**, 107.

2 *Ibid.*, p. 116.

3 R. B. Pilcher, *History of the Institute, 1877–1914*, Institute of Chemistry, London, 1914, p. 24.

4 Marshall Hall, *Chem. News*, 1877, **35**, 19, (12 January). Hall, a barrister, wrote to the Chemical Society Council with a request to see the relevant documents, but this was 'not acceded to' (Chem. Soc. Council minutes, 21 December 1876).

5 On Manning, see *Boase*.

6 Later Sir W. N. Hartley, from 1879 Professor at the Royal College of Science, Dublin; see *Proc. Roy. Soc.*, (A), 1914, **90**, vi–xiii.

7 See K. R. Webb, *J.R.I.C.*, 1962, **86**, 177–8.

8 See *J. Chem. Soc.*, 1882, **43**, 252–3.

9 See *DNB, J. Chem. Soc.*, 1909, **95**, 2213–15; and K. R. Webb, *J.R.I.C.*, 1960, **84**, 422–4.

10 On Tuson, see *Boase*.

11 On A. Voelcker, see *DNB, Boase*, and *J. Roy. Agric. Soc.*, 1885, **21**, 308–21.

12 *Report from the Select Committee on the Adulteration of Food Act (1872)*, (262), P.P. 1874, VI.

13 *Chem. News*, 1876, **33**, 27.

14 Papers relating to 'The Organisation of the Chemical Profession', at the Royal Institute of Chemistry, cited as *Organisation Papers*. Pilcher (note 3) obviously had access to these documents.

15 *Ibid.* a foolscap hand-written paper.

16 *Ibid.*, and Pilcher (note 3) pp. 31–2.

17 *Organisation Papers*, pp. 1–3.

18 *Chem. News*, 1876, **33**, 220. On Friswell see *J. Soc. Chem. Ind.*, 1908, **27**, 150.

19 *Chem. News*, 1876, **33**, 106–7.

20 On Neison, see *Proc. Inst. Chem.*, 1940, **64**, 68.

21 Pilcher (note 3), pp. 32–3.

22 Chem. Soc. Council minutes, 18 May 1876.

23 *Organisation Papers*, p. 11 (Organisation minutes, 18 May 1876).

24 *Chem. News*, 1876, **33**, 240–1.

25 N. S. Maskelyne, *ibid.*, pp. 246–7.

26 *Ibid.*, pp. 249–50.

27 *Ibid.*, pp. 250–1.

28 *Nature*, 1876, **14**, 169 (22 June), a response to a slightly frigid editorial (*ibid.*, p. 126).

29 Chem. Soc. Council papers with minutes for 15 June 1876. These papers have been extensively, though not completely, quoted by J. F. Thorpe in an address on 'The past and future of the Institute' at a meeting of the London and South-eastern Counties Section on 17 February 1937, and reproduced in *Proc. Inst. Chem.*, 1937, **61**, 162–72. Thorpe said he had relied 'almost entirely on the Council Minutes of the Chemical Society', and, though a former President of the Institute, appeared unaware of the *Organisation Papers* in its possession.

30 Chem. Soc. Council minutes, 15 June 1876.

31 *Ibid.*, 22 June 1876.

32 *Organisation Papers*, p. 19 (1 July).

33 Chem. Soc. minutes, 29 July 1876; Joshua Williams was then the leading expert in real property law, Professor to the Inns of Court and one of the most popular barristers of the day (see *DNB*).

34 Chem. Soc. minutes, 29 July 1876 (proposed by Attfield, seconded by Gladstone).

35 *Organisation Papers*, p. 23 (1 August). The diligent Pettengill on 6 August did, however, publish a further letter (*Chem. News*, 1876, **34**, 62–3), clarifying the position and inviting suggestions from readers.

36 *Organisation Papers*, p. 24 (13 October).

37 Chem. Soc. minutes, 26 October, 1876.

38 *Chem. News*, 1876, **33**, 269–71.

39 Pilcher (note 3), p. 36.

40 H. E. Armstrong, *Chem. & Ind.*, 1934, **12**, 464: 'In 1871 we had practically to force him to become President of the Chemical Society. I was a ring-leader.'

41 Autobiographical *Sketches from the Life of Sir Edward Frankland, edited and concluded by his two daughters M. N. W. and S. J. C.*, printed for private circulation, 1902, p. 162.

42 E. Frankland, *Experimental Researches in Pure, Applied, and Physical Chemistry*, London, 1877. The omission of any reference on the title-page to his connection with the Chemical Society (though many other affiliations are mentioned) may not have been such 'a curious oversight' as his obituarist supposed (H. McLeod, *J. Chem. Soc.*, 1905, **87**, 590; he also incorrectly cites the date as 1887).

43 *Organisation Papers*, p. 26 and attached printed Report (4 November).

44 *Ibid.*, pp. 31–7 (25 November); Frankland and Nelson were the others.

45 *Ibid.*, p. 38. The subcommittee's records before 23 June 1877 do not seem to have survived.

46 *Ibid.*, pp. 46–9, (minutes of Council, 19 June).

47 Pilcher (note 3), p. 42.

48 Plans for the Institute were cordially reported in the Pharmaceutical Society's organ in November 1876 and again in the following July and November (*Pharm. J.*, 1876–7, **7**, 375–6; 1877–8, **8**, 61, 403).

49 *Organisation Papers*, pp. 52–3 (minutes of subcommittee, 9 July).

50 Letter from Board of Trade to Pettengill, 2 July 1877, in Pilcher (note 3), pp. 41–2. The whole question of the attitude of the Pharmaceutical Society was quite complex and the subject of protracted correspondence. The following is an outline, derived chiefly from the Society's Council minutes (*PSC*) and those of its Law and Parliamentary Committee (*LPC*). All dates are 1877.

26 April Board of Trade (H. E. Calcraft) to Institute (Pettengill). Suggestions for modifying Articles of Association (*LPC*, pp. 102–3).

2 May Institute (Pettengill) to Board of Trade. Modifications acceptable. Licence requested on the basis that pharmacists and Institute members perform separate functions and public need protection in *both* cases (letter in *LPC*, pp. 102–4).

9 May Privy Council (E. L. Peel) to Pharm. Soc. Requests observations on Pettengill's proposals (letter in *LPC*, p. 102).

15 May Committee decide to seek clause to protect the powers and privileges of the Pharmaceutical Society (*LPC*, pp. 104–5).

18 May Pharm. Soc. to Privy Council.

5 June Institute (Frankland) to Pharm. Soc. Meets objections raised by Privy Council and reports Organisation Committee's proposed alteration in title to Institute of Chemistry and removal of certification clause (letter *PSC*, p. 62). (In fact the Committee did not consider this formally until 19 June.)

6 June Council resolves President and G. W. Sandford to look into proposed Articles and, if satisfied, to withdraw opposition (*PSC*, p. 62).

11 June J. Williams (Pres., Pharm. Soc.) to Frankland. 'On the part of the Council of the Pharmaceutical Society there exists every desire to facilitate the object which your Committee have in view, so far as is consistent with the duties entrusted to the Council.' But seeks some safeguard against later changes in Articles of Association, possibly in the Memorandum of Association (letter *LPC*, pp. 117–18).

16 June Board of Trade (H. E. Calcraft) to Pharm. Soc. In accordance with the exchange of letters between Williams and Frankland (5 and 11 June) Board proposes to settle Memorandum and amended Articles unless any further objection lodged (letter *LPC*, pp. 118–9).

19 June Pharm. Soc. (E. Brembridge, Secretary and Registrar) to Board of Trade. The Society 'can take no further exception to Registration of the Association' (letter *LPC*, p. 119).

22 June Board of Trade (H. E. Calcraft) to Pharm. Soc. Points out that although certification has been struck out of Clause 57 (*a*) it remains in 57 (*b*), and asks for this to be brought to attention of Council (letter *LPC*, pp. 119–20).

23 June Pharm. Soc. (Brembridge) to Board of Trade. Letter acknowledged (letter *LPC*, p. 120).

25 June Pharm. Soc. (Brembridge) to Board of Trade. Society had inferred from Board's letter of 16 June that removal of reference to certification would be 'not merely in one clause, but in all'. Goes on to say 'I am instructed by the President to say that the Pharmaceutical Society can take no objection to the granting "the rank or degree of Fellow or Associate" of the Institute of Chemistry to those connected therewith' (letter *LPC*, pp. 121–2).

In the light of this correspondence it is not difficult to understand the prevalence of the notion that the Pharmaceutical Society was urged to opposition by the Privy Council. This opinion, attributed to Attfield at the first General Meeting of the Institute (*Pharm. J.*, 1877–8, **8**, 643), was later denied by him and also contradicted by Sandford who argued that the real point at issue was the title of the new Institute (*ibid.*, p. 663). The battles over the right of the Pharmaceutical Society's exclusive use of the term 'chemist' continued for many years, though its solicitor, William Flux, hardly did the Institute's case justice as not being 'more than some idea of a sentimental character savouring of a breach of the 10th Commandment' (*PSC*, 23 April 1879).

51 Pilcher (note 3), p. 51.

52 *Ibid.*, p. 55.

53 *Pharm. J.*, 1877–8, **8**, 643.

54 Commencing with editorial comments advising 'real working analysts' to regard the scheme 'with considerable caution' (*Analyst*, 1877, **2,** 16).

55 *Ibid.*, p. 71.

56 *Ibid.*, p. 93.

57 *Ibid.*, p. 109.

58 *Pharm. J.*, 1877–8, **8,** 403.

59 These were F. Maxwell Lyte, H. C. Bartlett (who said he attended 'only by right as a Fellow of the Chemical Society' (*Analyst*, 1877, **2,** 31)), and G. W. Wigner. The latter sought to persuade the Council of the SPA to accept some involvement in the early discussions. Seeking to amend a motion (by Dupré and Heaton) 'that it is not at present desirable for the Society to take any action in the matter', he urged, with Muter, 'that it is desirable that some member attend the meeting in question as representing the Council and to explain the position of the Society in reference to the proposed organisation' (SPA Council minutes, 26 April 1876). The amendment was lost after the original motion was carried by 5 votes to 3. Wigner's gate-crashing was therefore entirely on his own personal initiative.

60 Pilcher (note 3), p. 38.

61 R. C. Chirnside and J. H. Hamence, *The 'Practising Chemists': a History of the Society for Analytical Chemistry 1874–1974*, SAC, London, 1974, p. 35.

62 The disinclination of the SPA is clearly evident from its minute books. Over the organization issue the Council was seriously divided, and it had other, more immediate, problems to settle, as the controversy with the Somerset House chemists and the problem of publishing its *Proceedings*. Moreover the Society was not a large one, attendances at meetings were extremely small and several Council meetings had to be abandoned for lack of a quorum. But above all it was a Society divided against itself, and it is no exaggeration to declare that it was racked with the bitterest in-fighting, much, but not all, of which was dominated by Wanklyn. At an Ordinary Meeting on 17 January 1877 reference was made to the resignations of President, one Vice-President and a Treasurer, to say nothing of seven others who had mostly ceased to be 'public analysts'.

CHAPTER IX

DEFINING PROFESSIONAL COMPETENCE: THE INSTITUTE'S QUALIFICATIONS TO 1920

Of all the issues, qualifications for chemists was the central one in the discussions leading to the establishment of the Institute of Chemistry. Those promoting the Institute clearly saw a connection between professional status and qualifications. The circular which called the public meeting that considered the 'Organisation of Chemists' in April 1876 indicated their goal: '. . . raising and establishing the status of the chemical profession, by drawing a marked distinction between duly qualified practitioners and others, and by promoting the acquisition of such knowledge and skills as are necessary . . .'[1] Once established, the Institute had to decide what this distinction should be, what knowledge and skills were necessary, and how it would promote their acquisition. In any period a definition of what constitutes the necessary knowledge and skills of a duly qualified chemical practitioner depends on the contemporary state of chemical knowledge and educational opportunities, as well as the range of tasks expected of such an individual. Similarly, in terms of gaining status and security for a particular group, a qualification, once defined by that group, is only valuable in so far as it receives public recognition. This depends on the public's criteria of evaluation. Such issues, raised at its very beginning, have been of continuing concern to the Institute of Chemistry.

1 The Initial Regulations: FIC as the Hallmark of Professional Competence

In 1877 the question of what should constitute a chemical qualification was complex. There were conflicting views about whether a qualification should be awarded on the basis of formal academic preparation alone, practical experience 'on the job' alone, or some combination of these. Furthermore, those who supported formal academic training, even if only as a small ingredient of a chemical qualification, did not always agree about which current pedagogical trend this should follow. Although the state of science education in Victorian Britain was often, with reason, lamented by many of those leading the movement for the professional organization of chemists, the Institute was established during a period of increasing opportunities for the study of chemistry when there was considerable public discussion about scientific and technical education (Chapter V). Therefore, unlike some other nineteenth-century professional institutions, the new Institute encountered an already well-elaborated educational structure within which it had to frame, or at least justify, its qualifications.[2]

In addition to problems of definition, the Institute had to face problems of authority. Until receiving a Royal Charter in 1885, it had no legal authority to grant certificates of competence. Under the original Act of Incorporation it could acquaint the public with its views about appropriate training for professional chemists and insist that its members had such training. While this had moral authority, since many founders of the Institute were well-known and respected academic chemists, members of the Institute could not claim any sort of legally-recognized qualification by virtue of their membership. The Charter eliminated this difficulty, but it did not grant the Institute a monopoly over chemical qualifications. So, in effect, in the early years under the Charter, the Institute's status still depended on the moral authority granted by the reputations of those associated with it. Indeed, it can be argued that this continues to be the case, although members in the 1970s enjoy the added authority conferred by the achievements of their predecessors during the past hundred years.

For the sake of public recognition, the initial membership criteria set up by the Institute were particularly important. They had to indicate that future members would also have reputations warranting respect. Internally, the initial regulations were also very important because of the problematic relationship between 'academic' and 'practising' chemists within the Institute. The educational objects of the Institute as set out in the Articles of Association make it clear that those framing the regulations had in mind primarily analytical and consulting chemists in private practice: 'To ensure that consulting and analytical chemists are duly qualified for the proper discharge of the duties they undertake by a thorough study of chemistry and allied sciences in their application to the Arts, Public Health, Agriculture and Technical Industry'.[3] To many contemporaries, analytical and consulting chemists were the professionals, while academic chemists were seen as professional educationalists, but 'amateur practitioners' when it came to applying chemistry to clients' problems.[4] The regulations that the Institute defined, however, showed very strongly the influence of its academics.

For the first six months of the Institute's existence, Council was to admit whomever it deemed a competent [analytical and consulting] chemist. For the following thirty months, it was to seek evidence of specific training and experience from candidates for its two grades of membership. Associates, the junior grade, had to be at least twenty-one years old and had to have passed a systematic course of three years' training in theoretical and analytical chemistry, physics and mathematics. The emphasis was on sound education in the principles of chemistry rather than specific vocational training. Fellows, the senior grade, had to be at least twenty-four years old, and had to have completed the same academic training as potential Associates. In addition, they had to show evidence of three years' subsequent experience either as an assistant to a chemist of repute, or as a professor or demonstrator of practical chemistry in a recognized teaching institution, or as a chemist in a technical industry. In lieu of this vocational experience, evidence of published research was accepted. In a final regulation, Council still, in effect, reserved the right to admit whomever it deemed competent.[5] Thus, in the initial regulations, the Associateship (AIC) was the badge of sound, general training, while the Fellowship (FIC) was the hallmark of professional competence (Figure 6, Chart 1).

Contemporary chemists found these regulations contentious. Council presented its initial right to admit whomever it cared to as a magnanimous open-admissions policy designed to help reputable chemists who never had the opportunity for formal study. Others saw this policy as an attempt to create an 'in-group' of chemists in order to gain monopoly powers over the practice of analytical and consulting chemistry by a clique of academics. The formal requirements also attracted this charge, probably with some justification. In the first place, with only two exceptions, all the members of the Institute's planning committee and of its first Council had had at least some formal training in practical chemistry either at well-known English institutions or abroad. Furthermore, the majority of both groups held teaching posts while doing analytical work on the side. Some analytical and consulting chemists in private practice, fearing an academic monopoly, viewed this latter tendency as professionally suspect and unjustly competitive. Academic chemists enjoyed an automatic and well-advertised reputation as experts which attracted customers, while at the same time they could charge lower fees than private practitioners because they had lower overheads.[6] The fact that the new Institute's regulations for the Fellowship, drawn up mainly by academics, offered as criteria of recognition for analytical competence experience in teaching and research increased suspicions while strengthening the academics' position.

Designating academics competent analytical and consulting chemists was not the only way in which the new regulations strengthened their position. The requirement of three years' systematic training in theoretical and analytical chemistry, physics and mathematics might be expected to have an effect on student numbers and expectations. Academics argued constantly that one of the difficulties in attracting students to study science was the lack of job opportunities afterwards.[7] If an organization was being set up which aimed to control new job opportunities, they felt it essential that academics should be in control of it. In fairness to the academics, it was also perfectly sensible and just that educational requirements should not be taken completely out of their hands. Nor were they the only group to favour such regulations; some analysts and industrialists also favoured strict academic training. Indeed, if the academics were to make any claim to be able to train prospective professional chemists given the facilities available in the 1870s their claim had to rest on the grounds that general training in the principles of the sciences by means of practical laboratory work would equip a student to undertake subsequently a chemical career in any branch of the subject. It was obviously impossible for any teaching institution to attempt to equip students specifically in all the variety of areas that required practising chemists. On the other hand, there were respected pedagogical reasons for this argument and most of the academics involved in the Institute advocated them, if only rhetorically.

In this case, current pedagogical rhetoric and practical necessity reinforced each other in the definition of what constituted the ideal curriculum for the prospective practising chemist. There were also non-pedagogical reasons for supporting the idea of a general scientific training for professional chemists. Since status was very much a concern of those involved in setting up the Institute, status was one of the things to be safeguarded by the membership. One effective way of doing this was to secure what might be termed a 'high-status' education for the Institute's members. That is, broad academic training would not only provide the chemist with his particular expertise, it would define him socially as an academic man, equivalent in status to members of the medical profession who had to undergo similar broad training in the sciences during their pre-clinical years.[8] The fact that the professional code would have to be voluntary reinforced the argument for 'gentlemanly' training for chemists. Furthermore, since the Institute had no statutory registration powers, but had to create a *de facto* 'register' of qualified chemical practitioners, exclusive qualifications were necessary. Then it could at least attempt to include all practitioners qualified according to its own criteria.

In addition to worries about academic self-interest in the framing of the Institute's regulations, there were also some quite legitimate queries as to whether this was in fact the best training for analytical and consulting chemists. Few questioned that prospective chemists needed theoretical training, but many argued that a systematic three years' course in a teaching institution was not the only way in which such training could be gained. A significant group argued that evening study combined with apprenticeship to a reputable practitioner was viable training. Many even argued that this would be preferable, because the student's practical work would then be directly relevant to his future career. Most analytical and consulting practices were highly specialized and those in such practices suggested that the expertise gained in dealing with complex, 'real' analytical situations could not be duplicated in the academic laboratory, however good the general analytical training offered.[9] Furthermore, the requirement of three years' systematic study was simply unrealistic for many of the sorts of people who had previously selected analytical careers. Such training was available in only a few centres. In addition, by depriving him of his role of educator, the Institute was ironically lowering the status of the analytical and consulting chemist, rather than raising it. The attempt to achieve a balance between these issues of principle and practice, between formal study in an educational institution and what might be called field work, have underlain almost all debates about qualifications within the Institute.

Once the Institute had determined what constituted sufficient training for a qualified chemist, it had to decide what would constitute sufficient evidence of this training. Among the possibilities were accepting personal testimonials, validating the chemistry examinations of existing institutions, and instituting its own examinations. This latter course was not strictly necessary and several professional associations played a useful qualifying role for many years without doing so.[10] However, given the controversies at the time of its establishment, it was clear that, whatever use the new Institute made of the other two possibilities, its founders definitely intended to organize practical examinations. The Institute soon established an Examinations Committee which arranged the first examinations in 1879. For the Associateship, the committee suggested that a good university degree covering the requisite subjects would be sufficient evidence of theoretical training, as would good results in the Science and Art Department examinations in chemistry, physics and mathematics. However, if such candidates, or any others, could not provide evidence of practical training, they had to undergo the Institute's own five-day practical examination in qualitative analysis (including the use of the microscope and spectroscope) and in quantitative analysis, both inorganic and organic.[11] Thus, from the start, the Institute emphasized the training of practical analysts; yet even the syllabus for the practical examination was broad and academic, testing candidates' general abilities as manipulative chemists across a range of techniques, rather than specific conditions that they would be liable to meet in a particular branch of practice.[12] In this way standard academic training, including evening classes with which the Science and Art Department examinations dealt, was endorsed as adequate for training chemists.[13] The Institute's qualification scheme was not dissimilar to that devised by the Society of Arts Committee on Technical Education in 1868 in which Frankland participated. For its lower grade, the Associateship, the Institute took maximum advantage of the training offered by existing institutions and insisted on sound theoretical grounding for which it tested the practical aspects. The higher grade required a further three years of approved experience in some branch of chemical practice. Council considered Fellowship applications individually and reserved the right to impose examinations in cases of doubt.

2 Modifications to the Initial Regulations

From the outset Council intended that the initial regulations should last only until 1881, after which admission to the Institute by examination would be made the norm.[14] Already in 1880, Council anticipated the revision by stipulating that all new members must first join as Associates and satisfy Council on grounds of formal education. It was hoped that this would reinforce the Institute's academic requirements and preclude applicants without the requisite academic training proceeding directly to the Fellowship.[15] Although schematically similar to the initial regulations, the revised regulations were a good deal tighter.[16] They were introduced in two stages. From 1881 to 1883, the only change was that the Institute began to run two examinations, one theoretical and one practical. All candidates for the Associateship had to sit the Institute's practical examination, although the earlier exemptions still applied to the theoretical examination. However, from the start of the 1883–4 session, the Institute would only accept a candidate's three years' study if it had been done at certain approved institutions, namely the existing universities and university colleges.[17] Furthermore, although it was not spelled out in the regulations, 'systematic study' came to mean full-time study during the day.[18] In addition the new regulations stipulated that the approved course work had to be validated by an approved examination. Those listed were first or second class honours university degrees in chemistry (except for Cambridge),[19] the associateships of the science colleges, or the Science and Art Department examinations in specified subjects. In lieu of these, the student could take a theoretical examination run by the Institute of Chemistry, and, to make this more feasible the Institute decided to allow its examinations to be held in various provincial centres which had college or university facilities capable of holding them (Figure 6, Chart 2).

Together these provisions, drawn up in 1881 to become operative in 1883, effectively excluded part-time courses and evening study, and therefore the Science and Art Department examinations, as routes to the Associateship. The Institute formally recognized the fact when it eventually published the 1883 regulations by excluding the Science and Art Department examinations from the exempting list.[20] In this way a whole range of institutions, which might have been quite attractive to practising chemists as places of study, were excluded and general academic training and the facilities of the academic establishment were emphasized even more. Significantly, this excluded the School of Pharmacy, possibly another ploy in the on-going debate about whether pharmacists deserved the title (and employment) of chemists.[21]

The new regulations did not attract new members. Indeed their announcement was followed by a four-year decline in membership.[22] It was rather sanguine to expect students with three years of systematic study to sit a new and unknown Institute examination when they were by virtue of the same course work entitled to a degree or similar recognized award. The irony of the Institute's situation was that it made its qualifications academically more stringent just at the time that industrial chemists, the group least likely to have had any formal academic training, let alone three years' systematic study, were beginning to organize for their own interests in the Society of Chemical Industry. Of the three classes of industrial personnel delineated by the Samuelson Committee, managers, foremen, and workmen, the Institute identified itself with the interests of the managers. By 1883, workers in industry had access to a widespread system of examinations through the City and Guilds of London Institute which had taken over the Society of Arts technological examinations in 1879. The City and Guilds operated a policy of subsidizing existing institutions in industrial centres which gave evening instruction to workmen and foremen on the application of scientific principles to the processes which they used every day. Students' performance was evaluated by a system of examinations which, the City and Guilds could claim proudly by 1883, were rapidly becoming recognized in industry as certificates of proficiency and were beginning to have the status of qualifications.[23] The Royal Commission on Technical Instruction, which sat from 1882 to 1884, noted that manufacturers in particular approved of the City and Guilds classes because they dealt with direct practical training. Indeed, the Commission went so far as to suggest that the Science and Art Department examinations should be made more practical and that the number of classes subsidized by the City and Guilds should be increased with local authority help.[24]

In contrast the curriculum required by the Institute stressed a thorough grounding in the general principles of science rather than its applications. The Institute's programme can be seen as a sort of academic backlash – a defence of the relevance to a chemical career of traditional university values from the challenge of successful specialist vocational instruction in the applied sciences. This is not to imply that the Institute's view was only self-serving since its defence of basic training in the principles of science represented a legitimate pedagogical point of view. However, this point of view separated the Institute from the technical education movement while many felt that the Institute should have been working within it. Where the Institute was in difficulty was that its university-level academics wanted to make sure that their students were as employable as those who followed the path of evening technical education. Ironically, the Institute offered a means of obtaining a technical qualification for students who enjoyed advantages denied to those who went through the *ad hoc* system of technical instruction.

3   The Influence of the 1885 Charter on the Institute's Regulations

The Institute's efforts to obtain a Royal Charter, granted in 1885, and thus achieve legal recognition of its qualifications, reinforced its academic tendencies. It was particularly necessary to demonstrate that the Institute intended neither to duplicate the learned society functions of the Chemical Society and the new Society of Chemical Industry, nor to operate for the commercial benefit of its members.[25] The Institute argued that chemical practitioners should enjoy status analogous to that of medical men; therefore, they should undergo the kind of academic training necessary for medical practice. Because of this, the Institute found itself excluding a large and important group of practising chemists who really provided its *raison d'être*.

The new regulations were problematic for industrial chemists; practising analysts also found them stringent. This group was more likely to have had some formal academic training at least in the rudiments of chemistry, but again three years of full-time study would be quite unusual, their normal procedure being to complete training as a sort of apprentice to an established analytical practitioner. There were, of course, strong protests from both industrial and analytical and consulting chemists.[26]

Council recognized this as a severe problem, particularly because the Institute's Charter, for all its academic sophistication, did not give it a monopoly over qualifications for the practice of chemistry. If substantial numbers of known reputable practitioners were excluded from membership, but continued to practice reputably, none the less, the Institute would lose all conviction as a qualifying body for chemists. On the other hand, if it operated too open an admissions policy, it could easily come to merit the charge that its qualifications were meaningless. Once the Charter was secured the Institute took steps to deal with the problems of potential members who were qualified by long experience and reputation rather than by formal training. It announced in the chemical press, under considerable pressure from analytical members of Council, that it would be willing to consider applications from such practitioners between June 1886 and March 1887.[27] In fact, this procedure, based on the precedents of the monopoly professions of medicine and pharmacy, was quite acceptable and membership figures did improve. The period of grace helped to stem some of the criticism of the Institute in the short term, but it did not really solve the fundamental dilemma.

For example some Fellows of the Institute who were practising analysts in Manchester and elsewhere in the North of England formed a pressure group. They were concerned that Council suffered the double domination of London and of academics. This northern group firmly supported the Institute's period of grace and urged reforms in the regulations which would recognize three years of approved experience under a Fellow in the laboratory of a private practice as equivalent to three years' systematic academic study for purposes of the Associateship. Furthermore, they wanted more provincial members on Council.[28] In 1889, partly to meet such objections, the regulations were altered slightly in favour of the practising chemists by accepting two years' study in a recognized institution and four years' training in the laboratory of a Fellow as equivalent to the three years' academic work. In addition, a new non-corporate grade of Student was created, partly in order to encourage prospective chemists in all forms of training to qualify through the Institute and partly to provide a means of keeping track of the progress of students working in private laboratories.[29] Analytical and consulting members of Council felt that these modifications did not go far enough. Some objected that the regulations devalued laboratory experience and placed a very heavy burden on the student who would select such a route.[30]

At the same time, some analyst members of the Institute raised again the virtually eternal complaint at the Chemical Society—that, because its membership was open and the Institute's regulations very stringent, suspect practitioners tended to use membership of the Chemical Society illegitimately as a qualification by appending FCS to their names. Discussion over the issue raged on in the chemical press and in the chemical institutions for more than two years.[31]

In May 1891, the Institute held a conference to deal with some of the key problems.[32] All the old grievances came out about the relative importance of analytical and consulting chemists and academics, of professional and professorial members, within the Institute. Analytical chemists were particularly concerned about the requirement that students had to obtain their training in a small number of recognized institutions.

> Nothing could be plainer: the Institute was founded *solely* and *absolutely* for the benefit of the analytical and consulting chemist. But within a few years, if not from the very commencement of the Institute of Chemistry, we have the strange spectacle of seeing that portion of our profession, that was in no way concerned in the objects of the Institute, conducting its council in direct opposition to the wishes of analytical chemists. Rules and regulations for admission and for training were laid down without consultation with the body of those who should have been competent judges—the analytical chemists.
>
> The policy adopted by the first council, and, unfortunately, hitherto upheld by succeeding councils, until now it has become sufficiently moss-grown and time-honoured to be considered a part of the Institute itself, was the natural outcome of the academical composition of the council. This policy, which has actually been partly incorporated into the charter—which charter was never submitted to the body of fellows until it was too late to discuss, much less to alter it—has been the rock on which the ship has stuck these 14 years. It may be summed up in three words: *'enforced college education'*.[33]

Analysts argued that London University provided adequate precedents for examining all comers regardless of where they received their training. Furthermore, the London BSc provided a loop-hole in the Institute's regulations since anyone who possessed this degree was exempt from the Institute's theoretical examination although he still had to do the practical. On a different tack, others argued that academic training had dubious relevance to real-life analytical work. Academics on the other hand deprecated premature specialization at the expense of a solid general grounding. Although both sides disagreed on the question of training, as Pilcher puts it 'there seemed to be a general consensus of opinion that the standard of the Associateship examination should be raised since the examination should be a real test in order to secure a high class of professional man'.[34] What Pilcher did

10   *Edward Frankland.*

11   *F. A. Abel.*

12   *James Bell.*

13   *Augustus Voelcker.*

14 *Michael Carteighe.*

15 *W. N. Hartley.*

16 *C. R. A. Wright.*

17 *C. T. Kingzett.*

Some past Officials of the Institute

18 *R. B. Pilcher.*

19 *R. C. Collett.*   20 *H. J. T. Ellingham.*

21 Senior members of staff at Russell Square.

From left to right: (standing) Dr I. R. McKinley (External Relations Officer), Mr B. A. Henman (Assistant Secretary, Professional Affairs), Mr R. W. Flack (Assistant Secretary, Examinations, Qualifications and Admissions), Mr J. F. Harding (Assistant Secretary, Services), Mr G. A. King (Professional Services Officer), Mr L. W. Winder (Assistant Registrar), Mr D. A. Arnold (Unification Committee Secretary). (seated) Miss J. Stockman (Member Services), Mrs D. Cameron (Examinations Officer), Mrs J. Thear (Members Services), Dr R. E. Parker (Secretary and Registrar), Mrs B. Gill (Qualifications Officer), Miss H. M. A. Garden (Secretary to Benevolent Fund Committee), Miss D. M. Woodrow (Personnel Officer).

not say, however, was that there was considerable disagreement over the direction that the upgrading of the examination should take. The analysts argued for detailed practical testing of specific 'professional' expertise, the academic faction urged ever more rigorous scientific knowledge. The upshot of the conference was that the regulations were revised yet again. William Tilden, then Professor of Chemistry at Mason College, Birmingham, and President of the Institute, prepared a draft for members to discuss. Tilden was firmly on the professorial side of the arguments within the Institute and his draft regulations reflect this.[35]

4 New Regulations: AIC as the Hallmark of Professional Competence

For the Associateship, Tilden kept the basic structure of the 1883 regulations with their 1889 modifications. However, he stiffened this considerably. No one was to become a candidate for the Studentship or the Associateship until he could show that his preliminary general education had reached a level equivalent to that required for university entrance by passing one of the standard examinations recognized for that purpose. In addition, Tilden prescribed continuous systematic, full-time, day study. Furthermore, he tightened up the regulations for admission to the Fellowship. Under the previous regulations an Associate could proceed to the Fellowship after three years' approved experience in some branch of chemistry, the results of which might be tested by an Institute examination. Alternatively, publications, patents, or a higher degree might be accepted as evidence of an individual's experience, but it was more often a matter of testimonials from existing Fellows. Tilden wanted to require a practical examination in a branch of pure or applied chemistry selected by the candidate, thus providing an actual examination of an individual's professional expertise much as the 'practising' faction within the Institute suggested. Research theses could be accepted as evidence of competence but, even then, Tilden reserved the right for examiners to require a practical examination to assure themselves on the question of professional competence. However, he did add the academic rider that a DSc in chemistry from any university in the United Kingdom should exempt any candidate from all further examinations.[36]

Certain analytical and consulting members of Council, particularly those who were embroiled in the debates over qualifications at the Chemical Society as well, objected strongly to this last clause. At this time, the London DSc was not a research degree but was awarded on the basis of examinations in pure chemistry and could hardly be called a test of professional competence. Council approved Tilden's suggestions *nem con*.[37] However, at the 1892 Annual General Meeting held a short time afterwards, two prominent analytical and consulting members of the Institute, both former Council members, requested that the revisions be discussed by the membership at large.

At this Annual General Meeting, Tilden clarified the reasoning behind his suggestions.[35] He opposed apprenticeship as a principal route to professional qualifications because few private laboratories could provide the facilities and supervised study available at British universities and university colleges, particularly the newer ones. Although Tilden did not of course say so, these institutions were trying hard during this period to attract students and build up their reputations as suitable centres of professional education.[38] He argued that the characteristic of a professional was that he was a gentleman, and the way to become a gentleman was, as it traditionally had been in Britain, by way of a university education. Apprenticeship could not provide this aspect of professional training. He also advanced the argument that the same general scientific training that would give the professional the desired social characteristics would prepare him to work in any of a number of detailed technical branches of applied chemistry.

When given the opportunity to discuss the revisions in May 1892 only some forty of the Institute's 825 members attended its conference.[39] Several prominent analytical and consulting chemists attended as did some teachers in the larger technical colleges. While all agreed that there should be high standards for membership tested by a stiff examination, many questioned whether restricting training to a few universities and colleges would help to achieve this. The technical college teachers were particularly concerned about this point as there were obvious implications for their enrolments. Otto Hehner[40] and Charles E. Cassal[41] reiterated points that they had both made before. Hehner argued that no amount of formal study could be equivalent to actual practice, and he cited instances of industrial disasters caused by chemists acting from first principles of theory with no respect for long practice. Furthermore, far from education creating a profession of gentlemen, Hehner felt that gentlemen were born rather than trained. Cassal suggested that the real bone of contention within the Institute was that all Fellows should be *bona fide* practising professional chemists; yet in terms of setting qualifications, it was the academics, who were not in this category, who seemed to have control. One industrial chemist even suggested that large industrial laboratories should be recognized as training centres for the Institute since many manufacturers preferred to employ chemists who had previous specialist experience.

Not surprisingly for a conference with such a critical purpose only a minority of recorded comments were from defenders. David Howard,[42] an original Fellow and prosperous chemical manufacturer, suggested that the reputation of the Institute was very closely linked to the reputation of the Institutions whose courses it recognized. Edward Frankland also emphasized this point and suggested that it was the curricular requirements of the Institute that made chemistry a profession rather than allowing it to degenerate into a trade. In fact, he argued that some of chemists' current problems, with respect to status, resulted from the lack of systematic training on the part of traditional practitioners (meaning, of course, analytical and consulting chemists). Frankland made another telling point. He noted with surprise, he claimed, the group's emphasis on examinations as an adequate test of professional expertise, while prevailing pedagogical thinking was turning against examination systems. Frankland suggested that a guarantee of good quality training was far better evidence of competence than any examination results.

As Frankland's remarks indicated, here again the Institute's policy on qualification has to be seen in relation to contemporary educational debates. During the late 1880s, there was a strong anti-examination movement. It was suggested that examination systems promoted sterile teaching, constricting syllabuses and rote learning merely to achieve examination passes rather than to foster knowledge. Criticism was levelled at the examinations of the University of London, the Science and Art Department and the City and Guilds.[43] It was argued that the examination system, particularly in science, led to overspecialization into readily examinable sub-disciplines and also stifled research initiative since only examination results received rewards. Also in the late 1880s, the technical education movement began to bear fruit. The Technical Instruction Act of 1889 allowed the new local authorities to levy rates to establish technical schools for instruction in 'the principles of science and art applicable to industries and the application of special branches of science and art to specific industries or employments'.[44] These schools were to be administered by the Science and Art Department, thus giving state sanction to the system of part-time evening instruction. Thus quite apart from any split between analytical and consulting chemists and academic chemists within the Institute, the Institute's requirement of continuous, systematic, full-time day study can be seen as a defensive move by university academics in the face of the potential increase in evening instruction. On the question of examinations, the Institute's defence had to be that its examinations were unique in testing practical achievements rather than book learning. As an example of this, it could point to its requirement that all examinees submit endorsed laboratory notebooks as evidence of the calibre of their work leading up to the examination.[45]

The practising faction did succeed in altering Tilden's draft, but their alterations were something of a pyrrhic victory. The general outline of the regulations which came into effect in October 1893 was retained until 1917. These regulations created two examination hurdles, in addition to evidence of preliminary education, for achieving the Associateship which became recognized as the professional qualification, rather than a preliminary to it. The first or Intermediate examination covered general theoretical and practical chemistry. The training for this examination was the stringent academic course work specified in Tilden's draft. Candidates with recognized university degrees or associateships with first and second class honours would be exempt from this examination. However, all candidates for the Associateship were required to do a second, Final examination which was a practical test in any branch of analytical chemistry they chose. The Fellowship became in effect merely a matter of spending a further three years reputably employed as a chemist, although Council reserved the right to impose examinations on dubious candidates (Figure 6, Chart 3).[46]

Thus the analytical and consulting faction had won its point—the Associateship became a professional qualification in the sense that it was awarded on the basis of a genuine test of professional competence in a specific branch of practice. Furthermore, it had succeeded in countering the professorial faction's claims that a first or second class honours university degree or its equivalent constituted a professional qualification on its own. However, the analytical and consulting faction did not succeed in eliminating the college or university training required for the Institute's qualifications which was their real complaint.

(a) Examination for Branch E

Once the 1893 regulations were in force, the Institute still faced the problem of getting its examinations officially (and unofficially) recognized as qualifications. It appointed a public relations committee to achieve this. But the committee recommended little more than constant publicity in the scientific and general press and circularizing public authorities and heads of departments responsible for chemical appointments, as well as making sure that the Institute's voice was heard in parliamentary committees dealing with issues relating to chemistry.[47] Public Analysts were a particular focus of the Institute's activities. This was partly because of the internal need to show the analytical community that the Institute's academic regulations were relevant to them. Public Analysts were now an effective pressure group via the Society of Public Analysts, which considered launching its own examinations during the very early 1890s.[48] Moreover, there was already recognition that Public Analysts needed qualifications. The Institute merely had to gain acceptance of its qualifications instead of fighting for the very idea of qualification.

In 1895, the Institute offered to testify to the Select Committee on Food Products and Adulterations about training qualifications. It appointed a committee to prepare the testimony which agreed that all candidates for Public Analyst posts should have a good general theoretical and practical training as well as special knowledge of the types of problems treated by Public Analysts. In fact the Institute was prepared to devise a special examination for candidates for such posts which would be open to its members if it could be recognized as a qualification. In the event, the Institute did not have the opportunity to submit evidence.[49] However, in 1896 when it rationalized its scheme of Final examinations for the AIC to allow candidates a limited number of options rather than a choice of any chemical field, the analysis of water, food, and drugs was one of the five branches (the subsequently well-known Branch E). At the same time, it decided to devise a syllabus to guide the training of prospective Public Analysts.[50]

The Institute was in an awkward position on this question, particularly in view of an impending revision of the Sale of Food and Drugs Act. It was on record with the view that the tasks of the Public Analyst were primarily chemical and that his training should reflect this. However, the Local Government Board still insisted on medical and microscopical knowledge in addition to chemical training and the Board continued to appoint medical men, particularly Medical Officers of Health (MOH), to Public Analyst posts. The Institute had to decide whether, in order to make its examination a required and unique qualification for Public Analyst posts, it should include medical and microscopical knowledge to gain immediate recognition. The alternative was to argue for the strictly chemical qualification in which it believed, risking total rejection by the Local Government Board and the new Act as well as possible further encroachment by MOHs. The decision to have a 'chemical' Branch E examination on the analysis of water, food, and drugs, backed up by required course work for prospective Public Analysts in therapeutics, pharmacology, and microscopy was a form of compromise. The examination plus the course work would entitle the candidate to a certificate, issued by the Institute, indicating that he was competent to practise as a Public Analyst.[51]

This compromise did not satisfy the Local Government Board. It was willing to recognize the Associateship as a qualification in chemistry only. It would not recognize AIC, in Branch E as *a*, let alone *the*, qualification for Public Analysts. In March 1897 Thomas Stevenson, a physician also trained in chemistry who was a lecturer in forensic medicine and toxicology at Guy's Hospital, Public Analyst for several places, Analyst to the Home Office, and immediate past President of the Society of Public Analysts, became President of the Institute. That such an individual was chosen by Council to hold the presidency at this time shows how important an issue the Public Analyst problem was for the Institute. In the face of any potential controversy with medical men, Stevenson, as an eminent medical man himself, was in an ideal position to support the chemical side of the Public Analyst's case. He would also serve to 'validate' any medical or microscopical training the Institute offered.

Stevenson's solution to the Institute's problem was to devise a two-tier examination structure for Public Analysts. In addition to Branch E in the analysis of water, food, and drugs, he instituted a second examination, in therapeutics, pharmacology and microscopy. Success in this latter examination earned a special Institute Certificate. Those Associates and Fellows who wanted additionally to gain a formal Public Analyst qualification would only have to sit the Certificate examination. However, future members, who hoped to qualify as Public Analysts at the same time as they qualified for the Institute, would have to sit both the Branch E examination and the Certificate examination which would be run jointly. In this way, the Institute felt that it had met the Local Government Board's medical and microscopical requirements without compromising the 'chemical' nature of its own qualifications.[52] In 1899, the Local Government Board agreed to accept the Institute's Certificate as *a* qualification for the many new Public Analyst posts that would become operative with the revised Sale of Food and Drugs Act in 1900. However, this Act did not give to the Institute its anticipated monopoly in such qualifications.[53]

(b) The examination in technical chemistry

The overall structure of the examinations scheme did not change until 1917, except for the addition of some more specialist examinations. In 1899, the list of examinations was extended by a Branch F in Biological Chemistry. The Institute saw this examination as sharing the characteristics of Branch E, that is of testing professional expertise, rather than just academic training. Indeed, in 1903, it opened the Branch F examination to existing Fellows and Associates, in a similar way to the arrangement for the certificates in therapeutics, pharmacology and microscopy under Branch E.[54] In the same year, a special committee of Council proposed that the Institute undertake what looked like a major change in educational policy, that is, that it should offer a set of examinations in various branches of technological chemistry in order to encourage the more efficient training of technical chemists.

As Pilcher points out, this proposal represented the Institute's reaction to contemporary discussions about the competitive position of the British chemical industry (among others) as it related to scientific training (p. 191).[55] In July 1902, a sub-committee of the London County Council Technical Education Board presented its conclusions about the reasons for Britain's deficiencies. It noted that (1) manufacturers lacked scientific training and consequently failed to appreciate the value of the application of science to industry, (2) a deficient secondary education system led to a lack of recruits for higher technological training, (3) Britain lacked individuals trained in both the principles of science and scientific methods *and* the applications of specific sciences to specific industries, (4) Britain lacked a well-funded and equipped institution for advanced technological training. While stressing the importance of a foundation of full-time general scientific training for prospective industrial chemists, the sub-committee stressed a need for postgraduate work in the applications of science to industrial processes as well as some training in their commercial aspects.[56] Also in 1902, a committee of the British Association for the Advancement of Science (BA), consisting of four academic chemists, three of whom were active in the Institute, compiled some statistics showing that few graduates entered chemical industry.[57] The President of the BA, Sir James Dewar, FIC (Jacksonian Professor of

Chemistry at Cambridge and Professor of Chemistry at the Royal Institution) suggested that even those British graduate chemists who did enter industry were not necessarily qualified for their work because of an over-emphasis on rote learning for examinations rather than on practical methods for approaching real chemical problems.

Here was a perfect opportunity for the Institute of Chemistry to be in the van of an educational movement. Through its examination system, it was ideally suited to take on the coordinating role called for by the London County Council Technical Education Board, and it had always stressed that its examinations went further than ordinary university degrees in the direction that Dewar sought. It was also an ideal opportunity for the Institute to show that it had more than the interest of analytical and consulting chemists in view. The Institute compiled its own statistics on the problem, showing that some 30 per cent of its members were graduates and a further 5 per cent had equivalent associateship qualifications from various institutions. Further, some 30 per cent of all Fellows and Associates were wholly engaged in private practice as analytical and consulting chemists, while 26.6 per cent were employed in industry, 16 per cent in teaching, 7.3 per cent in government service, and 19.6 per cent in two or more of these categories.[58] These statistics put the Institute in a strong position to argue that its record was no worse than the national average, and at least as good.

Neutral statistics were of course no answer to those who felt that the Institute should do something positive about promoting the training and proper qualification of industrial chemists.[59] That Council recognized this as an opportunity is indicated by its nomination of an industrial chemist for the first time as the Institute's next President, David Howard. As in the case of the choice of Stevenson for launching a new examination, Howard was a good choice for dealing with a difficult diplomatic situation within the Institute. Trained under Hofmann at the Royal College of Chemistry, he was head of a respected family firm that manufactured fine chemicals and was well known for his work in educational circles, on the Board of Education and through his association with the London Chamber of Commerce and the London County Council Technical Education Board. Furthermore, Howard's views were orthodox in terms of the Institute's academic requirements: he stood for sound general training, regardless of an individual's career choice and stressed the benefits of training in research methods as general training for the mind.[60] Thus Howard could be trusted to safeguard the academics' interests while simultaneously safeguarding and promoting those of the industrialists.

The 1903 proposal for an Institute of Chemistry technological examination scheme did not really depart from established Institute educational policy. The examinations in technical chemistry were to be postgraduate, thus taking up one of the London County Council (LCC) suggestions, that is, they were to be open only to Fellows and Associates who had been members for at least a year and would not constitute part of an individual's qualification to practice as a chemist. Furthermore, the committee insisted that the examination should only cover general principles and not the technologies of particular industries; this would avoid any problem of disclosing trade secrets. In addition, the committee suggested that the Institute should encourage the establishment of laboratories for technical training under teachers with technical experience.

It took Council two years to decide on instituting the technological examination scheme, as the consultation process was evidently complex.[61] Pilcher suggests that there was general harmony among manufacturers consulted about the scheme on the question of general training in the principles of science being preferred. However, this view underestimates the strength of feeling among manufacturers that general training was not very helpful to their employees while specialist training endangered trade secrets. There were also problems in setting the syllabus. While the emphasis on general principles was agreed, the examinees none the less had to have something specific to apply the principles to. One draft syllabus suggested that all students should study the sulphuric acid and town gas industries as these were sufficiently general, and inclusive of different types of chemical problems to provide a vehicle for examinees' discussions.[62] Eventually, it was decided that each candidate could elect to be examined in any branch of chemical industry.

There were the further problems of why anyone should want to take such an examination since it gave no qualification and was limited to those already qualified anyway. Indeed the Institute had long stood for the view that the basic training insisted on for the AIC qualification equipped an individual to practice in any field, so the scheme would seem to be redundant. In fact, although the scheme was proudly referred to in the Institute's literature, in practice it turned out to be superfluous and very few candidates sat the examinations.[63]

5 Gradual Reassessment of the 1893 Regulations

With the relative failure of the examinations in technical chemistry, other means were sought to make the Institute's qualifications attractive to industrial chemists. One industrial consultant suggested that the Institute should have another period of grace during which eminent senior industrial chemists might join without examination or fulfilling the academic criteria. He argued that this would not alter the character of the Institute as almost half of the Institute's industrial chemists, some thirteen per cent of the total membership, had joined before 1888 without examination. If the relaxation only applied to chemists over the age of forty, any new industrial members would be equivalent to a large section of the existing membership.[64] Council decided to proceed cautiously, inviting suitable people to apply and not publicizing the arrangements.

The same 1903 statistics which showed that the Institute's industrial membership was not insignificant in either internal or national terms also showed that the Institute was not attracting graduate chemists in proportion to the numbers being turned out of universities, particularly the majority of science graduates, who became teachers.[65] This group's argument was obvious—for teaching, a degree was essentially a professional qualification. Seeking membership in the Institute would mean, for them, merely another examination of dubious relevance to their career prospects. In his 1907 presidential address to the Institute, P. F. Frankland regretted that more academic chemists (meaning in this instance those in higher education) did not join the Institute, but at the same time he stressed the value of the Institute's examinations compared with university degrees. The former, he suggested, 'test what the candidate can actually perform when he is placed as far as possible under the same conditions as he would be if working in his own laboratory within reach of a good chemical library'. He noted that the practical man and the theoretical man were not always the same person. Yet in arguing against the university view that its examination system tested both, he argued ironically that both types ought to join the Institute via the Institute's examinations.[66]

During Frankland's presidency, some Council members suggested measures for easing the Institute's entry requirements. One possibility was that the list of examinations exempting candidates from the Institute's Intermediate AIC might be extended. Another, more radical, suggestion was that very good honours degrees might serve as exemptions from the Final AIC examination. Frankland did not approve and the movement subsided.[67] Speaking at the 1908 Annual General Meeting, he made it look as though the issue under discussion had been inverted, thus making his own view appear to be a defence of the status of university examinations. He noted that some Fellows felt that there should be no exemptions from the Intermediate examination, but held himself that a first or second class honours BSc was a good test at the Intermediate AIC level, and it helped to stress the Institute's belief in the value of university study. The results in the Final AIC examination over the preceding ten years showed that those exempt from the Intermediate did as well as those who took it. Cleverly, Frankland used this same argument as a justification for not extending the list of recognized institutions to include some of the higher technical colleges even though their numbers and standards were constantly improving: it was university training that the Institute valued, even though degrees could not be recognized as full professional qualifications.[68]

The Institute's regulations did not lack external critics and the next few years found it on the defensive.[69] Furthermore, expansion in higher education had reached the point where the Institute had to reconsider its twenty-year old requirements and examinations scheme. With increasing government support the scientific student body was expanding rapidly, as was the number of science graduates; the Institute however did not share this growth rate.[70] Furthermore, university degrees were becoming more specialized and there was a range of new technical degrees, while the value of examinations was again being questioned. Particularly disconcerting was the continued unpopularity of the technological chemistry examination, and Council decided to consult various professors of technical chemistry about the training of chemists. This idea was extended by Raphael Meldola, President of the Institute from 1912–15. A dye-works chemist from 1875 to 1883, then Professor of Chemistry at the Finsbury Technical College from 1885, Meldola had been among the witnesses during the LCC Technical Education Board's investigation of the application of science to industry in 1902. Finsbury, sponsored by the City and Guilds of London, was a pioneering technical college, and Meldola as past President of the Chemical Society (1905–7), the Society of Dyers and Colourists (1907–8), and the Society of Chemical Industry (1908–9), was well placed to initiate a new inquiry into the Institute's qualifications. He was particularly concerned to seek harmonization of the Institute's qualifications and those of educational institutions, as more coordination was needed. He attributed the lack of popularity of the Institute's technical examinations to its own failure to work sufficiently closely with either teachers of applied chemistry (because of its aloofness from technical colleges) or with manufacturers. At Meldola's suggestion, the Institute held an important conference of Professors of Chemistry in October 1913.[71]

The conference was attended by some sixty chemists; most universities and a range of other teaching institutions were represented, while Council members representing other branches of the profession also attended. Very diverse opinions were expressed. Most favoured the recognition of courses at technical colleges and equivalent institutions. In addition the university academics almost unanimously suggested that the Institute ought to welcome university graduates into the Associateship with no further examination. Some, in keeping with contemporary views about the relevance of examinations, suggested that the Institute should not hold its own examinations, but should instead act as external assessor to the examinations of educational institutions. Arthur Smithells, Professor of Chemistry at Leeds and well-known exponent of the teaching of applied science in universities, suggested that the Institute's examinations were counter-productive and 'particularly hostile to the right development of universities because they [the examinations] tend to perpetuate a mischievous antagonism between practical men and university teachers and between useful and "useless" knowledge'.[72] Thus the Institute was achieving the very opposite of its intentions in this view. Another northern professor of chemistry, H. B. Dixon[73] of Owens College, Manchester, went so far as to say that the Institute's qualifications were not well known in the North; he for one did not know what the Fellowship stood for and very few of his students sought its qualifications, although he sent, on average, twenty students per year into industry. Dixon echoed the common suggestion that the Institute should take a more positive attitude towards research and encourage research training, possibly making it a criterion for advance to the Fellowship. William Ramsay,[74] Professor of Chemistry at University College, London, and long an active member of the Institute suggested a model for a revised examination scheme that was in fact eventually adopted. He proposed that first and second class honours degrees in chemistry exempt candidates from all Associateship examinations, but that the regulations for proceeding from the Associateship to the Fellowship be tightened to include an examination in the practice of a particular branch of chemistry.

6 Some Tentative Revisions

Council set up a special committee to review the regulations in the light of the professors' conference. Although there was dissension on Council from certain analytical members, the committee decided fairly quickly to follow the lines indicated by Ramsay. At the same time, it hoped to be able to devise regulations under which eminent industrial and academic chemists could be invited to join.[75] The regulations had a rough passage through Council, complicated by the exceptional demands of war work. Practical chemists feared that new university graduates might receive a recognized qualification for no work, thereby diminishing the reputation of those who already held the qualification. Others argued that university degrees were too narrow and specialized to merit recognition as the general training always stood for by the Institute, while at the same time, they were no guarantee of practical experience. Finally, towards the end of 1916, Council approved in principle a modified set of revisions to the regulations which was circulated to all members.[76]

(a) Council's suggestions

The circular stressed two points, that some special provision had to be made for trained chemists who were prevented from taking examinations by the war, and to avoid the double examination of honours graduates. There were to be two routes to the Associateship. The first was by examination in general and theoretical chemistry. Candidates selecting this route must have studied four years full-time during the day at a recognized college or university, or have spent three years in such an institution with an additional two years under a Fellow of the Institute, or have earned a pass degree and been in practice for two years. There was no examination for the second route. A candidate could be elected to the Associateship on evidence of having a first or second class honours degree in chemistry plus three years' subsequent experience, or on evidence of having undergone four years of systematic course work with a subsequent two years' experience. Essentially, in an effort to meet both sides of the issue, approved experience was substituted for the Final AIC examination, which was meant to be a test of practical competence. At the same time, conditions for passing from the Associateship to the Fellowship were made more stringent. The candidate must have had three years' approved experience after gaining the AIC and have provided tangible evidence of achievement such as research results, patents, or an equivalent, or undergo an examination in one of the branches of the former Final AIC, though more specialized.

Only seven per cent of the Institute's members responded to the 1916 circular and this response was divided inconclusively: thirty were against the revisions, forty favoured them, and twenty favoured postponement of the entire issue until after the war. This was hardly a mandate for Council to bring about a radical alteration in the regulations, so what looked like fairly minimal revisions were approved by way of a compromise in July 1917. Candidates with first or second class honours degrees were exempt from the theoretical examination required of other candidates, but every one had to do the practical examination. The examination in technical chemistry at the same time became Branch G of the Associateship so that it could provide a qualification rather than just a certificate and possibly attract more industrial chemists. The 1917 regulations also contained a provision not included in the 1916 circular, but often mentioned in Council during the early twentieth century. 'In exceptional cases a candidate may be elected to the Associateship without examination by the Institute.' Under this clause Council could admit whomever it chose again, although it was probably aimed at younger industrial chemists who had not the requisite formal academic training in a recognized college or university. A circular accompanied the new regulations setting out one possible set of 'exceptional circumstances'. A special exemption from all AIC examinations, to apply during the war only, was to be granted to chemists in the services or doing other war work in the national interest providing they had degrees or equivalent qualifications and experience.[77]

(b) The influence of the provisional British Association of Chemists

Judging from reports in the contemporary press as well as the proceedings of meetings and disclaimers published by the Institute, the introduction of even these minimal revisions caused considerable ferment among the membership, and the fear of dilution of the qualification was widespread. Council published a statement noting the concern of members and assuring them that the admission of AICs without examination was only a temporary war measure which would end with the hostilities. It did not explain, however, whether the blanket enabling clause in the 1917 regulations was also temporary, or whether it would allow subsequently other forms of exemption.[78]

Any assessment of the reaction to the new regulations is complicated by the discussions with the provisional British Association of Chemists (BAC) which began to take place in the autumn of 1917 (p. 214). There was a strong industrial pressure group within the Institute for a broadening of qualifications in favour of industrial chemists along the lines suggested by the BAC organizers. Allied with the industrial group were the academics who favoured the recognition of university degrees as qualifications in themselves, and who increasingly saw industry as a promising destination for their students. At the same time, there was an active group of practising chemists, mainly analytical and consulting chemists, who opposed any broadening which might affect the status of the unique qualification which suited them very well.

The BAC proposed two levels of qualifications for membership. The first, or 'A' qualification, a university degree of any class, or equivalent diploma based on full- or part-time study at a university, or more particularly at a technical college, was in line with the Institute's thinking and would not have been difficult to accommodate. The second, or 'B' qualification, was seven years' experience in practice irrespective of formal training. This was to apply for a limited period only, in order to build up a register of qualified chemists. The Institute found this second qualification more difficult because of its responsibilities to existing qualified members. However, the Institute could not ignore the large body of chemical opinion behind the provisional BAC, nor the implications of the possible establishment of a second organization catering for what the Institute saw as its rightful constituency. In a statement of its objects and policies published widely in the chemical press just before the provisional BAC's inaugural meeting, the Institute tried to establish a defence against the new organization by showing that it already fulfilled all the BAC's aims. A précis of the 1917 regulations included in this statement added a new regulation to meet the BAC's terms. The Institute stated that it was willing to admit to examinations for its Associateship specially considered individuals who were at least twenty-seven years old and who had been in practice as chemists for a minimum of ten years and had reached a position of some responsibility.[79]

A committee set up to consider the BAC proposals suggested further modifications in the Institute's regulations in January 1918, including exempting first or second class graduates from all AIC examinations not just the theoretical one, and possibly admitting directly to the Associateship experienced chemists who were at least twenty-seven years old. Council's report to the Annual General Meeting in March 1918, suggested that the July 1917 regulations already included provision for admitting twenty-seven year-old candidates with ten years experience to the AIC examinations and for reserving the right of Council to consider applications for direct election to the Associateship.[80] The first suggestion, as we have seen, was not the case, while the second, although accurate and reflecting the spirit of Council's views at the time, conflicted with Council's August 1917 disclaimer that examination exemptions were a temporary war measure. Also, it could be said that Council's suggestion at the March 1918 AGM that the provisional BAC had not affected its views on the regulations was somewhat evasive. In the strict sense, the claim seems justified because Council had been heading in the direction of a less restricted Associateship from the time of the 1913 conference of professors, if not before. However, until stimulated by the possibility of the BAC's competition, Council deliberately had not pressed its views on a rather conservative (in the institutional sense) membership. Therefore, the provisional BAC did have a significant effect, urging Council along a path whose necessity it had long seen, but had been reluctant to take. This is not to accuse Council of chicanery. The regulations were in a fluid state, the Institute was in an awkward position, and Council's actions were perfectly within its powers under the Charter.

However, it is difficult to determine exactly what regulations were in force between July 1917 and March 1918, during which period 299 Associates were admitted. Figure 7 shows how dramatic this increase was.[81] As some members were quick to point out, and as J. J. Dobbie, President of the Institute,[82] had to agree, it was difficult to determine whether those admitted under the special war regulations had genuinely intended to apply for admission but for the interference of the war. Also, whether or not the wartime regulations were temporary in intention, since the Institute increased its membership by twenty per cent during the first few months of their operation, their effect was bound to be long term. In April 1918, an Extraordinary General Meeting was held to discuss the future of the Institute in the light of, 'modern developments', as President Herbert Jackson,[83] Professor of Chemistry at King's College London, described the discussions precipitated by the provisional BAC. By the time of this meeting, tempers had cooled somewhat and most members present seemed content to accept the regulations for admitting Associates without examination, so long as proceeding to the Fellowship ceased to be automatic after the passage of time. On the other side of the question, Council agreed to look into the possibility of recognizing technical colleges, and particularly, part-time evening work, providing that the training was equivalent to that of institutions it recognized already.[84]

7 The 1920 Regulations: FIC as the Hallmark of Professional Competence

Revised regulations, essentially a refined version of those of July 1917, were finally published in 1920.[85] Additional provisions were that honours graduates in chemistry were to be completely exempt from the Associateship examinations, and evening classes which were organized into systematic courses were to be recognized for students who were employed full-time as chemists during the day. The wartime exemptions for Associates were to end in 1920, but experienced practitioners who lacked academic training were still to be considered for admission until the end of 1921. In future there would be only one level of AIC examination, in general theoretical and practical chemistry, and the criteria for proceeding to the Fellowship were tightened. In lieu of evidence that a candidate had published research or patents, or otherwise distinguished himself, all Associates desiring to become Fellows would have to take an examination equivalent to the previous Final AIC in a branch of practice. The branches were:

A   Inorganic Chemistry
    I   Mineral products
    II   Metallurgy
    III   Manufactured products

B   Physical Chemistry

C   Organic Chemistry

D   Agricultural Chemistry

E   Chemistry (including Microscopy) of Food and Drugs and Water; Therapeutics, Pharmacology and Microscopy.

F   Biochemistry

G   Chemical Engineering

The first three branches were designed for those involved with industry, either directly in works or as analytical and consulting chemists. In each case the candidate had to elect a particular branch of industry on which to be examined (Figure 6, Chart 4).

This basic outline of regulations and qualifications remained in operation until 1956. There were of course periodic modifications in the subjects covered by the Branch examinations, and syllabuses varied as chemistry itself changed. In fact, the revised scheme of 1920 was little different in organization from that developed by Tilden in 1893 and both schemes in principle reflected the thinking of the 1860s on professional education. The main change between the 1893 and 1920 regulations was that the latter made the Associateship and the Fellowship two distinct grades. The Fellow was no longer basically a more mature Associate. Rather the Fellowship represented professional competence and achievement in a specific area of applied chemistry. The Associateship, as outlined in the 1920 regulations represented a solid general theoretical and practical training, a sign that the Associate had the potential for achieving professional competence.

This chapter has deliberately been quite detailed because the nuances of the various modifications of the regulations within a fairly constant general framework illustrate not only the difficulties faced by the Institute in attempting to coordinate groups with some conflicting interests, they also illuminate the complex structure of the profession of chemistry as well as its relationship with developments outside the profession. The 1920 regulations were probably so enduring because of the uneasy balance achieved in them between the principal factions within the Institute, the academic, the analytical, and the rising industrial.

GKR

NOTES AND REFERENCES

1 Papers relating to 'The Organisation of the Chemical Profession' at the Royal Institute of Chemistry.

2 Pharmacists, civil and mechanical engineers, and surveyors, for example, all enjoyed relative freedom in this respect. See A. M. Carr-Saunders and P. A. Wilson, *The Professions*, OUP, London, 1933; reprinted 1964.

3 R. B. Pilcher, *History of the Institute, 1877–1914*, Institute of Chemistry, London, 1914, p. 51.

4 For a retrospective use of this term, see 'Conference of Professors of Chemistry', *Proc. Inst. Chem.*, 1913, **37**, pamphlet bound in, p. 66.

5 Pilcher (note 3), p. 52; IC, Council Minutes, **1**, 1 February 1878.

6 See above, p. 121, where charlatans ironically were accused of the same offence, *The Analyst*, 1877, **2**, 109–11.

7 See for example the comments of Edward Frankland in *Report from the Select Committee on the Provisions for Giving Instruction in Theoretical and Applied Science to the Industrial Classes*, P.P. 1867–8, XV–I, qq. 8106–12, and *Chem. News*, 1876, **33**, 178–9.

8 Carr-Saunders and Wilson (note 2), pp. 372–3.

9 Otto Hehner, *Chem. Trade J.*, 1891, **9**, 75.

10 F. M. L. Thompson, *Chartered Surveyors: The Growth of a Profession*, Routledge, London, 1968, pp. 180–1; G. A. Millerson, *The Qualifying Associations: A Study in Professionalization*, Routledge, London, 1964, ch. V.

11 IC, Council Minutes, **1**, 7 May 1878.

12 *Ibid.*, 22 November 1878.

13 Note the implied equivalence of Science and Art Department and university examinations. As the Department's chemistry examiner, Frankland was well aware of the large numbers of chemistry entrants (p. 85) and their level. *Reports of the Royal Commission on Scientific Instruction and the Advancement of Science . . . , (c. 536)*, P.P. 1872, XXV, qq. 763–6. Practical examinations were held from 1878.

14 *Chem. News*, 1877, **36**, 193.

15 IC, Council Minutes, **1**, 23 January and 22 October 1880.

16 *Ibid.*, 28 January 1881, 10 January and 26 October 1883.

17 IC, Council Minutes, **2**, 2 March 1884 eased this requirement slightly by admitting candidates who had done approved 'courses', regardless of their institution.

18 Pilcher (note 3), p. 100; *Proc. Inst. Chem.*, 1891, **15**, pt. ii, 48–50; IC, Council Minutes, **2**, 23 January and 12 May 1891.

19 Cambridge was added later; IC, Council Minutes, **2**, 28 June 1889. It was not possible to sit a separate degree-level examination in chemistry at Cambridge until 1889.

20 IC, Council Minutes, **1**, 26 October 1883.

21 From 1884, it was of course open to pharmacy students to seek membership on the basis of their individual studies (note 17). The stringency of these regulations may be due

to the fact that the Institute was attempting to obtain statutory recognition at the time, see p. 201.

22 IC, Council Minutes, **2**, 12 January 1885 noted that there were many unqualified applicants.

23 *Royal Commission on Technical Instruction, 1882–4, Second Report,* (*c.* 3981–II), P.P. 1884, XXXI, pp. 401–7. In 1883, 2,397 candidates sat City and Guilds examinations in 154 centres. In 1883–4, it offered 34 examination subjects including several branches of applied chemistry.

24 *Ibid.*, pp. 528, 537. See also Michael Argles, *South Kensington to Robbins: An Account of English Technical and Scientific Education since 1851,* Longman, London, 1964, pp. 31–3; and D. S. L. Cardwell, *The Organisation of Science in England,* rev. edn., Heinemann, London, 1972, pp. 132–6.

25 See *Nature,* 1885, **33**, 73–7, 99; and *Chem. News,* 1885, **52**, 305–6.

26 Pilcher (note 3), pp. 84–5; *Chem. News,* 1885, **52**, 277, 318–9; 1886, **53**, 10.

27 IC, Council Minutes, **1**, 30 October 1885, 22 October 1886, and 24 June 1887.

28 *Chem. News,* 1886, **53**, 34, 59–60.

29 IC, Council Minutes, **1**, 23 March 1888 and 25 January 1889; **2**, 28 June 1889.

30 *Ibid.*, 24 December 1890.

31 *Chem. News,* 1889, **60**, 189, 201; 1890, **62**, 212–3.

32 Pilcher (note 3), pp. 103–5.

33 Note 9, pp. 75–6, emphasis in the original.

34 Pilcher (note 3), p. 104.

35 (a) IC, Council Minutes, **2**, 11 December 1891; (b) *Proc. Inst. Chem.,* 1891, **16**, pt. i, 14–23. Tilden had studied part-time himself, apprenticeship to London DSc taking fourteen years.

36 In the nineteenth century, the London DSc was an examined degree, ch. V, p. 84.

37 IC, Council Minutes, **2**, 11 December 1891, 22 January 1892; 1 March 1892.

38 Cardwell (note 24), p. 161; Michael Sanderson, *The Universities and British Industry, 1850–1970,* Routledge, London, 1972, chs. 3 and 4.

39 'Report of a Conference on the Present Regulations with Respect to Admission of Fellows and Associates to the Institute, 16 May 1892', *Proc. Inst. Chem.,* 1892, **16**, pamphlet bound in; see also, Pilcher (note 3), pp. 110–13.

40 On Hehner (1854–1924), see *Proc. Inst. Chem.,* 1924, **48**, 270; *Analyst,* 1924, **49**, 501–5.

41 On Cassal (1858–1921), see ch. X, note 9.

42 See note 60.

43 Cardwell (note 24), pp. 166–7; Argles (note 24), p. 34.

44 Technical Instruction Act, 1889, 52 & 53 Vict. c. 76; see also Cardwell (note 24), p. 160; Argles (note 24), pp. 35–41.

45 IC, Council Minutes, **2**, 23 January 1891.

46 *Ibid.*, 25 November 1892.

47 *Ibid.*, 13 October 1893, 26 October 1894.

48 B. Dyer and C. A. Mitchell, *The Society of Public Analysts and Other Analytical Chemists: Some Reminiscences of its First Fifty Years,* Heffer, Cambridge, 1932, p. 36.

49 IC, Council Minutes, **2**, 26 April 1895. Pilcher (note 3), p. 138.

50 IC, Council Minutes, **3**, 24 April 1896. The other four were: (a) Mineral Analysis, (b) Analysis and Assay of Metals, (c) Gas Analysis, (d) Organic Analysis.

51 *Ibid.*, 30 October 1896, 22 January 1897. Thomas Stevenson (*Proc. Inst. Chem.*, 1898, **22**, pt. i, 24) commented that '. . . if the Institute do not undertake this Examination [therapeutics, pharmacology and microscopy], the work will be done by some other body, and thus a slur will be cast upon the fulness of our qualification for the Office of Public Analyst'.

52 IC, Council Minutes, **3**, 21 January, 24 June 1898.

53 Pilcher (note 3), pp. 145, 147–9; IC, Council Minutes, **3**, 28 April 1899, *Proc. Inst. Chem.*, 1900, **24**, pt. i, 22. The Institute was, however, listed as one of the qualifying bodies for Public Analysts in the Local Government Board's regulations for implementing the new Act.

54 Pilcher (note 3), p. 150; IC, Council Minutes, **3**, 27 October 1899; **4**, 21 May 1903.

55 *Ibid.*, 27 November 1903; Pilcher (note 3), pp. 162–5. See also Cardwell (note 24), pp. 187–98, 204–8.

56 London County Council, Technical Education Board, *Report of the Special Subcommittee on the Application of Science to Industry, 15 July 1902*, London, 1902, pp. 5–7.

57 *Rep. Brit. Assoc.*, 1902, **72**, 15–18, 97–8; Cardwell (note 24), pp. 204–7; Pilcher (note 3), pp. 164–5.

58 *Proc. Inst. Chem.*, 1903, **27**, pt. i, 15–16.

59 Nor was it really an answer to those who suggested that the Institute was most active on behalf of private practitioners and controlled by a minority of academics in their own interests.

60 On Howard (1839–1916), see *J. R. I. C.*, 1956, **80**, 62. See also London County Council, Technical Education Board, *Report on the Teaching of Chemistry*, London, 1896, Appendix 2, pp. 16–17.

61 IC, Council Minutes, **5**, 24 November 1905; Pilcher (note 3), pp. 170–3.

62 IC, Council Minutes, **4**, 27 May 1905.

63 *Ibid.*, **5**, 26 October 1906.

64 *Ibid.*, 14 December 1906, 1 January 1907.

65 Cardwell (note 24), pp. 208–17.

66 *Proc. Inst. Chem.*, 1907, **31**, pt. ii, 18–19, 21. On Frankland (1858–1946), see ch. X note 6.

67 IC, Council Minutes, **5**, 25 October 1907.

68 *Proc. Inst. Chem.*, 1908, **32**, pt. ii, 15–20. Frankland's view prevailed although the Nominations and Examinations Committee disagreed; IC, Council Minutes, **6**, 22 May, 19 June 1908.

69 Some felt that the Institute should do more to encourage research by requiring it for the Fellowship (*Proc. Inst. Chem.*, 1909, **33**, pt. ii, 12–15).

70 Cardwell (note 24), pp. 203–6 shows that the number of full-time university level students doubled between 1900 and 1914, while the number taking degrees quadrupled.

71 On Meldola (1848–1915), see *Proc. Inst. Chem.*, 1916, **40**, pt. i, 36. On the conference, see IC, Council Minutes, **7**, 29 March 1912; and *Proc. Inst. Chem.*, 1913, **37**, pt. ii, 26–9.

72 'Conference of Professors', (note 4), p. 21. On Smithells (1860–1939), see A. J. Flintham, 'The Contribution of Arthur Smithells FRS (1860–1939) to the Development

of Science Education in England', Unpubl. MEd thesis, University of Leeds, 1974. See also, A. Smithells, 'Professors and Practical Men . . .', in *From a Modern University*, OUP, London, 1921; and *DNB*.

73 On Dixon (1852–1930), see *J. Chem. Soc.*, 1931, 3349.

74 On Ramsay (1852–1916), see ch. X, note 7.

75 IC, Council Minutes, **8**, 22 May and 27 November 1914.

76 *Ibid.*, **9**, 27 October 1916. The Institute recognized only 35 out of a possible 300 technical colleges and universities, *Proc. Inst. Chem.*, 1916, **40**, pt. i, 23–7.

77 (a) IC, Council Minutes, **9**, 20 July 1917; (b) *Proc. Inst Chem.*, 1918, **42**, pt. ii, **35**.

78 See for example, *Proc. Inst. Chem.*, 1917, **41**, pt. iv, 6–7; 1918, **42**, pt. ii, 8–20.

79 IC, Council Minutes, **9**, 2 November 1917.

80 *Ibid.*, 18 January 1918; *Proc. Inst. Chem.*, 1918, **42**, pt. ii, 10.

81 Note 77 (b), p. 30.

82 On Dobbie (1852–1924), see *Proc. Inst. Chem.*, 1924, **48**, 227.

83 On Jackson (1863–1936), see *DNB; Analyst*, 1937, **62**, 83–6; and *J. R.I.C.*, 1963, **87**, 195–7.

84 *Proc. Inst. Chem.*, 1918, **42**, pt. iii, 9–46. Council acted quickly on the last suggestion, recognizing several technical colleges which it had previously rejected. IC, Council Minutes, **10**, 5 July 1918.

85 *Proc. Inst. Chem.*, 1920, **44**, 109–18. In 1924, a Branch H on General Analytical Chemistry was added. It was dropped in 1927, but re-introduced in 1943.

CHAPTER X

THE PROFESSIONAL CHEMIST IN INDUSTRY 1877—1918

1 The Victorian Period and its Aftermath

A casual reader dipping into Pilcher's *History of the Institute*, which covers the period 1877–1914, might be forgiven for supposing that the Institute was obsessively preoccupied with the composition of chemical fertilizers. This would be grossly unfair as a serious judgement, for, as we have seen, much useful work was performed in the related matters of for example education, professional affairs, and in fact in many other areas as well. Yet of all the industrial matters that came to the Institute's attention in those early years agricultural chemistry seems to have been the most demanding. Its chief concern was with the Agricultural Analysts, a group whose activities were of much importance to the manufacturers of 'artificial manures'. On Tyneside, that great centre of the superphosphate industry in the 1870s, it was urged that their 'analytical results ought not to be translated into such a language as may mislead the farmer and annoy and cheat the manufacturers',[1] while loose and misleading statements on manure analysis should not 'come from the lips of a professional man'.[2] These exalted sentiments are reminiscent of those applied to the Public Analysts, a group with whom their agricultural colleagues shared some characteristics as, in other respects, they showed affinities with industrial chemists.

In 1893 the Board of Agriculture was approached by the Institute in connection with the Fertilizers and Feeding Stuffs Act of that year. The President, with three other members, obtained an interview with the Secretary of the Board to urge the importance of selecting properly qualified persons to perform analyses in connection with the Act, 'and to impress upon the Board the character of the qualification indicated by Fellowship of the Institute'.[3] Perhaps as a result of these representations by 1906 most analysts appointed were Fellows of the Institute.[4] The Board attempted to encourage technical and agricultural colleges to provide farmers with analyses either without cost or at purely nominal fees. In so doing it incurred the wrath of the Institute and withering scorn from its President, David Howard, who observed that if farmers were to get free chemical analyses they might as well have free medical and veterinary advice; and 'Why should not the smith have gratuitous analysis of his iron, the dyer of his dyes, the druggist of his drugs, and so forth? Why should we not all be fed with pap—at the public expense—with a Government spoon?'[5]

In 1906 a new Fertilizers and Feeding Stuffs Bill was presented to Parliament. Again the Institute sent a deputation to the Board of Agriculture, this time led by P. F. Frankland,[6] son of the founder and himself recently elected President of the Institute, supported by William Ramsay[7], the agricultural chemist E. W. Voelcker,[8] C. E. Cassal[9] (one of the black-ballers of the 1870s) and others. Frankland explained to the President of the Board, Earl Carrington, the aims and duties of the Institute and urged upon him the desirability of recognizing the Institute's qualifications as evidence of fitness for the role of Agricultural Analyst. On this point a favourable reply was later received, and most of the Institute's other recommendations were incorporated in the finally amended version of the Act which became law on 1 January 1907.[10] Several members of the Institute were later instrumental in framing methods of analysis which became officially adopted by the Board.

In 1907 an inquiry by the Board into agricultural education gave the Institute a further opportunity to press for a cessation of the practice of obtaining cheap analyses from agricultural colleges. As a result the Board's Committee affirmed that 'Analysis for commercial or trade purposes formed no part of the function of an agricultural college in receipt of state aid', though it considered 'that when an analytical work is distinctly of educational value it may properly be carried out by the chemist at such an institution'.[11]

Yet another issue which arose about this time was the question of tenure for Agricultural Analysts. In 1907 the Institute protested when an Agricultural Analyst in Scotland was dismissed without apparent reason, and in the following year, jointly with the Society of Public Analysts, it sent a further deputation to the Board. Sir William Ramsay draw attention to the quasi judicial character of such appointments and the possibility that they might be terminated at the caprice of interested parties exerting pressure on local authorities who would be unaware of the reasons for such activity. The Secretary of the Board, Sir Thomas Elliott, expressed sympathy with the points raised, but emphasized the problem of the relationship between central and local government as well as the difficulty of obtaining an amendment to so recent a statute.[12] However in the following year the Board recommended to local authorities that at least six months' notice should be given to their Agricultural Analysts, which went some way to meet the Institute case.[13]

A point made several times in representations regarding Agricultural Analysts was the disparity between their terms and conditions of service and those of the Public Analysts who enjoyed tenure. In the first twenty years of its life the Institute had been active on their behalf as well, particularly in connection with the Sale of Food and Drugs Act and its administration.

Activities of this kind are perfectly appropriate functions for a professional institution to engage in since they undoubtedly help to raise the status of its members, especially those engaged in analytical practice. In view of the origins of the Institute they are especially understandable. It may be doubted, however, whether they had much effect on the position of chemists in other kinds of industry or upon the shape of the chemical industry itself. Indeed it is hard to point to any specific action taken by the Institute during the nineteenth century which had more than marginal relevance to the manufacturing chemical industries (with the possible exception of analytical control). In other words the Institute before 1900 was hardly concerned with the situation of the chemist doing industrial research. At first sight this is all the more surprising since, as we have noted, academics tended to predominate to a large extent on its Council and at least five of its early presidents were notable for their research output: Frankland, Abel, Odling, Tilden[14] and Russell[15]. Although the Institute's policy looks extremely paradoxical there are several factors which helped to explain its lack of interest in industrial research.

In the first place there were in Britain very few chemists engaged in this kind of activity, a state of affairs in sad contrast to the growth of industrial research on the continent, particularly Switzerland and Germany. Where chemical research of this kind took place in the United Kingdom towards the end of the century it was often a sideline only. Two examples out of many must suffice to illustrate this point. One was the case of an establishment enjoying the highest prestige, the Royal Mint. Following the death of Thomas Graham, Master of the Mint, in 1869, C. W. Fremantle, the Deputy Master, wrote 'that the progress made of late years by the British Mint in the practical application of scientific knowledge to questions of Mint management have not kept pace with the advances which have been made by mints abroad'.[16] Many continental mints had laboratories attached for both assaying and for experiments 'bearing upon other questions affecting the interest or efficient management of the establishment'. Next year W. Chandler Roberts[17] was appointed as the first chemist with a salary of £200. During his early years of office he developed spectroscopic analysis for metals, worked on methods for removing brittleness from gold and studied capillary phenomena of molten metals. But all this was in addition to his responsibility as one of the assayers at the mint.

Another example of 'sideline research' in this period was the railway industry. Of this Sir Harold Hartley has written:

> Before the [1914] war original work of permanent value had been done in railway laboratories and workshops. It would be true to say, however, that these early investigations were made despite the lack of any definite research policy laid down by the Boards of the railway companies, and were mainly the pioneer inquiries of individuals.[18]

Thus at the Crewe laboratory Reddrop and his assistant Hugh Ramage (both Fellows of the Institute) developed the bismuthate method for the determination of manganese in steel,[19] while at Derby the chemist L. Archbutt[20] collaborated with the Locomotive Superintendent of the Midland Railway, R. M. Deeley, in some classic research on lubrication.[21]

But the chemists had to take vigorous action to make their presence felt in the industry which was sadly unaware of their services. Thus at Crewe in 1903 Reddrop's successor, F. C. Tipler, persuaded the General Manager of the LNWR to write to all departments urging that 'In future the freest use shall be made of the laboratory and testing shop for every necessary purpose in connection with your department, and I shall be glad of the assurance that the matter shall have your personal attention'.[22] Even so only the chief chemist and one assistant at Crewe were on salaried grades until 1910. In that year an enthusiastic student of chemistry was transferred at his own request from a clerical post to a more poorly paid position in the laboratory, retaining his salaried position. This raising of the status of the railway chemist was accomplished by an enthusiast who subsequently became known as Dr P. Lewis-Dale,[23] FIC, Chief Chemist to the LMS Railway.

The first industrial research laboratory in Britain appears to have been the Huddersfield dyestuffs firm of Read Holliday who by 1890 employed four or five research chemists, most of them from Germany.[24] Shortly after this the United Alkali Company was formed from forty-eight firms in an attempt to revive the declining fortunes of the Leblanc process for making soda. A central research and analytical laboratory was established under Ferdinand Hurter.[25] The departure from previous research activities in the alkali industry has been described like this:

[Workers] in the small laboratories of the individual factories . . . carried out researches in connection with their inventions and specific problems as they arose. With the Central Laboratory systematic research, covering all aspects of the chemical industry, began: a consistent campaign of investigation was launched to discover and evaluate new processes.[26]

A second reason for the Institute's apparent coolness towards industrial research at this time lay in the existence, from 1881, of the Society of Chemical Industry. The two chief objectives of this new organization were defined as follows: 'To enable persons interested in chemical industries to meet, to correspond, and to interchange ideas respecting improvement in the various processes' and 'to publish information relating to the aforesaid, by means of a journal or otherwise'. [27]

At the inaugural meeting at the Chemical Society's rooms in London, Roscoe as Chairman said that the new society would not interfere with the work of existing institutions, including the Institute of Chemistry. However, doubts about this were raised by Kingzett who argued that 'one of the objects of the Institute was to promote the interests of manufacturing chemistry and of all branches of the science allied thereto'. He was reassured by Abel, President of the Institute, who 'concluded that the objects proposed by this Society were entirely distinct'. Like other speakers he regarded the Society of

Chemical Industry as having similar functions to the Iron and Steel Institute.[28]

Of the committee members and other officers elected at this meeting the majority were also associated both with the Chemical Society and the Institute of Chemistry. An overlapping membership of this kind may make for good communication between the bodies concerned, but it can also define more rigidly the lines of demarcation between their separate functions. This, of course, has been a perennial difficulty in the Institute's position throughout its century of existence. But it cannot be a sufficient explanation, since the existence of the SPA did not inhibit it from acting in matters affecting the practice of analytical chemistry.

If a further reason is to be sought it is probably found in the paradoxical nature of what has been called the 'endowment of research movement'.[29] The Institute of Chemistry was born as this movement was gaining momentum, with the Devonshire Commission and the University Reform Acts as its most obvious manifestations. In the early days of the twentieth century, research was becoming accepted by the public at large as something worthy of government support and encouragement. The expression of this goodwill was chiefly in the creation of state fellowships for research, but the result was unexpected. A polarization had become evident between academic research on one hand and industry on the other, and the very existence of such fellowships tended to insert a wedge between the high-fliers (who usually chose academic research) and the rest who often settled for posts in industry. The availability of very limited funds from the government meant that a distinction between the brilliant and the mediocre was inevitable so the 'rank and file of science', as Huxley called them, were left to manage as best they could in industry, teaching or elsewhere.

The leaders of the Institute, academics themselves, tended to guard their academic preserves somewhat jealously. The old conflict between academics and practical men appeared in a new guise. As one writer has said recently: 'In a sense, the "researchers'" victory was a paradox. The public acceptance that brought them recognition in universities and research institutes also helped separate them from industry and society at large'.[30] Until World War I the rapid growth of higher education in the new institutions in the United Kingdom was more important than the application of science. In the Royal Society from 1881–1914 the percentage increase in academic Fellows was four times greater than the corresponding figure for applied scientists, for this was the great era of expansion in higher education.[31]

It is probably in terms like this that the Institute's attitude is to be understood. It is easy, with hindsight, to look back and criticize those in authority for failing to alert the profession as a whole, and the government and general public also, to the prime need for industrial research and for the promotion of that activity by all means within its power. Given the diversity of industrial needs, and the complications of dealing with both employers and employees, it is hard to see what the Institute could have done. Rather than blaming its leaders for accepting the *status quo* of industry it would be more reasonable today to see their dilemma as a product of the fragmentation of chemical institutions at the end of the Victorian era and draw the appropriate conclusions for ourselves.

About 1902 the tide began to turn in the Institute's affairs. With the passing of the Victorian age, and with an increasing awareness of Britain's slow industrial progress in comparison with its European and American competitors a new spirit was abroad and several events conspired to exert pressure on the Institute to turn its attention once more to the question of industrial research.

At the British Association meeting in 1902 the question was raised concerning the number of scientific chemists employed in British industry and a committee consisting of W. H. Perkin (Jnr),[32] G. G. Henderson,[33] H. E. Armstrong and G. T. Beilby[34] was set up to investigate. By means of circulars to the membership of the SCI they obtained the following data: 502 chemists replied, 107 being graduates, 59 of whom were graduates only of British universities, the rest having received at least one of their degrees abroad. As Professor Cardwell comments: 'This shows that even at that late date, the professional scientist in industry was to a large extent a foreign product.'[35] Of the 502 names 111 belonged to the Institute of Chemistry.

In his presidential address to the British Association Dewar talked expansively on the data presented by the committee, and by generously multiplying their data by three assumed there might be as many as 1500 chemists in British industry.[36] But even this rosily optimistic assessment compared very badly with Germany's known total of some 4000 chemists of whom eighty-four per cent were graduates while only thirty-four per cent of their British counterparts enjoyed similar qualifications.

In a detailed calculation based upon Dewar's estimate and numerous other data Cardwell has come to the following conclusions as to the employment position of chemical graduates about this time.

Secondary teaching	400 graduates
University and similar teaching	150 + graduates
Chemical industry	180–230 graduates

Thus, of the total number of professional chemistry graduates of 730–80 only about twenty-five per cent (thirty per cent at the most) were engaged in chemical industry. This was the situation to which the British Association was alerted in 1902.

In the same year the London County Council appointed a subcommittee to look at the application of science to industry in the light of increasing anxieties about the effect of foreign competition. The subcommittee heard evidence from ten Fellows of the Institute and concluded that inadequate scientific training was basically responsible in Britain.[37]

These two reports must have made a great impression upon the Institute and it is not without significance that the new President elected in March 1903, David Howard, was the first to occupy the Chair who could be genuinely said to be an industrial chemist. He was, as we have seen, one of the founder members of the Society of Chemical Industry. At the time of his election Council were considering a suggestion from E. J. Mills that it should establish examinations in chemical engineering and other branches of chemical technology. To study this proposal a special committee was appointed. Its inquiries amongst numerous manufacturers and others concerned with technical education soon led to an obvious conclusion. Pilcher puts the matter as follows:

> Whilst the replies indicated that the work of the Institute had been greatly appreciated, they pointed almost without exception to a desire for the establishment of a special examination. Since a sound and broad training in pure chemistry and physics was of primary importance to works' chemists, it was agreed that the examinations should be 'postgraduate', opinions being adverse to young men specialising too early in particular branches of work. A large number of manufacturers emphasised the view that they did not want chemists whose training and examinations had been confined to the technology of a particular industry, but those possessing knowledge, as wide as possible, of chemical processes generally.[38]

The outcome of the committee's deliberations was the establishment of an examination in chemical technology that was first held in October 1906 (p. 173). Its beginnings were not particularly auspicious, with only one out of the three candidates passing, and it was not an important departure in the Institute's policy.

Over the next few years the examinations in chemical technology continued to attract very low numbers of entrants although their influence was not confined to those who actually sat them. During this time much consideration was given as to how further to 'bridge over the gap between the college and the works' when in 1911 an important development was suggested by Professor H. Jackson.[39] This was to the effect that a lecture series should be started dealing with aspects of chemistry that were directly relevant to modern practice. This was fully in accord with the provisions of the Charter and this important series of publications began with the delivery of two lectures on cement in 1911 and continued with others on such diverse topics as cellulose, chlorine, chemistry in the gasworks, explosives, etc. In this way the Institute was beginning to play a big role in directing attention to the responsibilities and opportunities awaiting the chemist in industrial research. But now other and far more powerful forces were at work to the same end and in 1914 the outbreak of a European war changed for all time the attitudes of both the public and chemists to the importance of the chemical industry.

2 The Impact of World War I

The outbreak of war took both sides by surprise so far as chemical provisions were concerned. In Germany the army appeared to have assumed that its essential raw materials would still be supplied as in peace time, but in fact Germany was not prepared even for the shortages associated with a brief conflict.[40] Britain equally seemed to have grossly underestimated its dependence for raw materials on Germany itself. However the two sides differed profoundly in their response once war had been declared. British scientists were not differentiated from other citizens expected to join up, and many died at the Front, most memorably perhaps the young Oxford physicist, H. G. J. Moseley, killed in action in the Dardanelles in 1915. Thirty Fellows of the Chemical Society and fifty-five members of the Institute lost their lives on active service. Even P. F. Frankland advised his male students to volunteer for the forces for the first year or so of the war.[41] Many of the industries which produced essential raw materials were losing key personnel to the army or navy; the managing director of Lever's factory at Port Sunlight proclaimed that by 1915 'many of our best men had gone to the war',[42] while Crosfields at Warrington had released 665 men—a quarter of their male work force, and both these establishments were manufacturing that essential raw material for high explosives manufacture, glycerol. In Germany, by contrast, the research staff of the Kaiser Wilhelm Institute were diverted almost immediately into war research of various kinds[40] and the Knapsack carbide factories near Cologne increased their work force more than six-fold within a few months.[43]

One of the first deficiencies to make itself seriously felt in the United Kingdom was in the area of dyestuffs, so great had been our previous dependence upon Germany—over eighty per cent. Government authorization to violate German patents had little effect, for the industry was not geared for rapid changes, and so, as Tilden observed in late 1916, 'the dye-houses of Yorkshire and Lancashire are almost brought to a standstill for lack of material'.[44] Various moves by the government culminated in its sponsorship of a new company, British Dyes Ltd, in 1915, based on the Huddersfield firm of Read Holliday, with an injection of over £1 million of government money. Three years later the government promoted a merger between this company and its old (and embittered) rival, Levinsteins of Manchester into the British Dyestuffs Corporation. But the most important parliamentary action was the establishment of an Advisory Council which soon emphasized the need to establish research institutions to link industry with the universities.[45] In 1916 W. H. Perkin (Jnr) was appointed Chairman of the Advisory Council for British Dyes Limited which was able to establish small 'colonies' of chemists in different universities.[46]

The sudden dearth of dyestuffs was a serious blow to the nation not yet accustomed to the idea of 'total war'. Much more important in a military sense was the lack of raw materials with which to make explosives. Explosives based on nitroglycerin were derived from glycerol which was readily available from the soap makers. The chief propellant then used, cordite, was a blend of nitrocellulose and nitroglycerin obtained by mixing the two with acetone and this solvent had been hitherto only available as an import, originating either in the highly inefficient thermolysis of calcium acetate or else from wood-tar. Just before the war Weizmann in Manchester had discovered his fermentation process for making acetone but the offer of this process to the Admiralty was ignored until 1915.[47] In 1914 picric acid was the standard shell filler, made by nitrating phenol which was traditionally obtained from coal-tar. Attempts to supplement these limited supplies by synthesizing phenol had remained of limited success by Read Holliday (using the sulphonation method). Gradual replacement of picric acid by the non-acidic TNT led to a demand for toluene that was not then obtainable by synthesis. Some conservation of this material was possible by mixing TNT with ammonium nitrate. Pre-war studies by Brunner, Mond and Co were extended by F. A. Freeth to the point when, in 1915, it became possible to commence factory production of this material using a double decomposition reaction between imported nitrate and ammonium sulphate, several hundred thousand tons being made before 1918.[48]

All these explosive materials involved nitrogen in a high oxidation state. In Germany this was to pose a bigger problem than in the United Kingdom since an effective blockade deprived it of the Chile saltpetre upon which it was dependent for the production of nitric acid. To this urgent matter Haber turned his attention and before the war was over his process for the fixation of atmospheric nitrogen to ammonia (and its subsequent oxidation) was in full swing and producing half Germany's needs.[49] In Britain the Government did not make the technique a matter of investigation until 1917 and it was only six years later that the plant went into operation.[50]

The chemical upon which all the explosives industry depended was sulphuric acid. In the absence of a method for fixation of atmospheric nitrogen this was essential for the production of nitric acid (from imported nitrate) as well as its subsequent nitration reactions, only in the latter case a much higher concentration was essential and the acid produced by the traditional lead chamber process was not satisfactory unless afterwards concentrated by the expensive evaporation methods. For the pure anhydrous acid, and still more for oleum, the contact process was necessary, and very few such plants existed in pre-war Britain. For oleum there were only three, but by 1915 the Government's Advisory Committee on the Supply of Sulphuric Acid for the Production of Munitions came into being, encouraged such manufacturers as the United Alkali Co to set up contact plants and erected three under government supervision in Scotland. In this way production of oleum rose from its 1914 level of a few hundred tons per week to something like seven thousand tons.[51] In this way the need was avoided to import oleum in steel drums that frequently failed to survive a transatlantic journey with inevitably disastrous consequences.

Of course explosives were not the only outputs for the acid; but dyestuffs at that time almost all involved a nitration at some stage of their production or, in the case of those based on polynuclear hydrocarbons, a sulphonation. And over and above all this was the ever-present demand for sulphuric acid in the manufacture of superphosphate fertilizers.

These developments in the First World War emphasized in an entirely new way the importance to the economy of the scientist, especially the chemist. As we have seen the demands of war led to the establishment of an Advisory Council; this was responsible to a committee of the Privy Council for Scientific and Industrial Research which became shortly afterwards the Department of Scientific and Industrial Research and in due course the Science Research Council. Its rather patchily successful history cannot concern us now except in so far as its £1 million grant was a major step forward in government support and recognition of science. However welcome these parliamentary gestures were at the time, many recognized that an even more fundamental desideratum was wide public support for science, for without that government attitudes were not likely to remain sympathetic once the pressures of war were removed. In 1916 a meeting took place at the joint auspices of the Royal Society and the British Science Guild (a brainchild of Lockyer's) as a 'committee on the neglect of science'. One of its objectives was to break the stranglehold of the classics on higher Civil Service examinations and to open up those forbidden preserves to men of science. But its chief insistence was the need to bridge the gap between academic science and the ordinary man.[52]

This was a challenge accepted by the Institute of Chemistry, or rather by its Registrar and Secretary, R. B. Pilcher in conjunction with Frank Butler-Jones,[53] who from December 1916 to July 1917 contributed a series of articles to *The Engineer* under the title of 'What industry owes to science', observing in their opening remarks 'we have heard a good deal lately of our neglect of science'. The articles were well received, and in 1918 they were collected together as a book with the revised and slightly more accurate title *What industry owes to chemical science*.[54] A foreword by Sir George Beilby, a past President of the Institute, gave a 'Special message for parents and teachers' to the effect that 'Trained chemists will, in the near future, be in increased demand for industrial and official positions'.[55]

This book was slightly revised and issued as a Second Edition in 1923 and rapidly sold out. It was frankly an exercise in propaganda, but it was none the less an able and informed contribution and stimulus to the public debate that was then beginning to take place. It was also a stoutly patriotic defence of chemists in the U.K.:

> We have shown that though 'genius is of no country'. British men of science, often in the face of small encouragement, have played their part in industrial development. There is no reason to depreciate the value of their work, or to pay much attention to the Jeremiahs who seem to delight in bemoaning the industrial and commercial position of this country but are seldom able to offer any constructive criticism.[56]

This essay by the Institute in the realm of public relations was not quite a new departure but in its direct appeal to popular opinion certainly showed a new emphasis, one that was to become increasingly important in the inter-war years.

The appearance of Pilcher's *History of the Institute* in 1914 was seen by Council as a very timely event in the light of these developments, though how far it was of real value in the wider realm of public relations may be doubted. Certainly the Institute were trying to get rid of surplus copies well into the 1920s; one may perhaps be permitted to hope that this is not the fate of all historical writings in relation to the Institute of Chemistry! In fact we are told that Pilcher's *History* was prepared under the Chairmanship of E. W. Voelcker, who was then Vice-President and Chairman of the Proceedings Committee.[57]

The Institute's response to the needs of industry during the war were not confined to a general popularization of chemistry. Probably their most important role was in assisting and co-ordinating the recruitment of skilled chemists for the war effort. An Appointments Register had been instituted in 1908[58] but now it was to achieve a new role as the *Proceedings* for 1914 indicate:

> **Professional Chemistry and the War**—Immediately after the outbreak of war, the Registrar informed the Secretary of State for War that a number of Fellows and Associates of the Institute, with special knowledge in connection with the manufacture and examination of explosives and other war material, as well as with the examination of food, drugs and water, were available for scientific work on behalf of the country and willing to place their experience and services at the disposal of the Government. The Secretary of State, in reply, intimated that the offer was appreciated and would be noted. Later, two Fellows and one Associate were supplied for service at Woolwich Arsenal, whilst in other ways which need not be specified in detail the Institute and its Fellows have been useful to the War Office, the Admiralty, and other Government Departments.[59]

In the following year the Institute obtained for the Ministry of Munitions particulars of five hundred chemists, many of whom were appointed to government service.[60] By 1916 the number had reached six hundred and the President was not likely to have been far from the mark when he paid tribute to the unwearying efforts of 'the indefatigable Registrar', R. B. Pilcher, in this connection.[61] By the end of the war nearly two thousand names had been dealt with.[62]

In three other ways the Institute attempted to make a real contribution to the progress of chemical industry during the war. One of these was concerning the developing role it was to have, in conjunction with the Society of Public Analysts, as a clearing-house for information about scarce chemicals. As a result of its initial inquiries the Joint Committee of the Institute of Chemistry and the Society of Public Analysts was able to publish a *List of Reagents for Analytical Purposes*. By 1916 several firms were producing the more important reagents specified in that *List*.[63] Finally, the Institute set up a Glass Research Committee, under the Chairmanship of R. Meldola to discover ways of producing glassware for chemical use as a substitute for that made almost exclusively in Germany and Austria. A substitute also had to be found for one of the main ingredients, German potash. The results were very successful and led to the hope that in time British makers would 'excel the Germans in both quality and technique'.[64]

With the dramatic changes experienced by the chemical profession and the chemical industry within the next few years the achievement of such an objective would have been impossible. But it may be agreed that the Institute had done its best to capitalize upon the undeniable importance of chemists during the First World War and on its own contributions to their well-being and employment. CAR

NOTES AND REFERENCES

1 *Trans. Newcastle Chem. Soc.*, 1877–80, **4**, 127 (28 February 1878).

2 *Ibid.*, p. 130.

3 R. B. Pilcher, *History of the Institute, 1877–1914*, Institute of Chemistry, London, 1914, p. 127.

4 *Ibid.*, p. 195.

5 *Ibid.*, p. 184.

6 On P. F. Frankland see *Proc. R.I.C.*, 1946, **70**, 290, and L. H. Lampitt, 'Percy Faraday Frankland', *R.I.C. Lectures, Monographs and Reports*, 1949, no. 2 (1st P. F. Frankland Memorial Lecture).

7 See M. W. Travers, *A Life of Sir William Ramsay*, Arnold, London, 1956, and *idem*, *British Chemists*, A. Findlay and W. H. Mills (eds), Chem. Soc., London, 1947, pp. 146–75.

8 On E. W. Voelcker see *Proc. Inst. Chem.*, 1930, **54**, 344; *Analyst* 1931, **50**, 144–6.

9 Cassal's leading role in 'black-balling' emerges from his obituary, *Analyst*, 1922, **47**, 103.

10 Pilcher (note 3), pp. 195–8.

11 *Ibid.*, p. 204.

12 *Ibid.*, pp. 214–7.

13 *Proc. Inst. Chem.*, 1908, **32**, pt iv, 215–7.

14 See *J. Chem. Soc.*, 1927, 3190–202.

15 See *DNB*, *J. Chem. Soc.*, 1918, **113**, 339–50; J. R. Brown and J. L. Thornton, *Ann. Sci.*, 1955, **11**, 331–6; and K. R. Webb, *J.R.I.C.*, 1960, **84**, 272–4.

16 *1st Report Deputy Master of the Mint* (1870), (*c.* 303), P.P. 1871, XVI, p. 223.

17 On Chandler Roberts see *DNB*.

18 Sir Harold Hartley, 'Scientific Research on the London Midland and Scottish Railway', *J. Inst. Transport*, 1932, **14**, 497.

19 *J. Chem. Soc.*, 1895, **67**, 268.

20 See *Proc. Inst. Chem.*, 1935, **59**, 272. In 1912 the Society of Public Analysts and Other Analytical Chemists (the extended title dating from 1906) elected Archbutt as the first President not holding a Public Analyst's position.

21 L. Archbutt and R. M. Deeley, *Lubrication and Lubricants*, London, 1899.

22 Private communication from Mr M. T. Hall.

23 On Lewis-Dale see *J.R.I.C.*, 1960, **84**, 379.

24 D. S. L. Cardwell, *The Organisation of Science in England*, 2nd edn, Heinemann, London, 1972, p. 175.

25 On Hurter see D. W. F. Hardie, *A History of the Chemical Industry in Widnes*, ICI, London, 1950, ch. X. His advocacy of the Leblanc process in face of competition from electrochemical processes led W. J. Reader to remark 'it is unfortunate that when his advice became really influential, it turned out to be disastrous' (*Imperial Chemical Industries. A History*, vol. i, *The Forerunners 1870–1926*, OUP, London, 1970, p. 117).

26 Hardie (note 25), p. 177.

27 *J. Soc. Chem. Ind.*, 1931, **50**, 11.

28 *Ibid.*, p. 12.

29 On this topic see R. M. MacLeod, 'The Support of Victorian Science: The Endowment of Research Movement in Great Britain, 1868–1900', *Minerva*, 1971, **9**, 197–230.

30 *Ibid.*, p. 230.

31 Cardwell (note 24), p. 230.

32 See S. G. P. Plant in *British Chemists* (note 7), pp. 176–218.

33 See *Obit. Not. F.R.S.*, 1944, **4**, 491–502.

34 On Beilby see *DNB* and *Proc. Inst. Chem.*, 1924, **48**, 227.

35 Cardwell (note 24), p. 206.

36 *Rep. Brit. Assoc.*, 1902, **72**, 3–50 (especially 15–18).

37 Pilcher (note 3), pp. 162–4.

38 *Ibid.*, p. 171.

39 *Ibid.*, pp. 240–1.

40 J. E. Coates, 'The Haber Memorial Lecture', *Chemical Society Memorial Lectures*, Chem. Soc., London, 1951, vol. iv, p. 142.

41 Lampitt (note 6), p. 13.

42 C. Wilson, *The History of Unilever*, Cassell, London, 1970, vol. i, p. 222.

43 E. Baümler, *A Century of Chemistry*, trans. D. Goodman, Econ. Verlag, Düsseldorf, 1968, p. 66.

44 W. A. Tilden, *Chemical Discovery and Invention in the Twentieth Century*, Routledge, London, 1916, p. 4.

45 L. F. Haber, *The Chemical Industry 1900–1930*, Clarendon Press, Oxford, 1971, pp. 190–2.

46 Plant (note 32), p. 181.

47 F. Nathan, 'The Manufacture of Acetone', *J. Soc. Chem. Ind.*, 1919, **38,** 271T–273T.

48 F. A. Freeth, *New Scientist*, 1964, **23,** 274.

49 Haber (note 45), p. 203.

50 T. I. Williams, *The Chemical Industry*, E. P. Publishing, Wakefield, 1972, p. 71.

51 D. W. F. Hardie and J. Davidson Pratt, *A History of the Modern British Chemical Industry*, Pergamon, Oxford, 1966, p. 99.

52 Cardwell (note 24), p. 223; and *Proc. Inst. Chem.*, 1916, 40, pt iii, 4.

53 On Butler-Jones, an analyst with the Ministry of Munitions, see *Proc. Inst. Chem.*, 1943, **67,** 51.

54 *Op. cit.*, London, 1918; 2nd edn, 1923. A third, rewritten edn. appeared in 1945.

55 *Ibid.* (2nd edn.), p. viii.

56 *Ibid.*, p. 145.

57 *Proc. Inst. Chem.*, 1914, **38,** pt iii, 8.

58 Pilcher (note 3), p. 221.

59 *Proc. Inst. Chem.*, 1914, **38,** pt iv, 3.

60 *Ibid.*, 1915, **39,** pt iv, 3.

61 *Ibid.*, 1916, 40, pt ii, 21.

62 *Ibid.*, 1919, 43, 4.

63 *Ibid.*, 1920, 44, 202–14.

64 Pilcher and Butler-Jones (note 54, 2nd edn.), p. 77.

CHAPTER XI
ANALYSTS AND ACADEMICS: THE INSTITUTE AND PROFESSIONAL RELATIONS TO 1918

Once established, the Institute faced the immediate task of translating the rather abstract aims discussed by the organization movement into a set of policies which would achieve them. This was not straightforward. It was necessary to establish the reputation of the new Institute as a body which took seriously its responsibilities to the public at large.[1] At the same time, it was necessary to balance the sometimes disparate interests of the diverse groups practising as chemists. Until the First World War, the two principal groups involved in the Institute's discussions on professional affairs were academics and analytical and consulting chemists in private practice or official posts.[2] Many of the professional issues considered at the outset were raised again later as circumstances and membership changed. During the Institute's first forty years, Council repeatedly met such problems as the use of the title 'chemist', the statutory registration of chemical practitioners, the status of chemical appointments as compared with that of other government posts, competition between private practitioners and academics working in state-funded institutions, chemical ethics and etiquette, and the economic welfare of chemists. Indeed, some of these issues, although with different priority, are still of concern to Institute members.

Before turning to a detailed investigation of the Institute's professional affairs, one general point should be made. It is somewhat artificial to separate the discussion of qualifications from a discussion of the Institute's professional affairs generally. From the outset, its principal plank of policy was to establish and later maintain the reputation of sound qualifications for the practice of chemistry. The Institute argued that, if its qualifications were respected, its status with the public would be assured, and individual as well as collective well-being would follow. However, internal and external professional relations affected the Institute's views on what constituted sound qualifications (Chapter IX). The reverse was also true. All proposed policy changes in the sphere of professional relations were considered in the light of their possible effect on the reputation of the Institute's qualifications. This turned out to be both an asset and a liability for the Institute. It prevented hasty responses to short-term circumstances, but it sometimes also tended to inhibit worthwhile developments.

1 Registration

In addition to defining its qualifications, the Institute acted initially on two fronts: recruiting members and considering professional discipline. All of these were of course important for achieving status for its collective membership through public recognition, a main objective of any professional association. On the question of recruitment, a major decision had to be taken. Should the Institute attempt to form a comprehensive register of all chemists in practice and thus eventually constitute a licensing body for chemists? Or should the Institute limit its membership according to criteria of training or eminence? Medicine and pharmacy provided precedents for the former course, and such a policy would have the attraction of giving chemists the strength of numbers in governing both internal and external relations. Obviously any sanctions that such a professional institution might apply either to its own members or to the public would have force in proportion to the percentage of the profession it represented. If all chemists belonged, either by choice or by law, the new Institute would be in a very strong position. Comprehensive registration, whether compulsory or voluntary, did have weaknesses however. Contemporaries were particularly concerned that the many ill-qualified chemists likely to be admitted under such an arrangement would irremediably lower the standards which the Institute hoped to set.[3] In any case, the Pharmaceutical Society's position on the title 'chemist' precluded compulsory registration (p. 156).

On the other hand, a certain exclusiveness of membership would take advantage of the already existing individual reputations of initial members and therefore establish the new body's corporate reputation more quickly. Furthermore, the Board of Trade ruling that the Pharmaceutical Society already was a licensing authority in charge of chemists' qualifications, whose functions the new Institute would not be allowed to duplicate, made it necessary for the latter to adopt the policy of exclusive membership (p. 152). Indeed, until it obtained a Royal Charter in 1885, the Institute was even prevented from awarding qualifications, although it could restrict its membership according to whatever criteria it wished thereby creating *de facto* qualifications.[4]

In 1883, the Institute decided to seek reincorporation by means of an Act of Parliament. This would have afforded its register and qualifications statutory recognition. A Bill was drafted and approved by the membership, and forwarded early in 1884 for consideration by Parliament. In the event, Council was advised to withdraw the Bill and sought a Charter instead. Thereafter, the Institute tended to argue that its membership did constitute a unique register of those who were qualified to practise chemistry, even if not a comprehensive one. If all qualified chemists joined, statutory registration would be superfluous. In fact, the Institute formally called its list of members a register, even before the 1885 Charter granting it the power to issue certificates of competence. The Charter simply avoided the problem of the term 'chemist' by using a number of circumlocutions when referring to the Institute's members: 'persons practising the Profession of Analytical and Consulting Chemistry', 'persons competent to practise in analytical Chemistry and to advise in technological Chemistry', or 'persons desirous of qualifying themselves to be public and technical analysts and chemical advisers on scientific subjects of public importance'.[5]

The issue of registration temporarily lay dormant after the Charter, while the Institute framed its new regulations. However, the new regulations displeased analytical and consulting members because of the requirement that all training be undertaken in approved universities and colleges, thereby virtually excluding apprenticeship and part-time training (p. 163). This dissatisfaction led to renewed pressures for statutory registration. In 1889, two relatively new analytical and consulting Fellows of the Institute revived an old issue by suggesting to the Chemical Society that it ought to restrict its membership to chemists with scientific qualifications. They argued that since the Institute's requirements were so stringent, unqualified practitioners sought entry to the Chemical Society and incorrectly used the letters FCS as a qualification to practice. Such injudicious admissions to the Chemical Society, they suggested, tended to counteract the Institute's efforts to raise the status of the profession.[6] The Secretary of the Institute, Charles E. Groves, saw this as an attack on the Institute, the implication being that the Institute had accomplished little since the 1870s if the Chemical Society still provided a means for the unqualified to obtain 'qualifications' improperly.[7]

Although the young analysts denied any intention of attacking the Institute, their raising such issues when its regulations were under discussion anyway prompted a general evaluation of the Institute's progress (p. 166). Grievances and criticism reached such a pitch that in May 1891, the Institute held a conference to discuss some of the problems. William Odling spoke 'On the Relation of the Chemical Society to Professional Chemistry', Otto Hehner spoke on 'The Analytical Chemist in Relation to the Public, the Profession, and the Institute', C. R. A. Wright spoke 'On the Training Requisite for Professional Chemists,' and F. J. Lloyd spoke on 'The Best Training for an Analytical Chemist'.[8] Much to the annoyance of many analytical and consulting chemists, Council refused to publish the proceedings of the conference. Otto Hehner, one of the Institute's most vocal analyst critics published his talk separately in the *Chemical Trade Journal*.[9] This made it clear that the general issue underlying the specific discussions was the influence that academic and analytical and consulting members should enjoy respectively within the Institute. Hehner suggested that academics were antipathetic to the interests of analysts, yet, ironically, these same academics ran an institution that was formed for the benefit of analytical and consulting chemists.

> While thus the position of the analytical chemist becomes year by year of greater public importance, it is to be regretted that it continues to be held in but scant respect by the academical portion of the chemical profession, that so little is done for it in our colleges and schools so far as

education is concerned, so much less as regards scientific investigation of analytical problems . . . The fault lies largely with the teachers, who are out of touch with the large portion of the profession on whose behalf I am now venturing to speak. They are often not exactly conversant with the requirements of the public; they even look down upon analytical commercial chemistry as a mercenary and unscientific occupation. . . . Until it is recognized by all fractions of our profession, that every sincere and honest worker in the field . . . is, in the long run, equally useful in widening our science, and none has the right to assert that only he does useful work. Until that time arrives, I fear the split amongst chemists will only widen and intensify.[10]

After the conference, William Thomson, a Manchester analytical chemist, organized a protest group among colleagues in the North of England pressing for more representation for analytical and consulting members on the Council of the Institute. His Institute of Chemistry Reform Association argued that analytical and consulting chemists should constitute at least half of Council and that works chemists should be represented too. Groves, replying for Council, suggested that this was an attempt by the Society of Public Analysts to take over the Institute. But Otto Hehner, then President of the Society of Public Analysts, countered that only sixteen of the fifty-nine signatories of Thomson's petition were Public Analysts. Rather the petition should be seen as a protest by analytical and consulting chemists 'against the usurpation of their rights by those whose interest in the Institute is only secondary'.[11] The Annual General Meeting of March 1892 was particularly heated, as analytical and consulting members attempted, with some success, to put forward their own nominees for Council. Groves noted afterwards that fully one-third of the Institute's members were dissatisfied with Council.[12] Thomson kept up his campaign since the results of the Annual General Meeting were not altogether satisfactory. However, it was not really a question of numbers, but of influence.[13]

Meanwhile the young analysts, joined by Charles E. Cassal, veteran of the Chemical Society campaign of the 1870s (p. 117) and vocal analyst member of the Institute, kept pressing the qualifications issue at the Chemical Society. They even initiated another black-balling campaign in 1895.[14] Within the Institute, they successfully promoted the view that the Institute's Register should contain no designatory letters which might be viewed as chemical qualifications except 'FRS'. This of course excluded 'FCS' and even degrees.[15] Some academic members protested that this was unprofessional conduct on the part of a faction within the Institute. However, Tilden, as President, was already under considerable pressure from the analytical and consulting faction because of his advocacy of full-time university or college training for members (p. 167). He publicly supported the move on the grounds that the Fellowship of the Chemical Society was not a qualification.[16]

Not content with progress in the Chemical Society, given the views about open membership held by its President (H. E. Armstrong), the analysts continued to press the Council of the Institute to consider seeking legal sanction for compulsory registration of practising analytical and consulting chemists.[17] Such power in the Institute, they argued, would restrict misuse of Chemical Society membership. During 1896, Council investigated the possibility quite seriously but decided against it.[18] According to Pilcher, the main objection at this time was that any comprehensive register would have to include all of the individuals with extremely varied training who practised as analysts, even medical men and pharmaceutical chemists. Registration would grant them status equivalent to that of properly qualified members of the Institute, thereby weakening that body's position rather than strengthening it. Council stressed the argument that it was up to individual members to make the Institute's qualifications more widely known, so that charlatans would not be consulted.

2 Professional Ethics

Along with membership criteria and limitations, questions of professional conduct received early attention within the Institute. Any professional association seeking to establish a reputation must assure the public that, once qualified, its members can be relied upon to practice with integrity. This in turn helps to protect the position of members from the unfair competition of disreputable practitioners. In the case of analytical and consulting chemistry, several areas of abuse had emerged during the decade preceding the establishment of the Institute. Council initiated a series of conferences to discuss some of the more difficult problems members faced, and possibly to suggest some guidelines. Council had to hope that such open discussions would lead to a voluntary code of behaviour governing members' practice, as there were no sanctions that it could apply for non-adherence. General exhortation or the exercise of the moral authority of more eminent members by means of such devices as presidential admonitions were the only sanctions available, bar expulsion. In the early years, the latter could hardly have been a real threat; the Institute was anxious to increase its membership and expulsion from a young non-monopoly institution could not prevent anyone from practising in any case. Moreover, the Institute had no control over the behaviour of non-members.[19] And so that such justice as was possible could be seen to be done, Council followed the precedents of other professional bodies and fairly quickly appointed a panel of eminent chemists to serve as Censors. Although they were technically powerless, they did provide an aura of rectitude both within and outside the Institute which was important in creating a sound reputation.

In addition, the Censors could offer guidance on professional conduct. There were problems on which analytical and consulting chemists themselves felt they needed assistance and the Institute provided an important forum for airing them. Among the topics of the Institute's early conferences on questions of professional ethics were trade certificates, the relations of professional chemists to each other, their clients, and the public in legal cases, and general ethical issues facing analysts.[20] The first focussed on a question that was to recur quite regularly, and indeed eventually came to constitute the main business of the Censors; how analysts could prevent clients from misusing certificates of contents, purity, etc., either for advertising or for making false claims. For example, it was not uncommon for certificates based on a particular sample of a product to be used as a general testimonial for the whole of a firm's output. In other cases, firms advertised such certificates as 'scientific seals of approval' for their products. Moreover, the use of an analyst's name in such circumstances could also constitute an advertisement for the analyst, a practice strongly opposed by the Institute as being the mark of a tradesman rather than a professional.[21]

Also aired at these conferences were some difficulties raised by the 1874 Select Committee on the Adulteration of Food Act (1872). Who should be responsible for sampling? How should analysts deal with the problem that a client's suggested method of analysis might give different results from the analyst's preferred method? In a court case, should the analyst be his client's advocate, or an impartial observer? How should analysts present highly technical evidence to a court of laymen? Where two analysts' reports conflicted, what refereeing procedures should be used? For the most part, there were no straightforward answers to such questions, but the views recorded usually came down on the side of a policy of fair play underpinned by a reliance upon objectively determined natural laws. Such general advice was doubtless useful, but there was a constant demand for more specific action, for a clear definition of the distinction between a trade and a profession.

In 1893, the Censors drew up a list of 'practices discreditable to the profession of analytical and consulting chemist' in an attempt to specify the grounds for suspension or dismissal from the Institute which the Charter mentioned.[22] The list included:

(a) Advertising for practice in newspapers, journals, magazines or other published papers.
(b) Sending out by post, or otherwise, letters, circulars, or cards, offering professional services.
(c) Undertaking through another person or agency the performance of professional work at fees representing only a small fraction of the usual recognized scale of fees for analytical work.
(d) Supplying to other persons, not being qualified chemists, reports upon samples or processes with the knowledge that these other persons will issue such reports as their own work.

    (e) Issuing or allowing to be issued, certificates of purity or superiority concerning advertised commodities, such certificates being either not based upon the results of an analysis, or containing exaggerated, irrelevant, or merely laudatory expressions, designed to serve the purpose of a trade puff.

    (f) The unauthorized use of letters indicating University degrees.[23]

The particular actions designated discreditable at this time were of course a response to immediate contemporary problems, the main specific concern being unfair competition from unqualified practitioners. The list also illustrates one of the Institute's principal difficulties in its early years, balancing individual members' legitimate commercial activities with the corporate aim of seeking professional status. The fact that this list was so specific and narrow shows the difficulty of defining any code of professional conduct. It was all but impossible to legislate across the whole of chemical practice, as accepted standards varied both geographically and according to the branch of practice. In the end, the Institute had to rely on a somewhat abstract notion of gentlemanly behaviour. This tended to reinforce the 'academic' position within the Institute, as university education was a recognized hallmark of a gentleman in Victorian times.[24] Subsequently, there were periodic attempts to define a code of practice for chemists, generally in response to a specific set of incidents. All foundered on the difficulty of the diversity of chemical practice and sensibly adopted the approach of providing general guidelines rather than specific rules.[25]

3   Parliamentary Influence

Since the Institute was founded in the wake of legislation affecting chemists, another of its early and continuing concerns was to exert influence on government action regarding chemistry. The 1874 Select Committee on the Adulteration of Food Act (p. 106) demonstrated that analytical and consulting chemists lacked a public voice.[26] The Institute hoped to provide this voice, both indirectly, by establishing the reputation of its qualifications so that all posts created by legislation would eventually go to its members, and directly, by commenting on legislation in the making and in execution.

    Not surprisingly for a new body, the Institute's approach to dealings with the government was somewhat passive. It occasionally promoted discussions on actions which the government might take;[27] but it adhered to a policy of reacting to developments rather than initiating them. In 1878 Council appointed a Parliamentary Committee to monitor issues relevant to the chemical profession with which the government was dealing or ought to deal. Six months later, the Committee reported that it had retained a firm of parliamentary agents to do the monitoring while the Committee would decide on the Institute's response to any matters that arose.[28] Another approach was to seek direct support from MPs with chemical interests. This proved more useful when there were specific issues to be dealt with, or when some of the Institute's own members were MPs, rather than a general means of keeping in touch with the legislature. At times the Institute joined forces with other organizations, particularly the Society of Public Analysts, to press mutual causes. Since 1935 the Institute has been actively represented on the Parliamentary and Scientific Committee, which consists of members of both Houses of Parliament as well as representatives of many scientific institutions. The Institute has continued to use varied means to express professional chemists' views on legislation, as the success of any particular method of doing so has tended to depend on the individuals pursuing it rather than the method used.[29]

Perhaps more important than its efforts to influence legislation passing through Parliament were the Institute's efforts to influence the shape of legislation at the drafting stage and subsequently to make suggestions about its implementation. The *Proceedings of the Institute* contain instances far too numerous to list in which the Institute offered, or in later years, was invited to submit, evidence to Select Committees, Royal Commissions, and government departments. However, while it is a simple matter to show that the Institute was zealous in pressing its point of view, it is rather more difficult to evaluate its success in influencing public action in particular cases. Government response varied from ignoring the Institute's submissions altogether, acknowledging them but taking no action, to seriously considering and rejecting them. On other occasions Institute suggestions have been incorporated in the new legislation. The response has depended on the complexion of the Government of the day and the particular individuals involved on both sides as well as on the intrinsic merits of the Institute's position and the strength of its advocacy.[30]

4 The Status of Public Analysts

Until well after the Second World War, it was legislation affecting Public Analysts and holders of other public chemical posts that received most attention from the Institute, although from the First World War onwards, it commented increasingly on events affecting chemical industry (Chapter XII). There were several reasons for this orientation. In the first place, as the Institute argued when defending itself internally against charges of favouritism, as a chartered body it was committed to working for the public welfare and specifically prevented from working for the personal benefit of individuals when there was no issue of principle at stake. Since it was clearly in the public interest to have the most expert and efficient Public Analysts possible, it was also clearly in the public interest for the Institute to argue for improved terms, conditions, and remuneration on their behalf. Only by making such posts financially attractive and of sufficiently high status, could the government hope to recruit the highly qualified and responsible individuals it should want in such posts.[31] While they were in the public interest, these arguments were of course also in the interests of chemists.

Quite apart from the stipulations of the Charter there were doubtless practical considerations behind the Institute's constant activity on behalf of public appointees. Compared with other practitioners they were an identifiable and relatively homogeneous group, and the need for them to have qualifications was publicly acknowledged (Chapter IX). The same applied for other issues. Public Analysts taken collectively provided a concrete case, whereas industrial chemists were a disparate group for whom it was (and still is) difficult to advance any general argument. Furthermore, the Public Analysts' employers in local government were relatively few in number and were held publicly accountable. However inadequate the legislation and regulations affecting Public Analysts were, they at least gave the Institute a set of principles and standards about which to argue. Similar considerations underlay the Institute's advocacy of the cause of Official Agricultural Analysts appointed under the Fertilizers and Feedstuffs Act of 1893.[32]

Rhetorically at least, the Institute turned these circumstances to good account. The Local Government Board administered the Sale of Food and Drugs Act until World War I, after which the new Ministry of Health took over this function. These bodies had to approve all appointees to Public Analyst posts, although the appointments were made by local authorities. An unofficial intelligence network kept Council apprised of appointees, terms, and conditions for Public Analyst posts, and the Institute quickly notified the administering body of possible abuses. On the questions of terms, conditions, and remuneration, central administration had no legal jurisdiction until 1938 and usually referred the Institute unsatisfactorily to the local appointing authorities. With no statutory or central direction, they were free to fix remuneration at a level suiting the local budget. In an employers' market, there was no trouble filling posts. Indeed, even when the Institute publicly asked members not to apply for low-paid posts or those that set fees by inviting tenders, the posts were always filled, often by Institute members.[33] The Institute also challenged fairly frequent joint appointments of Medical Officer of Health and Public Analyst. Such appointments were obviously a blow to its claim that the Public Analyst's duties were primarily chemical, and it could quite truthfully assert that the analytical instruction given to prospective Medical Officers of Health was not adequate for such tasks. Central administration generally refused to recognize this objection since a medical qualification was legally permitted, but it met the Institute halfway by disapproving of dual appointments unless the Public Analyst's tasks in the particular area were known to be slight.[34] The Institute, however, continued to oppose joint appointments in principle. By the early 1900s almost eighty-five per cent of all Public Analysts holding ninety per cent of the available appointments were members of the Institute.[35] Indeed this near monopoly should have enhanced its bargaining position. There was doubtless an element of 'jobs for the boys' in the Institute's advocacy, but the real issue was one of status. Chemistry as performed by Public Analysts merited an independent post.

Another complaint was that Public Analysts were often subordinate to Medical Officers of Health (MOH) in local government public health hierarchies.[36] This was particularly irritating in view of the Institute's argument that the training and professional status of the chemist was equivalent to that of the medical man. Even more galling in these circumstances, the Public Analyst's superior chemical expertise could be overriden by the judgement of an MOH with little chemical training. Institute protests to local authorities generally met the response that there was a need for local rationalization and economy. Central administration approved of rationalization and felt that organization was a local matter; so long as the efficiency of neither post was impaired, it would not intervene.

5 The Economic Welfare of Chemists

Analytical and consulting chemists in private practice also appeared to be favoured within the Institute when contrasted with industrial chemists. Again, there were practical reasons for this. Any action reflecting on the status of Public Analysts and Official Agricultural Analysts also affected the status of analysts in private practice; most official posts were only part-time, so the incumbents were also private practitioners. Furthermore, analytical and consulting chemists were independent and self-employed. Therefore any regulations which the Institute might introduce affected only them and did not involve the delicate problem of attempting to influence employers. In addition, the Institute's very concept of a professional chemist was that of an individual in independent practice. When pressed about not catering for industrial chemists during the early years of the twentieth century, the Institute replied that it did aid them since many analytical and consulting chemists worked mainly for industrial clients. In addition, there were some fairly clear-cut issues affecting analytical and consulting chemists. For example, the Institute was always quick to object to any encroachment on the sphere of the private practitioner by publicly funded bodies. Its records are filled with protests against analytical work performed (ironically) by educational institutions, municipal laboratories, and other public bodies.[37]

(a) Remuneration

The possibility of defining a scale of fees for analytical and consulting work was among the early issues considered within the Institute.[38] As with so many other questions, the Select Committee on the Adulteration of Food Act had highlighted the problem: reputable analysts faced competition from unscrupulous practitioners who not only advertised for practice, but also offered their services for very low fees. These could not cover the costs of a thorough analysis, much less provide an income.[39] An official Institute scale of fees would give the public something against which to measure the claims of the unqualified. It would also provide reputable analysts with a quotable authority on fees in cases of controversy with clients. However, there were difficulties as well, and a committee appointed to construct a scale of fees in 1881 came to no very definite conclusions. In the first place there was concern that the public might interpret any scale as representing maxima rather than minima. This might work to the disadvantage of analytical practitioners. There was also the problem of balancing different styles of practice among the Institute's members. Should academics who could do analytical work with no overheads charge as much as private practitioners who had to pay for their own facilities? If academics charged less, would that not constitute unfair competition? Did junior members of the profession deserve as high fees as established practitioners? Ought any scale to allow for geographical differences in fee levels? In any case, would a scale of fees really provide a guarantee of professionalism to the public, or would the unscrupulous only improve their own income by following the Institute's suggestions? At a later discussion of the same issue, one Fellow of the Institute suggested that circulating a scale of fees in itself was unprofessional, as fees should depend on the circumstances of any particular case.[40]

Any scale of fees was only as useful as the degree to which members of the Institute themselves adhered to it. In Scotland in 1901, FICs constructed their own scale of fees and their own disciplinary panel. Council did not approve; it was for individual Fellows and Associates to create through their behaviour a 'proper feeling of professional responsibility' which would be followed by pecuniary rewards.[41] The realities of financial pressures, however, overrode feelings of professional responsibility during the competition for a number of public posts and Council was pressed to take firmer action. In the first instance this consisted of advising members privately not to apply for certain low-paid posts or those that invited tenders. With a lack of sanctions and a shortage of posts, such advice simply did not work.[42]

Matters came to a head in 1912 when one of the chemists in the War Department complained that there was growing dissatisfaction amongst members; they felt that the Institute should be more than just an examining body and an advocate of good conduct. The membership awaited a firm policy statement on ways to improve the status of analytical chemists in both public and private practice. This particular complaint may well have been motivated by personal frustration as the War Department chemical staff was in the midst of negotiations contesting the downgrading of its career and salary structure.[43] However, the general sentiment was widespread, and the protest was effective. The Institute submitted evidence on behalf of the Woolwich staff to the currently sitting Royal Commission on the Civil Service.[44] In addition, G. T. Beilby made the sort of policy statement demanded, in his 1912 presidential address to the Institute.[45] He suggested that the time had come for group action on behalf of Public Analysts and revealed the Institute's (unsuccessful) request, published the same day, that its members should not apply for specified posts. He committed the Institute for the first time to a public stand about the personal finances of members; the Institute considered £100 per annum to be the very minimum acceptable salary for a professional chemist, and then only for a newly qualified AIC. Beilby discounted current fears about overcrowding in the profession: 'there is a rapidly-increasing demand for trained chemists in industry, and industries are passing more directly under proper scientific control than hitherto'. This was perhaps an optimistic view of contemporary circumstances, but it did indicate the direction in which the Institute was to proceed.

In June 1912, the Institute held a conference on the remuneration and conditions of public appointments.[46] The main participants were seasoned combatants in Institute discussions, the young reformers of a previous generation. Indeed, the fact that the Institute had failed to instil such zeal into a new generation may have been part of its problem. William Tilden discussed the position of academics, while Otto Hehner and Charles E. Cassal focused on Public Analysts, and John A. Voelcker[47] discussed Agricultural Analysts. All agreed that the remuneration of the professional chemist did not create the status he deserved. Tilden implied and Hehner insisted that it was no longer possible for the Institute to separate the question of remuneration from the question of raising the status of the profession through education and qualifications. Hehner and Cassal both urged the Institute to designate the acceptance of low pay as unprofessional conduct constituting grounds for dismissal from membership of the Institute and to initiate a vigorous policy of boycotting unsuitable posts. In the case of Public Analysts, it was also necessary to take a strong stand on the matter of interference from MOHs. Otherwise, Cassal said, the Institute might as well close its doors.

After the conference, the Institute did begin to press the issues of remuneration and conditions in more specific terms, arguing for actual sums of money and quite detailed conditions for Public Analysts and chemists under other government departments. However, its main method still tended to be exhortation, if of a more intense variety. This placed a very heavy burden on the administrative officers. For example in 1913, Pilcher travelled to Edinburgh to make personal representations to the Corporation about its unsatisfactory Public Analyst post. He lobbied numerous officials and also personally attempted to persuade candidates to withdraw their applications.[48] In addition, periodicals were asked not to accept advertisements for posts with a salary of less than £100 and a committee was charged (successfully this time) with devising a publishable fee structure for substances analysed under the Food and Drugs Acts. It was still felt to be impracticable to devise a scale for private practitioners, but the committee drew up a set of typical fees for various branches of practice. This was not published but held for individual consultation at the Institute. However, none of the scales was made binding on members and no penalties for non-adherence were instituted. This, it was determined, was in keeping with the practice of other professional bodies.[49]

(b) The Appointments Register

The Institute's Appointments Register provided another means for pressing employers for improved terms, conditions, and remuneration. This was officially set up in 1908, although the Secretary had privately run an *ad hoc* appointments bureau since 1900.[50] The Register operated very simply. The Secretary kept a list of members of the Institute seeking either a new appointment or a change of employment, together with a list of posts either gleaned from advertisements or notified privately. Those seeking employment received a copy of the list of posts at regular intervals for a nominal fee. Pilcher screened all notified posts for suitable terms, conditions and remuneration and often tried to get them improved. It was his policy not to include jobs with salaries below a certain minimum (£100 during the pre-war years). The Appointments Register became one of the Institute's most valuable features; it was particularly useful to members at the start of their careers.[51]

Thus on the eve of the First World War, the Institute was beginning to execute its policies in the field of professional relations somewhat more vigorously, although the policies themselves and the methods of executing them would not have startled the Institute's Victorian founders. At the same time, developments in the academic world were inducing the Institute to re-evaluate its qualifications. The war brought circumstances which accelerated many of these developments by highlighting the Institute's strengths and its deficiencies.

6 World War I and Professional Affairs

The Institute's war record was deservedly a source of much pride in subsequent years, especially in connection with chemical reagents and glassware (p. 197). During the war, the Institute also took some important steps in the area of professional relations. Given a shortage of forces medical personnel, it urged the government to assign chemists instead of medical men to analyse water and food supplies, thereby releasing the latter for their 'proper' business of tending the wounded. Most significant however was the Institute's role in assisting a government that was notoriously disorganized about the proper utilization of its scientists with the mobilization of both Institute and non-Institute chemists for war work.[52]

The latter increased the demand for industrial chemists, brought them more into public view, and added to their list of grievances. The government's appreciation of the situation was so inadequate that while medical men were called up as officers, trained chemists were called up as sappers only to have to be recalled subsequently to staff the munitions factories. Woolwich Arsenal advertised for well-trained chemists at 2s 6d per week, inflicting the double indignity of classifying professional chemists as wage earners rather than salaried, and of offering a ludicrous wage at that, well below the Institute's minimum. For purposes of recruiting, chemists were classed with navvies and labourers in the Ministry of Labour's list. In any case, professional chemists felt it a social slur to have to deal with Labour Exchanges. Furthermore, public discussions about the aftermath of the war indicated that the future organization of British industry would be decided between employers, as represented by their associations, and employees, as represented by trade unions. There seemed no place for the professional man to state his case.[53] The Whitley Report of 1918 provided for the institutionalization of this scheme by the creation of a National Industrial Council for every industry to make policy decisions affecting employment for that industry. Each Council was to consist of the relevant employers' association and the relevant trade union. That a range of new chemists' organizations appeared, seeking in varied ways to establish a voice for chemists in their own future, is hardly surprising.

(a) New chemical organizations

The Institution of Chemical Technologists, for example, was established in 1913 in the wake of the internal controversies over the effectiveness of the Institute of Chemistry and the failure of its technical chemistry examination. Charles Cassal, one of the Institute's most active members, and most ardent critics, was among the promoters of the new Institution. During the early years of the war it argued its case strongly. The Institution was established to advance the study of technological chemistry and to obtain support and recognition for it; to bring about cooperation among professional chemists; to set high standards of professional conduct and responsibility; to secure a voice for technological chemistry; and to bring about a closer relationship between industry and education. In effect, the Institution of Chemical Technologists set out to be the professional body for works chemists and other chemists employed in industry, an area in which it felt that the Institute of Chemistry had failed.[54]

Another attempt to find a voice was the Conjoint Board of Scientific Societies organized by the Royal Society early in 1916. The Institute was represented on this Board, whose objects were to promote cooperation between pure and applied scientists; to supply means of public expression for scientific opinion on science, industry, and education; to promote the application of science; and to discuss questions requiring international cooperation.[55] At about the same time, another of the Institute's 'senior' internal critics, C. T. Kingzett, suggested that there be a similar organization for chemists. He called it a 'real Institute of Chemistry', which would include all existing chemical bodies and provide a coordinated and powerful voice so that chemistry and chemists would be properly valued.[56] Also in early 1916, H. E. Armstrong was trying to promote from within the SCI, the body that was eventually established in 1919 as the Federal Council for Pure and Applied Chemistry (FCC) with the object of voicing the interests of chemical science as distinct from the profession of chemistry and the chemical industry (p. 241).[57]

On a different level, chemical employers were also organizing. The Association of British Chemical Manufacturers was formed as a trade association in 1916 (p. 222). Meanwhile scientific employees formed new organizations: the National Union of Scientific Workers was founded in 1918 in order to bring about the integration of science and industry through trade union methods[58] and the National Association of Industrial Chemists (NAIC) started in Sheffield in June 1916. When founded, the latter was explicitly not a trade union, but was designed instead to prevent chemists from joining unions by pre-empting the issues. However, although not registered, its activities were certainly similar to those of trade unions. The NAIC's objects were: to promote the economic, intellectual, and social advance of industrial and metallurgical chemists; to promote their interests by collective action if necessary; to further the interests of young chemists; and to promote education for industrial chemists. Its main aim was to obtain recognition for the role of works chemists in the industrial life of the nation. It hoped to achieve this by seeking representation on government industrial committees, by pressing for adequate remuneration, by pressing for personal recognition of works chemists' discoveries, and by establishing an employment register. The NAIC had a very elaborate organization with local sections in centres throughout the North and in London as well as committees covering various branches of industry. It also specified regulations for admission, but these were not restrictive: full members had to be at least twenty-one and possess a university degree, or have three years' experience supplemented by part-time study, or have some equivalent experience approved by the Association. There was a junior grade of associate membership open to anyone over the age of sixteen employed in a laboratory. By early 1918, the Association's membership approached 1000.[59]

(b) The provisional British Association of Chemists

At first, the new wave of chemical institutions affected the Institute very little. For the most part, the functions of the new organizations either complemented those of the Institute, or were so far removed from them as to be of no importance to it. However, the provisional British Association of Chemists (BAC) presented a direct challenge. This was a self-conscious pressure group dedicated to 'persuading' the Institute of Chemistry to take more positive action on behalf of industrial chemists. If the Institute met its demands, the provisional BAC would not become a permanent body. If the

Institute did not comply the provisional BAC itself would erect the desired professional structure for industrial chemists.

The Institute took this challenge very seriously. In the first place, the movement was quite large. The inaugural meeting of the provisional BAC in Manchester in November 1917 was attended by 500 chemists, an unprecedented number. Furthermore, many Institute members were involved in the movement, and its constituency overlapped that of the Institute significantly. But perhaps most serious, almost all of the policies suggested by the provisional BAC had at one time or another been considered within the Institute and rejected. Obviously, their rejection had not stifled the issues behind the policies. The provisional BAC's aim was to improve the status of professional, particularly industrial, chemists. It did not set out to be a trade union and planned, like the Institute, to include employees and employers. Its declared objects were: to obtain power to act as the sole registration authority for chemists; to have the title 'chemist' legally redefined; to obtain legislation requiring that certain manufacturing processes must be under the control of qualified chemists; and to raise the intellectual status of the profession.[60]

Some of the early meetings of the provisional BAC were held under the auspices of SCI local sections. The SCI specifically declared its neutrality at these meetings, but a number of prominent SCI members were actively involved and the journal of the SCI gave provisional BAC events thorough coverage. In any case, it was definitely a movement of non-London, industrial chemists who must have had some source of funds, or at least overhead support, to make so organized a beginning. One contemporary suggested that the provisional BAC was an NAIC splinter group which had left the parent body because of its rather loose qualifications.[61]

The provisional BAC made several specific requests of the Institute. The first was that it make its membership more truly representative of the profession by widening its qualifications in order to attract the sixty-six per cent of qualified chemists who did not belong. The provisional BAC admitted all holders of degrees in chemistry to its 'A' qualification, regardless of class of degree, the institution in which the candidate had studied, or whether his course was full- or part-time, in the day or in the evening. It also had a 'B' qualification which was to apply for a limited period only. Under this heading, it admitted individuals who could demonstrate that they had had some general preliminary education and who had had seven years' experience in applying chemistry, latterly in a responsible or senior post. Thus, if the Institute were to adopt the provisional BAC's qualifications as suggested, it would also have to recognize a much wider range of teaching institutions, along with part-time and evening instruction, as suitable preparation for these qualifications.

Secondly, the provisional BAC saw the possible widening of the Institute's membership to include all qualified chemists as a preliminary to its seeking legal powers to compile a register. Victorian arguments about the benefits of a compulsory comprehensive register appeared again. However, there was now the additional specific argument that, in view of the establishment of the Whitley Industrial Councils, industrial chemists needed the representation that a powerful chemical body with statutory comprehensive membership could provide. Thirdly, the provisional BAC also suggested that, along with acquiring a stronger voice nationally, the Institute ought to run its internal affairs more democratically. It particularly wanted the Institute to establish local sections along the lines of those of the SCI so that provincial members would feel less remote. The sections should serve as local initiators and implementers of Institute policy and should keep in touch with headquarters by electing local representatives to Council. Fourthly, the provisional BAC asked that Council govern more openly, keeping members of the Institute better informed through the *Proceedings* than previously. Finally, the provisional BAC asked the Institute to take a stronger interest in members' financial welfare by establishing a Benevolent Fund, since many members would be facing financial hardship after the war.[62] For the most part then, the provisional BAC was attempting to persuade the Institute to take bolder strides in directions where it previously had always stopped after a few tentative steps.

The Institute's public response to the overtures of the provisional BAC was to express complete sympathy with its aims and objects and to imply that the movement was superfluous since the Institute already followed most of the policies suggested.[63] This was not a false claim, but the Institute's policies were closer to the 'letter' of the provisional BAC's suggestions than to their 'spirit'. After the provisional BAC's show of strength at the Manchester inaugural meeting however, the Institute established a General Purposes Committee to frame future policy. Pilcher was kept very busy defending the Institute around the country at meetings discussing the provisional BAC. Discussion within the Institute was intense and often heated. Council recognized that the Institute had to deal with the pressures from industrial chemists both because of new legislation and the changing national pattern of chemical employment. However, the difficulty was how to accommodate the industrial chemists without offending existing members. Academics within the Institute tended to favour the provisional BAC's suggestions and had indeed been pressing for wider membership for some years. Others however, protested strongly at what they saw as an erosion of the value of their hard-earned qualifications, and a possible long-term threat to the viability of private practice. The Institute's decisions about its qualifications are discussed in Chapter IX; it did open its doors somewhat more widely.

In fact Council put the pressure applied by the provisional BAC to good use. Pointing to these pressures, Council managed to push through reforms of membership policy which Institute members had previously rejected.

These met the provisional BAC's requirements in all but a few details. On the question of registration, the Institute held to its old argument that it already was the sole registering body for qualified chemists, and if all who were qualified would join, it would be a very comprehensive register indeed. It refused, however, to register chemists who did not hold the Institute's qualifications, or to create a third grade of membership to admit chemists with lesser qualifications, on the grounds that that would reduce the value of its existing qualifications. Furthermore, the Institute could point to quite recent discussions with the Pharmaceutical Society over the title 'chemist'. The outcome of these was not altogether satisfactory, but at least the Institute could show that it had been active. In addition, it very quickly agreed to establish Local Sections, to arrange for the election of representatives of Local Sections to Council, to institute a Benevolent Fund, and to upgrade the published *Proceedings*.[64]

The provisional BAC was largely satisfied with these changes and, according to its own policy statements, should have disbanded.[65] In fact, several active members of the provisional BAC were very surprised by the decision of a June 1918 executive committee and a July General Meeting to carry on. Some members of the provisional BAC thought that the Institute's reforms had been somewhat shallow, and that it had not made any great concessions on the question of membership. Others argued that the Institute's good faith deserved testing.[66] But the main reason for the BAC's continuing was the question of economics. J. W. Hinchley, one of the principal initiators of the BAC scheme made his views clear. The provisional movement had at least brought about a general expansion of the Institute and better consultation. That left a permanent movement free to deal with problems of registration and seeking recognition on the Industrial Councils. In fact, the final meeting of the executive committee of the provisional BAC recommended that all its members join the Institute of Chemistry, while the new BAC would deal with social and legal problems, attempt to influence parliament, establish local sections to look into individual problems of remuneration and employment, establish a friendly society, and look after the interests of junior chemists seeking qualifications.[67]

Thus, industrial chemists working for employers began to claim a more significant share of the Institute's attention after it had devoted forty years primarily to the professional interests of analytical and consulting chemists in independent practice. The academic community favoured this transition as it coincided with its own post-war interests. The reorganization of 1918 was to mark a turning point in the Institute's history. Nothing illustrates the magnitude of the change initiated then so well as the membership graph (Figure 7).

GKR

NOTES AND REFERENCES

1 F. M. L. Thompson, *Chartered Surveyors: The Growth of a Profession*, Routledge, London, 1968, pp. 148–50.

2 This is not to imply that the Institute did not include industrial chemists from the start, but rather that it was for the most part after the war that they became a significant group in Institute policies.

3 C. R. Alder Wright, *Chem. News*, 1876, **33,** 28, favoured the licensing authority approach (ch. VII, p. 123).

4 R. B. Pilcher, *History of the Institute, 1877–1914*, Institute of Chemistry, London, 1914, pp. 40–9 (43).

5 *Ibid.*, pp. 77–8 discusses the attempt to obtain statutory recognition. Royal Institute of Chemistry, *Charter of Incorporation, 1885; Supplemental Charter, 1944; Bye-laws—Revised 1924 and 1946*, London, 1947, *Charter*, pp. 6–7. The terms 'analytical and consulting chemist' and 'chemist' were used in the Charter, but not in the sections defining membership; *ibid.*, pp. 14, 18.

6 *Chem. News*, 1889, **60,** 189; F. L. Teed, *ibid.*, 1890, **62,** 212–13. Teed became FIC in 1888 and F. J. Lloyd, the other activist, in 1887. On Teed (1858–1937), see *Proc. Inst. Chem.*, 1937, **61,** 285. On Lloyd (1852–1923), see *ibid.*, 1923, **47,** 194.

7 *Chem. News*, 1890, **62, 225.**

8 Pilcher (note 4), pp. 103–5.

9 *Chem. Trade J.*, 1891, **9,** 73–6.

10 *Ibid.*, p. 75.

11 *Chem. News*, 1892, **65,** 85, 94, 95, 105.

12 IC, Council Minutes, **2,** 1 March 1892. The meeting was attended by about 180 members; *Chem. News*, 1892, **65,** 140–1, 143.

13 *Chem. News*, 1893, **67,** 23. In reply, W. N. Hartley, *ibid.*, p. 37, retorted that only 12 of the 35 members of Council were academics. However, Hartley may have been defining 'academic' somewhat narrowly. If lecturers in medical schools are counted, 17 Council members taught. Ten academics attended 50 per cent or more Council meetings as did 10 others. IC, Council Minutes, **2,** 1892.

14 *Chem. News*, 1892, **64,** 211–12; 1893, **66,** 249; 1894, **68,** 214–16, 255; 1895, **71,** 313.

15 IC, Council Minutes, **2,** 20 January 1893; Pilcher (note 4), p. 116.

16 *Chem. News*, 1893, **66,** 71, 83.

17 IC, Council Minutes, **2,** 1 March 1895; **3,** 1 March 1896.

18 *Ibid.*, 30 October 1896, 22 March 1897; Pilcher (note 4), pp. 140–1.

19 IC, Council Minutes, **1,** 25 January 1879, 25 June 1883. **3,** 25 March and 29 May 1898 consider a complaint by a Fellow about a non-member. Council ironically recommended that the Fellow seek the assistance of the Chemical Society since it happened that both parties were members of that body.

20 'Report of a Conference on Trade Certificates, 22 November 1878', *Proc. Inst. Chem.*, 1879, **2,** separate pamphlet bound in; 'Report of a Conference on the Ethics of Professional Chemistry, 8 December 1881', *ibid.*, 1882, **6,** separate pamphlet bound in; Pilcher (note 4), pp. 60–2, 70–1, 67–8.

21 Following the precedents of medical men in particular, the Institute argued that inclusion on a list of qualified chemists such as the Institute's *Register* should be all the

publicity that a chemist needed and all the information that the public needed. This remained the Institute's policy until 1965; RIC, Council Minutes, **55**, 23 July 1965.

22 Pilcher (note 4), p. 123.

23 IC, Council Minutes, **2**, 17 February 1893.

24 *Ibid.*, 21 December 1894; Pilcher (note 4), pp. 133–4.

25 In drafting the Institute's most recent statement on this subject in response to a government initiative, the Ethical Practices Committee came up against exactly the same problem; RIC Council Minutes, **62**, 21 July 1972; RIC, Council Minutes, n. vol., 14 December 1973. See also, 'The Path of Duty; Signposts for Members', *RIC Professional Bulletin*, no. 8, 25 June 1973.

26 'The Adulteration Act', *Lancet*, 4 July 1874, 18–20; 'The Public Analysts and the Report of the Adulteration of Food Committee', *Chem. News*, 1874, **30**, 69; *Report from the Select Committee on the Adulteration of Food Act (1872)*, (262), P.P. 1874, VI, 243.

27 See, for example, the discussion on 'The Relations of the Chemical Profession to Public Sanitation', in Pilcher (note 4), pp. 63–4.

28 IC, Council Minutes, **1**, 20 December 1878, 27 June 1879.

29 Report of the Professional Status Committee, *ibid.*, n. vol., 2 October 1973.

30 See, for example, the Institute's testimony to the Royal Commission on the Indian Civil Service, ch. XV.

31 See, for example, IC, Council Minutes, **2**, 12 May 1891; **7**, 25 November 1912; *Proc. Inst. Chem.*, 1938, **62**, 445.

32 For example, IC, Council Minutes, **2**, 13 October 1893; **5**, 26 May 1905, 25 May 1906, 25 October and 13 December 1907.

33 *Ibid.*, **3**, 20 January and 26 May 1899, 23 February 1900; **7**, 1 March 1912; R. B; Pilcher, *Chem. News*, 1912, **36**, 130 (5 March). For the results of this action, see IC, Council Minutes, **7**, 10 May 1912. Another case was recorded in *ibid.*, 17 March and 29 May 1913. and **8**, 29 May 1913 cont.

34 *Ibid.*, **2**, 20 January 1893; **4**, 31 January 1902.

35 David Howard, *Proc. Inst. Chem.*, 1904, **28**, pt. ii, 11.

36 See, for example, IC, Council Minutes, **7**, 30 March 1911; **8**, 19 December 1913.

37 Most of these protests were unsuccessful. There was a particularly rancorous dispute, in which the Institute was joined by other professional associations, over the right of the National Physical Laboratory to conduct routine tests of materials; *ibid.*, **5**, passim.

38 *Ibid.*, **1**, 25 November 1881.

39 *Report from the Select Committee on the Adulteration of Food Act (1872)*, (note 26).

40 *Proc. Inst. Chem.*, 1895, **19**, pt. i, 31.

41 IC, Council Minutes, **4**, 25 October 1901, 24 January 1904.

42 *Ibid.*, **6**, 24 April, 23 October 1908; 18 June, 18 July, 27 October, 14 December 1910.

43 *Ibid.*, **7**, 26 February 1912.

44 *Ibid.*, 14 June, 26 July, 25 November 1912; *Proc. Inst. Chem.*, 1913, **37**, pt. iii, 10–13.

45 G. T. Beilby, *Proc. Inst. Chem.*, 1912, **36**, pt. ii, 9–24; see note 33.

46 'Report of a Conference on the Remuneration and Conditions of Public Chemical Appointments', *Proc. Inst. Chem.*, 1912, **36**, pt. ii, separate pamphlet bound into RIC's copy.

47 On Voelcker (1854–1937), see *ibid.*, 1937, **61**, 520.

48 IC, Council Minutes, **7**, 25 April 1913; **8**, 29 May 1913. See also *Proc. Inst. Chem.*, 1913, **37**, pt. iv, 35–51.

49 On advertisements, see IC, Council Minutes, **8,** 22 November 1914. On fees, see *ibid.*, 7, 29 November 1912, 21 February 1913; **8,** 29 May 1915. See also, *Proc. Inst. Chem.*, 1913, **37,** pt. iii, 6, 10.

50 IC, Council Minutes, **3,** 25 May 1900; **4,** 30 October 1903; **6,** 22 May, 19 June, 23 October 1908. An employment bureau was proposed in 1896 but it was not instituted because of concern that running such a bureau might be viewed as touting; *ibid.*, **3,** 26 June, 30 October 1896.

51 The Appointments Register lasted until 1956 by which time the demand for chemists outstripped the supply. In 1968, the Institute initiated an appointment service to help young chemists return from abroad. In 1973, with somewhat bleak employment prospects for chemists, and the Institute again wanting to stress its professional utility, it formally re-established an appointments service. See 'Appointments Register', *J.R.I.C.*, 1956, **80,** 132; RIC, Council Minutes, **56,** 20 January 1967; **57,** 19 January 1968; n. vol., 12 October 1973.

52 R. B. Pilcher, *Proc. Inst. Chem.*, 1917, **41,** pt. i, 29–36; J. J. Dobbie, *ibid.*, 1918, **42,** pt. ii, 28.

53 IC, Council Minutes, **8,** 26 February, 30 April 1915; **9,** 27 October, 1 December 1916. See also, *Nature*, 1917, **100,** 106–7; *Chem. Trade J.*, 1917, **60,** 207; *Proc. Inst. Chem.*, 1918, **42,** pt. vi, 7.

54 *Chem. News*, 1915, **101,** 202–3, 211–14, 224–7; *Chem. Trade J.*, 1917, **60,** 266.

55 IC, Council Minutes, **9,** 20 March 1916; *Nature*, 1917, **100,** 211.

56 C. T. Kingzett, *Chem. Trade J.*, 1916, **57,** 319–20.

57 H. E. Armstrong, *ibid.*, 1919, **64,** 95.

58 *J. Soc. Chem. Ind.*, 1918, **37R,** 457.

59 *Ibid.*, p. 69; *Chem. Trade J.*, 1918, **62,** 187, 208.

60 *J. Soc. Chem. Ind.*, 1918, **37R,** 4–5; *Chem. Trade J.*, 1917, **61,** 413–15.

61 E. P. Lumley, *Chem. Trade J.*, 1918, **62,** 344.

62 IC, Council Minutes, **9,** 30 November 1917. The establishment of a Benevolent Fund had been suggested previously (*ibid.*, **2,** 1 March 1890), but the proposal lapsed due to lack of support from members.

63 R. B. Pilcher, *Chem. News*, 1917, **106,** 228–9. This statement was also sent out to all members resident in the Manchester area, urging them to attend the provisional BAC's inaugural meeting; IC, Council Minutes, **9,** 2 November 1918.

64 *Proc. Inst. Chem.*, 1918, **42,** pt. i, 11–12; pt. ii, 8–20; pt. iii, 9–46.

65 See note 60; IC, Council Minutes, **10,** 22 February 1918. British Association of Chemists, Minutes of Meetings of the Executive Committee, 20 April 1918; all BAC papers are held by the Association of Professional Scientists and Technologists.

66 BAC, 'National General Meeting', 15 July 1918 in BAC, Local Sections File. 'The Institute of Chemistry and the British Association of Chemists', Circular issued to the Birmingham Section of the BAC, 29 July 1918, in *ibid.*

67 On Hinchley (1871–1931), see *WWW*. 'Leeds and Bradford', 4 July 1918, in BAC, Local Sections File. See also C. A. F. Hastilow and L. P. Wilson, *Chem. Trade J.*, 1918, **63,** 248, 273. By the time it decided to become a permanent organization, the BAC had some 1500 provisional members. After rejecting the possibility of incorporation under the Companies Act, the BAC opted to register as a trade union, so that it could support strike action if necessary; BAC, Council Minutes, 25 September 1920 reports that registration was completed the preceding month.

CHAPTER XII
INDUSTRY AND THE PROFESSION AFTER 1918

1 Between the Wars

With the ending of the war in 1918, Britain was left with a chemical industry that had achieved more than anyone would have thought possible four years earlier. It was now to face an even greater challenge than that of wartime production. In a drastically changed world it was having to function with at least four impediments which made survival just that much harder.

In the first place there was an array of obsolescent plant which would otherwise have disappeared. Sometimes, as with chlorine production, the old plants (Deacon and Weldon) co-existed with newer (electrolytic) ones.[1] The survival of the Leblanc process into the 1920s would have been very unlikely in an industry that had not been stretched to its very limits. Secondly, the chemical industry was now equipped for over-production, a characteristic shared with Germany and many other countries. To take but one example, the estimated world demand for dyestuffs in 1920 was 100,000 tons, whereas world capacity was in the region of 280,000 tons.[2] Since this was a global phenomenon it presented not merely the problem of under-used capital assets but also the dangers of foreign undercutting, dumping and all the other ills associated with a stagnant market. Thirdly, there had been in Britain a marked tendency to concentrate on a relatively small number of products. These were not necessarily the most appropriate in peacetime—explosives being an obvious example.

The British chemical industry was relatively inflexible by comparison with Germany's and this will be encountered again. Finally, and closely related to the last point, the research orientation and commitment of many chemical manufacturers fell far short of what was needed to make progress in a world that included Germany, even a Germany that had been defeated in war.

All of this is not to suppose that the British chemical industry was about to be enveloped in a cloud of deepening gloom. After the armistice the reverse was the case for a while, and the general air of optimistic euphoria was intensified by the boom that began in 1919. The British Dyestuffs Corporation doubled the value of its exports to Switzerland in two years,[3] and speculation fever hit more than one major chemical producer in the U.K. But by mid-1920 the bubble had burst—two hundred years to the month since a similar fate overtook the famous South Sea Bubble.[4] The ensuing depression in the chemical industry lasted for about eighteen months. It saw raw material prices drop by half and imports slump to an alarming level, and together with the financial crisis and grim news of the Russian Revolution, engendered a sense of acute instability coupled with a determination to take whatever steps were possible to protect the industry's vulnerable economy. In fact the post-war situation called for a whole cluster of measures, not all of which were a direct result of the depression of the early 1920s.

A course of action that dated back to the war years was almost universally adopted after the armistice (except by Germany). This was the restriction on foreign trade by all manner of governmental devices, in the case of Britain by a combination of import licences and tariffs. In 1919 the Board of Trade designated a number of chemical intermediates which could not be imported without licence; then, in December of that year, an appeal against the impounding by Customs of a load of unlicensed pyrogallol was upheld by Mr Justice Sankey on a legal technicality regarding the original restriction. Thereafter foreign dyes began to flood the market as the boom referred to above gained momentum. A new Bill prohibiting imports of unlicensed dyes and dyestuffs intermediates was rushed through Parliament (despite opposition from the textile areas of Britain) at the end of 1920, but the adverse effects on the British Dyestuffs Corporation of unrestricted foreign competition, if only for a year or two, were plain for all to see.[5]

Chemicals other than these were the subject of an alternative kind of legislation, the Safeguarding of Industries Act of 1921. This imposed a $33\frac{1}{3}$ per cent *ad valorem* duty on a wide range of 'key' products that included several thousand synthetic organic chemicals and some inorganic substances —the Key Industries Duty. This Act, which survived until 1958, made discussions and litigation over the KID a familiar feature of the industrial chemical scene in Britain for nearly forty years, one of the last cases to come before the Tribunal being that of whether polyethylene was or was not a synthetic organic chemical.[6]

These measures, together with anti-dumping legislation, might have been expected to enable the U.K. chemical industry to thrive behind its protective walls. That it did so in due course is the result of other measures also, some initiated from within the industry itself. First, there came about the fulfilment of the alkali chemist's dream of the 1870s, not an Association of Manufacturing Chemists but rather the Association of British Chemical Manufacturers (ABCM) of 1916. Its German counterpart, Chemieverein, was far older, dating back to the foundation of the Institute in 1877. The ABCM, unlike the earlier proposal, was purely a trade association and through its representation many additional duties were imposed by the government.[7] The fertilizer trade was not included, but this had its own Fertilizer Manufacturers Association which successfully fought competition by imported superphosphate. Indeed specialization went even further than that with bodies like the British Sulphate of Ammonia Federation dedicated (successfully) to the protection of one single chemical compound. Much of this activity resulted from the institution of the Whitley Councils (Chapter XIII).

The formation of trade associations and, for that matter international cartels, had a powerfully inhibiting effect upon the international trade in chemical products in the years between the wars. Even more profound effects were engineered by the mergers, great and small that marked the chemical industry of this period. The takeover by Lever Brothers of Crosfields in 1919 and of John Knight in 1920, and the formation of the Fison Group in 1929 were important examples. They were far overshadowed by the biggest measure of them all, the formation of ICI (Imperial Chemical Industries) in 1926. This was a direct response to the changed status of a rival association overseas. The pooling association of German dyestuffs firms known as IG dated from the war years but, in 1925, it became a full amalgamation embracing other chemical industries as well: IG Farbenindustrie. The British reaction was clothed with patriotic sentiment— the new Imperial Chemical Industries were to promote trading interests of the British Empire 'the greatest single economic unit in the world'.[8] The new giant arose from a merger between the following firms:

(a) Brunner, Mond and Company, producers of about seventy-five per cent of alkali in the U.K.

(b) Nobel Industries, a holding company with interests as diverse as lacquers and General Motors of the U.S.A.

(c) The United Alkali Company, the last stronghold of the Leblanc process and later converted to the newer methods.

(d) British Dyestuffs Corporation.

With a large company like ICI a diversification to cut losses was possible, thus combatting the tendency of British industry to concentrate on just a few products. It was in the tradition of Brunner Mond which, before the merger, had added ammonia and nitrogenous fertilizers to its alkali production. However, diversification was not as conspicuous even in ICI as it was in Germany. Levinstein shrewdly observed that ICI 'depend for success on making comparatively few products extremely well and selling them at prices usually fixed by international agreement' whereas IG Farbenindustrie 'relies on making a large variety of substances constantly changing in range and new products appear in the laboratory and are taken up for large-scale manufacture because they seem to have profit-making capacity'.[9]

In our brief account so far we have concentrated on the commercial aspects at the expense of the chemical. Yet in fact these are always linked and it is worth recalling that one other remedy for the ills of the 1920s and 1930s lay in the hands of the industry itself—the development of fundamental and applied research. Of this subject Haber has well said that: 'In Britain, after 1914, money and resolution were suddenly and simultaneously combined with startling effects'.[10] Not only was this to offer the profession of chemistry a considerable challenge; it was also to provide the only sound basis for the development of the chemical industry.

Naturally the extent to which opportunities were seized varied from one firm to another. Brunner, Mond and Co was the British firm most consciously modelled on the German pattern;[11] the exploits of Freeth[12] and his colleagues demonstrate the success of that policy. However, Levinsteins had also incorporated this approach, but when Levinstein himself left the British Dyestuffs Corporation there was no one familiar with the dyestuffs industry on the board; from 1920–3 the number of research chemists dropped from eighty to thirty. But later on McGowan had a similar effect on Nobels by the rationalization measures he introduced. The final embodiment of the German research tradition was undoubtedly in ICI when, in 1927, Alfred Mond set up the Research Council, a body to link research in the universities with the industries. Outside members, mostly distinguished professors, were paid fifty guineas for their attendance (together with their expenses) and included Donnan,[13] Lindemann,[14] Robinson[15] and others. It met about twice a year and certainly succeeded in encouraging the development of research and, in a number of cases determined its direction. In 1928 occurred an enlargement of the research staff 'on a scale unprecedented in British industry';[16] no less than twenty-four extra chemists and engineers were engaged at one time. Oddly enough the Research Council was not popular with some of the ICI staff who felt a tension between the academics and industrialists and rather resented having to take on research dictated by those with an academic axe to grind. Its powers were severely cut down in 1935 when it was given a purely advisory function.[17]

It is necessary to appreciate the conditions that we have just described in order to understand the attitude of the Institute of Chemistry in the years between the wars. After the succession of small booms in the U.K. chemical industry in the 1920s, there came in the following decade, the depression whose effects were long to be felt in every industry in Britain and most other Western countries. In such circumstances as this it is hardly surprising that the Institute felt bound to concentrate its efforts upon the well-being of its members and the promotion of the chemical profession generally in a rather more narrow context than had been the case before the First World War.[18] To that end it continued its promotion campaign on behalf not only of itself but also of the profession of chemistry. In this campaign no one was more active than the indefatigable Secretary and Registrar, R. B. Pilcher, who continued his activities until his retirement in 1945 after over fifty years in the Institute's service.[19]. The post-war period saw the second edition of his *What Industry owes to Chemical Science* (1923) and also several editions of *The Profession of Chemistry* from 1919 to 1938, as well as *Chemistry as a Career* in 1923. The pages of the *Proceedings* are replete with references to his lecturing activities to schools and colleges and Local Sections on such subjects as 'Science as a Career' and on 27 September 1923 he gave a broadcast from 2 L.O. radio station on 'How to become a chemist'. But Pilcher was not left to do the job on his own, and many Members of Council and others engaged in similar activities. Indeed just after the war it was suggested that Fellows and Associates of the Institute should be prepared to deliver on appropriate occasions public lectures 'with a view to popularizing chemistry and its applications'.[20] When, in 1918, the first Local Sections were established the opportunity for further exercises of this nature became much greater.[21] However, despite these activities public ignorance of the Institute remained fairly high, and in 1933 complaints were heard to the effect that most people were not aware of what the initials FIC or AIC signified, since they were absent in all but a few of the lists of abbreviations in standard encyclopedias.[22]

But if ignorance was one enemy unemployment was another and a more serious one. As soon as the war was over the Ministry of Labour asked the Institute to appoint a representative to the Officers Resettlement Committee.[23] Three years later it was able to report that only thirteen members were unemployed although by 1922 that number had increased tenfold to around three per cent. Despite that the future was still regarded for chemists as being 'very promising'.[24] It is rather surprising to read that twelve years later the percentage of unemployed members of the Institute in the U.K. was still only just over three per cent, although the corresponding number for Germany was fifteen per cent.[25] In 1934 the three per cent figure still applied but the numbers of student members was now dropping alarmingly as people demonstrated an understandable reluctance to enter a profession that was both overcrowded and apparently dwindling. The response of the President (J. F. Thorpe) to the prospect of an overcrowded profession, was simply to impose higher standards of university and college entrance.[26] It must be to the credit of the Institute that the unemployment figures for chemists in this difficult economic period remained so constant. Much of this was due to the individual efforts made by officers of the Institute to secure places for members, by the issue of successive editions of Pilcher's *Official Chemical Appointments* (first published in 1906) as well as by the *Appointments Register* of the Institute.[27]

In other ways efforts were made to improve the professional status of the chemist and to safeguard his job. Thus in 1920 the Council of the Institute drew the attention of the DSIR to the dangers of appointing directors of research associations who were not experienced men of science but selected on the grounds of business acumen. They also observed that such staff should be British.[28] On several occasions the Institute sought to persuade the government to retain the measure of protection afforded by the Dyestuffs (Import Regulation) Bill; thus in 1924 it strenuously opposed the agreement then being considered between IG and the British Dyestuffs Corporation[29], while in 1930 it urged the government to retain the Act as it stood.[30] In similar vein Thorpe much later warned against 'too much reliance being placed upon the purchase of processes from abroad, rather than on encouraging research within our own industries, research institutions and the universities at home'.[31] The need for more industrial research was one of his favourite themes and in the same year he argued that the changing balance between coal and oil made this activity even more essential than before.[32]

These activities so manifestly directed to the welfare of its members cost the Institute dear in its negotiations with the Income Tax authorities. On 20 January 1933 the Council received the doleful tidings that the Special Commissioners for Income Tax had rejected the Institute's appeal for exemption from tax on the grounds that it was a charity. Their reasons are interesting. The Institute's claim that it was an educational body was countered with the objection that it ran no classes; its claim to be a scientific body met with an unfavourable comparison with the Institution of Civil Engineers whose claim had been allowed two years previously, but who were reported as having spent £400,000 on scientific literature. Clearly the advisers to the Commissioners had spent a great deal of time reading the *Proceedings* of the Institute and they 'felt that the weight of evidence which they had heard showed that the Institute had devoted so much attention to the professional interests of its members, that that must be taken to be a main or substantial object of the Institute. Their decision, therefore, must be against the appeal'.[33]

This judgement (which still applies)[34] was bitterly resented and certainly it does not seem to have taken into adequate account some of the other activities of the Institute which were certainly of wider benefit than only the professional well-being of its members. Thus in 1921 it sent a representative to the Joint Committee for Standardization on Scientific Glassware and two years later took over this committee providing secretarial service and accommodation. There were four subcommittees, one of which (on porcelain) never met, one (on volumetric glassware) held fourteen meetings which, amongst other achievements, recommended 'ml' instead of 'c.c.' as units and also secured the services of two members of ICI for its deliberations. Eventually its activities were taken over by the British Standards Institute.[35] Again in the early 1930s much time was spent on the consideration of the role of industrial administration in the training of the Institute's members, it being recognized that some understanding of the '£ s d side of affairs'[36] was essential for a chemist in modern industry. It was accepted that inadequate management skills were a valid criticism of many chemists and accordingly the Council commended a syllabus proposed by the Institute of Industrial Administration although it declined to 'overburden the already very comprehensive curriculum required for our Associateship qualification'.[37] Numerous other activities occupied the Institute secretariat and representatives during these years including numerous protests against the employment of aliens in the beet sugar industry, representations to government on the Pharmacy and Poisons Bill and much else of that nature. The activities of the Local Sections, often in conjunction with the Local Sections of the SCI, enabled members of the Institute to be kept abreast of numerous developments in industry as well as in the academic areas. But in the 1930s a new factor entered the industrial scene and this was to cause the Institute increasing concern and preoccupation.

The possibility of a second European war had been seriously considered in some quarters even in the 1920s and it has been rightly said that ICI was at least partly 'founded with war-like supply in mind',[38] although in 1933 less than two per cent of its turnover was in fact on war material and none on poison gases. This is in contrast to some popular rumours that were circulating at that time. Rearmament did not begin until 1935, but well before that time chemists were beginning to discuss their possible attitude to a further conflict. Thus a combined meeting of the Institute and the SCI in Bristol on 10 December 1934 was devoted to a lecture by Herbert Levinstein, a Member of Council, on 'Chemical defence'. He was not prepared to join in the somewhat general condemnation of chemical warfare, and stressed the value both of our dyestuffs industry and of the great resources of ICI in any preparations for war. Interestingly enough it was in this report on the activity of Local Sections that the Publication Committee inserted the following caveat:

> The Institute is not responsible for the views expressed in papers read, or in speeches delivered during discussions.[39]

This was possibly because Levinstein's remarks were quoted in very great detail.[40] Interestingly enough the same issue of *Proceedings* contains a brief note of the work by the Marxist biologist J. B. S. Haldane entitled *Callinicus: a Defence of Chemical Warfare*.[41]

Next year, at a celebration of the Newcastle-upon-Tyne and North East Coast Section, Sir William Morris, Principal of Armstrong College, Newcastle, thought the chemists 'had not made their science known to the man in the street' as well as physicists and astronomers had done, and because of the weapons of destruction at his disposal 'to the layman the chemist is a rather terrifying figure'.[42] This brought an instant rejoinder from the President, J. F. Thorpe, who thought that Morris 'did the chemists an injustice' if he accused them of 'being responsible for chemical warfare or anything connected therewith'.[43] In similar vein an editorial that year expressed anxiety that the idea should 'gain ground that chemistry is other than a good thing'.[44]

This editorial, entitled 'Science and War', was the subject of some correspondence in the next year and one member wrote urging on the Institute a pacifist policy arguing that 'the Institute should lead the way, rather than pursue a policy of *laissez-faire*'.[45] He looked for 'a determination on the part of the Institute, collectively and unconditionally, to outlaw war'.[46] The policy of encouraging free expressions of opinion in editorials and in correspondence, which was quite a new thing for the *Proceedings*, clearly caused the Committee some concern and this latest contribution led to real alarm lest the Institute should be diverted from the straight and narrow path of professional policy. Accordingly the following note was appended to an editorial later that year:

> The Publications Committee has decided that this discussion must be closed. The Committee cannot continue any longer to publish criticisms which either misinterpret views or which carry the discussion away from the original topic into regions of political and religious controversy beyond the province of a professional scientific institution.[47]

As the war became more and more a certainty and the deepening gloom descended on the late 1930s the Institute's external affairs became dominated by one thing. Frequent references are to be found to the study of the subject of air-raid precautions and the Council, in 1938, invited chemists to volunteer as Gas Detection Officers and decided to publish Davidson Pratt's monograph on *Gas Defence*.[48] Whatever else had dominated thinking about chemical industry from now on it was to be war.

2   The Second World War and its Aftermath

The onset of World War II found the chemical profession rather more prepared than had been the case in 1914. The chemical profession in 1939 was five times its size in 1914, and a catastrophic lack of chemical manpower was not envisaged, though it did seem likely that a large number of chemists would still be required.[49] One speaker at a Local Section meeting in East Anglia suggested, with remarkable prophetic insight, that the conflict might be termed 'a physicists' war', perhaps on the argument that the commodity in shortest supply determines the nature of the process.[50]

When general mobilization took place the Ministry of Labour decided that most of the 6,000 persons on the Central Register covering Pure and Industrial Chemistry should stay where they were. The Reserved Occupations, giving exemption from military service, included 'chemists (analytical, research, etc.)' and—for those over 25—'Laboratory assistant—skilled (chemical)'. This Register had been compiled with the help of the scientific societies and institutions, including the Institute of Chemistry. Thereafter the Institute was assiduous in keeping its members informed of changes in regulations, advising in cases of exemption and in other ways helping the direction of unemployed members into nationally important work.[51] Later in 1940 compulsory registration of all chemists and physicists was introduced,[52] and in 1941 the ages of reservation were raised and younger chemists were, where necessary, retained in industry by a system of deferment rather than reservation.[53]

Apart from playing a considerable role in assisting in the placing of chemists in industry during the war, the Institute also found itself engaged in considerable activity on behalf of those chemists who were serving as Gas Identification Officers in connection with Civil Defence. The question of hours of duty, compensation in case of injury and whether they should be treated differently from their other colleagues as 'highly qualified consultants' gave rise to much discussion and correspondence with A.R.P. headquarters[54] and a major paper by a Fellow of the Institute, G. W. Ferguson, reprinted in its *Proceedings* from the *Institute of Civil Defence Journal* of 1942.[55] More serious questions arose if examination of foodstuffs suspected of being contaminated was conducted by such persons other than in their capacity of chemists. The role of the Public Analyst would suffer in such an event,[56] as would that of private consultants if the Emergency Public Health Laboratory Service undertook analysis of water supplies. In the latter case the Institute's efforts were not too successful, and the President was moved to observe that 'he deplored the way in which the Ministry had treated the profession' by failing to restore lost work to consultants or otherwise to grant them compensation.[57]

The other main contribution of the Institute to industry during the war lay in the field of information. Inevitably, with severe restrictions on paper supplies, this was a very limited operation, but publication of a small number of lectures was possible through the war years. Their purpose seems to have been the dissemination of general rather than specialist information. They included several of historical interest, and a number on mineral resources, metallurgical chemistry, analytical techniques and biochemical topics.[58] Local Section lectures were reported briefly in the *Proceedings* and leaflets on *Laboratory Precautions* first appeared in the war.[59] The problems of the isolated chemist in wartime industry were also recognized in the encouragement of visits by Fellows to deliver lectures to small groups of chemists in the Ordnance Factories.[60]

Before the war was over the Institute was making its voice heard on the subject of post-war reconstruction. In 1943 a letter to the Press from its President (Findlay), William Bragg (President of the Institute of Physics) and R. H. Pickard (Chairman of the Joint Council of Professional Scientists) urged 'immediate preparation' for the tasks awaiting them after hostilities were over. At the same time they decisively rejected the notion that scientists should have a special influence on government since 'a scientific and soulless technocracy would be the worst form of despotism'.[61] In addition the Council took steps 'to remind the appropriate Departments of State of the organization of the Institute' in connection with the role of chemists in a post-war society,[62] and an anonymous article the following year went so far as to assert that the Institute, like the other 'great chartered professional organizations' was now 'practically part of the machinery of government' to whom 'the government constantly looks . . . for advice and assistance'.[63] Such confident affirmations, understandable enough in the afterglow of the recent 'Royal' accolade on the Institute, were perhaps a trifle premature, and certainly so in as much as the future of British industry was concerned. Nor is it to the detriment of the Institute to assert that this was so. Other organizations, as the ABCM and the SCI, were better placed to exert a direct influence on the course that chemical industry was to take in post-war Britain. With one exception (to which we return p. 232) the Institute's functions lay elsewhere. In fact the British industrial chemists were to witness a series of changes that any purely professional institution would have been largely powerless to prevent or even modify.

In the first place there was the effect of the war itself. Certainly the professional chemist had plenty to do. Figures quoted to the Institute by Sir Stafford Cripps, President of the Board of Trade, may presumably be taken with confidence. In 1939 the chemical industry employed about 160,000 people and wartime expansion led to a peak (in 1942) of nearly half a million. Thereafter numbers declined to 240,000 in November 1945.[64] We know also that, in 1944, about seventy per cent of the Institute's members were in industry,[65] so taking a figure of 300,000 for the total workforce at that time, together with the Institute's membership of over 9000,[66] we have roughly 6000 Institute members, or about two per cent of the total. Since not all industrial chemists were in the Institute the percentage of chemists in wartime Britain must have been rather over this figure. Even so it is clear that a well-qualified chemist was not likely to have too much difficulty in obtaining employment even in a contracted peacetime industry. This, in fact, proved to be the case and production of such personnel continued apace when the war was over. Without doubt this helped to accelerate the expansion of post-war industry to which further reference will be made shortly.

A further effect of the war on chemical industry has been identified in terms of the nature of the work done. W. J. Reader, in his history of ICI, has characterized World War II as 'the greatest source of business that ICI had ever had, but it never looked like an attractive business proposition. On the other hand . . . it got in the way of things that did'. Hence he refers to it as 'the Great Distraction'.[67] The consequence was an even stronger incentive for industry to make up for lost time after 1945 and expand in the desired directions as speedily as possible. What was true of ICI was likely to apply to some extent at least to most of the other chemical firms.

A second potent influence on the industry's future was the changing economic and political situation just after the war. Britain's economic problems were of course a legacy of the war, but they were not just that. The exceptionally hard winter of 1946–7 drained away much of the country's fuel stocks, with a consequent loss of £200 million in exports. Devaluation of the £ from $4.03 to $2.80 in 1949 entirely altered the pattern of dependence on American markets. The net result is familiar to all chemists: instead of importing American oil the U.K. turned to the Middle East and, in the early 1950s, embarked on an ambitious programme for installing refineries in the U.K. to deal with mainly Middle Eastern crude. Coinciding in time with a rapidly increasing demand for petrochemicals the installation of this plant enabled the chemical industry to expand at nearly twice the rate of other manufacturing industries in Britain during the period 1948–58.[68] By 1962 the U.K. was the largest petrochemical producer in Europe and the third in the world, with about seventy per cent of its organic chemicals being derived from petroleum.[69] This had important effects on the employment of chemists. A typical refinery in 1960 might have employed about 4,500 people, of whom perhaps 150 would have been qualified staff and another fifty management and executives.[70] Thus there would have been a ratio of 200 graduates to 4,500 total workforce, or nearly four and a half per cent. This is twice as high as the wartime figure and goes some way to explaining the continual demand for such personnel right into the 1960s. However, this must be seen in an international context, and it was reported in 1957 that in terms of research expenditure the U.K. was lagging behind its competitors, with less than two per cent of its turnover. This compares with over five per cent by the major German firms, four per cent in the United States and five per cent by Ciba in Switzerland.[71]

Perhaps this should have been received as a warning signal. The President of the Institute, Professor W. Wardlaw,[72] claimed that British chemistry could 'hold its head high' but asserted that in the chemical industry there was 'an urgent and continuing need for well-trained chemists to solve the many problems of research and development'.[68] Salutary though these words were to be, they were not able to stave off the economic problems that faced the chemical industry in the 1960s and 1970s. This third external constraint was complex in origin but certainly included the effects of depreciation in an industry that was highly capital-intensive. Pruning had to take place and many mergers in subsequent years reflected the aims expressed so tactfully by ICI when it contemplated a union of its Alkali and General Chemical Divisions in 1963, 'a better use of specialized manpower to facilitate further development and expansion'.[73] A rather more direct statement of the effects in the petrochemicals industry has recently (1972) been made, thus:

> Rationalization of individual companies' activities (concentration of production facilities, mergers with other firms, etc.) has been a feature of the industry in most countries for some years. It is part of a continuous process of seeking greater efficiency and has been another factor tending to restrict the growth of the industry's labour force. The economic and financial difficulties of the industry since 1970 have led to a widespread shake-out of employees in all fields of activity, which is still in progress.[74]

In the face of issues of this magnitude it may be argued that there was not a lot that the Institute could do, apart, of course, from its familiar activities associated with qualifications and professional matters generally. However, there was one additional role that had been perceived by Sir Stafford Cripps as far back as 1946, at the Institute's Anniversary Luncheon. Speaking of the importance of science in peace-time industrial competition he said 'The

Royal Institute of Chemistry, therefore, has a great part to play as the inspirational centre of our efforts in chemical science, whether in fundamental research at our universities, in education, or in applied chemistry in our industries'.[75] It is unlikely that this was merely post-prandial euphoria and the Institute does seem to have taken the charge seriously. During the years that followed it has undoubtedly played a valuable part in 'inspirational' activities in two main ways, by publications and by meetings. The former aspect can be immediately seen by a perusal of its *Proceedings* up to 1949 and the *Journal* that lasted from 1950 until 1965 (when *Chemistry in Britain*[76] became the combined organ of both Institute and Chemical Society). During the first twenty post-war years the Institute's periodical publication contained much material of wide interest to its members in industry as well as to those in education and academic research. In fact the very breadth of its coverage could be seen as a partial fulfilment of the role that Cripps had prescribed for it. This is still more true of the series of 'Lectures, Monographs and Reports' and its successor the 'RIC Lecture Series' that ran from 1961 to 1967. An attempted analysis of the contents of fifteen years' issues (1953–67) has shown how difficult it is to categorize any one as 'academic' or 'industrial', though the pattern that unmistakeably emerges is of a gradual move in emphasis towards the academic from very roughly 1 : 1 to (equally roughly) 2 : 1, with sundry topics of such general interest that they defy all attempts at classification. They were of sufficient substance— perhaps thirty pages each—to be more than potted introductions and yet not too daunting to the busy industrial chemist who wanted to enlarge his horizons. And, of course, the Local Section meetings, often in conjunction with the SCI or the Chemical Society, helped to fulfil the same objective. Such activities are hard to justify in any quantitative sense but at very least they provide evidence that the Institute conceived its role towards all sections of the profession very much as its Victorian predecessors had done: encouragement of the cultivation of a broad and general chemical knowledge and specialization after that. Only time will tell whether they were right.

CAR

NOTES AND REFERENCES

1 D. W. F. Hardie and J. Davidson Pratt, *A History of the Modern British Chemical Industry*, Pergamon, Oxford, 1966, p. 101.

2 L. F. Haber, *The Chemical Industry, 1900–1930*, Clarendon Press, Oxford, 1961, p. 252.

3 *Ibid.*, p. 250.

4 Charles Wilson, *The History of Unilever*, Cassell, London, 1970, vol. i, p. 253.

5 For details of this and subsequent legislation see Haber (note 2) chs. 8 and 9. The limitations on research imposed by the restrictions on fine chemicals from Germany led to attempts by academic members of the Institute's Council to activate the Institute into protest (IC, Council Minutes, 12, 31 October 1919). Over the next few months the Council were clearly divided over the matter. It was in the best interests of British manufacturing chemists that British industry should be supported, but research chemists badly

needed chemicals from abroad; *ibid.*, 19 December 1919, 23 April, 17 December 1920, 11 March 1921, etc.

6 *Chem. Age*, 1958, 80, 899, 935.

7 Hardie and Pratt (note 1), p. 111.

8 W. J. Reader, *Imperial Chemical Industries, a History*, vol i, *The Forerunners 1870–1926*, OUP, London, 1970, p. 326.

9 *J. Soc. Chem. Ind.*, 1931, 50, 251T.

10 Haber (note 2), p. 352.

11 See Reader (note 8), chs. 3, 6, 10 and 13 for an account of the history of Brunner, Mond & Co. to 1919.

12 F. A. Freeth, one of the first distinguished English chemists of modern times to have had an entirely English education, became Head of Research at Brunner, Mond & Co. and exerted a powerful influence on the development of post-war British chemical industry (see notes 2, 11). Obituary: E. Hunter, *Chem. Brit.*, 1971, 7, 28.

13 On Donnan see W. E. Garner, *Proc. Chem. Soc.*, 1957, 362–6.

14 On Lindemann see J. G. Crowther, *Statesmen of Science*, Cresset, London, 1965, pp. 339–76.

15 On Robinson see *Chem. Brit.*, 1974, 10, 54–7 (interview) and 1975, 11, 296 (obituary by Lord Todd).

16 Reader (note 8), vol. ii, *The First Quarter-Century 1926–1952*, OUP, London, 1975, p. 84.

17 *Ibid.*, p. 91; this action was taken by R. E. Slade, ICI's new Controller of Research.

18 Council were doubtless aware, with half an eye on the BAC (ch. XIII), that the membership would drop if action were *not* taken.

19 *Proc. R.I.C.*, 1945, 69, 67–8; obituary in *J.R.I.C.*, 1955, 79, 609–10.

20 *Proc. Inst. Chem.*, 1920, 44, 283.

21 *Ibid.*, 1918, 42, pt. iv, 3.

22 *Ibid.*, 1933, 57, 121.

23 *Ibid.*, 1918, 42, pt. iv, 6.

24 *Ibid.*, 1922, 46, 329.

25 *Ibid.*, 1932, 56, 102. Writing a few years later on 'The Profession of Chemistry during the Depression', Dennis Chapman suggested 'unemployment appears to have been at no time a serious problem for chemists as compared with the position of the industrial worker. This is probably for the reason . . . when in a depression it is a greater economy to employ a chemist than to discharge one'. (*Scientific Worker*, 1939 (Autumn) 74–81 (81).)

26 *Proc. Inst. Chem.*, 1934, 58, 102.

27 For his work in connection with the resettlement of officers and other chemists after the war, in addition to his other wartime services, Pilcher was awarded the OBE in 1920 (*J.R.I.C.*, 1955, 79, 609).

28 *Proc. Inst. Chem.*, 1920, 44, 28.

29 The Council experienced much internal tension at this time between pro- and anti-German factions. It was, in any case, far from clear what attitude would be in the best long-term interest of the profession. Dominating all discussions were understandable fears of undermining the chemical industry of Great Britain (IC, Council Minutes, 16, 29 February, 14 March 1924). Allusions to political differences had been published

in connection with the Council's reluctance to pronounce on the Dyestuffs (Import Regulation) Bill three years earlier (*Proc. Inst. Chem.*, 1921, **45**, 34, 135).

30 *Ibid.*, 1930, **54**, 282.

31 *Ibid.*, 1936, **60**, 113.

32 *Ibid.*, pp. 134–5.

33 *Ibid.*, 1933, **57**, 34.

34 I.e. in respect of profit-making activities (sale of literature etc.).

35 *Proc. Inst. Chem.*, 1932, **56**, 208–14.

36 *Ibid.*, p. 378.

37 *Ibid.*, 1933, **57**, 97.

38 Reader (note 16), p. 252.

39 *Proc. Inst. Chem.*, 1934, **58**, 404.

40 *Ibid.*, pp. 410–20.

41 *Ibid.*, p. 453. His argument was chiefly that use of gas would shorten the duration of a war and lessen the number of serious casualties.

42 *Ibid.*, 1935, **59**, 466.

43 *Ibid.*, p. 467.

44 *Ibid.*, p. 350.

45 *Ibid.*, 1936, **60**, 114.

46 *Ibid.*, p. 15.

47 *Ibid.*, p. 200.

48 *Ibid.*, 1938, **62**, 18.

49 Editorial, *Proc. Inst. Chem.*, 1939, **63**, 458.

50 R. S. Colbourne, *ibid.*, p. 471.

51 *Ibid.*, 1940, **64**, 163–6 and many later issues.

52 *Ibid.*, p. 268.

53 *Ibid.*, 1941, **65**, 303–5.

54 *E.g. ibid.*, 1941, **65**, 37–8.

55 *Ibid.*, 1942, **66**, 166–78.

56 *Ibid.*, 1941, **65**, 38.

57 *Ibid.*, 1944, **68**, 153.

58 *Ibid.*, 1940, **64**, 20; 1941, **65**, 16; 1942, **66**, 15; 1943, **67**, 10; 1944, **68**, 10; 1945, **69**, 10.

59 *Ibid.*, 1940, **64**, 20.

60 *Ibid.*, 1945, **69**, 60.

61 *Ibid.*, 1943, **67**, 150–1. This was presumably a reaction to 'Bernalism', the left-wing movement among certain scientists so nicknamed after J. D. Bernal, author of *The Social Function of Science*, 1939. The idea of research planned along the lines indicated by Bernal, though widely disliked, came back into prominence with the prospect of post-war reconstruction.

62 *Proc. Inst. Chem.*, 1943, **67**, 160.

63 *Ibid.*, 1944, **68**, 133.

64 *Ibid.*, 1946, **70**, 85.

65 *Ibid.*, 1944, **68**, 134.

66 *Ibid.*, p. 133.

67 Reader (note 16), p. 257.

68 W. Wardlaw, *J.R.I.C.*, 1958, **82**, 223.

69 *Chemicals Information Handbook 1972–73*, Shell, London, 1972.

70 E. LeQ. Herbert, *J.R.I.C.*, 1960, **84**, 129.

71 *Chem. Age*, 1957, **78**, 968.

72 On Wardlaw see E. G. Cox, *Proc. Chem. Soc.*, 1961, 397–400.

73 *Chem. Age*, 1963, **89**, 708.

74 *Chemicals Information Handbook* (note 69), p. 14.

75 *Proc. R.I.C.*, 1946, **70**, 86.

76 This new journal soon manifested the Institute's concern for questions of management in the chemical industry and related topics in reporting in its very first issue Lord Todd's Dalton Lecture 'Science, Industry and Government' (*Chem. Brit.*, 1965, **1**, 3–8). Subsequent issues made frequent reference to such questions, a trend that has continued ever since.

CHAPTER XIII

THE ERA OF THE INDUSTRIAL CHEMIST. PROFESSIONAL RELATIONS AND ORGANIZATION SINCE WORLD WAR I

There have been three turning points in the Institute's history with regard to professional relations and organization. Chronologically, these occurred in the aftermath of each of the world wars, and in the late 1960s. In all three periods, the Institute was faced with new government initiatives affecting science and technology and particularly difficult national economic circumstances. During each of these periods, the Institute investigated similar organizational solutions to contemporary problems, although with differing degrees of thoroughness: creation of a unified chemical body and registration, closer cooperation with other scientific and technological associations, and trade unionism. Underlying these developments has been a steadily increasing number of industrial chemists within the Institute.

1 Between the Wars

(a) Fulfilling the promises of the 1918 reforms

Although in 1918 the Institute and the British Association of Chemists decided to follow separate paths, it was obvious that the Institute would have to redouble its efforts to deal with the interests of industrial chemists. It will be seen that, except for a brief interlude during World War II, the Institute tended to reject BAC overtures seeking collaboration by arguing either that it had the matter well in hand on its own, or that BAC methods were inimical to a professional institution. However, although the Institute could refuse to collaborate with the BAC, it could not ignore the fact that, during the 1920s and 1930s particularly, many of its own most active members were also prominent in BAC affairs.[1] Furthermore, the Institute had to take account of the BAC's strength in the industrial Midlands and North, precisely where its own influence had been weakest. The possibility of the BAC's successfully tackling issues in place of the Institute could obviously cause difficulties in those areas. Thus, even after the Institute's 1918 promise of reforms which the provisional BAC deliberately motivated, the new BAC continued to function as a *de facto* pressure group on Institute activities, regardless of whether this was its official policy.[2]

The changes which the Institute initiated as a response to the provisional BAC movement themselves brought further pressures on Institute policies. In the first place, there was a rapid influx of new members and in addition the creation of the Local Section structure and the concomitant provision for the election of District members to Council meant that there were new formal channels of communication with headquarters. Thus the larger membership could also be much more articulate than before; Council had to at least be seen to be dealing with Members' initiatives. The Local Section structure was put into effect remarkably quickly, although it was not equally successful everywhere. Such speed was perhaps possible because the SCI local organization provided a model in many areas, and in some, a nucleus of members. The fact that the new BAC was organized on a local section basis may also have affected the Institute's timing. Indeed a number of vocal BAC members, who were also members of the Institute, became very active in the latter's Local Sections. The increase in travel expenses for the Administrative Officers and Council members during the early 1920s shows how seriously the Institute took this challenge.

However, the pressure was not all one way. Council managed to retain central control of policy decisions. For example, when the Local Sections first started, several suggested that the administration of the Institute might be decentralized. In particular, it was felt that Local Sections would be ideal units for making decisions on applications for membership. This would reintroduce an element of personal knowledge and evaluation of local circumstances into the selection procedures. Many felt that the Institute was inevitably losing its personal element due to its rapid growth and the consequent increasing unlikelihood of a small central committee's knowing individual applicants. The Local Sections also had other reasons for seeking to influence decisions about membership: many local members regretted Council's post-war policy of exempting candidates from the Institute's examinations (p. 178). Council defused the situation by setting up local panels for interviewing applicants. However, it stressed that final decisions would be taken centrally; the panels were to function only as advisory bodies. Council itself nominated the individual members of these panels, generally local academics and former Council members, on the grounds that it knew best who had the requisite experience of the intricacies of the Institute's regulations.[3] Furthermore, it took Council a full two years to decide to authorize reimbursement of fares for District Members and even longer to try to adjust the cycle of business so that they could participate properly when they did come.[4]

Council also had ways of making it look as though its own views had arisen in Local Sections. For example, although there were proposed Sections in Birmingham, Edinburgh, Glasgow, Gretna, Liverpool, Manchester and Swansea by November 1918, there did not seem to be much enthusiasm in the London area. (London chemists were well supplied with scientific institutions, and had ready access to the Institute.) Pilcher received instructions from Council to promote a London Section; G. S. Marlow, Assistant Secretary at the Institute, became its principal organizer and first

Honorary Secretary. During the 1920s, a number of resolutions suggesting actions contrary to those favoured by the northern Local Sections in particular were transmitted to Council from the London Section. The establishment of Local Students' Associations was one such matter. Most Local Sections opposed this suggestion, arguing that it was quite sufficient to admit Students of the Institute to their regular meetings. Marlow saw to it that London organized a separate body.[5] Once started, the London Section very quickly became the largest.[6] Ironically, it also included some very forceful BAC members.

From 1918, the Institute also began to take more positive action on the question of the economic welfare of members.[7] It made efforts to intensify the use of the Appointments Register, both as a means of finding employment for chemists and of suggesting appropriate salary levels to employers. The new post-war minimum salary was £300. But most important, particularly for its propaganda value, was the first chemists' Remuneration Survey in 1919. The Institute received several requests from chemists in public employment for assistance in claiming better remuneration. Lacking figures, the Institute found itself in a difficult position when bodies such as the Ministry of Supply replied to its suggestions that, compared to other posts, chemists under the Ministry already received adequate pay.[8] Repeated instances of low salaries for government posts, including some held by Council members, moved the Institute to make a policy statement. Council recognized that, if it did not deal with such problems, 'other' bodies might. Remuneration had to be among its interests, because the status of the professional man, once his level of qualification was assured, depended on his salary. However, Council's statement broke no new ground in terms of methods of furthering members' economic interests.[9]

In truth, Council dithered until O. L. Brady,[10] one of its younger members, transmitted a resolution from the London Section that the Institute be asked to collect confidential information on the salaries and conditions of employment of members. Brady himself worked at Woolwich Arsenal, one of the more notorious offenders on questions of pay and status, and was an active member of the London Sections of both the Institute and the BAC. Indeed, it was he who proposed the resolution to the London Section of the Institute; while, at virtually the same time, the London Section of the BAC was also looking into the question of chemists' salary structures.[11] The Institute was quite pleased with the rate of return of its questionnaires, but less pleased with the over-all financial position of its members. The general conclusion was that chemists were not paid as much as they were worth, but they were not drastically underpaid either (Figure 5). As expected, industrial chemists were the highest paid, government employed chemists were in the middle, and teaching members of the Institute lowered the average. A follow-up survey in the next year showed considerable improvement.[12] The generally favourable figures saved the Institute from an awkward problem.

It did not have to man battle stations on behalf of large groups of chemists and therefore it did not have to confront squarely the question of the extent to which it was willing to take on the functions of a protective association. The figures strengthened the arm of its policy of providing impartial, confidential advice to both the employer and the employee in any controversy over salary, and of seeking improved conditions in advertised posts. Individual members of the Institute also were not slow to use the remuneration survey figures as the basis of their own arguments for improved pay. The Remuneration Surveys became an important (if irregular in the early years) feature of the Institute's activities and a model for other institutions.

The early Remuneration Surveys also inquired about terms and conditions of service and revealed that these were quite varied. There was a good deal of uncertainty, particularly among younger industrial chemists, about what they were entitled to expect. The BAC had undertaken to provide legal advice on contracts for individual members, but the Institute could not do this under its Charter as such a service might lead to individual profit. However, the Institute prepared some general guidelines on what would make a reasonable contract from both the employee's and the employer's points of view. The Manchester Local Section with its high proportion of industrial chemists asked for a more specific model contract, but Council replied that it could not possibly provide a model that would suit the whole range of chemical industry without being unduly restricting. The guide-lines were regularly updated, latterly in collaboration with the ABCM.[13]

The early Remuneration Surveys and the guidelines on contracts helped to fulfil the implied promise in the 1918 reforms that the Institute intended to do more for industrial chemists. The former considered only salaried posts, and the latter dealt with circumstances facing industrial employers and employees. The Institute also unsuccessfully sought the right to represent chemists on the National Industrial Councils (Whitley Councils). Seeking such representation was one of the stated objects of the new BAC. Indeed, the BAC suggested collaboration on this issue, but the Institute preferred to act independently. At first, the Institute approached the Ministry of Labour informally through William MacNab, Council member and respected wartime adviser on explosives to the Ministry of Supply. His soundings were not encouraging: workmen were not likely to welcome the representation of technical staff on the Whitley Councils since the latter brought about resented innovations.[14] It seemed that professional men had been more justified than they knew in their alarm at being caught between management and the unions in future industrial organization.

The Institute persevered, arranging a formal deputation which was received by a rather more junior Ministry of Labour official than anticipated.[15] The Institute made a strong plea for scientists to have some voice in the machinery of industrial reconstruction. It pointed out that the State had already recognized the importance of science to the future of British industry by setting up the Department of Scientific and Industrial Research and providing for the establishment of the Industrial Research Associations.[16] But the latter covered only a very narrow range of industries, so full recovery still depended on the effective utilization of science by individual firms within each industry. Therefore, it was imperative that the value of the industrial scientist be recognized formally, and that his position be safeguarded.

At this meeting, the Institute indicated that it knew the weakness of the professional position. Chemists were dispersed in small numbers throughout a great many diverse industries. Even if industrial action were called for in any particular instance, chemists simply lacked the numerical power to make it effective. Their only real weapon was refusing employment in unsuitable firms, hardly more than a pinprick to a large establishment. Furthermore, such a policy was not likely to be successful in a period of economic stress, particularly since the Institute could apply no sanctions to its own members for non-adherence to a 'blacking' order and had no control at all over non-members.[17] The implication of this weakness was that even if the Institute were to contemplate adopting trade union practices, they would be unlikely to be effective. In any case, the Institute's formal position was that it could not act as a trade union since it included both employers and employees. Therefore, the Institute argued, it was vital that the Whitley machinery formally include professional scientists. Otherwise, they would have no voice.

The Institute put forward a possible mechanism. Having been advised by MacNab that the small number and diversity of chemical roles in industry precluded the Institute's obtaining authority to represent professional chemists directly on the Industrial Councils, it adopted his suggestion of forming an advisory panel. Such a panel of professional chemists could then be consulted by any of the Whitley Councils for industries involving chemistry, whenever necessary. The Institute asked that the establishment of such a panel receive official approval. However, the deputation achieved little. Pilcher pursued the matter further through private contacts, but was given the unpalatable advice that the Institute should not confine its efforts to its own membership, but should collaborate with the science unions such as the BAC and the National Union of Scientific Workers (NUSW). Otherwise, he was informed, the Institute should concentrate on propaganda and on advising its members to press for cooption on to specific Councils, as individuals, when technical matters were due for discussion.[18] As it happened, the National Industrial Councils were rather a non-event except in the sphere of government employment where the Institute was already a well-known advocate of chemists' standing. But the attempt to seek representation provided useful lessons about where the Institute's strength lay.

(b) A strong voice for chemists? Questions of the 1920s

Seeking their representation on the Whitley Councils was not the only way in which the Institute was involved in attempting to obtain a strong voice for chemists during this period. Discussions on this question within the Institute took place under a number of interrelated headings: joint action of some form with other chemical institutions, registration, the title 'chemist', a third grade of membership, joint action with other professional institutions, and trade unionism. In April 1918, the President of the Chemical Society called for the establishment of what in 1919 became the Federal Council for Pure and Applied Chemistry (to advance, safeguard, and voice the interests of chemical science). This FCC had been promoted since 1916 initially within the SCI (p. 214). Its purpose was to provide machinery through which the collective opinion of all workers in chemistry could be expressed. The new body was a federation of several chemical organizations, each of which was to retain its independence. They would unite only to consider matters of general concern. The original members of the FCC were the Chemical Society, the Society of Chemical Industry, and the Association of British Chemical Manufacturers each with three seats, the Faraday Society, the Society of Public Analysts, the Biochemical Society, the Institute of Brewing, the Society of Dyers and Colourists and the Society of Glass Technology each with a single seat.[19] The Iron and Steel Institute was soon added. The Institute of Chemistry did not join the FCC on the public grounds that, as a professional and qualifying body, it might prefer to act independently from the decisions of a body such as the FCC.[20] However, the Institute's interests were represented in the FCC by virtue of its president being a coopted member.

The new federation at once began to consider general issues of importance to the chemical profession and industry such as: standards of purity, the availability of chemicals for research and analysis, the provision of adequate financial assistance for the establishment of research fellowships by the Royal Society, the absence of experimental science from the education and training schemes of the army and so on. The FCC also showed some interest in the salaries paid to professional chemists. From the first the possibility of establishing an association or guild of chemical societies along the lines of the Royal Society of Medicine was discussed. It was hoped that eventually the FCC might have its own premises to house a central chemical library, meeting rooms, a lecture theatre and perhaps facilities for a Chemical Club.[21] In 1923 the SCI began to issue the Reviews section of its journal on a weekly basis under the title *Chemistry and Industry* and the FCC adopted this as its own official organ.

Quite apart from the external initiative of the FCC, the Institute had undertaken to look into the question of providing a stronger voice for chemists through registration at the time of its negotiations with the provisional BAC. The Institute's Local Sections, particularly Manchester and

Liverpool which included active BAC members, did not allow Council to overlook the fact. Most Sections wanted the Institute to include as many chemists as possible, but there were rather diverse views on how this should be done and which chemists should be included.[22] Council's opinion was the same as in the 1890s: restricting the use of the title 'chemist' and establishing a compulsory register of those entitled to use it would bring more problems than benefits to the profession. Some minimum qualification, doubtless below the level of the AIC, would have to be defined. This would lead to a dilution of the Institute's standards, and threaten the reputation of its existing qualifications. Furthermore, the latitude of qualification that would have to be allowed in the early years might strengthen the Institute's bargaining position by virtue of numbers, but it would also weaken it in terms of the collective value of the individuals involved. Council admitted the value of a register in areas of chemical practice dealing directly with the public or affecting their health or safety. But it did not see how manufacturers would find a compulsory register any more valuable than the voluntary one which the Institute already provided. Furthermore, the restriction of the title 'chemist' was probably best achieved by an educative process. Discussions with the Pharmaceutical Society indicated that their members were using the term 'pharmacist' more often now, but that there were still practical problems such as shop signs and public habits which prevented their giving up the title completely. In 1922, Council formally asked the Local Sections to discuss the whole problem (although they had been discussing it ever since their establishment and forwarding comments to Russell Square).[23]

Discussions within the Local Sections ranged widely, mainly covering points that had been debated often before within the Institute. Some chemists tried to bring a new urgency to the issue. In the very early 1920s, the spectre of overcrowding was raised in chemistry as well as other professions. The rapid increase in the Institute's membership fuelled these worries and made many chemists press for closer collaboration among the existing chemical institutions to attempt to exercise some control over the situation.[24] The question of control was also important for other reasons as E. F. Armstrong, President of the SCI, pointed out early in 1923 in an address to the London Section of the Institute.[25] Managing Director of Joseph Crosfield & Sons as well as Chairman of the Soap Manufacturers' Employers' Federation and Chairman of the Whitley Council for the soap industry, Armstrong expressed concern that chemists were losing the influence which they had gained during the war. In contrast, the trade unions seemed to be ever stronger. Therefore, it was vital that chemists organize effectively so that their voices might influence the government. The question for Armstrong was not whether chemists should organize, but whether they were willing to face the consequences of not doing so. He suggested that the FCC was ineffective because the Conjoint Board of Scientific Societies overlapped it in functions. Thus, even if the government should decide to consult chemists over any particular issue, it had to face two bodies for a start. Armstrong called for an organization unifying the existing chemical societies, particularly the three chartered bodies, a central headquarters for chemistry, and a rationalization of chemical publications.

R. L. Collett, Council member of the Institute and an active member of the London Section, maintained during the discussion of Armstrong's address that all chemists recognized the need for some form of confederation, but it was difficult to overcome the vested interests of the three chartered bodies. Collett, who was to become Assistant Secretary to the Institute two years later, cited the Chemical Society in particular.[26] He suggested that the Federal Council was weak because it had no control over any capital, which limited its actions. Collett felt that the FCC had only come into existence because of a number of unsuccessful attempts to induce the Councils of the three chartered bodies to meet and take joint action. He supported Armstrong's views, noting a vast change in status of workmen's unions since 1910 and suggesting that chemists had not enjoyed comparable progress.

There were proposals for joint action with other institutions as well. In 1923, Professor E. C. C. Baly of Liverpool who was active in both the BAC and the Institute suggested that the latter should not ignore the former. He wanted the Institute to create a third (lower) grade of membership in order to include the routine testers and others who formed the bulk of BAC members. Otherwise, the Institute and the BAC might find their actions in conflict rather than in harmony. In fact, Baly proposed that with a third grade, the Institute might well be able to absorb the BAC or at least form a joint protective association with it. Council replied that the Institute had made its peace with the provisional BAC in 1918 and had no intention of reopening negotiations with the newer body.[27] At the same time, the Liverpool Section asked that the Institute hold a national conference somewhere in the provinces, since judging from the lack of response to a number of Liverpool initiatives, Council was still rather remote from the membership. A conference was held in Liverpool and one of the principal subjects was a motion by Baly and Professor I. M. Heilbron[28] that the Institute initiate the establishment of a National Federation of Men of Science and a General Science Council. Broadly the former was to be a federation of the Institute of Physics, the Institute of Chemistry, the engineering institutions, the BAC (not as a trade union but as a qualifying body for lower grades of works chemists), and subject subcommittees of the NUSW (for those disciplines which did not already have separate professional organizations). This would provide a strong voice for all professional scientists and technologists, while the General Science Council would be a licensing body for the practice of science. The proposal was much discussed, but it got nowhere.[29]

The Local Sections and the BAC did not allow the questions of registration and collaboration amongst chemical bodies to lie dormant.[30] Liverpool and Manchester particularly promoted both the expansion of the Institute's register by the creation of a third grade of membership and a statutory licensing monopoly. They saw these actions as first steps towards complete self-government of the profession of chemistry, subject perhaps only to the control of the Privy Council. This was a particularly vexed issue at the time since, while in Government, Ramsay MacDonald as Prime Minister and Sidney Webb at the Board of Trade had deliberately refused to put scientists in top administrative posts affecting science, on the grounds that more objective decisions were made by laymen who had access to scientific advisers. The Presidents of the main chartered scientific and technological institutions protested jointly.[31]

In 1926 Council's Special Committee on Registration rejected compulsory registration as impractical at the time and of dubious applicability to industry, and it did not encourage a comprehensive voluntary register. In addition to the old argument that the Institute already administered a voluntary register, the Committee compiled statistics which implied that further voluntary registration might fail, thereby weakening rather than strengthening the position of the Institute. The Committee also opposed a third grade of membership for the old reason that it would devalue the Fellowship and the Associateship.[32] This report unleashed a storm of protest in the provinces. The BAC, which had been optimistically leaving the issue up to the Institute decided to promote voluntary registration by establishing a General Chemical Council. Predictably, the Liverpool Section of the Institute forwarded a resolution to Council that it take part in this new body. Meanwhile, the SCI was attempting to promote unity amongst chemists through a Congress of Chemists, and the FCC through a joint register of members of all chemical bodies.[33] A *Nature* leader applauded the move toward registration amongst chemists, hoping that it would counter a tendency toward fragmentation along specialist lines. If chemists did not form a register, their identity as a group might be dissipated.[34]

(c) A strong voice for chemists? Answers of the 1930s

In response to these activities, successive Presidents of the Institute called for solidarity on the question of its right to be the sole registering authority for chemists, while Council reiterated its view that restricting the practice of chemistry would weaken rather than strengthen the profession.[35] In fact, Council wanted the whole problem of the use of the title 'chemist', registration, and a third grade of membership deferred, pending the report of a Departmental Committee investigating the Poisons and Pharmacy Acts. When the Committee reported in 1930, after sitting for four years, the reason for Council's delay became clear. The Committee recommended that chemists be entitled to call themselves 'chemists', although it would not recommend that pharmacists be forbidden to use the title. Council decided to seek a Supplemental Charter to claim a distinct title for Institute members in order to clearly distinguish chemists from pharmacists. The suggested title was 'Chartered Chemist', which would bring the Institute into line with the terminology used by some other professional associations. Although Council did not say so explicitly, while distinguishing chemists from pharmacists, this title would also distinguish members of the Institute from other chemists. Thus, while members of the Institute would be able to enjoy a unique and accurate description of their calling, other chemists would still be subject to confusion with pharmacists. Hopefully, this distinction would make Institute membership more attractive. In any case, it would provide Council with a very good reason *not* to pursue general registration of the profession. The Institute had come down firmly on the side of voluntary exclusive registration rather than compulsory (or voluntary) comprehensive registration.

Council had very little feedback from the membership about its proposed petition, only fifty-five members bothering to comment. However, some members attending the AGM which discussed it argued forcefully that such a move was divisive and ran directly opposite to prevailing efforts to unify the chemical profession. The dissenters exercised their right to call for a postal vote which in fact went against them, 2,406 members favouring the new title and 698 opposing it. Furthermore, the Pharmaceutical Society expressed reservations. Despite the favourable vote, the Institute deferred the petition while it tried to meet the Pharmaceutical Society's points. In the event, MacDonald's first National Government fell before the Pharmacy and Poisons Bill was passed, so the Institute postponed the Supplemental Charter petition indefinitely.[36] In 1933 under the Second National Government, the Poisons and Pharmacy Bill became law, opening up the title 'chemist' as anticipated. However, the Institute did not proceed with the Supplemental Charter in view of a new spate of negotiations for closer cooperation among the existing chemical bodies. Although the Institute wanted to preserve an independent line in resisting any move toward compulsory and comprehensive registration or actual unification, it would hardly have been politic for it to have taken so obviously a separatist action.[37]

During the late 1920s and early 1930s, there were various moves to bring about closer collaboration among the chemical institutions. In view of its attempts to gain exclusive rights for its members, the Institute's response to such overtures tended to be cautious. For example, the Chemical Society suggested that it would be logical to amalgamate the Local Sections of the Institute and the SCI since they already sponsored many meetings jointly. At the same time, the Chemical Society itself wanted to institute a local section structure which it hoped to combine with that of the other two bodies. Speaking at a Birmingham Local Section meeting, Pilcher put Council's point of view. The current informal collaboration between Institute and SCI Local Sections, on occasions when there were topics of mutual interest, seemed to work quite well; there was no reason for Chemical Society members not to be invited to such meetings as guests. Of course, the implication of Pilcher's comments was that Chemical Society members who were anxious to attend Institute Local Section events regularly could do so easily by the simple expedient of joining the Institute, provided they possessed suitable qualifications. Pilcher also indicated Council's view on the general question of collaboration: complete federation of the chemical institutions was not feasible because of their very mixed standards of qualifications. The Institute could not countenance its members being considered equivalent to individuals with lesser qualifications. What was desirable, however, was much better coordination and a clearer distribution of non-overlapping responsibilities among the existing organizations.[38]

The Chemical Society's independent initiative having proved unsuccessful, another move toward increased collaboration came from the FCC. It will be remembered that the Institute was not a constituent of this body, although its views were represented on it, while the Chemical Society and the SCI were full members (p. 241). By 1931, the FCC included some sixteen chemical organizations. In October 1931, it set up a committee '. . . to consider how the resources of the various bodies concerned with the professional and scientific welfare of chemists can most economically and efficiently be utilized'.[39]

This committee proposed a scheme for the unification and consolidation of the chemical profession which the FCC unanimously adopted in January 1933. It called for a new chartered 'Society of Chemistry' with objects comparable to those of the various royal societies concerned with other specific sciences. The main constituents were to be the Chemical Society, the Institute, and the SCI, all of whose members were to become members of the new body. The way was to be left open for other organizations concerned with chemistry to enter as constituent bodies. There was to be a weekly journal and the chemical library was to be available equally to all members. It was envisaged that the Councils and Committees of the constituent bodies would continue to have some autonomy within the new Society, but all administrative, secretarial and accountancy work was to be centralized for economy. Ultimately it was expected that a similar centralization of all libraries belonging to constituent bodies and of all editorial and publishing work would take place. Lastly, along the lines of the Chemical Society's earlier proposal it was suggested that all local sections outside London should belong to the new Society and be open to all members of constituent bodies.

Although it was claimed that this scheme 'would go far towards the unification of the chemical profession' and would promote closer association and better understanding between bodies which represented competing and even conflicting interests, the proposed body was still no more than a federation.[40]

Given its current attempts to make its register more exclusive and its

22   *Entrance and main stairs at 30 Russell Square, since 1914 the home of the (Royal) Institute of Chemistry.*

27 *Specialist laboratory, Russell Square.*

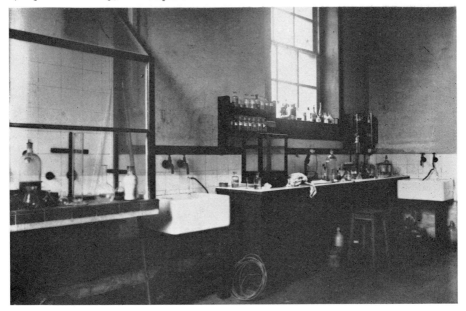

28 *Metallurgical laboratory, Russell Square.*

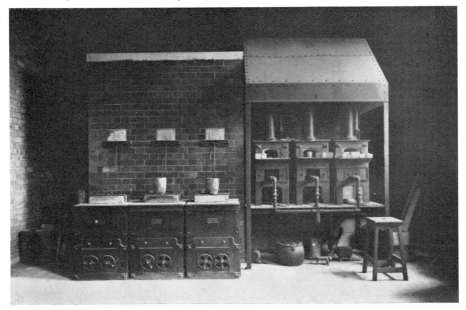

previous rejection of the Chemical Society's proposal regarding Local Sections, it is hardly surprising that the Institute opposed this scheme. However, this time, rather than awaiting further external proposals, the Institute set up its own committee to consider means of cooperation among the chemical bodies. What were effectively this committee's suggestions for the establishment of a Chemical Council were ratified in July 1935 for a seven-year trial period, after much discussion by a Joint Committee of the three principal bodies involved.[41] The Chemical Council was to consist of twelve members; the Institute, the Chemical Society, and the SCI were each to nominate three members, and there were to be three further representatives of chemical industry nominated by the Association of British Chemical Manufacturers. In addition the Chemical Council was to be empowered to admit other bodies to membership but only with the separate approval of the Councils of the three principal bodies.

The proposed objects of the Chemical Council were:[42]

1 The coordination of the activities of the constituent bodies.

2 The collection and allocation of funds contributed by the constituent bodies and from sources for the support of publications and of the objects approved by each of the Councils of the constituent bodies.

3 The centralization of the secretarial and administrative work of the constituent bodies.

4 The business control of publications and of the library.

5 The promotion of any other objects of general interest to and approved by each of the Councils of the constituent bodies.

Initially, the Chemical Council concentrated on financing existing chemical publications (particularly abstracts) and the Chemical Library. Previously, the cost of the former had been borne by individual societies, while the cost of the latter had been borne mainly by the Chemical Society. As a remedy, the Chemical Council set up two appeal funds, hoping that each would reach £100,000. It was anticipated that industrialists would recognize the importance of the work of the chemical institutions for their own enterprises and contribute generously.[43]

While the Institute was involved in shaping the Chemical Council, there were also developments on the question of registration. In 1935, the Poisons Board set up under the 1933 Poisons and Pharmacy Act reported on the regulations devised for its administration. It noted that under modern circumstances, many drugs were prepared industrially rather than by individual pharmacists. Consequently the Board ruled that anyone involved in the manufacture of pharmaceutical preparations containing poisonous substances must have a recognized pharmaceutical or chemical qualification. The Institute's qualifications were cited as the only acceptable chemical ones. The Board ruled that mere possession of a degree was no guarantee of professional competence. In any case, a degree could not be revoked, whereas the Institute had disciplinary powers comparable to those of the Pharmaceutical Society and could remove unacceptable practitioners. The Board suggested that this would not adversely affect graduates since the Institute made ample provision for their admission. Members of the Institute who favoured compulsory registration were very pleased with these regulations; the numbers in the particular industry were small, but the principle was important. Others, however, saw the ruling as an encroachment of government in yet another area. The universities particularly opposed the establishment of a principle which might throw doubt on the value of degrees, and which might in the long run reflect on university autonomy. The Institute was clearly in an awkward position. It offered to organize a licensing system for non-Institute members who wished to work in the pharmaceutical industry, but the Poisons Board turned down the suggestion.[44]

The Committee of Vice-Chancellors and Principals of Universities and University Colleges approached the Institute about the problem in 1936. In March of that year, Robert Howson Pickard became President of the Institute for a three-year term. He was Director of the British Cotton Industry Research Association and had been a member of the University of London Senate since 1926. He was an ideal President to deal with this tricky problem of balancing the legitimate, but conflicting, interests of the Institute's academic and industrial members. In 1937, while the discussions were going on, he became Vice-Chancellor of the University of London.[45] In the event the Institute proposed another Supplemental Charter with two main provisions. Firstly, to promote better communications with universities, it sought power for the universities to nominate a certain number of members to Council so that they would have direct representation. Secondly, a third grade of membership was proposed with the title 'Graduates Registered by the Institute'. Members of this category were to have exactly the same qualifications as those graduates who entered the Associateship by exemption. However, the new group would pay a smaller fee and enjoy no privileges of the Institute such as receiving publications or participating as voting members at meetings. As corporate members, however, they would be subject to disciplinary procedures. Essentially then, the Institute was trying to provide the licence which the Poisons Board had vetoed, and was taking steps in the direction of registration which it had long resisted.[46]

Understandably many members of the Institute were outraged by these proposals.[47] The very idea of formal university members of Council, even if the universities chose their representatives from an Institute list of nominees, was particularly repugant. In the first place, there was the old grievance about the relative positions of academic and practical chemists within the Institute. Furthermore, many were concerned that this was the thin end of the wedge leading to a loss of the Institute's powers of self-government. If the universities had a voice in Institute affairs, did the ABCM and other bodies not have just as much a right to one? Furthermore, as the President himself pointed out, there always were university members of Council. One academic noted with some asperity that the fifty-strong (1937–8) Council included amongst its members, ten professors, four or five lecturers, and one Vice-Chancellor. Surely they could make the academic point of view heard between them. Therefore, some members suggested, the universities would not seem to have much to gain, while the Institute would seem to have a lot to lose.

In addition, the proposals disturbed some of those in favour of registration as well as some of those against. The former regretted that such a move was limited to graduates, having promoted a broader register of practising chemists all along. Those against registration objected to the proposals as a step in the wrong direction. Furthermore, there was a good deal of concern about the effect of the new grade on the status of Associates. Council argued that undoubtedly many members who joined the new grade as a short-term expedient would be attracted to the full Associateship. Others protested that people who were not willing to make a wholehearted commitment of both funds and energies to the Institute would enjoy the same status in terms of certain posts as longstanding Associates. In connection with the registration issue, Associates had been pressing since at least 1927 to have a few of their number on Council. Council resisted this move because among the duties of all Council members was dealing with promotion of Associates to the Fellowship. There was concern that a conflict of interest might arise. However, Associates saw their presence on Council as a way of increasing the voice of industrial members of the Institute as well as making known the views of the majority group.[48] The proposed new grade of membership was a case in point. Associates did not welcome the potential erosion of their position.

Sir Robert Robinson, however, really threw the cat among the pigeons at a special General Meeting discussing the Supplemental Charter. Eminent Waynflete Professor of Chemistry at Oxford, Robinson suggested that the universities would take strong action if the Institute rejected these proposals.

> The poisons matter was nothing but the spark. It is only the thing which drew attention to a very serious situation, namely that University Graduates, qualified in chemistry, are gradually being excluded, to put it quite plainly, from important jobs.[49]

Other Council members quickly denied that the Institute was under any form of threat, but the damage has been done. A postal vote showed 1,386 in favour of petitioning for a Supplemental Charter and 1,446 against, with roughly forty per cent of the eligible voters participating in the poll. Pickard attributed the adverse vote directly to unjustified fears about university coercion.[50] He stressed that despite the results of the poll, Council still favoured the proposals because: (i) Departments of State might require a register, (ii) the Institute was the only body with authority to maintain a register of chemists, and universities would recognize this as *quid pro quo*, (iii) the Institute provided professional discipline which the government saw as necessary for some purposes, (iv) in order to make as complete a register as possible the Institute had to include all qualified chemists even if it meant tolerating those who were not interested. Council did, however, make some concessions to the memberships' views. It agreed to admit to the new grade anyone who was ordinarily exempt from the Institute's examinations, including those with certain technical college qualifications. Furthermore, it retreated from the idea of direct university nominees to Council, though suggesting that Council should always include six university professors.[51]

2   The Effects of World War II: Old Questions and Old Answers

The proposed Supplemental Charter was put into abeyance when it became obvious that the imminent war would make a very different sort of register necessary. In the Second World War as in the First, the Institute played a very important role in helping to mobilize chemists effectively for war work. The importance of this work was recognized in 1944 when the Institute was given a Royal Command to change its name to the Royal Institute of Chemistry. The government itself was rather better organized this time with respect to the utilization of scientific and technical personnel, but this did not make the Institute's task any easier due to the vastly increased numbers and a much reduced staff. The Administrative Officers helped many individual members with mobilization problems and constantly pressed that professional chemists be taken on at the level they deserved. From 1940, the government required all scientific and technical personnel with more than a very minimal qualification to submit their names to the Central Register of the Ministry of Labour. The statistics thus produced gave the Institute food for thought. By March 1942, the Central Register included the names of 20,000 chemists who had at least some qualification, although not necessarily up to the Institute's level. The Institute and the other chartered chemical bodies embraced a total membership of about 12,000, the Institute alone having approximately 8,000 members. If a further 1,000 BAC members were included, this still meant that there were 7,000 chemists who had no institutional affiliations at all, and 12,000 outside the Institute. These figures could not be ignored and the discussions of registration took a new turn. The suggested third grade of membership now became a 'licentiateship' lower grade to attract as many chemists as possible. Furthermore, these statistics promoted the case of those who had been suggesting for some time that the Institute ought to have a thorough review of policy.

A committee was set up to carry out this review with a very extensive brief:

to examine the relationship of the Institute to the State;

to examine the extent to which the Institute might exert itself on the behalf of individuals with employment problems;

to take steps to maintain the standards of the existing qualifications;

to investigate possible new grades of membership;

to investigate the possibility of further cooperation and possible unification with other chemical bodies;

to investigate means of publicizing chemistry and chemists;

to consider proposals for a central 'Chemistry House'.[52]

All these issues were widely discussed within the Institute despite the exigencies of wartime. Rather than a lower corporate grade, Council tended to favour a temporary grade between the student level and the Associateship level.[53] However, the issue was deferred until after the war since it was unclear whether the Ministry of Labour Central Register would continue, and this would obviously affect the Institute's role in registration. On the question of unification, results were similarly inconclusive. There was considerable pressure from within the Institute and the chemical community at large to proceed for a much closer liaison among the chartered chemical bodies than afforded by the Chemical Council.

In 1942, the original seven-year agreement of the Chemical Council expired. From 1940, a new agreement had somewhat extended the cooperation among the three chartered chemical bodies through new arrangements for financing the publication of abstracts and through a joint subscription scheme. The Institute administered the latter. By 1942 a Conjoint Chemical Office, a very small step in the direction of a Chemistry House, was set up.[54] In 1943, a letter appeared in *Chemistry and Industry* signed eventually by almost 500 eminent chemists, including most immediate past and present officers and members of the Institute's Council and those of the other chartered societies. Noting that there was already a good deal of *ad hoc* collaboration at the Local Section level, they petitioned the Chemical Council to investigate the feasibility of either enlarging its own scope or fostering some new Federal Body comprising the three chartered bodies. The important point was that the new body must cater for all that professional chemists required in a concerted and unified way: publications, scientific meetings, high standards of qualification and registration (whether recognized *de jure* or only *de facto* by the government), publicity, social security, and social functions.

> Chemists are undoubtedly cast to play an important part in planning and building the post-war world; they can only play it if they are willing to remodel their own organization where this is necessary to meet the real needs of the future.[55]

Some Local Sections strongly supported unification, but the Institute tended to follow the line of its current President, Alexander Findlay.[56] He had signed the letter, but favoured the Institute's 1930s policy of collaboration rather than unification. Emeritus Professor of Chemistry at Aberdeen, Findlay also followed the 1930s hard line on qualifications and exclusive registration. He was not alarmed by the Central Register's statistics because, according to his criteria, seventy-five per cent of chemists qualified to join the Institute had already done so. He suggested that the unification of chemists should not be confused with the unification of chemical societies. The Institute was set fair to accomplish the former already. Furthermore, there was no point in creating another registration body since the Institute already enjoyed government recognition for this purpose. Moreover, the Institute always had done a great deal to safeguard the economic interests of its members, both collectively and individually. As for the unification of chemical societies, Findlay favoured rationalization of overlapping functions and collaboration, but he noted that participation in the joint membership scheme of the Chemical Council scarcely indicated an extensive grass-roots movement in its favour.[57]

After Findlay's presidency, there were no further attempts to bring about a unified chemical body until the end of the post-war scientific boom led to the events of the late 1960s discussed in Chapter XVI. Rather what Findlay accomplished was to reaffirm the Institute's independent functions as a professional organization for chemists. Under his lead, a petition for a new Charter reflecting modern circumstances and allowing scope for future developments was devised. It came into effect in 1949. Findlay felt that it was particularly necessary for the Institute to seek a clear statement *de jure* that it represented the profession as a whole and not just the analytical and consulting chemists specified in the 1885 Charter. He estimated that, by the middle 1940s, seventy-five per cent of the Institute's members were employed in industry, so *de facto* it already did represent the whole of the profession. Furthermore, the war had brought a wave of social legislation, including changes in educational policy, which would affect the Institute. While maintaining the standards of its qualifications, the RIC would need flexibility regarding grades of membership. A growing organization (such as the Institute had again become during the war) would also need flexibility regarding its own governing structure. Findlay hoped that in future the Institute would serve not only to bring chemists together but to provide them with advice and guidance in a more positive manner than previously. He also felt that the Institute had to accept a responsibility for the economic welfare of chemists.[58]

It was during Findlay's presidency that Pilcher retired and H. J. T. Ellingham joined the Institute as Secretary. He largely carried on the consolidation initiated during this period.[59]

As was the case during the First World War, the Second World War had brought problems of the economic welfare and status of chemists to the fore. Under the latter heading, the Institute was particularly concerned that science be properly utilized. Together with other professional organizations, it complained in 1941 that the government's Science Advisory Council was too pure science oriented and that it ought to take more account of applied science by including representatives of physics and chemistry with industrial experience.[60] A short time later the Institute agreed to establish for the duration of the war a Joint Council of Professional Scientists, together with the Institute of Physics and representatives of other scientific disciplines. The Joint Council's general remit was to voice collective opinions on public matters and bring about more coordinated action amongst the scientific professions on such issues as the proper utilization of scientists, the education, training, supply and employment of scientists, publicity for science, and the maintenance of standards of qualifications and ethics. Specifically, it considered the Ministry of Labour's recommendations on minimum hours, the possibility of urging the government to establish a Central Scientific and Technical Board, the influence on professional standards of shortened wartime degrees, the promotion of a national policy on research and development work, and the post-war utilization of scientists.[61]

While dealing with these general issues, the Institute also looked into some more specific problems. Jointly with the Society of Public Analysts it deluged the Ministry of Health with complaints and deputations because the Ministry's Emergency Public Health Laboratories interfered severely with private practitioners accustomed to analysing water supplies. When it appeared that these laboratories would become permanent under the new National Health Service, the Institute created a new Branch I examination in Water Supply and the Treatment of Sewage and Trade Effluents, so that Institute members would not become excluded from such practice under the new arrangements.[62] After the war, the Institute investigated the position of hospital biochemists. In an effort to raise their status, it created another new examination, Branch D–I in Clinical Chemistry.[63] Underlying both of these cases was an old worry in modern guise, that inevitable rationalization under the Health Service would lead to the exclusion of chemists in favour of medical men.

In addition to issues of status and standards, wartime conditions induced the Institute to take a stronger line on questions of individual remuneration. The Association of Scientific Workers which was in the Trades Union Congress (TUC) was pursuing questions of renumeration particularly forcefully; members of the Institute asked Council to take a stand as well. It rejected collaboration with the AScW and its more blatant methods, arguing that the Institute had always found private, neutral advice to both parties in a dispute the most effective means for dealing with individual problems. However, echoing worries of World War I (p. 239), there was genuine concern among members that post-war circumstances would again see a strengthening of the trade unions and employers' federations at the expense of professional men.[64] The effects of possible nationalization caused particular concern. Consequently, the Institute agreed to a *rapprochement* with the BAC, which was not in the TUC, for the duration of the war. The two organizations established a joint committee to consider the position of chemists.[65]

In 1945, Council made a major policy statement on 'The Economic Welfare of Members'. The Institute was not barred from dealing with this issue by its Charter, indeed it recognized members' economic problems as one of its major responsibilities. The statement reviewed the Institute's past activities in this area and mentioned principles for the future. It could not agree to collective bargaining for professionals since the qualities determining professional advance were very much a matter of individual merit. However, the Institute would use its standard methods of seeking economic advancement more vigorously. It would seek wider recognition as an advisory body to government departments and industrial firms, and it would set up a standing committee to approve applications from employers for advertisements in the Appointments Register and to seek legal advice on principles affecting groups of chemists.[66] In fact, this was no great departure in principle for the Institute, Council was merely taking on formally tasks which the Administrative Officers had been performing on an *ad hoc* basis for years.

The Institute's claim that its methods worked was certainly not false, judging from members' correspondence. There were some notable successes and some notable failures. Success really depended on the reasons for a firm's inadequate conditions in the first place. Larger firms with established procedures and several chemists were harder to persuade than small firms employing a chemist for the first time.[67] There were problems with the Institute's methods. One was the old difficulty of lack of sanctions, although in the employees' market of the post-war period this was less of a problem. Another was simply that of numbers. The annual Report for 1948 proudly pointed out that the Administrative Officers had been consulted on remuneration and related issues some one hundred times in the preceding year. Such consultations were very time-consuming for the already overworked officers, and one hundred was only one per cent of the total membership. A further problem was that the overall results that the Institute achieved for the profession were gradual, cumulative and not spectacularly visible; it was difficult to prove in actual £.s.d. that it had brought about any improvement.[68]

In 1946, the South Yorkshire Section added a specific grievance to the more general concern about the professional man's loss of status. It pointed to recent wage rises in nationalized industries for unskilled workmen which eroded the standing of the chemists in those industries.[69] The government was again creating sets of Whitley Councils, to deal with the new nationalized industries. As was the case after World War I, the Councils consisted of employers' groups and unions (p. 239)—the government had left the professional man out again. The Joint Council of Professional

Scientists was kept in existence specifically to try to deal with this problem.[70]

Meanwhile, the Institute adopted the same position it had been forced to after the First World War. It did not claim to represent chemists on the staff side of the Whitley Councils although this would have been possible under the new Charter. Instead it acted in an advisory capacity for both sides. At the same time, it advised members who were forced to join unions, as in the case of the coal industry, to join the BAC. Indeed, the Institute even toyed with the idea of more active collaboration with the BAC.[71]

In his 1950 presidential address to the Institute, J. W. Cook discussed the problems facing professional men. He was against unionization, but felt that if the government continued its policy of establishing Whitley Councils, the Institute might have to reconsider. However, he saw the same problem that faced the Institute in its efforts to deal with Whitley Councils some thirty years before: no tiny sectional union, such as professional chemists might form, could possibly compete with the big workers' unions. Furthermore, there seemed to be a trend toward the establishment of salary scales which made little allowance for the recognition of individual merit, the traditional means whereby professionals advanced. He produced statistics to show that the position of the professional man had fallen significantly over the decade 1938–48. This was not just a British problem, but that did not make the circumstances any more palatable. So ironically, while there was an unprecedented demand for professional scientists and technologists after the war (p. 267), they were relatively worse off financially than before the war.[72]

The financial issue dominated the early fifties. The Institute even considered becoming involved in formal negotiations on salaries and conditions of service for specialized groups of chemists, if the majority of a particular group were members of the Institute. Significantly, it hoped to start with the Public Analysts, one of the few coherent groups within the Institute. But they decided to establish their own professional association.[73] For the most part the Institute kept to its usual activities of acting as an advisor (with some success in the case of the coal industry and the National Health Service), publicizing the status of chemists, and pursuing an active recruitment campaign so that the Institute would become as strong as possible. By 1953, there was some optimism. Salaries had improved considerably and the demand for trained personnel was still keeping pace with the supply. The Institute estimated somewhat optimistically that seventy per cent of those who were eligible to join actually did so.[74] Throughout the rest of the fifties and early sixties, professional chemists enjoyed relatively full employment (with the exception of some older chemists) and the Institute carried on along the lines defined after the war.[75] Its main area of expansion of activities during this period was in the field of education and qualifications discussed in Chapter XIV.

3 Old Questions, New Answers: Professional Relations since the 1960s

In the middle sixties, with Dr R. E. Parker[70] well settled in the role of Secretary and Registrar which he had assumed in 1962, the Institute paused to assess its future. The Professional Status and Ethical Practices Committee prepared a report reviewing past policy and suggesting future activities.[77] The Committee noted that recent trends in education made it likely that the Institute's role as an examining and qualifying body would change. The former would almost certainly diminish; but the future of the latter was unclear, it might well increase. The Report also suggested that this reassessment was needed in the light of recent social and economic changes. It mentioned no specific circumstances except for the possible effects on the Institute of Britain's application for entry into the European Economic Community. However, this review was undertaken just after a period of significant reorganization of the administration of science and technology by the Labour Government following the 1964 election in which the integration of science, technology, and industry had been a major issue. In addition to increased central planning, another new note entered discussions about science and technology from 1965. National economic difficulties forced cut-backs in programmes approved as recently as the year before. The Institute's Remuneration Surveys indicate that the personal circumstances of chemists (except for senior chemists) were not adversely affected until the more serious reverses of the early seventies. However, the long post-war boom in science and technology appeared to be slackening, or at any rate, entering a very different phase.[78]

Furthermore, the Institute's Professional Status and Ethical Practices Committee noted that 'new concepts of professional rights and obligations and the rapidly diminishing proportions of professional people who are self-employed were causing all the representative organizations to give more attention to the advancement or safeguarding of their members' economic interests, their standing in society, and their relations with the public and their employers'.[79] In its suggestions for future policies, the Committee reaffirmed the soundness of principles that had long been in practice within the Institute. However, it suggested that these principles should be more vigorously pursued in some directions and that some previously discarded policies be revived. In the first place, it proposed that *Chemistry in Britain* should include more articles of relevance to professional interests on such topics as laboratory design, safety measures, public health regulations, and legislation affecting the practice of chemistry, as well as managerial problems. The Committee also wanted members of the Institute to extend their relationships on a personal level with members of the Government and legislature as well as civil servants. It was felt that this would smooth the Institute's path when it wanted to comment on current problems. Furthermore, the Committee wanted the Institute to show more initiative in offering evidence to government departments and committees, rather than waiting to be invited to testify. Lastly the Committee recommended the Institute to attend more to the public image of chemistry via its new Information Officer making sure that, when chemical news broke, there would be competent chemists available to comment on it.

On the question of economic welfare, this 1966 reassessment suggested no new principles. Noting the generally favourable employment situation for chemists, it suggested that a modified form of the old Appointments Register be re-introduced in order to help the one sector that did seem to be in difficulty, the senior chemists. In addition, it recommended that a general review of the working of Local Sections be undertaken and that they assume a more active local role in professional affairs by organizing Local Employment Advisory Panels to assist both younger and older chemists in changing jobs or during disputes. It also suggested that more chemical posts with statutory qualifications be promoted, particularly in areas of high responsibility. Furthermore, in view of the number of issues affecting professionals as a group, some generated by the Government, others not, more collaboration with other professional associations was recommended.

The report concluded by pointing out that:

> much of the Institute's work—and especially its activities in promoting and safeguarding members' professional interests—must be, in part, in response to external developments. For this reason it is impossible to draw up a long-term development plan in great detail. However, the Committee believes that the guiding principles and specific projects outlined above will provide a reasonable basis for progress in the next few years.[80]

The Committee was justified in this view. The 1966 reassessment was firmly rooted in the Institute's past and proposed a model for gradual evolution following long-established principles. In execution however, because of external developments, it brought about far more sweeping changes during the next decade. In fact, the late sixties became another turning point in the Institute's history. Perhaps the most far-reaching of the changes, a new movement for unification among the three chartered chemical bodies (Chapter XVI), was not foreseen in the 1966 report, although it was obvious by then that the Chemical Council had outlived its usefulness.[81] But the report did provide the context for developments.

Some members urged a more democratic and more genuinely representative governing structure for the Institute. There was particular concern that industrial chemists were not represented on Council in proportion to their numbers in the membership at large.[82] Various reforms to the structure and business cycle of Council were introduced. In 1969, a re-evaluation of Local Section structure, suggested in 1966, proposed drastic changes in order to give the Sections new life. Redistricting was proposed so that Sections contained more nearly equal numbers of members. The most fundamental suggestion was that the Institute's activities eventually should be far more decentralized, the new-style Local Sections having more responsibilities and possibly some full-time staff. This contrasted with public developments of increased central planning for science. Formal channels of communication were also proposed between District Council Members and their constituencies, a notoriously weak link in the past.[83] As it happened, the new local structure (regionalization) was instituted at the same time as amalgamation. The Institute's new local structure was superimposed on that of the Chemical Society in such a way that while Institute members were responsible for administering fairly large regions, Chemical Society members were responsible for administering the subdivisions of these units.

This was a logical division since many of the Institute's Local Section events had been of the learned society type anyway. Furthermore, if decentralization of professional functions were to take place, the fragmentary Local Section structure, which served learned society activities admirably, would not be practical. The effect of this however, was to make many Institute members feel isolated from Institute activities, and it tended to prevent discussion of professional affairs on a local level as there was no suitable forum. This policy also tended to highlight and indeed increase the differences in identity felt between the academic and the industrial communities. Thus a policy intended to strengthen the Institute's local functions had in fact weakened them. The Local Employment Advisory Panels were disbanded since they were rarely consulted and in 1973, Council decided that it would be preferable if all Local Sections became joint CS/RIC bodies. By 1975, the situation was much improved, although there were still some local queries about the need for a two-tier structure.[84]

During this period, the Institute also broadened its contacts with other professional bodies in the face of increasing government involvement in science planning, the 'brain drain' and a changing economic pattern. In 1968, while the possibility of unifying the chemical bodies was seriously assessed, the RIC agreed to join in the establishment of the Council of Science and Technology Institutes (CSTI) which included, the Institute of Physics, the Institute of Biology, the Institute of Mathematics and its Applications, and the Institute of Metallurgists. An obvious cousin of the old Joint Council of Professional Scientists which disbanded in 1958, the new CSTI conspicuously lacked the membership of the Institution of Chemical Engineers. The CSTI took on objects very similar to those of its ancestor, primarily to provide a joint voice to influence government on matters of mutual interest. For a time, it was thought that the Council of Engineering Institutions (CEI) might also join forces with this new body to form a very large pressure group.

In 1971 when the proposed Industrial Relations Bill made professional organizations think in terms of unionization again, the RIC fostered the Association of Professional Scientists and Technologists which became the union for members of CSTI organizations.[85] In addition to these activities, as the financial stringencies and economic reverses of the early 1970s took hold, the RIC began to be very active in protesting various restrictions on pay that imposed particular hardships on professional men who were not on incremental scales. Its Remuneration Surveys also proved valuable, if distressing, to chemists. Re-echoing sentiments heard in periods of stress immediately after both wars, the Institute received an invitation in 1974 to participate in a Forum of Professional and Service Institutions which hoped to provide a sort of middle body to look after the interests of professional men who fell between the interests of capital and the interests of labour.[86]

Thus the Institute's views on professional relations have formed an interesting pattern. At various points in its history, during periods of economic difficulty and government initiatives affecting science, the Institute has been presented with similar problems and similar choices of answers. After the First World War, the Institute dealt with the possibility of unification of the chemical bodies by opening its own doors more widely and particularly becoming more accessible to industrial chemists. At this time, it favoured *ad hoc* collaboration with other professional institutions and rejected trade unionism altogether, preferring to maintain its own private initiatives as adviser in dealing with members' problems, which it still does. After the Second World War, the Institute rejected the idea of unification among the chemical bodies and concentrated on consolidating its independent position as a professional institution. As part of this effort, it participated actively in a consultative body of scientific professional associations. It rejected trade unionism as a proper direction for a professional association, but did advise its members to join a separate professional trade union. In the latest phase, the Institute wholeheartedly embraced all three organizational solutions; it has pursued unification among the chartered chemical bodies, joined in a federation of scientific and technological associations, and actively promoted the establishment of a trade union for professional scientists and technologists. The Institute's pattern of policy-making in the area of professional relations during its first one hundred years can best be characterized as one of gradual evolution through response to circumstances that arose, rather than bold departures in new directions. This attitude of constructive conservatism has perhaps resulted from the necessity of balancing the diverse aims of the varied groups practising as chemists, indeed from the nature of the chemical enterprise itself.   GKR

NOTES AND REFERENCES

1 IC, Council Minutes, **18,** 22 May 1925 records that 26 per cent of BAC members also belonged to the Institute.

2 There were mixed views within the BAC about this, some members favouring such tactics as only voting for 'BAC approved' nominees to the Institute's Council. B. Hickson, Letter to H. W. Rowell, 4 February 1919 in BAC, Institute of Chemistry File, all BAC papers held by the Association of Professional Scientists and Technologists.

3 IC, Council Minutes, 10, 24 January, 28 February 1919; 11, 28 March, 2 May, 30 May 1919.

4 *Ibid.*, 16, 25 May, 29 June 1923.

5 *Ibid.*, 10, 29 November 1918; 'Registered Students', *Proc. Inst. Chem.*, 1922, 46, 113–14. It was short-lived.

6 IC, Council Minutes, 12, 23 April 1920 records that the London and South-Eastern Counties Section had 1095 members, while the next largest had only 292 members.

7 cf. ch. XII for the industrial context of this move.

8 IC, Council Minutes, 10, 29 November 1918.

9 *Ibid.*, 11, 28 March 1919; *Proc. Inst. Chem.*, 1919, 43, pt. ii, 50–2.

10 On Brady (1890–1968), see *Chem. Brit.*, 1968, 4, 554. Brady was also first president of the NUSW.

11 IC, Council Minutes, 11, 27 June 1919; *Proc. Inst. Chem.*, 1919, 43, pt. iii, 27; BAC, Council Minutes, 2, 23 August 1919. Brady felt, however, that professional associations and trade unions should remain separate, *Proc. Inst. Chem.*, 1919, 43, pt. ii, 22.

12 (a) *Ibid.*, 1920, 44, 31–41; (b) *ibid.*, 1921, 45, 44–54. In fact, except for a dip just after the Second World War, the Remuneration Surveys revealed fairly comfortable circumstances for chemists other than teachers right up to the 1966 pay freeze; IC, Council Minutes, 56, 20 January 1967.

13 Note 12 (a); *Proc. Inst. Chem.*, 1921, 45, 109–299; IC, Council Minutes, 17, 21 November 1924; see also 'Contracts of Service', *Proc. Inst. Chem.*, 1925, 49, separate pamphlet bound in; *J.R.I.C.*, 1950, 74, 213–17.

14 IC, Council Minutes, 11, 30 May, 29 June 1919. On MacNab (1858–1941), see *Chem. and Ind.*, 1941, 60, 680.

15 IC, Council Minutes, 10, 26 July 1918; 11, 30 May, 29 June, 10 October 1919.

16 R. M. MacLeod and E. K. Andrews, 'The Origins of the DSIR: Reflections on Ideas and Men, 1915–1916', *Public Admin.*, 1970, 48, 23–48; see p. 195.

17 IC, Council Minutes, 16, 27 July 1923; 17, 16 June 1924.

18 *Ibid.*, 11, 31 October 1919; 12, 27 February 1920; *Proc. Inst. Chem.*, 1919, 43, pt. iii, 15–17.

19 H. E. Armstrong, (a) *Chem. Trade J.*, 1919, 64, 95; (b) *J. Soc. Chem. Ind.*, 1919, 38R, 18–19, 59.

20 *Proc. Inst. Chem.*, 1918, 42, pt. iv, 3–4.

21 Note 19 (b).

22 *Proc. Inst. Chem.*, 1920, 44, 177, 182–4; 1921, 45, 55–61, 142–5; IC, Council Minutes, 12, 23 April 1920; 13, 22 April 1921.

23 *Proc. Inst. Chem.*, 1920, 44, 87; 1922, 46, 36–44; IC, Council Minutes, 13, 21 January 1921. This was another issue on which the Institute rejected BAC collaboration; *ibid.*, 28 January 1921.

24 *Proc. Inst. Chem.*, 1922, 46, 51–6, 111; 1920, 44, 103–7; G. G. Henderson, *ibid.*, 1926, 50, 77.

25 *Ibid.*, 1923, 47, 39–46. On E. F. Armstrong (1878–1945), see *ibid.*, 1946, 70, 56.

26 This may just have been 'politics' since he was replying to the president of the SCI at an IC meeting. On Collett (1886–1955), see *ibid.*, 1955, **79**, 483.

27 IC, Council Minutes, **15**, 27 April 1923. On Baly (1871–1948), see *Proc. R.I.C.*, 1948, **72**, 120. He later served as Registrar to the BAC.

28 On Heilbron (1886–1959), see *ibid.*, 1959, **83** 737.

29 'Conference at Liverpool, 18 October 1923', *ibid.*, 1923, **47**, separate pamphlet bound in.

30 'Conference at York, July 1925', *ibid.*, 1925, **49**, 233–60.

31 G. G. Henderson, *ibid.*, p. 95; 1930, **54**, 205.

32 *Ibid.*, 1926, **50**, 174–82. The Committee calculated that the major chemical bodies together had 10,000 members. The Institute's own membership was near 5,000 and there were at least 2,000 chemical graduates in teaching who had no institutional affiliations. G. G. Henderson, *ibid.*, 1927, **51**, 83, estimated that there were about 1,000 new first- and second-class honours graduates in chemistry each year, whereas the Institute's annual intake fell steadily from 491 in 1921 to 242 in 1927.

33 BAC, Council Minutes, **3**, 30 September, 30 October, 11 December 1926, 26 November 1927; *The Chemical Practitioner*, 1928, **1**, no. 5, 3; no. 6, 2; no. 7, 1. *Proc. Inst. Chem.*, 1927, **51**, 148–50; 'Annual Report for 1926', *ibid.*, p. 19. The Institute opposed the joint register, not wanting outside chemists to claim equivalence with its own members.

34 *Nature*, 1927, **119**, 903.

35 G. G. Henderson, *Proc. Inst. Chem.*, 1927, **51**, 87; A. Smithells, *ibid.*, 1928, **52**, 79; 283–95.

36 IC, Council Minutes, **19**, 22 October 1926 includes a copy of the Institute's testimony to the committee. The Supplemental Charter is discussed in *Proc. Inst. Chem.*, 1930, **54**, 97, 245, 309; 1931, **55**, 79–97, 104, 145, 279.

37 *Ibid.*, 1934, **58**, 10, 262–3; 1935, **59**, 214, 219; 1936, **60**, 41–4. During this period, the Institute was in a strong position to get its views represented in both Houses of Parliament. G. C. Clayton, a director of ICI and member of Council from 1926 until 1936 (president for 1930–3), sat in the Commons. Robert Francis, Lord Henly, took his seat in the Lords in 1925 and served on Council during 1931–4. On Clayton (1869–1945), see *ibid.*, 1945, **69**, 153; on Lord Henly (1877–1962), see *ibid.*, 1962, **86**, 448.

38 *Ibid.*, 1930, **54**, 206, 319–21.

39 IC, Council Minutes, **24**, 17 February 1933.

40 *Ibid.*

41 *Ibid.*, **25**, 19 January, 19 December 1934; **26**, 21 June 1935. For the view that this arrangement should mark a first step toward amalgamation of the three chartered bodies, see *Chem. & Ind.*, 1935, **54**, 253–4. For the Institute's disagreement with this view, see *ibid.*, p. 593.

42 IC, Council Minutes, **26**, 21 June 1935.

43 *Ibid.*, **27**, 18 December 1936; *Proc. Inst. Chem.*, 1936, **60**, 201–6. By the end of 1936, £23,410 had been promised of which £8,712 had been received.

44 *Proc. Inst. Chem.*, 1935, **59**, 297–302.

45 On Pickard (1873–1949), see *ibid.*, 1949, **73**, 558.

46 R. H. Pickard, *ibid.*, 1937, **61**, 305–7. 'Special General Meeting, 19 October 1937', *ibid.*, separate pamphlet bound in.

47 *Ibid.*, pp. 435–63.

48 *Ibid.*, 1927, **51**, 98; 1935, **59**, 218.

49 Note 47, p. 460. This concern was evidently fairly widespread within the universities, but not totally justified. See Michael Sanderson, *The Universities and British Industry, 1850–1970*, Routledge, London, 1972, ch. X.

50 Note 47, p. 465; R. H. Pickard, *Proc. Inst. Chem.*, 1938, **62**, 121.

51 *Proc. Inst. Chem.*, 1938, **62**, p. 388; 1939, **63**, 350.

52 *Ibid.*, 1942, **66**, 69, 75.

53 *Ibid.*, p. 193; 1945, **69**, 57. *Ibid.*, p. 11 shows that 35 per cent of the eligible FICs and 28 per cent of the eligible AICs voted about the third grade (53 per cent for, 47 per cent against).

54 IC, Council Minutes, **31**, 21 June 1940. By 1943, there was concern about the lack of growth of the two publishing societies.

55 *Chem. and Ind.*, 1943, **62**, 62–3.

56 On Findlay (1874–1966), see *WWW*; *Chem. Brit.*, 1967, **3**, 24–5.

57 Findlay travelled extensively around the country fostering these views; *Proc. Inst. Chem.*, 1943, **67**, 71–5, 172–3, 205, 209; 1944, **68**, 211–6.

58 Alexander Findlay, *ibid.*, 1946, **70**, 79–83; 1949, **73**, 159–62.

59 On Ellingham (1897–1975), see *ibid.*, 1963, **87**, 31–4; *Chem. Brit.*, 1976, **12**, 322–3.

60 *Ibid.*, 1941, **65**, 208.

61 *Ibid.*, 1942, **66**, 270–1; 1944, **68**, 181–2.

62 See for example, *ibid.*, 1942, **66**, 191; 1949, **73**, 66.

63 J. W. Cook, *ibid.*, 1950, **74**, 106–7.

64 *Ibid.*, 1940, **64**, 38; 1942, **66**, 153, 254–5.

65 *Ibid.*, 1944, **68**, 122. The collaboration lasted until 1949.

66 *Ibid.*, 1945, **69**, 80–1.

67 R. L. Collett, *ibid.*, 1951, **75**, 13.

68 *Ibid.*, 1945, **69**, 140; 1948, **72**, 66.

69 *Ibid.*, 1946, **70**, 162.

70 RIC, Council Minutes, **48**, 20 June 1958.

71 72 per cent of ARICs and 62 per cent of FRICs replying to a Manchester Section questionnaire said they would approve the Institute's representing them in employer/employee relations. Over 40 per cent of all those replying indicated that they would countenance its becoming a trade union. *Proc. R.I.C.*, 1946, **70**, 175; 1948, **72**, 45, 67, 295; 1949, **73**, 508–9.

72 Note 63, pp. 108–10. On Cook (1900–75), see *WW*; *Proc. R.I.C.*, 1949, **73**, 162–4; *Chem. Brit.*, 1976, **12**, 60–1.

73 *Proc. R.I.C.*, 1952, **76**, 10; 1953, **77**, 18.

74 *Ibid.*, pp. 61–3.

75 'Activities of the Institute in Matters Affecting the Professional Status, Conditions of Employment and Welfare of Members', Office Note to the Professional Status Committee, RIC, Council Minutes, **48**, 4 July 1958 confirms this view. An 'office note' is a statement prepared by the Administrative Officers to act as a basis for Council's discussions.

76 On Parker, see *J.R.I.C.*, 1962, **86**, 361–2.

77 'The Future Role of the Institute as a Professional Body', Report of the Professional Status and Ethical Practices Committee, RIC, Council Minutes, **56**, 14 October 1966.

78 For a contemporary expression of this view, see *Nature*, 1965, **207**, 1113–15.

79 Note 77, p. 1.

80 *Ibid.*, p. 9.

81 There already were a number of joint activities among the three bodies. In 1966, the Institute promoted a joint register for the CS, the SCI, and the RIC. The project foundered for various practical reasons, but it is interesting that one industrial member of Council objected on the grounds that the value of RIC qualifications would be diminished if its register were amalgamated with those of two non-qualifying bodies; RIC, Council Minutes, **56**, 20 January 1965; cf. note 33. The Chemical Council was disbanded in June 1966.

82 RIC, Council Minutes, **57**, 13 October 1967; 38 per cent of Council was industrial.

83 *Ibid.*, **59**, 18 July 1969; P. Corbett, *Chem. Brit.*, 1972, **8**, 543–5.

84 RIC, Council Minutes, **62**, 13 October, 15 December 1972, 30 March 1973.

85 *Ibid.*, **58**, 26 July 1968; **61**, 21 May 1971; F. A. Robinson, *Chem. Brit.*, 1973, **9**, 312–16.

86 RIC, Council Minutes, n. vol., 8 February 1974, 20 March 1975.

CHAPTER XIV

ACADEMIC WORK OR EXPERIENCE?

THE INSTITUTES QUALIFICATIONS SINCE 1920

The changes in regulations instituted during the First World War and consolidated in 1920 had an immediate and significant effect on the character of the Institute's membership. Associates quickly began to outnumber Fellows and the Associateship soon became the normal grade of membership (Figure 7). However, members expressed concern that the Institute's qualifications were being devalued under the new arrangements. In the first place, once they had the basic qualification, many practising Associates lacked opportunity or inclination, or both, to prepare for further examinations. This meant that the majority of members of the Institute would have a lower level of qualification than previously. Then in order to counter this effect, the Institute began to place more emphasis on the criteria exempting Associates from the Fellowship examinations. This distressed many members who had only agreed to the exemption of honours graduates from Associateship examinations on the assurance that promotion to the Fellowship would become more rigorous. There was particular concern that the Institute's higher qualification could be awarded without a candidate's ever having undergone the traditional formal practical examination of professional expertise. So, in the eyes of some, the Fellowship was being weakened because it lacked members and because entrance criteria were not stiff enough.[1] At the same time, some members saw a further threat to the Institute's standards in an (unsuccessful) movement on the part of some academics to seek exemption from the AIC examination for students with degrees in applied chemistry or with BSc (Tech) in chemically related subjects such as metallurgy.[2]

1   The Institute and Part-time Technical Education

(a)   Register of Chemical Assistants

In addition to altering the regulations for its own professional qualifications, the Institute also began to take on a broader educational role. In 1920 it organized a Register of Chemical Assistants and, in 1921, it accepted an invitation from the Board of Education to collaborate in its new National Certificate scheme in chemistry. The purpose of the Register of Chemical Assistants was to foster systematic part-time training among junior industrial staff. Too often, the Institute noted, junior staff with a capacity for academic work were allowed to drift, discovering their lack of systematic training and lost career opportunities too late. At that very time, under its new regulations, the Institute was admitting for a limited period only just such people who had achieved responsible positions in industry through talent and intelligence, but who lacked the basic knowledge to take them further. It was hoped that the new Register would prevent such cases in future by making sure that the part-time efforts of junior staff were usefully oriented towards eventual professional qualification. Such a system only became possible under the new regulations, since they reversed the Institute's long-held position on the suitability of part-time training and technical colleges for study at professional level. This programme may have been in part a response to the indirect influence exerted on the Institute by the new BAC which planned to foster the training of junior chemical staff amongst its other activities.[3]

(b) The National Certificate system

The National Certificate system was a post-war reconstruction venture of the Board of Education. In collaboration with the professional institutions, it hoped to systematize technical education. Since the end of the Science and the Art Department examination system in the early part of the century, every technical school and college had run its own courses and given its own awards. These achieved local recognition, but it was difficult for students thus trained to move about. Furthermore, students tended to study rather random selections of subjects, which limited their utility and career prospects. The National Certificate scheme was designed to alter this situation. National Certificates were to be awarded to part-time students who systematically followed and passed examinations in approved groups of courses at non-university institutions. Syllabuses were to be designed locally in order to suit the needs of local industries, but they had to conform to certain broad national guidelines and be approved centrally. The National Certificate scheme was specifically meant to attract part-time students working in industry, and special emphasis was to be laid on relevant practical training. There were to be two levels of award, the lower (eventually called the Ordinary [ONC]) required three years of part-time work and the upper (eventually called the Higher [HNC]) required a further two years. The latter was originally meant to be roughly equivalent in standard to the Final BSc at pass degree level.[4]

The role of the Institute, like that of other professional associations, was to act jointly with the Board of Education as external assessor of local facilities, syllabuses, and examinations in its own discipline, chemistry. The BAC's known interest in the area of part-time technical college training may have influenced the Institute's decision to undertake the task.[5] Under the Institute's guidance the core of the National Certificates in chemistry became broad training in the principles of chemistry, physics and mathematics. Any applied studies included in later years of the course had to be based on a general investigation of the *principles* of the particular industry involved, not works techniques. Having just weathered an internal uproar over qualifications, the Institute particularly insisted that any joint award at the level envisaged by the Board of Education would explicitly *not* constitute a professional hallmark. Indeed, the Institute would not recognize the National Certificate courses as constituting part of the training for its own professional qualifications either, although some of the engineering institutions did for theirs. The Institute's position was that the National Certificates did not include the requirement of preliminary general education that was essential for the AIC, that some of the courses tended to be too specialist, and that the standards reached in the basic sciences were not high enough.[6] This was certainly a perfectly understandable view in the early 1920s, particularly considering the Institute's concern to consolidate the reputation of its qualifications under the new regulations. However, once it adopted this position, the Institute kept to it rather firmly (although it made exceptions in individual cases) until World War II, and it did not make any formal changes until 1956. Indeed, the position of National Certificate holders figures in most of the debates about a third grade of membership discussed in Chapter XIII.

Within a decade, it was reported that the National Certificate scheme had had the desired effect of bringing about significant improvements in the quality of chemistry teaching and facilities in many technical colleges. Heads of chemistry departments found the external support of the Institute and the Board of Education very useful in obtaining funds from Local Education Authorities. However, from the point of view of the Board of Education, the National Certificate scheme was not an unqualified success. Its original intention had been to promote more practical vocational training rather than general professional training. In the case of chemistry, the effect was further complicated by the fact that the Certificates were based on general training but did not lead to a professional qualification. The overall drop-out rate was quite high since the courses were demanding in themselves; there were the added demands of the scheme being based on part-time study. The reward did not seem commensurate with the effort required. In comparison to Certificate schemes run by other professional institutions, the chemistry enrolment was low.[7]

It has to be pointed out in the Institute's defence that it was in an awkward position. Members' worries about the reputation of existing qualifications were genuine and any broadening in the direction of providing HNC's with a route to the Associateship would have exacerbated these. Further, the possibility of providing a new membership grade for HNC's, and equivalents such as pass BSc's, had serious 'political' ramifications outside the Institute, within the larger chemical community (Chapter XIII). During the 1930s, the Institute discreetly relied on its well-established principles. After all, if everyone who was already eligible to enter under the existing regulations did so, it would have been a large and powerful body. Thus it did not seem necessary to widen its regulations for the sake of numbers. Membership grew steadily, but not dramatically.

2 Consolidation in the 1930s

The Institute's growth rate was in keeping with the general situation in university-level scientific training, it was essentially a period of consolidation.[8] There were some alarms at the rise of general science teaching in schools at the expense of the amount of time devoted to pure chemistry. However, in the end this was decided to be a development in accordance with the Institute's principles of favouring broad preliminary education.[9] Similarly, some members suggested that the Institute might consider including some form of management training in its curricula (p. 226). But Council decided that the basic principles of its system would not admit such a course, and in any case industrialists and academics alike were divided on the value of such training.[10]

In 1937, J. F. Thorpe, Professor of Organic Chemistry at Imperial College and past-President of the Institute, indicated that the Institute might have to re-evaluate its role as a qualifying and examining body. In answer to those who thought that the Institute might become superfluous because of the development of university education, Thorpe suggested that, on the contrary, this might give the Institute an even more important role. Thorpe foresaw a significant change of emphasis. He thought it likely that in future the Institute would become the examining body for those who did not have the opportunity to undertake formal university study. In addition, he noted a tendency toward increased specialization in university courses. He suggested that these were consequently becoming beyond the intellectual reach of many students who could none the less be very useful chemists if given broad general training. This group might find the Institute's examinations preferable to university degrees in future.[11] These comments of course had profound implications for the Institute's qualifications. However, in the event, it was again the circumstances of war and its aftermath that induced the Institute to reconsider its policies.

3 Wartime Changes and Chemical Education

During the war, the government re-evaluated the total provision of education in Britain. Since war made the necessity for scientifically and technologically trained personnel for Britain's industrial future even more obvious, these areas came under particular scrutiny.[12] The White Paper of 1943, while calling for more thorough provision of elementary and secondary education, also suggested that it should be a duty rather than an option of Local Education Authorities to provide facilities for technical education in the further education sector. Furthermore, integration between the needs of local industry and local technical education provision had to be improved. The Institute immediately prepared a statement responding to the White Paper, reiterating its long held views that the only foundation for a scientist or technologist was broad general education in the principles of science. It deprecated recent tendencies toward specialization in the schools and consequent premature specialization at more advanced levels. This, it felt, was achieved at the expense of general principles.[13] Here, the Institute had clearly seen the writing on the wall. Shortly after the 1943 White Paper, the new-style Ministry of Education requested that National Certificate courses be made more relevant to local industries, that is more practical in the vocational sense including a larger applied science component in both the ONC and HNC. The Institute categorically refused, but the Ministry did not give up easily. As a compromise, the Institute suggested that a second National Certificate scheme, in applied chemistry, be introduced. This was eventually started in 1947, but there was one period when feeling ran so high that the Institute almost withdrew from National Certificates altogether. In order to win its case for general training in the Chemistry National Certificates, the Institute suggested that it might moderate its position about the possibility of these leading to a professional qualification.[14]

Also important to the Institute were the Report on Higher Technological Education (the Percy Report) of 1945 and the Report on Scientific Manpower (the Barlow Report) of 1946, both dealing with the need for more scientists and technologists. The Percy Report recommended rationalization of the existing plural provision. It suggested that a certain number of technical colleges should develop applied science courses of university standard and postgraduate specialist courses relevant to particular industries. It called for the establishment of Regional Advisory Councils to coordinate technological studies in universities and colleges and to liaise with industry. A similar national body, responsible for publicizing the value of trained personnel in industry, was also suggested, which might also create for the new programmes special awards (distinct from degrees). In addition, industrial administration should be included in technological curricula. The Barlow Report focused more specifically on the provision of scientists, supporting the broad recommendations of Percy. The Barlow Report however, quantified the problems. If Britain were to achieve its manpower targets in science and technology, the output from universities would have to be doubled. A corollary of this was that there would have to be vastly increased provision of science teachers at all levels.[15] From this time onward, the Institute and other professional organizations began to lobby more consistently for improved pay and conditions for school science teachers and to become more concerned with school science generally. It was obvious that future manpower expansion depended on circumstances in the schools. Ironically, the post-war increase in demand for scientists and technologists further eroded the numbers going into school teaching since it became less and less attractive in comparison to many new opportunities in industry. While pressing the case for teachers in general, the Institute renewed its efforts begun in the 1920s, to get the Burnham Committee's recognition for salary purposes of the ARIC as an honours degree equivalent.[16]

The Institute welcomed the proposed expansion and its members were soon serving on the new Regional Advisory Councils. It suggested that Local Sections should look into technical education in their areas so that the Institute would be able to offer useful advice. However, it did not agree with all the policies of the two reports. When invited to comment on the first report of the National Advisory Council on Education for Industry and Commerce (the body charged with designing the detailed implementation of the wartime recommendations), the Institute reacted strongly, implying that the new proposals were tantamount to throwing out the baby with the bath water. It objected to a new system of awards and a new awarding body for degree level work. In the case of chemistry at any rate, the RIC itself already provided a recognized and respected set of awards. If some new monitoring body were needed, it suggested that the existing Joint Council of Professional Scientists would provide a nucleus of expertise and accepted standards. Furthermore, rather than creating elaborate and costly new institutions, the real financial effort should go into putting existing technical colleges on a sound footing. The Institute opposed the introduction of very specialist degree level courses, re-iterating its view that the basis of a sound technological education had to be broad general training in the principles of science.[17]

4 Post-war Changes and the Institute's Qualifications

Therefore, it is not surprising that in 1950, after an extensive review of its qualifications, taking into account pressures from the post-war increase in HNC's as well as the increase in university output, the Institute decided not to change its regulations. In fact those for proceeding from ARIC had been altered somewhat in 1948. The three FRIC branch examinations (A, B, C), testing academic work rather than specific professional expertise, were to be eliminated. In addition all candidates would be requested to submit a statement of their experience and output, after which they might or might not be referred to the Board of Examiners for formal examination. It was hoped that this would counter the difficulty of ARIC's not applying for the Fellowship.[18] From 1947 Council had agreed to consider applications for ARIC from HNC holders on an *ad hoc* basis. Also in the late forties, the Institute collaborated with the AScW, the AUT, the BAC, some members of the Joint Council of Professional Scientists, as well as the Science Masters' Association in promoting a City & Guilds examination for laboratory technicians and agreed that it might be appropriate to foster their organization in a separate institution.[19] Thus technicians were declared not to be in the province of the Institute, while technologists were.

(a) *The emergence of GradRIC: ARIC again the hallmark of professional competence*

However, during the early 1950s, a number of issues came together to make the Institute reconsider its views on qualifications. In the first place, evidence from the Local Sections showed that there were increasing instances where technical colleges correlated their teaching for the HNC and the ARIC examinations. The Sections pointed out that this was an efficient use of technical college and student time. If students entering Higher National Certificate courses were properly prepared with respect to preliminary education (which was likely to be more common in future with the spread of the new General Certificate of Education [GCE] system), such correlated teaching might eventually make up a route to professional qualifications.[20] This was to be particularly recommended in view of the increased number of HNC students due to the widespread acceptance of day release arrangements. Council's reply to this view was given in an editorial in the *Journal*. It applauded the rationalization of use of facilities by technical colleges, but still disagreed that the HNC should become a definite step to the Associateship. The HNC was viewed by the Institute as a qualification for technical assistants and it should be valued as such. To paraphrase an argument that it used in the same context on another occasion, Council felt that it was important to encourage a class of first-rate assistants, rather than fourth-rate technologists.[21]

However, at about the same time, the University of London revised the regulations for its external degree in chemistry in such a way that more part-time students might wish to qualify directly through the ARIC examination rather than indirectly by exemption based on a London degree. At the same time it was noted that the pass rate in the ARIC examination had been declining steadily over the preceding decade from fifty-seven to twenty-five per cent of the entry.[22] The current London external BSc pass rate was considerably higher. It was recognized that the fact that the latter was done in two stages might well weed out the weaker candidates. Furthermore, there was the perennial problem that most ARIC's entered by degree exemption, yet the Institute was not growing at the same rate as the number of graduates.

In addition, discussions on a national level, regarding a national technological qualification, were still proceeding. If the Institute wanted to press its case for its qualifications along with the other professional institutions, it made good sense to harmonize its overall pattern with theirs. The major engineering institutions and the Institute of Physics did not admit graduates directly, but required evidence of varying periods of practical experience for their Associateships. Furthermore, during the early 1950s the possibility that the Institute might have to assume the functions of a protective association made the possibility of additional qualified chemists joining their ranks quite attractive (Chapter XIII). However, as Ellingham pointed out in an editorial, they were not merely after numbers for numbers' sake.[23]

As a result of considering these issues during 1954, Council announced a new set of regulations in 1955 to become effective in 1956.[24] The main principle behind the new regulations was a return to the 1892 concept that the Associateship should be the sign of professional competence, rather than just recognition of academic work. To certify basic training, a new non-corporate, transitional grade was introduced, Graduate Membership. This would be the examined grade, divided into two parts. The same systematic pre-examination training was still required. Part I would consist of a theory examination in the three basic branches of chemistry, but no practical test. Its level was meant to be approximately equivalent to that of a pass degree. The Part II examination would resemble the former ARIC examination, including the by now characteristic and well-known practical examination. Part II was to be equivalent to Honours degree standard. A good honours degree would exempt the candidate from all Institute examinations, and significantly, a good HNC would exempt the candidate from Part I. Thus the HNC was brought into the structure of the Institute's professional qualifications. The Part II stage would be followed by two years in the practice or application of chemistry which would entitle the graduate to the Associateship.

The award of the Fellowship would become a senior honour, a sign that the member had obtained a standard of professional maturity and responsibility. Finally, the Branch examinations for the Fellowship were to be discontinued, to be replaced by post-Associate diplomas in the professional subjects that were not related to the Fellowship.[25] With the Associateship 'promoted', it was hoped that membership would increase. These regulations were brought into existence under the presidency of an industrial man, Sir Harry Jephcott.[26]

Predictably, members from various camps expressed concern about some features of the new regulations. Some academics regretted the imposition of a new hurdle before honours degree chemists. Others felt that someone who qualified by part-time study would already have a good deal of experience in the application of chemistry and would find a further requirement of experience superfluous. Still others suggested that the 'promotion' of the Associateship, contrary to Council's expectations, would prevent even more people from seeking the higher grade. Another group suggested that the Institute should create a corporate grade of membership which would serve as a definite qualification at the GradRIC Part I level for those who did not aspire to higher academic attainments.[27]

(b)   A third permanent grade of membership, the Licentiateship

Council seriously considered the question of a third permanent grade in 1956, but was reluctant to institute one for the reasons presented in an unfavourable Office Note:

Since the war there have been, however, many other changes that may be considered to weaken the case for a permanent third grade of membership. In particular a clearer distinction has been drawn between *technicians*, on the one hand, and *scientists and technologists*, on the other. The former, often highly skilled, are nevertheless limited in general to working under direction; the latter are expected to have a clearer and deeper understanding of fundamental principles and an ability to apply them in dealing with new problems of any kind, and to accept full professional responsibility for their work. It has also been recognized that skilled technicians are required in much greater numbers; 4–5 to every qualified scientist or technologist, if the latter are to be relieved of routine work and exercise their proper functions. Most technicians are now able to secure well paid posts in industry and the Government service and the best of them can rise to positions of notable responsibility.

The question that arises is therefore whether a place should be found for 'chemical technicians' within the membership of the Institute. Would the Institute gain or lose by their inclusion? Are there alternative ways of looking after their interests? In many other professions, especially those where this distinction has long been more fully recognized the conclusion has been that the professional body should not admit the corresponding technicians to any grade of its membership or to any form of association that might be mistaken for a grade of membership, but that the professional body should encourage technicians to form associations of their own and give guidance and help in forming them.[28]

The Office Note pointed out that the only category of student in a difficult position was the full-time technical college student who stopped at the Part I level. There was no recognized award to which he could aspire. However, the part-time student at the same level could receive an HNC. The Institute argued that this award should be considered a qualification in itself, indeed employers seemed to be recognizing it as such. The Higher National Diploma (HND), the full-time or sandwich equivalent of the HNC, was introduced in 1958 to eliminate the discrimination against these students. Thus in the Institute's view, there already existed qualifications at the GradRIC Part I level.

Council deferred the matter. However, the British Association of Chemists did not. In 1958, it noted in the *British Chemist* that an annual average of 2,000 HNC and HND recipients, who were definitely chemists, had no institutional home since the RIC made no provision for them.[29] In 1959, the BAC proposed to foster the establishment of an Institute of Chemical Technologists. A lower grade, or Associateship, would be set at the level of HNC/HND plus a further year's study. Five years' experience would entitle the Associate of the new institute to proceed to its Fellowship. Although the RIC had to admit that it had long ago accepted the principle that it might be necessary to organize a separate body for chemical technicians it had some misgivings about the BAC's proposal. In the first place, there was the direct association with the BAC, a trade union. In addition, it regretted the use of the word 'technologists' in the title of the proposed body, because the RIC had long been arguing that HNC/HND represented a technician level of expertise and that 'technologist' ought to be reserved for the independent worker.[30]

The BAC held an open conference attended by many heads and teachers in technical college chemistry departments. At this conference, a new proposal for an Institute of Applied Chemistry arose. The soundings of the RIC observer who attended indicated that technical college academics would in fact welcome a counter-initiative from the RIC, with which they had long-established relations on questions of curricula and qualifications. Thus, much as during the period after the First World War, a BAC initiative was successful in stimulating the RIC to move in a direction that it did not particularly favour. The RIC reopened the issue of providing for the interests of the 'underqualified'.[31] Council felt that there was a considerable gap between the level of the HNC and the level of the GradRIC Part II. Therefore, it proposed a two-tier arrangement to accommodate two general types of HNC holder. For those who wished to stop their formal training at the HNC, Council suggested that the RIC might foster an affiliated technicians' association. For those who wished to proceed beyond HNC, a new non-corporate grade of the Institute was proposed, the Licentiateship. For this grade, which was seen as equivalent to pass degree level, in addition to the HNC, it was to be necessary to successfully complete a further year's study in a chemical subject, or to complete the GradRIC Part I, and to go through a period of supervised experience on the job. Basically, the Institute was trying to draw a line between those whom it should designate as technicians and those who could be placed at the bottom of the scientist/technologist level. Noting that if this grade were to have full voting rights it might significantly influence Institute policy, the RIC decided to proceed with these proposals as a basis for general discussion.[32]

Consultations with the Honorary Secretaries of Local Sections and the Liaison Officers in Technical Colleges indicated that there was little support for the lower tier proposal of an affiliated technicians' association. However, there was widespread support for the idea of a third permanent grade of membership, provided that it were made a *corporate* grade instead of a non-corporate grade as suggested by Council. The Liaison Officers were concerned that, if the Institute did not act, 'another body' would.[33] Thus the RIC was to remain an organization catering for the qualifications of scientists and technologists.

Early in 1961, Council conducted a referendum of the corporate members about the new grade. It proposed that the new Licentiateship should be a corporate grade with academic requirements of the usual preliminary general education, basic training in physics and mathematics plus systematic study in chemistry or applied chemistry to the level of pass degree (HNC plus a further year or GradRIC Part I, or equivalent). A period of recognized experience was also specified. The new grade would not carry voting rights at General Meetings. Furthermore, to relieve the predictably stated fears that the admission of a less qualified group would ultimately dilute the value of the Associateship, Council proposed that the regulation providing for the admission of mature chemists in responsible posts directly to the Associateship would be abolished. However, Licentiates could progress to the upper professional grades by further academic study to the GradRIC Part II level. In fact, Council argued that, rather than lower the status of the existing grades, the new grade would make them seem higher by comparison—rather a reversal of its earlier view. In February 1961, a vote of 5,617 for the proposal and 1,376 against was recorded, forty-seven per cent of the corporate members having voted.[34] The new grade of membership was instituted in 1962. It is noteworthy that when a third permanent grade of membership was finally instituted, the issues in connection with which it was first discussed—registration and the unification of chemistry—were dormant.

5 The National Council for Technological Awards

These developments in qualifications, the creation of the non-corporate GradRIC and the corporate LRIC grades, were based on educational policies which the Institute had long followed. However, far-reaching national changes in the sphere of higher education from the late 1950s onwards began to affect the RIC's well-established policies, leading eventually to a major post-amalgamation review in the early 1970s and suggestions for several new directions. The doubling in the rate of output of university scientists and technologists called for by the post-war Barlow Report took only five years to achieve instead of the projected ten. In addition, the overall proportion of students doing pure and applied science in universities increased significantly. Until the middle 1950s, demand for graduate scientists was considerably in excess of supply.[35] Except in so far as they affected potential numbers of entrants, this expansion did not affect the Institute's policies.

There had been a similar rapid increase in the output of the technical colleges, aided by the expansion of day release and block release programmes.[36] This expansion was accompanied by developments in government policy following from the implications of the Percy Report. Thus despite the objections of the Institute and other professional associations, which felt that they could do the job, the Government created in 1955 the National Council for Technological Awards which organized a new Diploma in Technology. The 1956 White Paper proceeded to recommend a further fifty per cent increase in output of advanced level students from the technical colleges. The major advanced award would be the Diploma in Technology which would be awarded for individually approved courses within the existing technical colleges.[37] In 1956, in face of these changes, the Institute held a conference on the Education and Training of the Chemist.[38] There was support from the industrial side for the addition of a slightly more vocationally oriented component in the final year of university study. The feeling was that the current final honours year was really preparation for specialist research; there ought to be an alternative final year programme for students destined for industry. However, the Institute's basic belief in a foundation of general scientific training was reaffirmed. It was just at this time that the Institute was instituting the GradRIC, with the effect of returning its Associateship to its former status of a mark of professional competence, and withdrawing automatic recognition as professionally qualified from university graduates. Thus the Institute could take on the new Diplomas in Technology on their own ground. In fact, the Institute treated these awards in chemical subjects as equivalent to honours degrees for purposes of exemption.[39] By 1958, the Institute noted with satisfaction that the trend in technical colleges in recent years had been away from the London External BSc toward the GradRIC and the new DipTech.[40] The latter two qualifications complemented each other nicely and the Institute's future seemed assured. In 1959, the Institute created its own research diploma, a logical extension of its own GradRIC qualification and the DipTech; the diploma was designed to be equivalent to the PhD. The National Council for Technological Awards had no award at that level.[41]

At the same time, the Institute's very success in this area put a strain on its resources. Moreover, there was some concern that externally examined students fared worse than those who sat internal examinations. This might affect students' decisions about whether to pursue an award such as the DipTech or the GradRIC. In 1958, to ease this problem, the Special Relationship scheme was instituted for the GradRIC Part II examination. This was basically a devolution measure. Five colleges with large numbers of entrants, together accounting for twenty-five per cent of all entrants, and good pass rates were invited to conduct their own Part II examination.[42]

6 The CNAA

A bit later the Institute broadened its educational activities in other directions. In 1962, it formed the British Committee on Chemical Education jointly with the Royal Society. It began to sponsor such activities as refresher courses for chemistry teachers. In addition, in 1964, the Institute started the journal, *Education in Chemistry*. Its intention was to bring new methods to the attention of teachers, with an eye to their training future Institute members.

In 1963, the Robbins Committee on Higher Education reported. It called for still further expansion in this area, more integration between various types of institutions, and some new higher technological institutions of university status. It called for the abolition of the National Council for Technological Awards and its replacement by a National Council for Academic Awards (CNAA), which would award degrees to students in the technical colleges. The Robbins Report was meant to deal with the provision of full-time higher education. However, it was immediately obvious to the Institute that the proposals, particularly that the new National Council award degrees, if applied to part-time education, might have a significant effect on the Institute as an examining body.

> If such degrees were available to part-time as well as full-time students, the recommendations would have major repercussions for the Institute as an examining body. The number of candidates for the external GradRIC might well decline considerably and even the need for a Part I examination might substantially disappear. Instead, membership of the Institute at Licentiateship and Associateship grades could become essentially a matter of satisfying the academic requirements by suitable exemptions rather than by direct examination, and one of the Institute's tasks in the future might be to ensure that adequate standards are reached in establishing new degree courses in chemistry and applied chemistry. These and other relevant matters, such as the Special Relationship scheme, will require careful debate by Council and its Committee in the next few months.[43]

Professor H. J. Eméleus expanded on this theme in his 1964 presidential address.[44] His concern was that, with the projected doubling or trebling of university places, students who currently qualified by part-time work would most likely be able to study full time. While this was desirable, the effects on the Institute might be considerable. In the first place, there had recently been a marked reluctance on the part of graduates to join the Institute.[45] This was probably an effect of the introduction of the requirement of postgraduate experience. In fact, in view of its 1956 regulations and the DipTech the Institute concentrated increasingly on the technical college sector. As always, it was difficult for it to put over the benefits of membership in tangible terms. By this time, it appeared likely that what became the CNAA would not deal in part-time awards for the time being, so Eméleus could say with confidence that the Institute would have a continuing examining role, if a diminished one. He emphasized that the Institute's function was to provide an examination for those who needed one, whatever their numbers. With the financial stringencies starting in the late 1960s, this became less realistic a sentiment. He also called for some means other than further academic work for Licentiates to proceed to the higher grades.

7 Gradual Reassessment of the Institute's Examining and Qualifying Role

In 1965, while the Professional Status and Ethical Practices Committee was reviewing the Institute's future role, a Study Group on Qualifications also reported. It suggested that the GradRIC Part II examination needed rethinking. The theoretical part did not give the student much scope to display his knowledge over a range of chemistry and the practical examination was no longer relevant to modern needs. It emphasized straight analytical skill rather than the student's ability to apply theory. The idea that the Institute should cease to hold a practical examination was rejected. Quite apart from any intellectual merits, the practical examination had come to symbolize the distinction between the Institute and 'academic' chemistry. But it was suggested that the difficulties with the practical examination favoured the move toward internal examinations in the colleges. Some university academics on Council questioned the value of practical examinations as opposed to continuous assessment of laboratory work at honours level.[46] At the same time, the fall in quality and quantity in the Branch E examinations was noted. Ironically, the numbers had fallen off considerably since the Institute's examination had at last become a compulsory qualification for Public Analysts in 1955. The upshot of these discussions was that the last vestiges of the old qualifications system, the Branch examinations, were reorganized. From 1966, the Institute offered four postgraduate qualifications. The Research Diploma, the Diploma in Applied Chemistry (Branch E), the Diploma in Pharmaceutical Analysis (instituted jointly with the Pharmaceutical Society in 1964), and the Mastership in Clinical Biochemistry (a replacement for the old Branch D1, instituted in 1966). Furthermore, in 1966, the Eaborn Committee which was appointed by the British Committee on Chemical Education began its investigations on compatibility between university chemical teaching and the chemical industry. The Institute also called a useful meeting among the heads of chemistry departments.

The Institute's involvement with other bodies continued to increase. In 1967, the Chemical Industries Training Board came into existence and the Institute pressed for representation on it. This was a product of the 1964 Industrial Training Act, whose objects were to secure a supply of trained personnel for industry in keeping with the Labour Government's stated policy of promoting industrial advance directly through technology. The Act was also designed to help to improve the quality and efficiency of industrial training, and to spread the cost of that training more evenly among firms. The Chemical Industries Training Board presented the Institute with some difficulties. Only day release courses qualified to claim grants under the Board, so full-time GradRIC students were excluded. Furthermore, the Institute had reservations about the Board's emphasis on the City & Guilds technician certificates at the expense of higher qualifications for technologists such as the HNC.[47]

During the late 1960s, a newly noted national trend was beginning to complicate the picture. At school level, both the quality and quantity of science teaching was diminishing. During the early 1970s, just after the Eaborn Committee reported that, in fact, chemistry and industry were rather better integrated than was commonly thought and that existing university special degrees provided quite suitable training for industry,[48] the move away from science was causing academics to re-evaluate their programmes to make them more attractive to students. As a result of the Eaborn Committee's work, a Standing Committee on the Relationships between Education and Industry was established. Over the next few years, it began to modify some of the conclusions of the parent committee. For example, the poorer employment prospects for chemists in industry made it advisable for chemistry degrees to be broadened after all, particularly in the direction of business and managerial training, so that students would have ample career options.[49]

These varied events affecting education also began to affect Institute policies. In 1969, an Office Note by the Education Officer and the Examinations Officer recommended that the Institute think of carrying on its role as an examining body for only another five years. Developments favouring the polytechnics and the increasing role of the CNAA made it likely that the Institute's examinations would become superfluous anyway. But there were also problems within the examinations themselves. The pass rate of the external GradRIC examination was considerably lower than that of GradRIC Part II examination under the special relationship scheme. Furthermore, teachers wanted more autonomy such as they enjoyed under the CNAA. The GradRIC needed pedagogical modernization. In addition, the CNAA covered a wide range of colleges, giving students more choice. It was agreed that there should be gradual devolution of the GradRIC Part I and Part II examinations to the technical colleges. There was not uniform support for this move within the colleges which already operated the Special Relationship scheme. Some feared that this would have the effect of spreading top students too thinly among numerous colleges and detract from their own enrolments. In 1975, this process was completed.[50] In a related way, the CNAA took over the Institute's Research Diploma scheme in 1973.[51]

8 Counselled Experience: A New Assessment of Professional Expertise

In 1971, an Office Note on Qualifications and Professional Relations put some hard facts before Council. The Institute could only claim to include about sixty per cent of those who were qualified to join, while there were many chemists of marginal or lower qualifications outside. In the light of the Industrial Relations Bill, it was necessary to think about qualifications in terms of 'bargaining power'. Council suggested some half measures but did not really grasp the nettle with regard to the point of principle behind the

Office Note. However, five days later, there was a meeting between the President, the past President and the Executive Officers of the Institute; a special President's Committee was set up to investigate the future development of the Institute's qualifying and examining function.[52] The Committee's brief was to investigate these in relation to the professional relations aspects of the Institute's work, its main concerns being to consider the recent trends in degree courses and the effect on qualifications of setting up the Association of Professional Scientists and Technologists (APST). Ironically, just at this time, the Institute's Educational Executive Committee was wound up and the Chemical Society took on all educational functions under the new amalgamation arrangements.[53]

The President's Committee's investigations were far-reaching, and their implications are still being dealt with. The Committee recommended that the Institute should reorient its emphasis toward the professional rather than the academic side of its qualifications. Among the committee's specific suggestions were that the GradRIC and LRIC grades be amalgamated into a single corporate third grade of membership. Depending on an individual's aspirations and opportunities, the grade would either be transitional or permanent. The Committee also suggested that a route be devized making it possible to progress from the Licentiateship to the Associateship via 'counselled experience'. This would assist in the goal of stressing that the Associateship was a mark of professional competence. Predictably, the report was not greeted with uniform acclaim, various of its provisions affecting established notions and long-held principles. The detailed proposals of the Committee's work need not detain us here. The important point is that in view of the changing nature of national educational provision, the need to make decisions about this new direction was pressed as a matter of urgency. Recruitment had always been a problem, but now, unless the Institute's qualifications had something to offer that a degree did not, recruitment would become impossible.[54] This was a particular problem as technical college students, the Institute's main constituency since the late 1950s, could aspire to CNAA degrees. Furthermore, chemistry degrees were becoming much broader and the Institute would have to rethink what its exemptions meant. Stressing experience for its qualifications would help the Institute circumvent the difficulty of whether degrees with less and less chemistry could lead to professional competence. A Working Party on Regulations was charged with implementing the committee's recommendations.

The possibility of a route from LRIC to ARIC via counselled experience was not a new one in 1972. It had been suggested in 1966, but rejected, partly for the reasons explained in the memorandum which accompanied the referendum about the establishment of the Licentiateship in 1961. There were fears of lowering the academic standard of the Associateship. While the President's Committee was sitting, a new consideration arose. It became necessary to evaluate the possible influence of Britain's entry into the EEC on the Institute's qualifications. In order to suit the requirements of the EEC and to make sure that RIC chemists were not excluded from international posts, a new designation for Associates and Fellows of the Institute was pressed through—Chartered Chemist. Because of its lesser academic qualifications, the Licentiateship grade was not included in this designation. Feeling ran high among Licentiates who were concerned that they would become even more second-class citizens than they already were. The creation of Chartered Chemist status almost foundered on their opposition, but this was prevented by a resolution at the relevant General Meeting to the effect that a 'counselled experience' route be created as a matter of urgency. In fact, Council made a commitment to complete this by early 1975. Applications began to arrive in 1975.[55] Another effect of entry into the EEC on the Institute's qualifications is the possibility that they might begin to be accepted internationally (Chapter XV).

Finally other changes are probable in the National Certificate and Diploma area. In 1972, the Haslegrove Committee on Technician Courses and Examinations recommended that the administration of all National Certificate and Diploma schemes be transferred from the professional institutions concerned to the City & Guilds. The new qualifications would be run under a Technician Education Council. The transfer, ludicrously, was supposed to take place by 1973. The Institute and other professional associations opposed this move. It was not that their own establishments were being affected, so much as the way in which this was happening. The City & Guilds had always been responsible for the lower level, clearly assistant technician calibre, whereas the National Certificate had catered for the higher level technicians who, though they might not work independently, were expected to show initiative and independent scientific insight. The professional associations' fear was that this level would be lowered. In the case of the RIC, this might make it necessary to introduce its own qualification at HNC level because of the relation of the HNC to its grades of membership. In the event, the immediate threat was staved off, as such speed was impracticable, if for no other reason. However, the Technician Education Council was formally established in 1973 and is represented on the Joint Committee of the Department of Education and Science (DES) and the RIC for National Certificates and Diplomas. Its future schedule is unclear.[56]

Perhaps a suggestion that was put at the last Council meeting of 1975 would sort out some of the difficulties: that Chartered Chemist, the term that now covers two grades, be considered a single grade. Thus the Institute will have come full circle.

GKR

NOTES AND REFERENCES

1 See *Proc. Inst. Chem.*, 1925, **49**, 233–60 for members' worries. Council's position is explained in R. L. Collett, *ibid.*, 1929, **53**, 97–9, 137–42.

2 'Conference on the Place of Applied Chemistry in the Training of Chemists', *ibid.*, 1925, 49, separate pamphlet bound in.

3 *Ibid.*, 1920, 44, 151–4, 275–80. 'Leeds and Bradford', 4 July 1918 in BAC, Local Sections File; BAC, Council Minutes, 2, 20 November 1920, 7 May 1921; all BAC papers held by Association of Professional Scientists and Technologists.

4 F. E. Foden, 'The National Certificate', *Vocational Aspect*, 1951, 3, 38–46; Ministry of Education, *Education, 1900–1950*, H.M.S.O., London, 1950, 49–50. See also, Institute of Chemistry, National Certificates. Joint Committee Minutes, 1, 20 June 1921. Hereafter, IC, N.C. Joint Committee Minutes.

5 The BAC was certainly disappointed to hear that the Institute was doing so; BAC, Council Minutes, 2, 26 November 1921, 21 January 1922.

6 IC, N.C. Joint Committee Minutes, 1, 20 July 1921; 27 April 1922.

7 Foden, (note 4) pp. 39, 43–5; *J.R.I.C.*, 1952, 76, 233–5. Ministry of Education, (note 4) p. 50 gives the following:

	1923	1931	1939	1944	1950
Electrical engineering					
ONC	—	592	1133	1035	2915
HNC	—	279	421	388	1394
Chemistry					
ONC	57	108	196	167	615
HNC	46	47	58	64	222
Mechanical engineering					
ONC	606	974	1833	2536	5614
HNC	122	327	632	837	2435

8 Michael Sanderson, *The Universities and British Industry, 1850–1970*, Routledge, London, 1972, pp. 243, 261.

9 *Proc. Inst. Chem.*, 1934, 58, 116–29; J. F. Thorpe, *ibid.*, 1935, 59, 122; 1937, 61, 3–5.

10 *Ibid.*, 1932, 56, 291–5; 1937, 61, 333–4; See also, Sanderson (note 8) 264–75. At the same time, the Institute consistently argued that chemists should avoid narrowness of outlook and seek managerial positions.

11 J. F. Thorpe, *Proc. Inst. Chem.*, 1937, 61, 170. On Thorpe (1872–1940), *ibid.*, 1940, 64, 273.

12 Descriptive comments are based on Michael Argles, *South Kensington to Robbins: An Account of English Technical and Scientific Education since 1851*, Longman, London, 1964, ch. VII; Sanderson (note 8), pp. 348–59.

13 'Report of the Chemistry Education Advisory Board', *Proc. Inst. Chem.*, 1943, 67, separate pamphlet bound in.

14 IC, N.C. Joint Committee Minutes, 2, 16 August 1944, 11 February 1947. See also, files of 'Correspondence between the Royal Institute of Chemistry and the Ministry of Education', 1944–5; particularly a summary statement by Alexander Findlay, 21 February 1945. See further, *Proc. R.I.C.*, 1945, 69, 138; 1947, 71, 112.

15 *Ibid.*, 1946, 70, 221–2.

	1950	1955	
Estimated need	70	90	$\left.\right\} \times 10^3$
Estimated output at current rate	60	64	

16 RIC, Council Minutes, 13, 26 November 1920; *J.R.I.C.*, 1954, 78, 347. In 1972, the Burnham Committee recognized GrandRIC, Part II. At issue was not the Institute's particular qualification, but Burnham's general policy about professional qualifications. RIC, Council Minutes, 62, 13 October 1972.

17 *Proc. R.I.C.*, 1950, **74**, 458–63.

18 *Ibid.*, p. 265; 1948, **72**, 240–1; RIC, *Regulations*, RIC, London, 1947, p. 14.

19 *Proc. R.I.C.*, 1947, **71**, 234.

20 RIC, Council Minutes, **41**, 15 June, 17 October 1951.

21 *J.R.I.C.*, 1952, **76**, 236–9; 1950, **74**, 367.

22 RIC, Council Minutes, **42**, 16 May, 20 June 1952. F. J. Smith, *J.R.I.C.*, 1953, **77**, 21–2. 'Annual Report of Council, 1953', *ibid.*, 1954, **78**, 10, pointed out however that the number of successful ARIC examinees had been increasing (43 in 1930, 85 in 1940, 109 in 1950).

23 H. J. T. Ellingham, *ibid.*, 1954, **78**, 71–2; 'Annual Report of Council, 1955', *ibid.*, 1955, **79**, 1–3.

24 RIC, Council Minutes, **43**, 15 May 1953; **44**, 16 July, 15 October, 17 December 1954. Office memoranda, particularly the views of Ellingham, figured largely in the discussions.

25 'Annual Report of Council, 1954', *J.R.I.C.*, 1955, **79**, 1–2, 229–33.

26 On Jephcott see *ibid.*, 1953, **77**, 219. See also *ibid.*, 1955, **79**, 261–9, 384.

27 *Ibid.*, p. 401; 1956, **80**, 51, 109, 244, 375.

28 'Suggested Permanent Third Grade of Membership', Office Note I, RIC, Council Minutes, **46**, 20 July 1956. The London Section particularly promoted this, *ibid.*, **47**, 17 May 1957; see also, *J.R.I.C.*, 1956, **80**, 630.

29 RIC, Council Minutes, **48**, 20 March 1958.

30 'Report of the Professional Status Committee', *ibid.*, **49**, 16 October 1959.

31 *Ibid.*, 20 November 1959.

32 *Ibid.*, 18 December 1959.

33 *Ibid.*, **50**, 15 July, 21 October 1960; *J.R.I.C.*, 1960, **84**, 398.

34 The Royal Institute of Chemistry, 'Memorandum issued by the Council in Connection with a Referendum on the Proposal to Establish a New Grade of Membership (Licentiateship) of the Institute', in RIC, Council Minutes, **50**, 18 November 1960; *J.R.I.C.*, 1961, **85**, 103.

35 Sanderson (note 8), pp. 349–59.

36 IC, N.C. Joint Committee Minutes, *passim* show that chemistry was no exception, although its absolute numbers were small compared to other subjects (cf. note 7).

37 Argles (note 12), pp. 104–7.

38 *J.R.I.C.*, 1956, **80**, 496–517, 671–93.

39 *Ibid.*, 1958, **82**, 481.

40 *Ibid.*, p. 291.

41 RIC, Council Minutes, **48**, 19 December 1958, 20 March 1959.

42 *Ibid.*, **47**, 17 May, 15 November 1957; **48**, 20 June 1958. The scheme worked well and was extended in 1967 to a further eight colleges; *ibid.*, **57**, 19 May 1967.

43 *J.R.I.C.*, 1963, **87**, 405. He might have added that the proposed new Council's schemes made the RIC's research diploma less urgent.

44 H. J. Emeléus, *ibid.*, 1964, **88**, 100–3. On Emeléus see *ibid.*, 1963, **87**, 99.

45 'Annual Report of Council', *ibid.*, 1964, **88**, 2–3.

46 RIC, Council Minutes, **55**, 21 May, 23 July, 8 October 1965; 18 March 1966.

47 *Ibid.*, **57,** 16 October 1967. Cf. this view with earlier discussions on the level of the HNC (p. 272).

48 *Report of the Committee of Enquiry into the Relationship between University Courses in Chemistry and the Needs of Industry*, RIC, London, 1970, pp. 4–9.

49 See Reports of the Committee on the Relationships between Education and Industry, RIC, Council Minutes, n.vol., 18 June, 12 October, 14 December 1973; 8 February 1974.

50 *Ibid.*, **58,** 14 February, 20 March 1969.

51 *Ibid.*, n. vol., 18 May 1973. During its 10 years' existence, 42 research diplomas were issued (*ibid.*, **61,** 15 October 1971).

52 *Ibid.*, 21 July, 15 October 1971.

53 *Ibid.*, 21 July 1971.

54 *Ibid.*, **62,** 21 July 1972; n. vol., 6 June, 20 July 1973.

55 *Ibid.*, 8 February, 13 December 1974. See also, 'Chartered Chemist', *RIC Professional Bulletin*, no. 19, 1 November 1975, and RIC, Council Minutes, n. vol., 12 December 1975.

56 RIC, Council Minutes, **62,** 19 May, 13 October 1972. Thus, the Institute has become a champion of HNC level training as a route to professional qualification.

CHAPTER XV
THE INSTITUTE'S INFLUENCE OVERSEAS

1   Some Problems of Chemists Abroad

From the earliest years of the Institute's history there have been members residing abroad, especially in the former Dominions. Whilst the problems of safeguarding the interests of its members in this country have always been difficult enough, those of its foreign members have often proved much more so. Problems involving employers and governments overseas could generally only be solved by those chemists who were directly affected by them. The Institute could only offer advice which must inevitably be coloured by its experience at home, even though the Council constantly sought the opinions of senior Fellows who were in close contact with conditions 'on the ground'. In this they have been helped very significantly by the existence of Local Sections overseas,[1] but it was frequently necessary to remind such Local Sections that they could not properly be said to 'represent' the Institute, nor were they empowered to make any executive decisions on its behalf. Partly for this reason and partly no doubt from the development of feelings of national identity, national institutes for chemistry have been founded which sometimes, as in South Africa, have felt themselves to be in competition with the Local Sections. The Institute always had in mind parity of esteem between the memberships of Chemical Institutes in the various countries and to this end has constantly suggested the adoption of standards of qualification comparable with its own. This has not always been easy where the total number engaged in chemical work is substantial but the proportion of these workers who could claim to be fully trained chemists is low. The tendency has often been to lower the required entry qualifications in order to produce a viable group to support meetings and other activities.

To adopt this expedient is to reduce the professional status of the chemist. This has always been a primary problem for the Institute.[2] It was particularly marked in India, where chemists in government service were accorded a lower rank than those in other branches whose qualifications and training were certainly no more rigorous. The difficulty of assessing the true value of degrees awarded in the Indian subcontinent has posed a continuing problem for the Institute and the only possible expedient has been to review each case individually. In New Zealand, the newly formed Local Section at once proposed that a professional Register of Chemists should be prepared. This, though attractive in principle, is difficult in practice as we have already seen; it is a problem which has faced the Institute since its inception and which has never been satisfactorily resolved. It was suggested in 1908 that a Fellow should be elected to the Council to represent Indian affairs, but this was rejected. Instead Honorary Local Secretaries were appointed,[3] in South Africa (Transvaal, Cape Colony, Natal); Australia (Queensland, New South Wales, Victoria, South Australia); India (Bengal, Bombay, Madras); New Zealand; West Indies; Canada (Ontario, Quebec) and at Cairo. These representatives, all Fellows of the Institute, were intended to act as advisers (a) to prospective candidates wishing to join the Institute and (b) to the Council in London on chemical matters of local professional interest. They were not asked to convene Local Sections, nor were they empowered to act as agents of the Institute. It was hoped that they would advise the Council on situations such as existed in India and be prepared to convey the advice of the Council to members in their areas.

It clearly would be impossible to attempt to discuss every case in which the Institute has been approached or involved in activities overseas. Instead, we shall examine some important examples which will serve to illustrate recurring problems and the approach adopted by the Institute towards them. We shall begin with the difficult question of the chemist in the Indian sub-continent.

2   The Institute in India, 1907–50

(a) The status of the chemist

The Institute has always had members working in India, usually in some branch of government service. The first members were British subjects, having qualified for membership in this country, who had gone out to India to work, but as early as 1883 an examination for the Associateship was held in India itself.[4] A list of chemical appointments under the India Office was maintained but this did not include chemists employed in the cordite factory at Aruvankadu who were appointed by the Ordnance Department of the Indian Government and were not members of the Indian Civil Service. Such posts were listed amongst subordinate appointments in 'Army Regulations India', and this lowered the status of chemists.[5]

Many chemical posts in the Indian Government Service were filled by members of the Indian Medical Service and steps had already been taken to encourage officers of this service to qualify in chemistry.[6] Qualified chemists in the Indian Ordnance Department on the other hand, were classed as 'civil mechanics'[7] and placed in positions subordinate to military officers with lower or no chemical qualifications. Even though on appointment in England they were ranked as gazetted officers with all the privileges that this entailed, they found on arrival in India that they were treated as subordinate to non-commissioned officers and the privileges they had been led to expect with regard to leave and pay did not materialize.

A Royal Commission on the Public Services in India was set up in 1913. This was not directly concerned with the scientific professions in general nor with chemists in particular; however, in the professions to be examined many chemists were employed and the Institute seized this opportunity to make recommendations to the Commission. Accordingly a Special Committee was appointed under the Chairmanship of Sir Alexander Pedler and a memorandum was prepared.[8] In its general remarks the memorandum first emphasized that the Institute represented consulting, analytical and technological chemists, but not pharmaceutical chemists. It went on to point out that European qualified chemists had experienced considerable difficulties in India regarding the status to which their education and training entitled them. The education of a professional chemist is analogous to that of other professional men, extending as it does over at least four years' systematic training, and involving at least an equal standard of general culture and the maintenance of an equal social status.[9] Council also expressed concern that too many chemical appointments were filled by men with a medical or military training, neither of which fitted them for competent chemical work.

> The Council [of the Institute of Chemistry] would point out that a medical training does not fit men for the practice of analytical chemistry, and that a military training is not an essential qualification for the management of a chemical factory or the control of scientific operations.[10]

Repeated accounts of official slights had come to the notice of the Council, though it was admitted that these were mostly probably unintentional and 'due to lack of knowledge and a proper appreciation of a comparatively recently organized profession'.

The Institute recommended that for the recruitment of chemists for various Departments of the Government of India, the Secretary of State should appoint to the Boards entrusted with such appointments, scientific men with experience of conditions in India who would be able to assess the suitability of candidates for work there. The Institute's memorandum then went on to consider specific areas of appointment.

(b) The Institute's suggestions ignored

Council pressed the Commission to consider favourably their recommendations regarding the pay, status and conditions of service of professional chemists to ensure that suitably qualified chemists might be attracted to the service of the Indian Government. The memorandum, dated 24 October 1913, was presented to the Commission sitting in Calcutta in January 1914. On 8 May, Sir Alexander Pedler was called before the Commission in London to give evidence on behalf of the Council. He was told that the Commission did not wish to take evidence on pay, allowances, leave or pensions, nor were they required to take evidence with respect to chemists attached to the Ordnance Department. Thus it would seem that almost all the recommendations of the Institute, designed to establish the professional status of the chemist in the service of the Indian Government, had fallen on deaf ears. Nevertheless, Sir Alexander was questioned about the general conditions affecting appointments and the views of the Council on the recruitment of professional chemists for government service. He suggested that chemical appointments should be filled by professional chemists and not necessarily military officers or medical men. The Commission asked whether this would make for economy. Sir Alexander replied that he was less concerned about expense but that it would certainly improve *efficiency*.

Little notice appears to have been taken of the recommendations of the Institute; dissatisfaction about the status and prospects of chemists was still being expressed in 1919. It was still the case that chemists in government service were treated less generously than engineers of the Public Works Department, Police Officers, and members of the Indian Medical and Forestry Services. The Institute therefore warned Fellows and Associates that in accepting appointments in India they:

> should have regard to the conditions and prospects offered to them, especially in view of the fact that it is practically impossible for a married gazetted officer to bear the expense of maintaining and educating properly a family of medium size, since his children must be sent home as soon as they are of school age, and his wife should be able to go to the hills in the hot season.[11]

(c) Admission of Indian graduates to membership

Another problem which continually faced the Institute was that of assessing the relative value of Indian university degrees when Indian candidates applied for admission to the Associateship or Fellowship of the Institute. In 1921 a conference was held between members of the Institute's Nominations, Examinations and Institutions Committee and some Fellows of the Institute, usually resident in India, at home on leave.[12]

It was considered that the average Indian BSc degree was in no way comparable with an English BSc or Scottish MA, although some Indian MSc degrees were comparable with an English Honours BSc. Professor Krall thought that since the standards of training varied so much in Indian universities and education in India was undergoing so much change it would be unwise to recognize any degree of an Indian University as equivalent to the Associateship examination. It was held that in general the practical skill of candidates with Indian degrees was lower than their theoretical knowledge. Krall advocated that all Indian candidates should be examined in India, the exercises to be set and work appraised by the Board of Examiners in London. On the advice of the Conference a Special Advisory Committee for India was set up in 1921 to advise the Nominations, Examinations and Institutions Committee on each individual application by Indian candidates for admission to the Fellowship or Associateship. This Committee was given a free hand to make such inquiries as were thought necessary into the technical and personal qualifications of candidates.

But the unfair treatment of chemists in India continued.[13] In 1924 a letter was received from Arthur Marshall, Chief Inspector of the Indian Ordnance Department, complaining that the only chemists in the Ordnance Department who were placed in the Warrant of Precedence in India were the Chief Inspector and the Manager of the Cordite Factory, and they were both in the lowest category of all. Other civil servants of their general age and standing were all placed higher and in view of the importance of precedence in India he suggested that this should be taken up with the Secretary of State.[14]

(d) Establishment of Local Sections in India and Pakistan

In 1948 Professor Alexander Findlay, at the end of his term of office as President of the Institute, visited India and Pakistan to investigate the situation there at first hand. He attended the Annual General Meeting of the Indian Section of the Institute held at Patna in January 1948 when a resolution was passed requesting the Institute to divide the existing Indian Section into four separate Local Sections centred on Bombay, Calcutta, Delhi and Madras–Bangalore respectively.[15] Findlay wrote to the Council strongly supporting this resolution which had already been communicated to the Institute by Mr Sen, Honorary Secretary of the Indian Section. The following month a request was received from senior chemists in Pakistan for a Local Section in Lahore[16] because chemists in Pakistan could not be expected to attend meetings held in India. Findlay suggested that the Institute might appoint an Honorary Secretary and Organizer for the proposed Pakistan Section and this was done.

It was hoped that these Local Sections would prove capable of interesting and organizing chemists in India so that in due course the activities of the Institute might be handed over to an Indian organization for chemists such as the Indian Institute of Chemistry, but the initiative had to come from the Indian members themselves and not from the Institute in London. Findlay feared that the enthusiasm expressed in many quarters during his visit might evaporate as he left and in the event although the Local Sections established at Bangalore and in Western India were soon in full commission whilst that in Madras, which started later, was also very active, the other sections proved far less successful.

In his report Findlay pointed out that whilst in the past the Institute had never really functioned or been recognized as the professional body for chemists in India, the new organization was proposed in part to facilitate this, so that the Institute through its Local Sections and Branches might assume the responsibilities and functions of a professional body. Certainly he believed that the Institute's qualifications would continue to be sought after by reason of their high standards and he felt that consideration should be given to ways in which the examinations system and other machinery for the election of Fellows and Associates might need to be modified to suit candidates in India.

The most important aspect of Findlay's visit however was the long-term issue of the establishment of an Indian Institute of Chemistry with standards similar to those of the RIC. Findlay had suggested to the Indian chemists that the Institute would be both willing and anxious to offer help in this direction, although it had to be realized that there was some sensitivity towards the idea that there might be any attempt to force British institutions on them. There was felt to be some similarity to the situation in Southern Ireland[17] and Findlay suggested that the time might come when the RIC stood at the centre of a world-wide group of similar, autonomous institutions each having been modelled upon it and perhaps helped by it in various ways to become established. Certainly Findlay came away from India in 1948 with the feeling that there was a strong desire amongst Indian chemists to establish ultimately an association on the lines of the RIC, whilst in the meantime accepting the RIC itself as the professional body for chemists in India.

(e) Developing autonomy

In 1951 a statement was issued by the RIC announcing some changes in its relationships with chemists in India and Pakistan.[18] It had been made absolutely clear by Findlay's visit in 1947–8 that the profession of chemistry in India and Pakistan had not yet reached a stage of development which could be said to parallel that of the profession in other countries (e.g. Australia, Canada, New Zealand and South Africa). Each of these countries had its own Institute of Chemistry with objectives, organizations and standards of qualification closely similar to those of the RIC. It was hoped that India and Pakistan would ultimately follow this trend, but it was felt that until this position had been reached the interests of the chemical profession were best served through the Local Sections of the RIC in India and Pakistan. These had developed since Findlay's visit and were centred on Bangalore, Bombay, Madras and Delhi with another Local Section to be formed around Calcutta. In addition to these sections there were also Honorary Corresponding Secretaries in other centres and this whole structure now seemed adequate to replace the previous system in which there had been only one Honorary Corresponding Secretary for the whole subcontinent.

This position had been filled for some years by Dr G. J. Fowler who had also acted as Honorary Secretary to the Indian Advisory Committee, a group of distinguished Indian chemists which had been responsible for scrutinizing the applications of Indian chemists for election to the Associateship or Fellowship of the RIC. Dr Fowler had asked to be relieved of his duties and the Institute took this opportunity of changing their *modus operandi*. As from 1 April 1951 all Indian applicants would be required to send their applications direct to the Registrar of the Institute in London. Any information required by an applicant in filling in the forms would be available to him in India by consultation with the Honorary Secretary of his Local Section or with the Honorary Corresponding Secretary of the Institute in areas where no Local Section yet existed. Both the post of Honorary Secretary for India and the Indian Advisory Committee were discontinued.

One effect of these changes was to place more responsibility for the Institute's affairs directly in the hands of the Indian chemists themselves. It was pointed out that the existence of the Local Sections was intended to act as a stepping stone towards the establishment of an Indian Institute of Chemistry and that until this had been done the RIC would hold a watching brief on professional standards amongst chemists in India.[19]

There is now an Indian Institute of Chemistry and also an Indian Chemical Society, although neither is very active and the RIC has found it necessary to maintain its own Local Section structure. In 1976 there were altogether seven Local Sections in India, Pakistan, Bangladesh and Sri Lanka. Most of these were very small and most appeared to be falling slowly in numbers possibly due to the difficulties of paying subscriptions in sterling to London. In general the Local Sections have had good relationships with the Indian Institute of Chemistry and with the Indian Chemical Society, although it might be said that the hopes cherished by the RIC, that the existence of their Local Sections and the influence exerted by chemists holding RIC qualifications might encourage the establishment of comparable standards by the Indian Institute, have not been realized so far.

3   The Establishment of the Australian Institute of Chemistry

As we have already seen, four Honorary Secretaries to represent the Institute of Chemistry were appointed in Australia in 1908, and in 1918 the formation of an Australian Chemical Institute was reported by Dr Thomas Cooksey, Honorary Secretary in New South Wales. The aim of the Australian Institute was to follow as closely as possible the precedent of the home Institute, holding examinations and seeking a charter from the Federal Government. Cooksey was seeking general advice about regulations, policy and the question of registration of professional chemists. By 26 November 1920 application had already been made for a Charter. The Australian Chemical Institute argued that the position of the chemist in Australia in 1920 was similar to that of the chemist in Britain in 1877. It was therefore necessary, they maintained, to accept somewhat lower standards for membership. In fact Associateship in the Australian Institute was to be available on the basis of a pass degree in chemistry, or two years of an honours course plus two years' approved laboratory experience.

The Australian Chemical Institute felt itself justified by the strong feeling for local control which rendered the Local Sections of the Institute virtually ineffective. However, the Council of the Institute opposed the application for a Royal Charter by the Australian Chemical Institute on the grounds that the latter was tending to undo all the good work put in by the Council of the Institute over the years to raise the status and level of technical education of chemists in Great Britain and the Dominions. A memorandum was therefore prepared and circulated to members of the Institute in Australia setting out the Council's position and reasons for opposing the Australian Chemical Institute's actions. The Council felt that the profession of chemistry being worldwide, the standards of attainment should be uniform and it was not accepted that the standards adopted in Australia in 1920 should be comparable with those attainable in 1877. However, in December 1920 a letter was sent to the Australian Chemical Institute in which the need to raise the standards of attainment necessary for their Associateship was emphasized. In fact it was suggested that the same standards as for Associateship and Fellowship of the Institute in Great Britain should be applied and any present members of the Australian Institute who were unable to comply with these standards should be retained in a lower grade of membership. The Council of the Australian Institute would be made up entirely of Fellows and would therefore consist of senior, experienced chemists. One reason urged for the establishment of uniform standards was the possibility of the introduction of registration, since it would clearly be desirable for registering authorities in each country to be able to accept the qualifications of the others. The letter ended with a request for a copy of the draft Charter for consideration by the Council of the Institute.[20]

The comments made by the Institute on the draft Charter submitted by the Australian Chemical Institute were all concerned with academic and professional standards. For instance it was pointed out that degrees in chemistry were already being awarded by Australian universities as a result of courses and examinations, to a decidedly higher standard than that being demanded by the Australian Chemical Institute for entry to its Associateship.

This being so the Council of the Institute felt entirely justified in urging the Australian Chemical Institute to raise its entry requirements. It was pointed out that to seek to compare their own position with that in England in 1877 was totally unrealistic, since there were many reputable courses in chemistry and plenty of establishments at which to study, whereas it was claimed that in 1877 there had been very few in England and no definite courses of training for the profession of chemistry had been prescribed then. The Institute also expressed reservations about the powers which the Australian Chemical Institute wished to retain to admit Associates without examination. It was felt that the ability to do this was made too easy by the draft Charter.

These comments were received and acted upon and the Institute informed the Privy Council that it was satisfied with the amended terms. The Royal Charter was therefore granted to the Australian Chemical Institute in November 1931.

4   New Zealand Chemists and the Problems of Registration

The New Zealand Section of the Institute was formed in 1928 and immediately the question of the formation of a Register of Chemists was brought up. This Register was to contain the names of chemists earning their living in the Dominion mainly by the practice of chemistry. When prepared it contained 104 names of which 33 were Fellows or Associates of the Institute. The list included professors and lecturers, consultants and analysts, works chemists, research chemists and government chemists. The arguments urged in favour of legal registration were that it would assist chemists and others in giving an adequate service to the public, whilst at the same time providing chemists with a means of receiving recognition and of being distinguished from pharmacists. It would also be a means of consolidating the profession and would show that minority amongst the public, who recognize the merits and services of the chemical profession, that chemists are in earnest in seeking legal recognition.

In England the Institute was already considering the possibility of petitioning for a Supplemental Charter which would deal in part with the problems of registration.[21] In the event this proposed Supplemental Charter did not materialize until 1937, but the Council felt that it would be necessary to deal carefully with the request for support from the New Zealand chemists so as to avoid pre-empting any decisions which might later be taken in England. The fact that the New Zealand Section wished to restrict only the use of a title to its registered members and not to restrict the practice of their profession seemed right to the Council of the Institute and general sympathy with the aims of the New Zealand Section was expressed provided that these were desired by the general body of chemists in New Zealand.

In any scheme for registration of chemists there is a problem regarding a title which would serve to differentiate industrial, research or educational chemists from pharmacists. The Institute suggested that the most suitable title would be 'professional chemist' although 'chemical practitioner' would be a possible alternative. Whatever title was adopted it would be necessary to introduce into any Act a clause excluding pharmacists; at the same time, in the new Pharmacy Bill then before the New Zealand Parliament, a clause excluding 'chemists' was needed. A Registration Board would have to be established and criteria for registration set up.

The Committee in London suggested that in the wording of the Bill presented to the House of Representatives there should be a statement such as 'Nothing in the Professional Chemists' Registration Act shall apply to legally qualified pharmacists and chemists and druggists, provided that they do not practice as professional chemists'. Reciprocal wording was suggested for insertion into the new Pharmacy Bill then under examination.

To give the process of registration some 'teeth' there would have to be penalties for offences—especially regarding the use of the restricted title by unregistered persons. Provision would be needed for those who had practiced for not less than twenty years, but who were not qualified to register under the Act. These chemists were to be allowed to continue and to use the restricted designation providing they lodged their names with the Ministry of Science and Industrial Research within twelve months of the commencement of the Act.

These conclusions were then communicated to the New Zealand Section in November 1928. They were accompanied by a study paper prepared by the Council of the Institute.[22] In this paper it was suggested that the establishment of a professional register, and enforcement of the requirement to register on all who wish to practise in that profession, is usually intended to protect the public rather than to foster the interests of the members of that profession. Registration may be restrictive or non-restrictive. In the former case any unregistered person practising the profession is liable to a fine or summary conviction in a court of law. In the latter case non-registered practitioners are free to offer their services within certain limitations and it is up to the public to decide whether they are proficient or not. One problem within the chemical profession is that over ninety per cent of its members are in salaried employment. Many of these cannot be said to have reached a sufficiently high educational standard to be registered as independent practitioners, yet they can do repetitive chemical operations quite satisfactorily. Compulsory registration of chemists implies the establishment of minimum academic standards and the closure of the profession to all except fully qualified personnel—not in the selfish interests of the profession, but for the protection of the public. Whereas it might be both possible and beneficial to all concerned to introduce a register for those engaged in private practice, the enforcement of registration for chemists in industry is quite another matter. In order to ensure that industrial firms did not employ non-registered chemists for certain prescribed duties it would be necessary to institute forms of inspection which might be unacceptable to employers. Also a chemist in a given industry must be specially trained whilst employed on the job, since it is not possible to learn to do many specialized operations in colleges.

5   The Federation of European Chemical Societies

All the European countries except Luxembourg have one or more chemical societies, but in general these bodies are far more concerned with the advancement of the discipline than with the *professional* status of the chemist. Indeed, the RIC is almost unique amongst European chemical societies in offering its own academic and professional qualifications and has had vastly more experience than any other European chemical society in safeguarding and enhancing the professional status of its members. It is therefore not surprising to find the RIC taking a leading role in activities concerned with the profession of chemistry in the European Community. Activities in this respect have been greatly facilitated by the existence of the Federation of European Chemical Societies, established in 1970. It happened by coincidence in 1963 that both the Congress and the Conference of IUPAC were held in London and the Secretary of the Chemical Institute of Canada suggested to the RIC that the IUPAC occasion would provide a very good opportunity to hold a meeting of the Secretaries of Chemical Institutes of the Commonwealth since so many of them would be present in London anyway. A meeting was therefore arranged with Professor Eméleus, then President of the RIC, in the chair. It was attended by the Secretaries of the Australian, Canadian, New Zealand and South African Institutes of Chemistry, whilst the Secretaries of French, German and Dutch Chemical Societies were also invited to attend. This meeting proved so successful that it was repeated two years later at the IUPAC Conference in Paris and thereafter meetings were held annually. In 1966 fifteen Chemical Societies including European Societies as well as the American Chemical Society were represented at a meeting in Budapest. This group was formalized in 1970 and the first meeting of the General Assembly of the Federation of European Chemical Societies was held in Prague. Since then, the meetings have been held alternately in East and West European cities. The RIC as a founder member has held the Secretariat of this Federation, jointly with the Hungarian Chemical Society (Magyar Kémikusok Egyesülete) since its inception, but in 1976 the Secretariat was handed over to the German Chemical Society at the General Assembly in Helsinki.

In 1975 there were twenty-six member Societies,[23] the only notable absentee being Russia, but in April 1976 the Mendeleef Society announced its intention of joining the Federation and this was expected to herald also the entry of the East German and Bulgarian Societies. This would then leave only Greece and Portugal outside the Federation.

During 1974–5 a working party was set up entitled the Committee on Chemical Education in Europe (CCEE) to collect information about the activities in the educational field of all the chemical societies throughout Europe.[24] The purpose of the inventory was to describe the situation as it existed in 1974–5, to stimulate new activities and to make names and addresses available to Societies who wished to embark on new fields and who felt the need of advice. The inventory would also form the basis of international European coordination of activities in the field of chemical education and would provide some backing for the Committees dealing with problems of the mutual recognition of European qualifications in chemistry.

The existence of the Federation has made negotiations regarding European legislation concerning the rights and duties of chemists easier than they might otherwise have been. Contacts between the chemical societies of the member countries of the EEC already existed and a measure of mutual understanding and agreement had already been established so that issues of mutual concern to chemists in all the member countries of the EEC could be approached with some common ground already prepared. By 1976 agreement on full professional qualifications had been virtually finalized on the basis of a four-year, full-time university course beyond university entry at age eighteen which is common in most European countries.[25]

A large number of draft directives has issued from the European Parliament in Brussels. Indeed when the Community was enlarged in 1973 there were about forty of these relative to various professional matters, all of which were under discussion. No agreement had been reached with regard to mutual recognition of qualifications, largely because the approach had been to consider courses quantitatively, comparing the total numbers of hours spent in studying each part of the course. In 1973 Dr Dahrendorf, a German Commissioner, took a different approach, selecting the profession of medicine and considering the training of doctors in the European countries qualitatively. A general meeting was held in October 1974 which led to legislation in 1975 laying down minimum requirements for the training of doctors in all member countries of the EEC.

This legislation, which has to pass through the national assemblies of all the member countries, lays down regulations for all kinds of doctors including specialists, and in doing so it raises a problem for certain chemists.

Amongst the medical men covered by the new legislation are the chemical pathologists who work side-by-side with clinical chemists. Indeed the two titles are merely different names for the same profession and both doctors and chemists may compete for the same posts—viz. heads or senior members of hospital laboratories. The only difference is that the chemical pathologist has had an initial training in medicine and is therefore considered to be a doctor, whilst the clinical chemist began his training as a chemist and cannot therefore be regarded as a doctor.

Since there is now a situation in which there is legislation for the medical profession but not for chemists, the clinical chemists, who have their own associations in various European countries, have become very worried. They feel that vacancies occurring in hospital laboratories may well in future be filled by chemical pathologists whose profession has been recognized in law, whilst the clinical chemist will be passed over. The clinical chemists, who are not sufficiently numerous to have their own committee, turned to the European Communities Chemistry Committee for help, and a meeting was held at 30 Russell Square in January 1976 when the Irish, Dutch and British Associations of Clinical Chemists met under the Chairmanship of Dr R. E. Parker who is also Chairman of the ECCC. The problem was then taken up in March at a meeting of the ECCC after which a letter was sent to Dr Schuster, the Director General for Research, Science and Education, whose department is concerned with the recognition of qualifications. The problem is now recognized but so far no need has been felt to amend the legislation[26].

Another area in which the ECCC has been concerned with legislation leading to professional registration is that of the directives concerned with the free movement of pharmaceutical products. This requires that the quality of pharmaceutical products must be certified in any one country to standards accepted by all other member countries and it is clearly necessary to lay down conditions by which the required qualifications for the 'qualified person' who signs the certificate of quality are defined. A situation had grown up whereby some countries, notably France, Belgium, Holland and Luxembourg, had given this power solely to pharmacists. In the United Kingdom, Ireland, Germany and Italy on the other hand, either chemists or pharmacists could hold these positions. A survey taken in the United Kingdom in 1974 showed that there were about twice as many chemists as pharmacists in such posts and in Germany too there were more chemists than pharmacists engaged in certifying the quality of pharmaceuticals. When Britain entered the Common Market the draft directive on this subject which would have imposed the French system, was nearly complete. Thus the monopoly would have been given to pharmacists although a clause would have been inserted allowing those now in post to continue. This threatened state of affairs was strongly opposed through the ECCC and by individual chemical societies through their own governments. The RIC fought it through the Department of Health as well as through the ECCC in Brussels and to a large extent the campaign was successful.

The directive actually signed in 1975 allows that not only pharmacists, but also chemists, may act as qualified persons to certify the quality of pharmaceutical products. The directive is, however, something of a compromise for it requires the competent authority (i.e. the government) to satisfy itself that whatever basic qualification a person may have, whether in pharmacy, chemistry or even biology, he shall have covered a number of specific topics which form part of most pharmacy courses. The Pharmaceutical Society of Great Britain has maintained that *only* a pharmacy degree fulfils all the requirements, but the RIC disputes this and is keeping a careful watching brief on the subject to ensure that the new directive is properly interpreted.

The question of registration of chemists therefore, whether nationally or internationally, is closely linked with the development of specialization. It is an objective which can only be pursued piecemeal and in this connection the Institute's postgraduate diplomas play a very important role.

As far as the EEC is concerned it is always necessary to tailor qualifications to *occupations* for these are what the Commission is concerned with. This being so, it follows that chemists have greater problems than, say, doctors or pharmacists. Doctors have only one principal employer whereas chemists have literally hundreds of employers and so whilst it is relatively easy to set up registration in a profession such as medicine it is virtually impossible to do so in chemistry as a whole. Thus the piecemeal approach seems to be the only viable one. So far it has had a fair degree of success, at least in the European arena.

NGC

NOTES AND REFERENCES

1 There are at present 12 Local Sections overseas viz. Deccan, Eastern India, Western India, Madras, Northern India, Pakistan, Sri Lanka, East Africa, Cape, Nigeria, Malaysia and New York. Most of these Sections are quite small in numbers, the American Section being the largest with 471 members.

2 The American Institute of Chemistry (later The American Institute of Chemists) was founded in 1923 strictly as a professional Association to promote the welfare of the chemical worker. E. B. Carmichael, *Chemist*, 1974 (September), 22–3.

3 IC, Council Minutes, **6,** 18 May 1909.

4 R. B. Pilcher, *History of the Institute, 1877–1914*, Institute of Chemistry, London, 1914, p. 73.

5 In 1907 Institute members seeking appointments in India were advised to make sure that their professional status was properly recognized. IC, Council Minutes, **5,** 21 November 1907, 30 January 1908.

6 Pilcher (note 4), p. 174.

7 *Ibid.*, p. 233; IC, Council Minutes, **6,** 22 May 1908.

8 Pilcher (note 4), p. 277; IC, Council Minutes, **8,** 24 October 1913. On Pedler see *WWW*. Pedler died in 1918.

9 Memorandum for the Royal Commission on the Public Services in India, 1914, p. 2. IC, Council Minutes, *loc. cit.*, note 8.

10 *Ibid.*, p. 4.

11 *Ibid.*, **12,** 17 December 1919.

12 *Ibid.*, **14,** 22 July 1921. The Fellows resident in India included K. S. Caldwell, G. J. Fowler, H. Krall, R. V. Norris and J. J. Sudborough.

13 Thus in 1921 Sir William Pope, on a visit to India, requested the Indian Government to grant overseas allowances to chemists in line with the practice for other regular services. Two years later some minor concessions were obtained for chemists in the ordnance factory at Aruvankadu. *Ibid.*, 28 October 1921; **16,** 27 April 1923.

14 The Chief Inspector's salary was raised, but his status remained unchanged. *Ibid.*, **17,** 18 January 1924.

15 *Ibid.*, **38,** 15 July 1948; *Proc. R.I.C.*, 1946, **70,** 93; 1948, **72,** 121.

16 RIC, Council Minutes, **37,** 20 February 1948.

17 *Proc. R.I.C.*, 1948, **72,** 146.

18 *Ibid.*, 1951, **75;** RIC, Council Minutes, **41,** 11 January 1951.

19 In 1946 it was decided to resume the Associateship examination in India, RIC, Council Minutes, **36,** 13 December 1946. This was done two years later, *ibid.*, **38,** 19 March 1948, but demand did not justify annual examinations in India.

20 *Ibid.*, **13,** 17 December 1920.

21 Although, as has already become clear (chs XI and XIII), the Institute had grave doubts about the feasibility of general Registration for chemists.

22 A study of the subject of Registration, IC, Council Minutes, **20,** 16 November 1928. The question of Registration had arisen even before the Institute was founded, Pilcher (note 4), p. 36.

23 The Federation of European Chemical Societies published a booklet giving basic information about the activities of all these societies in 1972 (2nd edn. 1974, 3rd edn. in preparation). The member societies in 1974 were:

Verein Öesterreichischer Chemiker
Société Chimique de Belgique
Flemish Chemical Society
Czechoslovak Chemical Society
Slovak Chemical Society
Danish Chemical Society
Assocation of Finnish Chemical Societies
Société Chimique de France
Société de Chimie Physique
Schweizerische Chemische Gesellschaft
Société Chimique de Turquie
The Chemical Society/The Royal Institute of Chemistry
Union of Chemical Societies of Yugoslavia
Hungarian Chemical Society
Institute of Chemistry of Ireland
Italian Chemical Society
Royal Netherlands Chemical Society
Norwegian Chemical Society
Société Chimique de Pologne
Spanish Royal Society of Physics and Chemistry
Swedish Chemical Society

24 *Inventory of National Activities in Chemical Education*, Federation of European Chemical Societies, London 1975, p. 29.

25 Three-year degree courses common in the United Kingdom have been accepted in view of the more specialized sixth-form courses in British schools. These are considered equivalent to the first year of a University degree course.

26 *Chem. Brit.*, 1976, **12**, 402.

CHAPTER XVI
AMALGAMATION—THE SEARCH FOR A FORMULA

1 The Organization of the Chemical Fraternity in Britain

In his Presidential Address to the Chemical Society in 1967 Sir Harry Melville[1] argued persuasively for rationalization of the activities of the main chemical bodies in the United Kingdom.[2] The previous decade had seen an enormous expansion of the universities with a corresponding increase in the number of chemistry graduates. Chemical industry had remained relatively buoyant during this period, with an average increase in output of seven per cent per annum between 1954 and 1965, even though the rest of British industry had passed through a period of stagnation. Rearrangements in the big industrial organizations combined with political and economic developments in Europe and America had resulted in changes in the patterns of academic research and in requirements for graduates, but the demand for chemists had remained high and the numbers coming forward in the subject had maintained a steady increase. This apparently satisfactory situation had been complicated during the 1960s by the large-scale exodus of qualified scientists including chemists from Britain and other European countries to the U.S.A. Clearly measures were needed to reduce this one way traffic, the 'brain drain', and in addition to government intervention, a strong well-organized professional association might help to provide added incentives (for chemists) to remain in Britain. A further worrying trend for the future was also becoming apparent in that the numbers of secondary school pupils electing to read chemistry in universities and polytechnics was showing a sharp decline and it seemed doubtful whether the supply of chemists could be maintained at its present level without some concerted effort to encourage young people to take up the subject whilst still at school. New and more relevant methods of chemistry teaching seemed to be called for whilst a fuller appreciation of the relation between academic chemistry and its applications in industry was clearly essential if sixteen-year-olds were to be fired with enthusiasm for the subject. Thus, although there had been rapid expansion in the numbers of chemists, and the subject was undoubtedly of growing importance in both industrial and government affairs nationally and internationally, there were serious questions regarding the organization of chemistry itself and of the activities of its practitioners which required urgent attention.

Chemistry, occupying a central place in the 'spectrum' of scientific activities, itself extends over an ever-widening field from chemical physics at one extremity to the chemistry of natural products at the other; from the preparation of ultra-pure substances to that of complex pharmaceutical products with the vast operations of large-scale organic chemistry in between. In all of these developments, as Sir Harry pointed out, new specializations were constantly arising, yet the dividing lines between the various activities were never clear-cut. New developments occurring on the periphery of the subject, usually encroaching on areas traditionally regarded as separate, had tended to lead to the isolation of those involved in the pioneering work. New 'languages' had grown up and journals devoted to the new specialist areas appear from time to time. Now, although in the interests of the developing subject these channels of communication are necessary, they create a dilemma as they lead towards fragmentation of chemistry as a discipline. Of course, the diversions between organic, physical and industrial chemistry are really artificial and there is a need to find methods of binding such specialisms into a unified whole again.

Melville saw this danger of fragmentation in chemistry and the mutual exclusion of specialist groups of chemists as a very real one which was reflected in the activities of the major chemical bodies. Thus the Chemical Society, Faraday Society and SCI were all doing very similar things and all three had specialist groups concerned with various aspects of academic and industrial chemistry. The RIC, too, tended to duplicate some of these activities, although it was different in that it was (and is) concerned with the professional status of chemists in industry and elsewhere. In London all the different chemical bodies had been in the habit of running their affairs in isolation from each other and meetings arranged by any one of them were generally very poorly attended, even when addressed by prominent chemists. On the other hand, in the regions where programmes of activities by Local Sections were often combined and joint meetings held, good attendances were much more common. It seemed that in practice the various specialist groups could indeed find common ground and Melville proposed that this fact should be recognized by some form of merger or confederation which would ensure the unification of specialist groups of chemists into one common Society in which group activities could be rationalized and duplication of effort avoided. This single body resulting from an outright merger could then speak with a common voice for chemistry. It would become a body whose opinions on chemical matters would be both sought by governments and heeded nationally and internationally. On a practical note cooperation between the various chemical bodies would lead to the rationalization of publications in chemistry and the wider availability of information.

This proposal was laid before the Councils of the Chemical Society, RIC and the SCI (the three Chartered bodies), and it was decided to open negotiations with the object of working out a scheme for amalgamating or unifying the three bodies. The first step was to appoint an independent adviser to study the problem and Sir Eric Bingen was asked to accept this commission on the basis of his extensive knowledge of industrial mergers and take-overs. Sir Eric began his investigations in August 1967, but unfortunately he fell ill shortly afterwards and was obliged to withdraw. There was then a brief interval until early in 1968 when Sir James Taylor agreed to take on the task, he had already been instrumental in bringing about the merger between the Institute of Physics and the Physical Society in 1960 and was therefore well aware of the problems involved in such a difficult operation.[3] A working group was established consisting of five representatives from the Councils of each of the three bodies, with Sir James, who was himself a member of all three, as Chairman. By the end of 1968 the investigations were well in hand.

2 The RIC and the Proposed Amalgamation

The RIC view of the possibilities of integration had been set out in a memorandum of 14 November 1967[4], discussed and received without dissent by Council on 12 December. The memorandum which had already been sent to Sir Eric Bingen, made clear that the RIC fully supported the integration of the three major bodies if this should prove possible, but if not then the RIC would be prepared to consider integration with either of the other two bodies. What the RIC did not favour, however, was the idea of any form of loose confederation since this would simply seem to make four bodies out of the present three. Such a move could hardly be expected to be more successful in uniting the various branches of chemistry than the Chemical Council had proved to be. The eight basic objectives for the organization of the science and profession of chemistry put forward by the RIC were:

(i)   To extend and refine the fields of pure knowledge on which it is based, and to disseminate this knowledge.

(ii)   To widen and improve understanding of the practical applications of that knowledge, and to disseminate this understanding.

(iii)   To provide channels of communication between chemists for their mutual benefit in professional and social relations.

(iv)   To set up and maintain adequate standards of theoretical knowledge and practical competence by establishing examinations and prescribing qualifications.

(v)   To ensure that suitable persons are able to receive the necessary education and training and to ensure an adequate supply of properly trained entrants to the profession.

(vi)   To promote or safeguard the status and general interests of chemists in their relations with other professions and the general public.

(vii)   To further—and, when necessary, protect—the legal rights, economic interests, conditions of practice or employment, and, in general, the material welfare of chemists.

(viii)   To set standards of ethical conduct and to uphold compliance with such standards by disciplinary action.

Of these the Chemical Society and SCI were already concerned with the first three items whilst the RIC was mainly involved in points (iii)–(viii).

The Council of the RIC expressed a firm intention to maintain its functions as an examining and qualifying body and as an educational and professional body. Coupled with this there was also the need to retain its role as a disciplinary body in any known cases of unprofessional conduct amongst its members. Nevertheless, the RIC was anxious not to appear merely in a protective role, acting solely in the interests of its own members and oblivious to those of the rest of the chemical community. In any case, as a chartered body the RIC was bound to act in the public interest and for the well-being of the chemical profession as a whole and not merely in the interests of its own members or of any other chemists.

Council was furthermore careful to point out that the RIC was not a trade union. This recurrent issue had become a fine point in 1968 since the Industrial Relations Bill was then being hotly debated. The RIC had expressed its intention to maintain and indeed intensify its professional activities in respect of remuneration surveys and advice to its members on terms and conditions of service and it seemed that if any really effective policy were to be carried out in this field, the RIC might be forced to register as a trade union. This prospect deterred the SCI in the negotiations from the outset since its membership included managers and employers of chemists and it seemed possible that at some future time there might well be a confrontation between employer and employee within the Society. The RIC discounted this since its own membership had always included employers as well as employees. In the end the possibility that the RIC might become a trade union was given as one of the reasons for the withdrawal of the SCI from the negotiations.

With regard to the exchange of information, the RIC shared with the Chemical Society and SCI the aim of bringing chemists together and providing a forum for exchange of information, the spread of knowledge and fostering of a sense of professional unity and fellowship.

For this reason the RIC acted as a publishing house, organized meetings through its Local Sections (thirty-two in the United Kingdom and eleven overseas) and helped to sponsor some feeling of professional unity and mutual responsibility through the RIC Benevolent Fund.

The Council of the RIC gave two fundamental reasons for supporting the proposed amalgamation, viz., consolidation of support and unification of control, for since there is no limit to what could be done if there were unlimited resources, it seemed highly desirable to prepare and pursue an organized programme with priorities decided by one overall authority so as to make the most effective use of the limited resources which were available.

3 The Case for Integration as Seen by the RIC[5]

There were four main arguments in favour of amalgamation as seen by the Council of the RIC. In the first place there was the importance of a single *powerful voice for chemists*. At the heart of RIC thinking stood the belief that:

> . . . their professional and economic interests would best be served if chemists joined together to form one powerful assemblage and, in particular, with the Government and with those who employ chemists.[6]

On the other hand the Chemical Society had wider aims in that the common voice was to be an outgoing advisory voice to which the Government and Civil Service would turn when chemical questions had to be decided.

Secondly, *the creation of a single focus of support for all chemists* with separate bodies was seen to be important. The individual chemist would often support only those activities which served his own interests and tended to ignore his responsibilities to all the rest. In any case many chemists feel that the main weight of their responsibilities must be directed elsewhere, to their universities or employers or even with the advent of the EEC in the wider international scene, rather than to their fellow chemists. This situation was felt particularly by the RIC because it seemed that the services it provided for the advancement of the professional and economic interests of chemists were less tangible than those provided by the Chemical Society or the Society of Chemical Industry. The RIC stated that in its opinion *every* practising chemist in the United Kingdom should be expected to support the work and further the interests of the profession *as a whole*.

But, 'Until membership of one body is virtually essential for every chemist this aim of focussing support will not be feasible'.[7] There would seem to be some desire by the RIC to exert a degree of coercion here in strong contrast to its stance in earlier years. It appears that the RIC would like to have seen a unified chemical body with an important, possibly even statutory qualifying function in a manner similar to that of the Pharmaceutical Society or the Institute of Patent Agents. That is to say, a professional body whose diplomas limit the entry to and practice of the profession, and whose membership is restricted to those so qualified. This could not have been a reasonable aim in the eyes of the Chemical Society or SCI, both of whom include in their membership people interested in or concerned with chemistry but without formal qualifications in the subject. Even if this class of membership could be catered for some friction might still arise between those who sought membership for professional purposes and those who joined the Chemical Society out of interest as amateurs only.

In the third place there was the *coordination of views and interests*. Three independent bodies must inevitably create some overlap and duplication of activities, although in practice this was less than it might be because there was already a desire for cooperation amongst the members. Nevertheless each body was principally concerned with the activities it was formed to carry out and was not so worried about the complementary activities of the other two. If all activities were coordinated under a single control there could be much more rationalization and the effort involved in providing the various services could be more effectively deployed. This would naturally lead to economies in time, and money.

Lastly, *improved efficiency in the administration* of the combined society could be achieved by combining closely related activities and so eliminating overlap and competition between the three bodies. Rationalizing the use of premises, amenities, equipment and staff for greater efficiency and creating one governing body by reducing the powers of the three separate Councils, or even abolishing them altogether. The Council of the RIC thought that apart from establishing the structure and powers of the governing body the other problems of rationalization should be left to the permanent officers to work out as soon as practicable, after integration.

4 Problems of Integration

Despite the obvious advantages to be gained by integration the Council of the RIC saw that there would be major obstacles to be overcome and four areas in which problems might be anticipated were identified. Firstly there was the question of the various types of membership (Figures 7–8).

By the terms of its Charter the RIC is obliged to require every corporate member of whatever grade to furnish evidence of training, qualifications, knowledge, skill and experience as a chemist and also of being of good repute. Corporate membership, unlike membership of the Chemical Society or SCI, is a qualification. The RIC would clearly need to preserve these qualifications within the structure of the larger organization, but it was thought that the Privy Council might allow the establishment of a further grade of corporate but non-qualifying membership, either through a supplementary charter or through a new charter for the joint body.

Coupled with membership was the difficult question of subscriptions about which the three societies had different views. Thus, the Chemical Society had always called for a low annual subscription and charged economic if preferential rates to its members for its publications. In this way the members of the Chemical Society could select only those publications they wanted and were required to pay for nothing more. This system is clearly satisfactory for a Society whose main activity is that of *publishing*. The RIC on the other hand, engaged in activities that are for the general good of the profession of chemistry as a whole, and which could not readily be charged for on an individual basis.

TABLE 2   Membership and Fees for some British Chemical
Societies in 1966[8]

Society	Membership	Fees
Biochemical Society	3,500	£5
Pharmaceutical Society	28,847	£5 5s
Faraday Society	2,400	£6 (under 27 £3)
Institution of Chemical Engineers	6,800	Member £9 9s Associate Member £7 7s
Society of Chemical Industry	8,000	£4
Royal Institute of Chemistry	17,500	Fellow £5 5s Associate £4 4s (under 35 £3 3s) Licentiate £3 3s
Chemical Society	14,000	£2 2s

Most of the RIC's work in safeguarding the interests of chemists bears no special reference to individuals. The SCI already levied an annual subscription and it was really the low subscription charged by the Chemical Society which caused the problems in this area since this would not provide sufficient revenue to support all the activities envisaged for the new joint body. Once more the RIC stated that in its opinion,

> every chemist in the United Kingdom should be expected to make his fixed contribution to the activities and services for the collective benefit of chemists and then pay favourable though not highly subsidized prices for services that he might need as an individual.[9]

The only really notable overlap in the activities of the three Societies in 1967–8 was the question of the two chemical news journals. In compliance with the terms of its Charter the SCI published *Chemistry and Industry* (circulation 10,000) as a weekly journal, whilst the RIC and Chemical Society jointly issued *Chemistry in Britain* (circulation 40,000) on a monthly basis. This latter journal was itself a replacement for the RIC's *Journal* and the Chemical Society's *Proceedings*. The question of amalgamating the two journals, *Chemistry in Britain* and *Chemistry and Industry* was discussed, but complete amalgamation was ruled out by the economic problems of producing a weekly chemical journal with a circulation of 40,000. Moreover the SCI were unwilling to agree to the replacement of *Chemistry and Industry* by a joint publication produced less frequently. However, by bringing down the production costs of both journals the possibility of issuing them on a weekly or fortnightly basis was becoming ever nearer.

The RIC did not consider that agreement on the details of such a merger of publications need precede or even immediately follow the integration of the three bodies. It seemed too that there might be problems arising from the desirability of retaining a charitable status as far as possible. Both the Chemical Society and the SCI are regarded as charities but the RIC might have found some difficulty in being so regarded because of its Charter provisions, and it was doubtful whether a joint body could be if it were to include in its objectives a direct reference to the promotion of *professional* interests. Still, some activities of the RIC were eligible for charitable status and these were channelled through its fund for the development of education in chemistry. From time to time there was also the very valuable service to members of the RIC or their dependents in need offered through the Benevolent Fund.

The last major area in which problems were foreseen concerned the question of the three Charters. This occupied the attention of Sir James Taylor and was dealt with in detail by him in his report to the Councils of the Chemical Society, SCI and RIC. It will be discussed more fully below.

5   Sir James Taylor's Report[10]

With the memorandum from the RIC and other documents before him Sir James Taylor began to study the problem and his report was presented to the RIC at a Council Meeting on 26 July 1968. In it Sir James pointed out that any new body must be capable of encompassing the three main aspects of chemical activity in this country, viz. 'academic' chemistry, the profession of chemistry and chemical industry. The activities of the Chemical Society and SCI would need to be maintained as charities and the name 'Chemical Society' should be preserved since it belonged to the oldest national chemical society in the world. There must be no restrictions as to qualifications for Fellowship of the Chemical Society or membership of the SCI (including foreign membership and the possibility for the SCI to have a foreign President). The reading, discussion and publication of original papers must continue and the Chemical Society Library must be maintained. The SCI wished also to continue its liaison with the Chemical Industries Association, to maintain its specialist groups and add to them as required, and to continue the free distribution of *Chemistry and Industry* to its members, although not necessarily weekly.

The essential conditions for the RIC were rather different since its professional structure must remain intact and the membership of the RIC be restricted to British (or ex-British) subjects. Only the non-professional activities of the RIC could continue to be a 'charity' whilst its professional activities must remain the sole responsibility of the Corporate Membership of the RIC in any merger. For the benefit of chemistry in this country and the encouragement of original research, all three bodies should maintain their individual medals and awards systems. From this summary, it seems clear on paper at least, that the Chemical Society and SCI as learned societies had more in common with each other than the RIC.

In his Report, Sir James next considered the problem of naming the new body. In the light of his earlier experience with the physicists he suggested that the negotiations for a merger of the chemical bodies would only succeed if the current names could be maintained in one form or another. The corporate members of the RIC had a vested interest in the name of their institution since it formed part of their professional qualifications whilst the term 'Chemical Society' with its historic associations should be retained. He could not accommodate the RIC view that *all* chemists in the United Kingdom should be required to support professional activities, since there were many Fellows of the Chemical Society who had no interest in these and some members of the SCI who, though concerned with chemical industry, were not themselves chemists.

The next difficulty arose from the fact that all three of the chemical bodies had its own Charter. This meant that the merging of the physicists could not serve as a model for the chemists since the former were merely limited liability companies for which new Articles of Association were no more restrictive than older ones which in any case included nothing of great value to be preserved. The same is not true of charters, which are granted by the Crown on the advice of the Privy Council and are intended to operate in perpetuity. Sir James considered that new charters were almost always more restricted and restrictive than older ones which consequently should not lightly be relinquished. In fact he was probably being over-cautious. It is true that newly established organizations may nowadays be granted charters in more precise and restrictive terms than was often the case in former years, but old-established bodies like the Chemical Society, with more than a century of 'good behaviour' to their credit would probably be leniently treated. Most, if not all the benefits of the old charters could probably be incorporated into a new one, especially if the same name were to be retained.

In industry the merging of companies can often be accomplished by a 'take-over' but this solution was not feasible for the chemical bodies. Neither the Chemical Society nor the SCI could take over the rest since neither Charter included the examining and qualifying roles of a professional body. On the other hand the RIC could not take-over the other two without creating privileged and underprivileged classes of membership.

So none of the three existing Charters could freely and adequately by itself cover all the various activities of the three bodies. Sir James pointed out that chartered bodies as part of the establishment are in a privileged position relative to non-chartered ones and argued persuasively for the retention of all three Charters. He considered that the Chemical Society Charter, by virtue of being the oldest, included various rights which would almost certainly be lost in any new charter. In addition its Charter does not require Privy Council approval for changes in its bye-laws—a situation which he thought could not be retained. So the *a priori* case for retaining the three Charters seemed overwhelming.

Nevertheless Sir James conceded that the question of relinquishing the present Charters in order to obtain a new one would be a possible approach.

He thought too that it would be feasible, though difficult to retain the enormous advantages of charitable status for the combined body, even though the RIC continued to be concerned with professional activities. On the whole, he was strongly opposed to any attempt to obtain a single new charter in exchange for the three existing ones and felt that the dangers in attempting to dissolve the current chartered bodies were such as to make it not worthwhile.

All three Charters charge the Councils with the management and supervision of the affairs of the body and also determine the duties of the Executive Officers, but all include powers of delegation. The bye-laws of the Chemical Society gave its Council power to appoint committees with delegated powers and to cooperate with other bodies. Powers of cooperation and joint action are written directly into the Charter of the RIC and are also contained in the bye-laws, whilst the SCI is similarly authorized. Thus the three Councils already had adequate powers to delegate authority in such a way as to make possible the joint running of their affairs with a uniform policy and financial control. Within this unity Taylor proposed that each body should retain its own name and be concerned with its own appropriate activities, and went on to elaborate these as laid down in the Charters.

6 Division of Responsibility in the 'New' Chemical Society

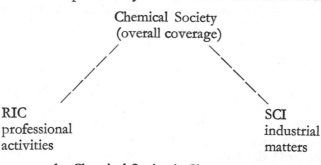

Chemical Society
(overall coverage)

RIC
professional
activities

SCI
industrial
matters

As we have seen the Chemical Society's Charter was set out in broad terms and was concerned with the promotion of chemistry as a discipline. The Chemical Society's Library established under its Charter remains amongst its most valuable assets. The 1885 Charter of the RIC gave its objectives as those of promoting the profession of analytical and consulting chemistry and of raising the status of chemists engaged in such work, by means of qualifications of good standing.[11] The 1949 Charter refers to 'maintaining and raising the status of the profession of chemistry and promoting the usefulness of persons practising the same'. The RIC is also required by its Charter to compel the observance of a code of ethical behaviour in order to ensure the integrity of its membership and to maintain a high standard of scientific and practical efficiency. The SCI was established in 1881 'To advance applied chemistry in all its branches'.[12] It was intended to provide a forum for its members and to extend opportunities for the interchange of ideas regarding improvements in the various chemical industries. The 1907 Charter of the SCI expanded upon these objects and also specifically precluded the power or right to act as an examining body for the purpose of conferring degrees, qualifications or authority to practice, or to use any distinctive title.

In broad terms the Council of the SCI saw the activities of the three Chartered Bodies as: The Chemical Society concerned with basic chemistry; the RIC with the professional status of the chemist; and the SCI with applied chemistry at home and overseas, with particular application to management and economies. Sir James accepted the SCI's view as basically sound and proposed the appointment of a Chief Executive who would have the job of general supervision of all the activities of the three bodies. He would need to be a man of such calibre as would make him willingly acceptable to all three Presidents. He ought preferably to be independent. Possible models for the supra-structure could be drawn either from the old Chemical Council or from the Charter of the Council of the Engineering Institutions. The participant institutions of CEI are separate corporations described as Constituent Members, and there is power to add to them and also to accept 'Affiliates' with limited privileges.

Another possible model would have been to set up Councils with a common membership and to hold Council meetings concurrently or consecutively on the same day. This is a move often made in industry—but it would have needed some changes in the bye-laws if it were to be applied to the chemical bodies.

The consolidation of the finance departments of the three bodies and rationalization of members' dues was also seen to be needed as a matter of urgency. With regard to members' dues there were two views; either members should be asked to pay a subscription large enough to subsidize the activities of the organization or the members' subscriptions should be small and all activities should be self-supporting. Many felt that members should be asked to pay only for what they want and not to be asked to contribute to activities from which they derived no benefits. The matter to be decided then was whether the members' subscriptions should be as low as possible and they should be asked to pay at economic rates for publications, symposia, etc. The Chemical Society had always taken this view.

Assuming then that all three Charters were to be retained, a big step towards unification would be taken if there were a common membership. Taylor suggested that all the members of the three chemical bodies should become members of the Chemical Society—and this could be achieved without increasing any of the membership fees. The greatest disparity was between the subscriptions for the Chemical Society and those for the SCI, but these might be brought into line if the SCI's *Journal* were incorporated in *Chemistry in Britain*. Alternatively if SCI members still wanted their own

Journal then they might be asked to pay for it as an extra publication, whilst receiving *Chemistry in Britain* (with SCI news included) free. Sir James felt that the whole question of subscriptions had to be studied in detail before it could be clearly stated what practical advantages might accrue to members.

7 Reception of the Taylor Report

As we have already seen (p. 301) the RIC favoured complete amalgamation (unification) under a single charter in contrast to the SCI which favoured a federation with the three constituent bodies retaining virtually complete autonomy. Discussions went on into 1969 with the aim of attempting to resolve this fundamental difference but although very close agreement was achieved between the Chemical Society and the RIC, the SCI remained adamant. By May 1969 it had become clear that the early amalgamation of all three bodies was unlikely. In view of this the Council of the RIC decided to explore the possibility of a two-body amalgamation between the RIC and the Chemical Society only. At the Joint Annual Meetings in Nottingham representatives of the RIC and Chemical Society drew up an outline scheme for a joint organization. A further meeting was planned for 3 June to produce agreed recommendations with regard to the 'top structure' of an RIC/Chemical Society amalgamation to be communicated to the SCI, SAC and Faraday Society on 17 June. This then was the point of decision at which the RIC and Chemical Society decided to press on without the SCI, whilst leaving the way open for the SCI (and other bodies) to join in (possibly in some form of confederation) at a later date. From this time onwards although the SCI was kept informed of progress made, the principal participants in the discussions were to be the RIC and Chemical Society.

Although separate detailed negotiations towards amalgamation only began in April 1969, there was so much common ground that rapid progress was made. In May the Councils of the two bodies agreed to consider Sir James Taylor's Report on a scheme for amalgamation tabled at a meeting of the RIC Council on 26 July 1968, together with a statement of the Case for Amalgamation, also by Sir James, and a statement by the President of the RIC summarizing the history of the negotiations and the attitude of the RIC towards Sir James's Report.[13] The Council of the Chemical Society had already given approval to the two documents submitted by Sir James and in principle to the Scheme of Amalgamation. Council of the RIC unanimously approved the proposals in principle.

It became apparent, however, that two or more chartered bodies could not legally be governed except by their own councils so long as they retained their individual charters. The two Councils would have to be preserved and arrangements for cross-representation made. This was reported to the RIC Council at a meeting of 10 October when a three-stage process was outlined as follows:

Stage 1 Association of the participating bodies with a Grand Council consisting of the individual Councils added together and a Quorum Council of minimum size, both empowered only so far as delegated by the RIC and Chemical Society Councils.

Stage 2 All members of the participating bodies become Fellows of the Chemical Society and all common activities to be brought under the *aegis* of the enlarged Society.

Stage 3 Complete amalgamation into one body with a single Charter.

It will be noted that Stage 3 has not yet been achieved although discussions towards this end are still actively going on.

The amalgamation proposals were published in *Chemistry in Britain* in October 1969 and it still seemed that there might be a good prospect of the SCI deciding to participate whilst there were positive indications that the Faraday Society and SAC might wish to join. No decisions had been taken by any of these bodies at that time, but a five-body link up seemed to some to be within reach.

At the RIC Council meeting of 12 December 1969 the President was able to report that discussions on important matters of detail in the negotiations connected with the amalgamation proposals had progressed well. The representatives of the Faraday Society and SAC had accepted assurances with regard to the preservation of the interests of their societies should they decide to enter the Scheme of Amalgamation and it was expected that the Councils of these two bodies would shortly take formal decisions in favour of full participation. On the other hand the SCI had decided to turn its attentions to the Institution of Chemical Engineers; SCI representatives would continue to attend the meetings of the Joint Negotiating Committee, but a decision by the SCI to join the Scheme of Amalgamation had by this time become improbable.

8 Heads of Agreement

At a meeting on 9 December 1969 the Joint Negotiating Committee had drawn up a Letter of Intent and Heads of Agreement which, after further legal advice and slight amendment, were accepted and signed on 5 February 1970 by Sir Ronald Nyholm[14] for the Chemical Society and Mr L. H. Williams for the RIC.

> It was agreed that,
> The Councils of the Chemical Society and Royal Institute of Chemistry wish to carry out all their respective activities so far as is legally and constitutionally possible, in unity, with a common membership.[15]

Now, although the Councils of the Chemical Society and RIC were in agreement, it was felt that such an important change should be presented to the membership so as to determine the extent to which it was found to be acceptable among the members. Each society proposing to join in the Scheme of Amalgamation therefore decided to hold a referendum among its members and it was agreed in July that the RIC referendum should be addressed to the corporate members of the Institute in January 1970 with a closing date for the receipt of votes by the end of January or early in February.[16]

In fact it was the middle of January before the referendum could be set up and the final date for votes to be received was fixed for 28 February 1970. The Chemical Society, SCI, Faraday Society and SAC also held referenda during 1970 and the voting patterns were as follows:

TABLE 3   Responses to the Referenda[17]

	per cent response	per cent response in favour	per cent membership in favour
Chemical Society	40	93.9	37.5
RIC	51.3	92.8	47.6
SCI	54.3	68.3	37.1
Faraday Society	58	82.4	46
SAC	c50	94.3	c47

9 Results of the Referenda, 1970

The polls recorded by all these societies indicate a high degree of apathy amongst their members, or possibly the fact that a great deal of cooperation already existed and many joint meetings were regularly held by Local Sections throughout the country diminished the urgency of moves to amalgamate. In any case it seems clear that pressure towards amalgamation was coming from the top and was not very strongly felt at the grass-roots. The results of the RIC ballot were declared in April and received at the Council Meeting on 15 May. Early in April the Council of the SCI had decided by majority vote to pursue discussions with the Institution of Chemical Engineers with a view to establishing a joint learned Society, but there still seemed the remote possibility that the SCI might yet amalgamate with the chemical bodies and the way for this was left open.

As far as the Chemical Society and RIC were concerned the decision to proceed towards Amalgamation as from 1 January 1972 was taken immediately after the results of their referenda were known in April. The SAC requested the right of withdrawal from the Scheme and it was understood that this request hinged on their wish to retain some measure of autonomy at least until that Society had celebrated its centenary in 1974. The President of the RIC thought that although it was important to see the Amalgamation arrangements as permanent it would be unwise to press smaller bodies too strongly in this respect at first.

10 The 'Profession of Chemistry'

At the Annual Meeting of the RIC held in Edinburgh in 1970, the President, Mr Leslie Williams, spoke of the 'Role of the RIC in the seventies'.[18] The main issue he raised centred around the protection of the professional interests of the corporate members. The question—a very important one for the Amalgamation discussions—was to what extent, if at all, it would be right or desirable for the RIC to act as a trade union entering into salary negotiations on behalf of its members, as part of its professional activities. There were three broad points of view. Many considered that the individual chemist must always be prepared to 'find his own level' in the profession, but that more activity by the RIC in generally raising the status and advancing the interests and welfare of chemists, especially those employed in industry, was necessary.

Others felt that a non-chartered protective association was required. This would then be able to carry out all the educational and qualifying activities of the RIC whilst protecting the interests of its members, but would not be empowered to enter into salary negotiations either in general or in particular cases.

On the other hand, a more militant section of the membership thought that outright unionization, either through one or more of the existing unions or through a newly formed body to be registered as a trade union, was urgently necessary.

The distinction between a protective association and a trade union is that the latter has the legal power to impose sanctions on employers and can therefore take militant action if necessary. A chartered body is not usually empowered to promote the status and economic interests of its members because it is a fundamental tenet of all charters that the public interest is of prime importance. Thus in any conflict between the interests of its members and the public weal it is for the chartered body to resolve the issue without taking a partisan line. Within the RIC there was also the further complication that the members include both employers and employees, a factor which might well lead to internal conflict.

The RIC has always been involved in activities designed to improve or protect the status and material welfare of its members, but it has not always acted vigorously in this direction. Remuneration surveys amongst RIC members have been carried out spasmodically since 1919 and have become a regular feature since the Second World War. Occasional articles or documents on conditions of employment have been published, whilst help and advice has long been offered to members on an unofficial and individual basis and the latter function has been growing progressively over the last two decades. In general though, the RIC has been both passive and powerless in regard to salary negotiations for the benefit of the general body of members.

The summer of 1970 witnessed a spate of activity within the RIC concerned with self-assessment and revaluation in the light of the proposed Amalgamation, for it was clear that the RIC must in future turn its attention almost exclusively to its qualifying and examining procedures on the one hand and its professional activities on the other.[19] It was highly desirable that the RIC should be seen to be both vigorous and effective. It was therefore essential to devise a viable policy for future action, considering that the two aspects of its work being interdependent, must flourish or decline together. Three possible lines of action presented themselves. The RIC might continue to take a limited interest in the general welfare of the profession of chemistry, while offering some help to individual members, as at present. Alternatively a more positive stance with regard to the professional status of its members might be adopted. In this case it would be possible to leave much of the actual work to other bodies, which might either be under the control of the RIC, under some joint control, or even fully independent.

Thirdly, as a more problematic alternative, the RIC might be able to accept for *itself* a greatly enlarged sphere of responsibility, including even direct action on a considerable scale, with a view to improving both the status and economic prospects of its members.

Of these alternatives it was felt that the first might well lead to the establishment of *other* independent bodies to act as protective associations or trade unions for qualified chemists and in this way the value of the services offered by the RIC to its members would be reduced. This would act to the detriment not only of the RIC but also of the new Chemical Society.

The other suggestions might be constitutionally possible, although previously as an arbiter the RIC always had taken an impartial view and decisions not to act as a negotiator in a dispute were on record. Consequently any strengthening of direct action would involve a change of stance by the RIC and the question now was whether future policy should be slanted towards more positive action of this kind, bearing in mind the volume of work the Institute could reasonably undertake.

The RIC Charter specifically permits action as an advisory or negotiating body on salaries and conditions of employment, and it has a long tradition of positive, if limited and little publicized, action in such matters. Furthermore the RIC is larger and more conscious of its responsibilities as a *professional* body than the other chemical bodies which have always tended to regard themselves as learned societies. An area in which it was suggested that the RIC should be more active was in the provision of information and advice to individual members and especially younger members. To this end it was suggested that advisory panels might be set up in various parts of the country in collaboration with Regional Committees and Local Sections. These panels would be available to any member who wished to discuss employment problems. Before this it would be necessary to publish information of terms of engagement including a handbook on formal Service Agreements and Conditions of Employment. The Professional Executive

Committee put the following recommendation forward for the consideration of the Council.

> That the Institute should accept for itself a greatly enlarged sphere of responsibility, including direct concern and possibly direct action on a considerable scale, for improving and safeguarding the status, economic interests and general welfare of its members, with special reference to their remuneration and other conditions of employment.[20]

This resolution which was passed by the Council was intended to be a firm statement of future policy to be pursued as energetically and enthusiastically as possible. In passing the resolution the Council committed the Institute to a comprehensive expansion of professional activities. The Professional Executive Committee was asked to prepare a policy statement to be approved by all members of the Council and a working party on the Status and Conditions of Employment of Chemists was set up.

This change of emphasis in the RIC's policies was reported in *The Times* newspaper on 28 September under the heading 'Trade Union tactics for Royal Institute of Chemistry'. Nothing could have been more damaging to the delicate state of negotiations with the SCI, and coupled with other events in October and November 1970 it was undoubtedly an important factor leading in the end to the withdrawal of the SCI from any further discussions concerning its part in the new Chemical Society.

11 Point of Decision for the SCI

As we have seen, the referendum held by the SCI in September 1970 had indicated that only thirty-seven per cent of the membership of that Society was known to be definitely in favour of Amalgamation. This left the SCI Council in a difficult position and it was decided to seek legal advice. Opinion of Counsel, delivered in November 1970,[21] urged caution with regard to the entry of SCI into the Scheme of Amalgamation in view of the low proportion of the membership in favour. The referendum having revealed that a substantial proportion of the membership was opposed to Amalgamation, Counsel warned that a very difficult situation had been created and indeed whether or not they could legally proceed towards Amalgamation in the absence of unanimity could probably only be determined in the Courts. Counsel feared the possibility of dissident members filing a suit against the SCI Council on the grounds that the wishes of the membership had been ignored. There were legal precedents for such action and it seemed at least possible that it might succeed. In any event considerable embarrassment could be caused for the Council and the general conclusion was that entry of the SCI into the Scheme of Amalgamation would be inadvisable.

Mr L. Williams, in his Presidential Address to the RIC in July 1970, outlined the case for a common membership between the RIC and the Chemical

Society and argued in favour of a wholly professional membership and there appeared to be no place in his view for any member of the new Chemical Society who could not claim to be a professional chemist.[22] The dual prospect of the RIC as a trade union and of a uniform membership of the new Chemical Society restricted to professionally qualified chemists, caused further grave concern for the Council of the SCI and in particular for their President, Mr G. H. Beeby.

On his election in 1970 Beeby had taken steps to re-open negotiations with the RIC and Chemical Society but by November he had come to the conclusion that it would be both impractical and undesirable for the SCI to enter into Amalgamation with any combined chemical organization which included the RIC.

In November 1970 Mr Beeby issued a personal statement in which he set out his own objections to the proposed Scheme of Amalgamation and the reasons which led him to believe that the SCI could not join it. These reasons are interesting and cogent in themselves, though whether or not they are biased or well founded must be left to the reader to judge. Mr Beeby said:

> It is my considered opinion that so long as the RIC remains an entirely autonomous entity—and I accept that this is unavoidable—there can *never* be a true amalgamation.[23]

He felt that the RIC with seven seats as a permanent right was being accorded too strong a representation on the new Chemical Society Council and suggested that instead the RIC should be concerned solely with qualifying and professional matters and should remain separate from the new Chemical Society which would take over all other activities now undertaken by the RIC.

Mr Beeby went on to quote from the end of Mr Williams's Presidential Address:

> Although we shall all be members of the enlarged Chemical Society, there will still be a considerable number of Chemical Society members who will not be members of the Institute and no doubt they have their own good reasons. We hope that they can be persuaded to change their minds and if, in the different circumstances in which the Institute will be conducting its affairs, it can demonstrate its greater effectiveness as a professional body, that they will be encouraged to join. In the meantime, they should recognize that, collectively, they constitute the main barrier in the way of taking amalgamation to its logical and desirable end, that of a one-charter organization. Clearly, therefore, the Institute's main task in the seventies will be to do everything possible to encourage a common membership and as this would be in the best interests of all chemists we shall hope for the support of the Chemical Society Council.[24]
> [Commenting, Mr Beeby said], 'In my view, this amounts to an explicit statement that the RIC and, it hopes, the Council of the Chemical

Society, will not welcome as members of the 'new' Chemical Society people who are not professionally qualified chemists; scarcely an attractive prospect for the many senior and distinguished members of SCI who are not chemists, and whose membership is one of the distinctive features of our Society'.[25]

He then went on to remark on the 'new policy' declaration issued by the RIC in October, and said that he felt that the RIC would be forced to register as a trade union if it were to carry out its proposed policy effectively. Whether or not the RIC did, in fact, register, he said, 'there can be no doubt whatever that RIC intends to operate in every way short of strike action (a self-denial which does not of itself confer exemption) as a trade union'. He felt that the SCI should not amalgamate with a body which is linked in any way to a trade union.

Many members of the SCI are, of course, employers or in management and the implications of any form of trade union activity are obvious. However, there are also considerable numbers of RIC members who are employers, managers or self-employed and their positions too would have to be considered if the RIC were to take up any strong or militant stance on behalf of its members.

Mr Beeby concluded his statement as follows:

I have always been, and I remain of the opinion that an amalgamation of SCI with the old Chemical Society and other scientific but non-qualifying bodies such as the SAC and the Faraday Society would have been both possible and advantageous to all. What I do not favour, indeed what I believe to be both undesirable and impracticable, is an amalgamation of *any* non-professional 'learned society' with the whole or with part of *any* body with mandatory qualifying functions which must retain its identity and its autonomy.[26]

Thus when the SCI Council met in November to consider its future course of action there was considerable weight both of evidence and opinion against entering into the Scheme of Amalgamation. Council members were in possession of the Draft Heads of Agreement between SCI and Chemical Society drawn up by Sir James Taylor and of Mr Beeby's personal statement, but the Opinion of Counsel was withheld until after the vote had been taken. It was also proposed, though in contradiction of Sir James Taylor's recommendations, that ultimately the Charters of the SCI and Chemical Society should be merged into one. This would mean, in effect, that the SCI would forfeit its own Charter—though not necessarily its name, since it was proposed that the SCI should become a division of the new Chemical Society. Nevertheless, it appeared to many that the SCI was being asked to sacrifice a great deal for little return and the motion to proceed with negotiations towards Amalgamation was defeated by 25 to 16 with 6 abstentions.

With this the SCI withdrew from the negotiations and proceeded both to consolidate its own position as far as possible and to continue talks already begun with the object of establishing closer links with the Institute of Chemical Engineers.

12 Amalgamation and the Work of the RIC

During 1971 arrangements went ahead in preparation for the implementation of the four-body Amalgamation as from 1 January 1972 (the SAC came in on 1 January 1975). Deeds of Agreement were signed between the Chemical Society and each of the other three bodies and it was agreed to set up six divisions to deal with academic matters. These were to include Faraday and Analytical Divisions derived from the FS and SAC respectively. There was also to be an Industrial Division which in the absence of SCI from the joint body would be in competition with the activities of that Society. The new Chemical Society was also to have a Regional structure of Local Sections derived with some modification from the existing structure.[27] Provision was made to enlarge the membership of the Council to include representation by the Divisions and Local Sections, whilst the RIC was to retain its own Council with responsibilities for professional affairs and for qualifications and examinations. All this information was presented to the memberships of the four bodies together with an explanatory introduction relating the history of the negotiations by Sir James Taylor for consideration at their AGMs.[28] The RIC voted unanimously in favour of the necessary changes in the bye-laws as did the Chemical Society and by July 1971 all the new Boards, Committees and Divisional Councils had been appointed. Sir James Taylor's Joint Negotiating Committee was able to hand over all its responsibilities and to discontinue its meetings, and by October 1971 the educational activities, the Local Sections and the publishing activities of the RIC had all been transferred to the Chemical Society.

For some time the RIC had been giving careful attention to its own future role. On the surface this appeared to be dramatically reduced by Amalgamation, but events outside the chemical world itself were changing so rapidly that in fact the RIC was to find its capacity to fulfil all the aspects of its new role taxed to the full. In 1971 there were two vitally important issues requiring attention, both connected with the Industrial Relations Bill. The provisions of this Bill envisaged industrial relations entirely in terms of negotiations between employers and *trade unions*.[29] The RIC along with some other chartered bodies made vigorous representations to the Government and clauses were introduced into the Bill which would enable chartered bodies to have some of the rights and immunities accorded to registered unions. Seats on the new Industrial Relations Commissions were also secured so that the voice of the professions could be heard, but the membership of the RIC is very diverse and there were many for whom the Institute held responsibilities who did not fit neatly into any of the categories for which the Industrial Relations Bill catered. The interests of chemists at senior levels in industry often differed from those of larger groups of workers in the same industry. Such professional chemists it seemed, might be obliged to join or at least be represented by, unions which could neither look after their interests properly, nor respect their loyalties and obligations to their professional institutions. The government seemed reluctant to recognize the dilemma of professional people and a campaign was launched to enlist the support of MP's and Peers in order to press for some amendments to the Bill. Some modest success was achieved which fell far short of what the RIC had hoped, although they did include specific references to professional qualifications, whilst the Code of Industrial Practice urged employers and unions to give due regard to the codes of conduct of professional employees.

However, the Industrial Relations Bill by encouraging collective bargaining and imposing a more rigid structure on the negotiating machinery, made it necessary for the RIC to relinquish its earlier plans for extending its activities to include direct participation in official negotiating machinery for salaries and for terms and conditions of service. There was clearly a need for union representation for chemists in industry and so the RIC joined with other science institutes to establish the Association of Professional Scientists and Technologists (APST), which was duly registered as a trade union on 4 November 1971. The RIC made clear its relationship to the new union,

> . . . The Institute will continue to be active in collecting and disseminating information about the status and general welfare of chemists; including their conditions of employment, just as it has done in the past, and it will retain its close links with employing organizations. The Institute will also continue to advise its members on a personal basis and will be prepared to intervene informally on their behalf in appropriate circumstances, *but it will leave collective bargaining and direct negotiations with employers to the APST.*[30]

Meanwhile, all the other professional activities of the RIC continued unabated. The Remuneration Survey was carried out in spite of the postal strike in the early weeks of the year. It appeared that chemists' earnings were barely keeping pace with the rises in the Index of Average Earnings, indeed for older chemists earnings were falling distinctly behind the average. Figures from the Survey were received in time to be presented to the Civil Service Arbitration Tribunal, but were rejected on the grounds that the Tribunal could not accept data from a third party. Since the same information had been supplied by the RIC to the Institution of Professional Civil Servants this rebuff had no real substance and merely cast doubt on the capacity of the Tribunal itself.

Thus, after amalgamation the RIC redoubled its efforts to promote the professional interests of chemists, but the fact that Local Sections were now under the Chemical Society tended to make some RIC members feel that they had lost effective contact with their Institute. As a result in 1973 a change was introduced by which all Local Sections were attached to the Chemical Society and RIC jointly. On the whole, amalgamation made far more immediate difference to the activities undertaken by the Chemical Society than to those of the RIC and there was some criticism that too many new activities were being started by the Chemical Society. In the professional field the RIC continued to develop links with other bodies such as the Confederation of Scientific and Technical Institutes and the Federation of European Chemical Societies of which the RIC took on the Secretariat jointly with the Hungarian Chemical Society. We have already noted that the professional activities of the RIC began to extend to the European scene particularly after the entry of Britain into the Common Market.

Nevertheless, professional matters at home have not been neglected. Work has progressed on toxic substances in connection with the Robens' Report on Safety and Health at Work and on preparing evidence for submission to the Royal Commission on Environmental Pollution regarding the most desirable qualifications and training for professional chemists responsible for the monitoring and control of pollution. In another area a great deal of effort was devoted to the preparation of a written code of conduct for chemists. This proved to be a difficult and lengthy task, although a booklet with the title *Professional Conduct—Guidance for Chemists* was prepared in 1973 for distribution in the following year. In addition to these major projects the RIC also maintained its other professional activities, including the production of the bi-monthly Professional Bulletin and the maintenance of a whole range of advisory services to its members.

13 The Prospect for Unification

Although the Scheme of Amalgamation has worked successfully in many respects it still leaves a great deal to be desired. The scheme has not really created a single powerful voice for chemistry, nor could it ever do so whilst professional activities are treated separately by the RIC. For various purposes which have no relevance to the needs of chemists or the organization of chemistry either as an academic discipline or as a profession, arbitrary dividing lines must be drawn between the activities proper to the CS as a learned society with charitable status and those which must be undertaken by the RIC. Many, indeed most, of the activities of these two bodies overlap and it is virtually impossible to disentangle them on any viable *chemical* criteria. In practice the result has been that the CS is the body whose voice is heard on behalf of chemistry most of the time, but intermittently another voice—that of the RIC—must be heard and it could be that this voice might become increasingly unfamiliar if the present amalgamation were to be perpetuated too long. Nevertheless, it must be said that the period since

1972 has been a very valuable intermediate stage in the movement towards unification. During this time various lessons have been learned and mistakes of organization or practice which might otherwise have been made can now be avoided.

With regard to the question of a single focus of support for chemists, the Scheme of Amalgamation has been far from perfect. Indeed there is here an incipient weakness in the scheme and a possible source of future disruption since there is a strong inducement for all chemists to support the CS whereas there is no corresponding inducement for *all* chemists to support the professional activities of the RIC. Superficially this seems to suggest that an unfair share of the financial burden has been falling upon RIC members, though in fact the real position is not quite so disproportionate as it may appear. The CS has valuable assets to offer and these must be considered to the advantage of RIC members who now receive CS membership at no extra cost. Nevertheless, it would be a valuable step forward if any feelings of injustice amongst certain sections of the membership could be removed.

As we have seen, it was the intention of Sir Harry Melville that there should be a single body to represent all the interests of chemists and chemistry in this country. Both the CS and RIC were in agreement with this view and the Scheme of Amalgamation was only brought in as a compromise resulting from the warnings and fears expressed by Sir James Taylor. The chief obstacles of Unification which we saw were concerned mainly with the Charters and the problems of membership in a new Society which must include the qualifying role of the RIC. Now although such problems were real enough to make it difficult if not impossible to create a single Society at once, none of the objections raised in 1967 were so intractable that they could not be removed or overcome, although this might involve some minor sacrifices. For instance the RIC might have to forego its right to act as an advisory body in matters relating to conditions of employment whilst the CS might well lose the privilege of changing its bye-laws without reference to the Privy Council. Would such changes be unthinkable? In the end it will be for the memberships to decide, but the Councils of the CS and RIC were anxious to explore further the possibility of Unification and in October 1973 a joint working party was set up to reconsider the problem.[31] It was agreed that if Unification could be achieved without any major curtailment of real privileges, it would be advantageous in nearly all respects.

It was decided from the start that the new Charter would either be based on the CS Charter, or alternatively the CS would apply for a Supplemental Charter to cover qualifying examining and professional activities. Within this new or Supplemental Charter a change of name was envisaged in line with the retention of designatory letters for corporate grades of membership. The question of reducing the number of grades was also considered together with the possibility of fixing a single subscription rate applicable to all members.

Early in 1975 it was agreed to go ahead with a thorough re-examination of the possibility of creating a unified body and the Unification Committee was set up 'to develop a plan and strategy for a complete merger of the Chemical Society and the Royal Institute of Chemistry'. The benefits appeared to be psychological rather than material. Most of the latter had either been obtained already under the Scheme of Amalgamation, or could be derived from it by further refinement. On the other hand the benefit to chemists of having a single focus of support could be very great and the increased interest and support which might well ensue could be of enormous value to the well-being of the discipline and profession in Britain.

The fundamental objectives sought by the Unification Committee were first that the new body should have a constitution which would include all the powers and range of activities of the existing bodies, and second that the privileges and concessions enjoyed by the CS as a learned society and recognized charity should be preserved. It was recognized that these two objectives might be difficult to reconcile, but that unless they could be achieved any Scheme of Unification without them would be unacceptable to the memberships.

The decisive factor in considering the new constitution was the need to ensure charitable status. On closer examination it appeared that neither of the existing Charters could be modified to allow for this, nor would Supplemental Charters provide the solution. Hence it seemed clear that both the CS and RIC would have to give up their existing Charters in favour of a new one bringing into existence a reconstituted Society with a new name and extended powers. Within the new Charter the heritage of the CS with its valuable advantages would be preserved whilst the history of the RIC would be referred to and express provision for the continuance of its activities would be made.

Regarding the choice of a name for the new Society several criteria had to be fulfilled. In the first place the new name should not be too similar to the name of any other chartered body. The initials used to denote membership should not be too similar to those used by any other such body nor to any abbreviations already in common use. Besides this the name should characterize the two bodies. Clearly the continuance of the Chemical Society's role would be imperative, but many also favoured the inclusion of the word 'Royal'. To accommodate all these considerations and provide a name which would involve only a minimal change in the designatory letters for qualified members it has been suggested that the new Society might be called 'The Royal Society of Chemistry' and investigations were initiated to discover the prospects of this name receiving official approval.

It was proposed that the membership of the new Society should be open to all who were interested in chemistry and duly sponsored. Such membership would not represent a qualification, but within this general membership there would be certain categories open only to those who could meet stringent academic requirements including 'counselled experience'. Membership in these grades *would* represent a professional qualification and some rights and responsibilities would be restricted to members in these 'qualified grades'. This would be a further development in line with the introduction in 1956 of the GradRIC as a non-corporate grade of membership with progression to the Associateship after a period of counselled experience. If, with the establishment of the new Society, this period were to be extended to a full three years, its professional qualifications would take on an added value and significance. It was suggested that the annual subscriptions should not be substantially different for any of the various categories of membership in the new Society. In 1975 it was realized that there was still a long way to go before Unification could be accomplished, but a time scale of about five years was envisaged and it was hoped that the new Society might come into being towards the end of 1979 and be fully operative in 1980. Negotiations are still in hand,[32] but one thing is certain, Unification will mean far more to the professional status of the chemist in this country than a mere organizational rearrangement in his representative Societies.

NGC

NOTES AND REFERENCES

1 Sir Harry Melville, *WW* (1976); Frank Hartley, President of the RIC, immediately welcomed the suggestion of Amalgamation.

2 *Chem. Brit.*, 1967, **3,** 212–16.

3 J. Taylor, *The Scientific Community*, OUP, London, 1973, p. 45.

4 RIC, Council Minutes, **57,** 15 December 1967.

5 *Ibid.*, Memorandum submitted by the RIC on integration of the three major chemical bodies.

6 *Ibid.*, p. 5.

7 *Ibid.*

8 Table compiled from *Scientific and Learned Societies of Great Britain*, Allen and Unwin, London, 1967. Figures relate to 1965–6.

9 RIC, Council Minutes (note 5), p. 8.

10 J. Taylor, *Chem. Brit.*, 1969, **5,** 439–43.

11 For a discussion of the 1885 Charter see R. B. Pilcher, *History of the Institute, 1877–1914*, Institute of Chemistry, London, 1914, pp. 77–81 and ch. XI above.

12 See ch. IV.

13 *Chem. Brit.*, 1969, **5,** 436.

14 Sir Ronald Nyholm was a powerful advocate and indefatigable worker in the cause of Amalgamation; his tragic death in a motor accident on 4 December 1971 was a major loss to all concerned in the negotiation. See *Chem. Brit.*, 1972, **8,** 3, 341.

15 RIC, Council Minutes, **59,** 13 February 1970.

16 All the relevant documents were published in *The Amalgamation Proposals*, issued with *Chem. Brit.*, 1970, **6,** for the information of voting members.

17 Figures supplied by SCI. SCI, Council Minutes, 13 November 1970, p. 613.

18 *Chem. Brit.*, 1970, **6,** 296–300. Dr Williams, an industrial chemist, had been President of the Institute from 1967–70; his term of office was extended by a temporary change in the bye-laws to enable him to continue his part in the Amalgamation talks.

19 These procedures were in any case under review due to the establishment of the CNAA and the recommendations of the Robbins Report.

20 RIC, Council Minutes, **60,** 29 July 1970.

21 Copy provided by SCI.

22 L. H. Williams, *loc. cit.*, note 18.

23 G. H. Beeby, SCI, Council Minutes, 1970, p. 620.

24 *Ibid.*, p. 621.

25 *Ibid.*

26 *Ibid.*, p. 622. These sentiments were repeated by Mr Beeby in his Presidential Address to the Annual Meeting of the SCI at Leeds, 12 July 1972. *Chem. & Ind.*, 1972, 554–7.

27 This proved to be a mistake. Many RIC members began to feel isolated from their Institute since Local Sections under the Chemical Society were unable to provide an adequate forum for the discussion of Institute business concerned with professional matters. There was much bad feeling until the Local Sections were attached to the Chemical Society and RIC jointly in 1973, (ch. XIII, pp. 257–8).

28 *The Amalgamation Proposals*, 1971.

29 RIC, Annual Report, 1971, pp. 2–3.

30 *Ibid.*, p. 3 (my stress).

31 This working party held its first meeting at Russell Square on 2 October 1973 under the Chairmanship of Dr F. A. Robinson.

32 Progress is being reported periodically. See *Chem. Brit.*, 1976, **12,** 141–2; 1977, **13,** 82–4.

APPENDIX

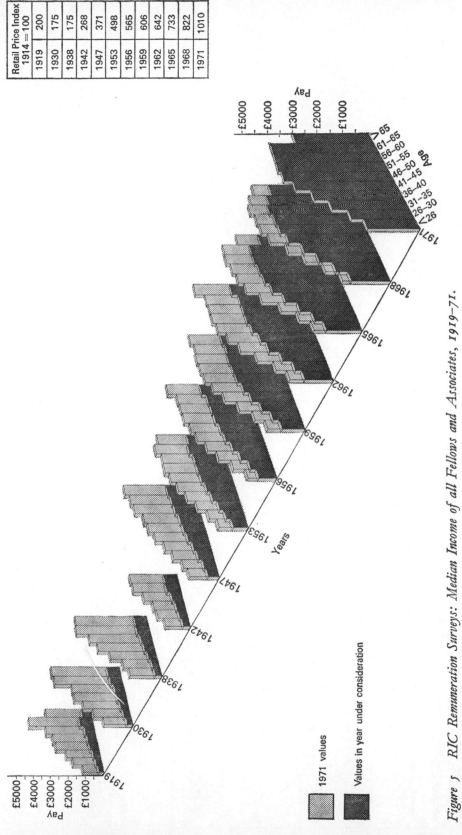

Retail Price Index 1914 = 100	
1919	200
1930	175
1938	175
1942	268
1947	371
1953	498
1956	565
1959	606
1962	642
1965	733
1968	822
1971	1010

Figure 5   RIC Remuneration Surveys: Median Income of all Fellows and Associates, 1919–71.

(Source: RIC Professional Bulletin, no. 11, 1 December 1973, pp. 2–3.)

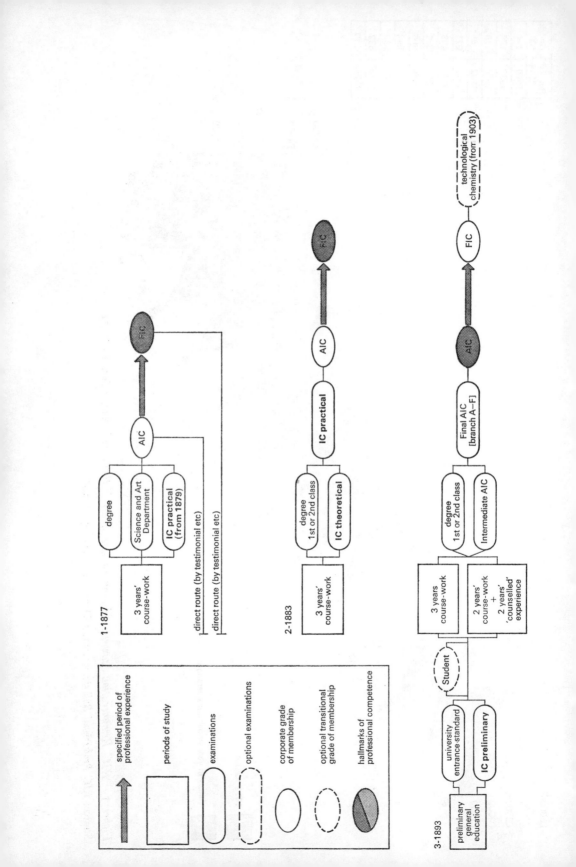

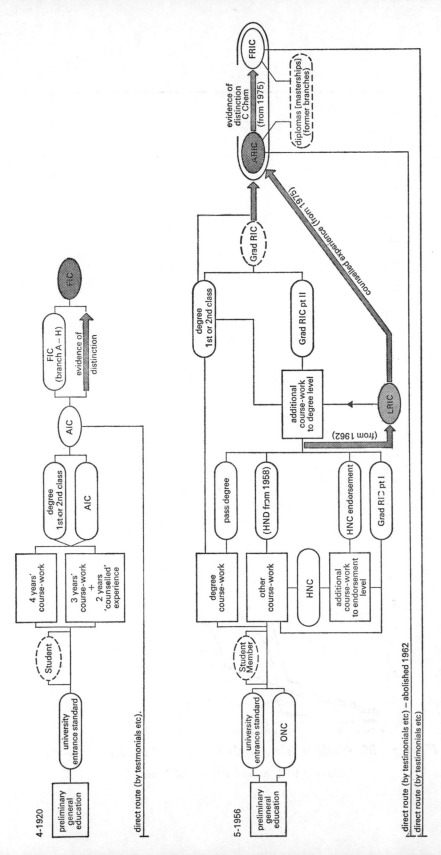

Figure 6 The Institute's Qualifications.

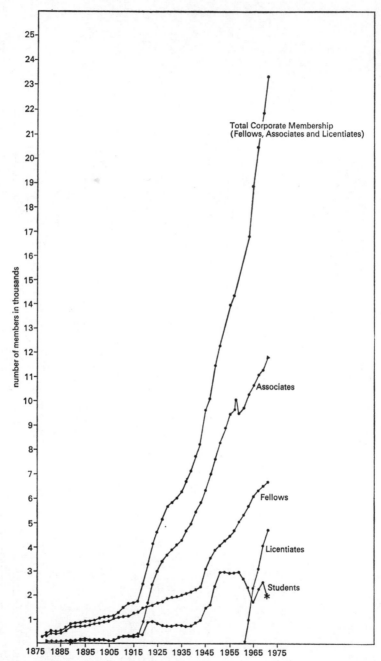

Figure 7   Membership of the (Royal) Institute of Chemistry, 1878–1971.

(Source: RIC, Annual Reports of Council.)

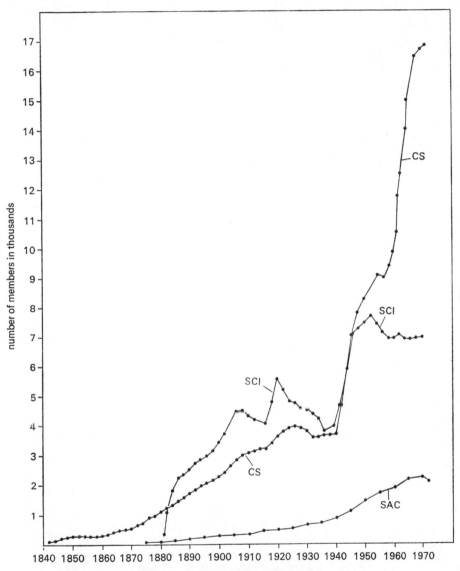

Figure 8   Membership of the Chemical Society, 1841–1971.
Membership of the Society of Chemical Industry, 1881–1971.
Membership of the Society for Analytical Chemistry, 1874–1971.

(Sources: CS, Annual Reports of Council; SCI, Annual Reports of
Council to 1965, thereafter, *The World of Learning*, Europa Publications,
London; R. C. Chirnside and J. H. Hamence, *The 'Practising Chemists':
a History of the Society for Analytical Chemistry*, SAC, London, 1974.)

SUBJECT INDEX

NAME INDEX

A

Abel, F. A., 78, 92, 136, 138, 144–5, 149–51, 188–9, Plate 11.
Accum, F., 35, 58, 72, 103.
Agricola, 12.
Albertus Magnus, 7.
Alldred, C. H., 122.
Allen, A. H., 108–9, 112, 124–5, 150.
Allen, W., 46–7.
Allhusen, C., 40–1, 53.
Airy, Sir G., 99, 110, 130.
Archbutt, L., 188, 198.
Aristotle, 16.
Armstrong, E. F., 242–3, 260.
Armstrong, H. E., 38, 52, 150, 155, 191, 204, 214.
Attfield, J., 149–50, 155.
Austen, J., 24.
Austin, J. B., 59.
Avicenna, 16, 19.
Ayrton, A. S., 130–1.

B

Babbage, C., 54, 57, 66–7, 74.
Bacon, F., 22, 28.
Bacon, R., 8.
Baly, E. C. C., 243, 261.
Bartlett, H. C., 138, 157.
Beddoes, T., 25.
Beeby, G. H., 316–17, 324.
Beguin, J., 17–18.
Beilby, G. T., 191, 195, 198, 210–11.
Bell, Sir I. L., 61, 73–4, 97, 110, 150.
Bell, Jacob, 47, 53–4.
Bell, James, 106, 112, 150, Plate 12.
Bell, John, 46–7.
Bernal, J. D., 234.
Berzelius, J. J., 49, 54, 70, 96.
Betley, R., 96.
Bingen, Sir E., 300–1.
Biringuccio, V., 12.
Birkbeck, G., 59–60.
Bloxam, C. L., 150.
Bonus, P., 27.
Bottinger, H., 37–8.
Bouch, W., 97.
Boyle, R., 28.
Brady, O. L., 238, 260.
Bragg, W., 229.
Bramwell, F. J., 126.
Brande, W. T., 14–15, 27, 57, 125.

Brembridge, E., 156.
Brewster, D., 66–7.
Brodie, B. C., 149.
Brooke, H. J., 70.
Brougham, Lord H., 45, 56, 58.
Browell, E. I. J., 96–7.
Brown, A. C., 150–1.
Bullock, J. L., 75.
Bunsen, R. W., 43, 95–6, 99–100, 116.
Butler-Jones, F., 195, 199.

C

Caldwell, K. S., 297.
Campbell, A., 65.
Campbell, D., 136, 139, 150, 154.
Cannizzaro, S., 131.
Carrington, Earl, 187.
Carteighe, M., 136, 139–40, 143–4, 149–51, Plate 14.
Cassal, C. E., 168, 187, 197, 203, 211, 213.
Cavendish, H., 28, 128.
Charles II, 9.
Chaucer, G., 7, 9.
Clapham, A., 41.
Clapham, R. C., 62.
Clark, J. G., 36.
Clayton, G. C., 261.
Clegg, S., 35, 99–100.
Collett, R. T., 243, Plate 19.
Cook, J. W., 262.
Cooksey, T., 290.
Cooper, J. F., 41.
Cramer, J. A., 14.
Cripps, Sir S., 230–2.
Crookes, W., 78, 89, 92, 115, 140, 150.
Crosfield, G., 36.
Crosfield, J., 36
Crowder, W., 73.
Crum, W., 32.

D

Dahrendorf, R. D., 295.
Dalton, J., 34–6, 67, 74, 82.
Dante, I., 7.
Davis, G. E., 64–5, 73–4, 150.
Davy, Sir H., 24–6, 28, 35, 57.
Deacon, H., 39–41, 53, 221.
Deeley, R. M., 188.
De la Rue, W., 78–80, 92.
Devonshire, 7th Duke of, 128.
Dewar, Sir J., 150, 172–3, 191.